Middle Eastern Flute Magic

Play the Nay

Finger Charts for Arabic Music Scales

Cameron Powers

Middle Eastern Flute Magic: Play the Nay
Finger Charts for Arabic Music Scales
-- First Edition

Original Copyright © 2015 by Cameron Powers
Published by GL Design, Boulder, Colorado, USA

All rights reserved. No part of this book may be reproduced in any form or by any electronic or mechanical means including information storage and retrieval systems without permission in writing from the publisher, except by a reviewer, who may quote brief passages in a review.

Library of Congress Control Number: 2019905933
ISBN: 1-933983-21-3
ISBN Complete: 978-1-933983-21-9

Contents

Play the Nay

Magical Legacy of the Nay	6
Essential Quartertone Terminology	7
Introduction	8
Playing with Omar Faruk at my home in Boulder, Colorado in 2001	9
History of the Nay	10
Your First Note	12
Finger Positions	13
Maqamat	14
Note Names of Expanded Basic Arabic Scale	14
Supporting the Nay: Two Basic Alternate Fingerings	16
Notes Found on the Dukah "D" Nay	17
The Lowest Notes	18
Mapping the Maqams onto the Dukah Nay	33
Jins or Ajnas - Building Blocks	33
Jins Rast on C	34
Jins Nahawand on C	34
Jins Nawa Athar on C	35
Jins Bayati on D	35
Jins Saba on D	36
Jins Hijaz on D	36
Jins Kurd on D	37
Jins Sikah on E half-flat	37
Jins Ajam on Bb	38
Jins Saba Zamzama on D	38
Jins Athar Kurd on C	39
Leading Low Notes	40
Maqam Charts	40
List of Maqams for Dukah Nay	41

Maqams Basic to the Nay 42
    Maqam Sultani Yaka (Nahawand 2 on G) 46
    Maqam Yak-Gah (Rast on G) (Rast Nawa) 48
    Maqam Shawki Tarab (Kurd on A with Saba) 50
    Maqam Busalik Ushayran (Bayati on A) 52
    Maqam Bayati Ushayran (Bayatayn on A) 54
    Maqam Hijazi Ushayran (Shuri on A) 56
    Maqam Ajam Ushayran (Bb Major) 58
    Maqam Shawq Afza 60
    Maqam Rahat el Arwah (Huzam on B half-flat) 62
    Maqam Irak (Huzam on B half-flat with Bayati) 64
    Maqam Bastanikar (Huzam on B half-flat with Saba) 66
    Maqam Rast 68
    Maqam Suznak 70
    Maqam Dalanshin 72
    Maqam Nahawand 1 74
    Maqam Nahawand 2 76
    Maqam Nakriz 78
    Maqam Nawa Athar 80
    Maqam Athar Kurd 82
    Maqam Basandidah 84
    Maqam Bayati 86
    Maqam Husayni 88
    Maqam Saba 90
    Maqam Saba Zamzama 92
    Maqam Shuri 94
    Maqam Hijaz 96
    Maqam Hijaz Awji 98
    Maqam Shehnaz 100
    Maqam Kurd 102
    Maqam Shehnaz Kurdi 104
    Maqam Ajam on Eb (Eb Major) 106
    Maqam Huzam 108
    Maqam Sikah 110
    Maqam Awshar 112
    Maqam Jaharakah 114
    Maqam Jaharakah Turki (Shehnaz on F) 116
Doubled Low Notes - The Bridge 118
Alternative Low Note Fingerings Illustrated 119

Collection of Nays 120
Curled Nays 121
Nays in Different Keys 122
Turkish Sufi Kiz "B" Nay 122
Rast "C" Nay 123
Dukah "D" Nay 124
Busalik "E" Nay 125
Jaharka "F" Nay 126
Nawa "G" Nay 127
Huseyni "A" Nay 128
Ajam "Bb" Nay 129
Nay Construction 130
Glossary of Terms 136
Acknowledgments 139
Cameron Powers -- Biography 140
Musical Fun by the Red Sea in Aqaba, Jordan 141
Other Books and CD's by Cameron Powers 142
Harmonic Secrets of Arabic Music Scales 142
Arabic Musical Scales 143
Maqam Practice Tracks 144
Soulscapes 145
Love Without Borders 146
Singing in Baghdad 147
Spiritual Traveler 148
Naked Wild and Free in the Grand Canyon 149
Cameron Powers Project CD 150
Baghdad & Beyond CD 151
Middle Eastern Moods 152
Dancing with Your Soul 153

Magical Legacy of the Nay

Ancient Reed Flute of Love and Longing

> *There is a story told about the origins of the nay.*
> *A man was walking beside a river. Suddenly he heard a voice! It was the voice of God who revealed to this man the secret of the universe. The man felt an amazing flood of ecstatic energies filling his soul and became very excited.*
> *"But," added God, "you must not reveal this secret to anybody else!"*
> *The man was having trouble containing his excitement. He so wanted to share the secret. He obeyed God and told no one directly but he was unable to resist whispering the secret into a well.*
> *Soon some reeds grew up in the mud in the bottom of the well. A passing musician cut the reeds and made one into a flute... a nay.*
> *Forever after, when the sound of the nay is heard, the secret of the universe is revealed.*
>
> *-- Oral Tradition of the Nay; This story is wide-spread, and may not have a single attribution*

Essential Quartertone Terminology

Quartertones are pitches approximately halfway between the equal-tempered notes. Equal tempered notes are all defined by either "whole-step" or "half-step" intervals. "Three-quarter-step" intervals create what we are calling "quartertones."

So you will see lots of notes labeled "half-flat" or "half-sharp."
Half-flat can be abbreviated "hf" while half-sharp can be abbreviated "hs."

Other terms you will see which come from Middle-Eastern solfege are:
bemol = flat
diese = sharp
nuss-bemol = reboton = half flat
nuss diese = half sharp

For more definitions see the Glossary of Terms toward the end of the book.

"Nay" in Arabic Letters:

Introduction

It was around 1975. I had returned to the USA from living in Athens, Greece. I could now play bouzouki as well as guitar and sing and speak in Greek. I formed a little band and began to perform in my home town of Boulder, Colorado for local folks who loved both Greek line dancing and belly dancing. Soon the belly dancers told me,"We love the Greek music you are playing, but if you really want to play for us you should learn Egyptian music!" I found an Armenian friend who could sell me an oud and I asked an Iraqi friend to help me learn some Arabic music. Soon I was listening to tapes which my dancer friends had provided and I discovered a mysterious sound!

There was an instrument being played which sounded like a rush of liquid sensual fire. I had no idea what it was. By the mid-1980's I was spending a week every summer in Mendocino, California at Middle Eastern Music Camp. Omar Faruk Tekbilek was one of the instructors and I found out what had been making that amazing sound: the Nay!

> *There is an ancient legend about the Nay. It seems that a Sufi heard the voice of the divine as he was walking through the countryside. "Listen carefully and I will reveal a great secret!" came from the voice of God. The Sufi listened and became enlightened. "But you cannot pass that secret to any others. I have revealed it to you alone!" insisted the voice. The Sufi could not contain himself. He whispered the secret into a well. God did not punish him for this as the Sufi had not revealed anything directly. But after some time a fresh crop of reeds grew from the mud in the bottom of the well. A passing shepherd harvested some of these reeds and made them into flutes... into Nays. Forever thereafter it became possible by listening deeply to the sound of the Nay to hear and feel the ultimate divine secret.*

Between 1986 and the year 2000 I attended Middle Eastern Music Camp about ten times. I also attended the Arabic Music Retreat on the East Coast and studied oud with Simon Shaheen. But it was Bassam Saba, another Nay player, who hypnotized me the most deeply with his musical magic. Jihad Racy, who also offered instruction at Simon Shaheen's Retreat, could also perform to perfection on the Nay. But it had been Omar Faruk who had inspired me to finally purchase a nay from him and take his introductory course. For years I had listened to him play with so many other fine Middle Eastern musicians. He could do anything with those little reed flutes: drive a high-speed hot dance melody or float endlessly in long wailing improvisational taqasims.

The objective of Faruk's introductory week-long course was nothing more nor less than to produce a sound... a note... any note... that would be enough! I think I accidentally produced a couple of notes but certainly not during our microscopic "performance" at the end of the week. I left the camp with my new little Nay stuck in a handy sun-visor crack above the dashboard in my van.

During the next year or so the simple secret of getting a note, any note, eluded me. I became frustrated and forgot to even try. But there came a time when I was driving across Oklahoma on a long stretch of arrow-straight interstate highway. I was listening to a tape of Arabic music and I took my nay and, while easily steering with my knees, began to pretend that I was playing along. Suddenly, to my great surprise, I was! I mean sort of... anyway... I was fluttering my fingers over the holes and blowing at the proper angle and some notes were emerging!

I could then begin to actually practice! I realized that, along with other mistakes I had been making, I had been blowing too hard! To play the Nay I needed to just barely pass my breath over the end of the reed... nothing much more...

It was at about that time that my own extensive performance tours through Egypt, Jordan, Syria, Lebanon and Iraq became all-consuming and I never made it back to Middle Eastern Music Camp to progress further with Faruk. But when he passed through Colorado on his own performance tour he came to my house for a visit. I threw a party in his honor and we played together... with me sticking to performance on my primary instrument, the oud.

Playing with Omar Faruk at my home in Boulder, Colorado in 2001

I had also discovered that just getting notes out of the Nay was not enough. It was a certain double octave technique which produced the real magic. This requires infinite delicacy but once achieved the ultimate cosmic Nay secrets could be revealed. The higher notes could be supported by identical notes from an octave below. Two notes could emerge at once and that thick smoky almost-human sound of musical breath would suddenly manifest.

I have never acquired the agility on the Nay to perform at high speed. But if the mood is right and my audience is patient I can produce those slow melodies or improvisations which I love so much.

Since I have written two books which reveal the structure of the maqam systems of indigenous Middle Eastern music scales I was apparently the perfect person to decipher and describe the musical maps finger-hole by finger-hole on the most common Dukah Nay. I have also provided maqam lists for Nays of different sizes which begin from different tonics or keys. I haven't seen this information published elsewhere so I will present that in this little book.

-Cameron Powers 2019

History of the Nay

Although the Nay is now included in most orchestras in the Arabic world, Persia, and Turkey, it started over 5,000 years ago in Ancient Egypt. Pictures of the nay appear on Egyptian tomb paintings. A nay master, known as a "a nayeti," is the product of thousands of years of experience.

In Arab music the nay is considered to be the perfect wind instrument since its richly harmonic tone, mellow and slightly husky, most closely approximates the sound of the human voice. Despite its relatively simple construction, the nay's clear sound has been declared to be the "soul instrument" and the "salt and pepper" in Arabic music. The sound of the nay is felt to be a vehicle that originates from a place even deeper than the human voice: it has a husky and mournful tone that symbolizes the breath of life. Its modulations are harmonically rich and create effects that go beyond traditional music-making. Even in the Western world, when people first hear the sound of the Nay, they may be powerfully drawn and won't be able to stop searching until they finally discover what is making that sound!

The current name for this flute is the word "Nay" which is Persian for "reed." Because of the different dialects of Arabic, the name may be written in different forms in the English Language. In some parts of Egypt, a Nay or "Ney" is referred to as "Qassaba" which is the colloquial Egyptian word for a piece of reed. This instrument had many different names in the thousands of years of its past history.

The traditional Nay is made of Nile Reed. It is an end-blown flute with seven finger holes. Six in the front and one in the back. The Nay is made of a nine-segment section of reed. This is very important for the Nay to work properly.

Arab style playing is generally more rhythmic than in Turkish or Persian styles which stems from the shepherd association, as the nay is commonly a pastoral instrument. The classical nay is usually longer, the folk models shorter. The Turkish style is more smooth and flowing, resulting from the Dervish association. In Turkey , the Mevlevi (Whirling Dervishes) long ago adopted the nay as their main instrument in the sema, the spiritual service that includes the trance dancing spinning. The pastoral association is weaker in Turkey , the nay being a learned, urban Classical instrument. In Armenia various types of kaval, smaller flutes, fill in the folk world.

Actual nays surviving from 4,500-5,000 years ago have been found in the excavations in Egypt and in the ancient Mesopotamian city of Ur. Recently some of these ancient flutes were given to the best modern Egyptian players and recordings were made to discover how these ancient nays were tuned.

Most of these nays were made to play the same 8-note diatonic scale used in modern Middle Eastern music. But one of them had its holes drilled to yield the even more ancient pentatonic scale having the F-note as a base note and missing the third and seventh notes of the diatonic scale.

These flutes are relics from hundreds of years and hundreds of kilometers apart but seem to generally be tuned to either F or A would suggest that there was a kind of a source of standard musical notes. Perhaps there was a sacred flute in a principal temple that was used as a yardstick for tuning.

Your First Note

If you don't give up you will succeed! Most players choose to hold the nay so that it angles toward the right side. This means that your right hand will be used to cover the thumb hole and the upper three holes while your left hand covers the lower three holes.

Some players, including my inspirational favorite players Omar Faruk and Bassam Saba, have chosen to hold it the opposite way so that it angles toward the left. Either way is fine but in this book the illustrations will show the nay angled toward the right.

Hold the nay in front of you pointing downward and to the right. There will be a place on the left side of the aperture, the end of the tube, which will be used by your lips to split the flow of air which issues from your lips.

As you bring the nay to your lips you can experiment with finding a way to seal the right side of the aperture while gently blowing. If you purse your lips in the same kind of way you do when you whistle it will help. It may help to actually whistle with your lips while you bring the nay to approach your lips and see what happens. At some point you may hear your own whistled note and then get hints of sounds from the nay. Gradually reduce the sound of your own whistle and find the sound of the nay in stronger ways until you have success. There is no need to try and finger any notes while gaining this first success. Just use your right hand to hold the nay and focus on the aperture and your lips.

It is possible to blow across the end of the nay as if it was a soda bottle and get a sound. Don't waste your time doing this as it will not lead to being able to play the instrument.

If you already have some skill playing another type of flute and your lips have a habitual embouchure or position which works with that instrument this may work against you. There may be too much tension in your lips and you may have to learn to relax them in order to coax your first sounds from the nay.

Most beginners also blow way too hard. The nay comes to life most easily with a very gentle and soft stream of air. If you are feeling dizzy, that means that you are trying too hard.

Another problem which I had to overcome was my tendency to want to smile or otherwise facially express my delight when I finally succeeded in coaxing out a sound. Smiling lips accidentally kill the sound. Sad but true.

Finger Positions

Once you have learned to reliably elicit a sound from the nay you can begin to pay attention to your fingers. Omar Faruk made light of this enterprise when he told me, "Once you can make a sound on the instrument then your fingers will find the notes!" He seemed to imply that this was so easy that teaching would hardly be necessary. I disagree. My fingers are not so brilliant as his. So I had to discover quite a few things about how to place and use my fingers.

There are two extreme approaches from which to begin experimenting. The first is used by Turkish classical players. They train themselves to use only the pads under the middle joints of the fingers to cover the holes. The advantage of this is that gradual covering and uncovering of the holes is very easy and natural so that subtle and fluid pitch changes are made. The disadvantage is that it takes a lot of training to stretch the muscles in your fingers, hands and arms so that playing in this position does not cause pain and tension. Also it is more difficult to awaken the nerve endings under the middle joints of your fingers so that you can accurately feel and discern complete and incomplete hole coverage. *Incomplete hole coverage leads to complete loss of pitch control!*

The other extreme is to use only the pads under the end joints of the fingers to cover the holes. The advantage of this is that the most sensitive and discerning nerve endings in your fingers can be utilized and complete hole coverage with no leaks is most easily achieved. The disadvantage is that rocking the pads under the end joints very slowly and subtly to achieve gradual pitch changes is more difficult.

Everyone's structure is different and you will need to experiment in order to find what is best for you. With the exception of the highly trained classical Turkish players it seems that most players end up using pads under the middle joints to cover higher holes that are closer to the mouth and pads under the end joints for the lower holes.

For the smaller nays in higher keys the end joint finger pads may be exclusively used if you have large fingers because they are narrower and fit more easily side by side.

A Craftsman Pulled a Reed ...
A craftsman pulled a reed from the reedbed,
cut holes in it, and called it a human being.

Since then, it's been wailing a tender agony
of parting, never mentioning the skill that gave it life as a flute.

-- Jalāl al-Dīn Rūmī, from Mathnawi, excerpted from a translation in The Essential Rumi by Coleman Barks and John Moyne

Maqamat

I have come to believe that the entire musical scale system known in the Middle East and the Orient as "maqam" (plural: "maqamat") has probably evolved from the Nay.

If you really want to play equally-tempered music with it's keyboard-based European music scales then you should be studying Balkan Kaval which is a Nay with 8 holes drilled in entirely different places. The Kaval is extensively used in Serbia, Macedonia, Bulgaria and Greece and does not work for maqam-based music. The Balkan Kaval is not the same as the Arabic Kawal which is a short Nay without a thumb hole.

The Nay has 7 holes: one for the thumb and three for the fingers on each hand. As you will see from the charts at the end of this book, the lowest Arabic music notes begin on G. The European music traditions have settled on C as the most basic beginning note because playing only the white keys on the piano puts one into the key of C and the keyboard has become the king of European music. This is not so in the Middle East although in recent decades keyboards have made big inroads in the Orient with the adoption of the harmonium in Pakistan and India and 'quarter-tone' keyboards in the Middle East.

But the Nay holds us into the ancient origins of music in the Middle East and I will present fingering charts which reflect the importance of the note G in maqam theory. The Dukah Nay, which is most basic and the first one to be learned is thought of as facilitating the key of D. But as we shall see it equally facilitates the use of all the basic maqam tonic notes. 'Qarar' is the Arabic word for 'tonic.' This labels the basic 'key' in which one is playing. Middle Eastern music can seem complicated to Westerners because from the equal-tempered point of view it is 'micro-tonal.' But maqam-based tunings were being used wherever the silk road caravans traveled for many centuries before Europeans took the keyboard with it's equally-tempered intervals and its fondness for the key of C as a standard.

The primary Nay, called the "Re/Dukah Nay," facilitates playing maqamat in the keys of G, A, Bb, B half-flat, C, D, , Eb, E half-flat and F. It gets even simpler when we realize that all maqamat are built from a few "Ajnas" (plural for "jins") which are 3 or 4 or 5-note sequences which form the basic building blocks of the maqamat. And the resulting maqamat only begin to appear complex when unusual combinations of Ajnas are chosen or when fancy modulations from one scale to another are achieved.

As we become familiar with the maqamat and with their building blocks, the ajnas, we find things falling into place in a very simple way which makes easy sense. And it seems to me that the simple design of the Dukah Nay has led to the creation of the whole system.

So I will present the maqamat in a way which is most basic for the Nay. We will begin from the note G, or "Yaka," as it's called in Arabic.

Note Names of Expanded Basic Arabic Scale

Note: the double hyphen "--" indicates the presence of another possible quartertone pitch for which the words "nim" (lower) and "tik" (higher) would be used before the nearest note name to provide a label.
Example: two notes called "G half-sharp" or "Tik Yakah" and "A half-flat" or "Nim Ushayran" could be added to the following table but would remain largely irrelevant as they would not ever be used in commonly played keys.

G:	Sol	Yakah (Old name = Nahuft)
--		
Ab/G#	La bemol/Sol diese	Qarar Hisar
--		
A:	La	Ushayran
--		
Bb	Si bemol	Ajam Ushayran
B hf:	Si nuss-bemol	Iraq
B	Si	Kawasht
--		
C:	Do	Rast or "Jawab el-Do"
--		
Db/C#	Re bemol/ Do diese	Zirkulah
--		
D:	Re	Dukah
--		
Eb/D#	Mi bemol/Re Diese	Kurd
E hf:	Mi nuss-bemol	Sikah
E	Mi	Busalik
--		
F:	Fa	Jaharka
Fhs	Fa nuss diese	Jaharka Tik
Gb/F#	Sol bemol/Fa diese	Hijaz
--		
G:	Sol	Nawa
--		
Ab/G#	La bemol/Sol diese	Hisar
--		
A:	La	Husayni
--		
Bb	Si bemol	Ajam
B hf:	Si nuss-bemol	Awj
B	Si	Mahur
--		
C:	Do	Kirdan
--		
Db/C#	Re bemol/ Do diese	Shahnaz
--		
D:	Re	Muhayyar
--		
Eb/D#	Mi bemol	Sinbulah
E hf:	Mi nuss-bemol	Buzrak
E:	Mi	Jawab Busalik
--		
F:	Fa	Mahuran
Fhs	Fa nuss diese	Mahuran Tik
Gb/F#	Sol bemol/Fa diese	Jawab Hijaz
--		
G:	Sol	Nawa or Ramal Tuti or Jawab Nawa or Saham

Note: these names are not always known by modern musicians.
These note names do not necessarily correlate with maqam names but it is possible to see obvious relationships.
Some of these words are originally Persian while others are Arabic. The presence of the Persian words doesn't mean that the scales used in contemporary Persian music are related to maqamat. Persian, Afghani, Pakistani and Hindu music scales have more similarity to each other than to the Arabic and Turkish scale system being taught in this book. It should also be noted that this book presents scales primarily from the Arabic way of teaching rather than the Turkish. But there is a great deal of overlap.

Supporting the Nay: Two Basic Alternate Fingerings

Holding the nay firmly and steadily is required so that the delicate lip positions can be consistently achieved which bring perfection to the qualities of sound. So the long end of the instrument cannot be left waving in the breeze. This means that the right hand must continue to hold the nay even when the holes being covered are not necessary for pitch control.

So you will see two primary alternate finger positions which exist only for the purpose of support.

This holding alternative position, one of many ways to finger a G, is convenient for maqams which do not include the Eb such as Rast.

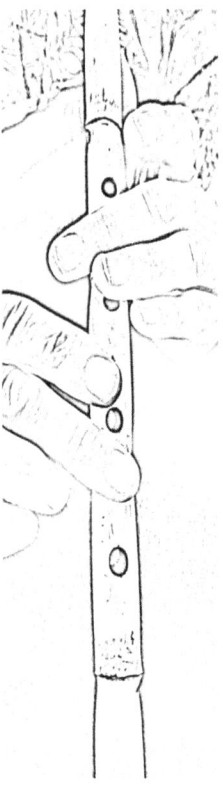

This holding alternative position, another of many ways to finger a G, is convenient for maqams which do include the Eb such as Kurd and Hijaz.

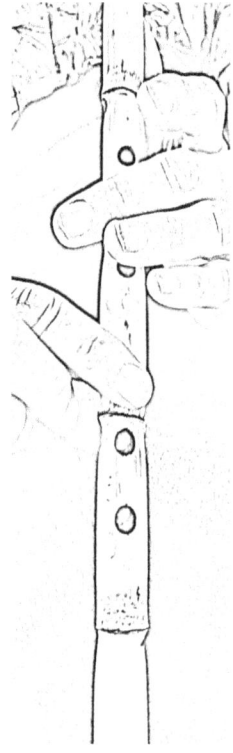

You will discover that by employing these alternative finger positions you will be able to more rapidly through multiple notes in your maqam of choice without having to clumsily arrange the fingers on your right hand.
And if you follow the finger charts for the different maqams illustrated in this book you will be guided to use the most efficient finger positions for each maqam or music scale.

> *Take Down a Musical Instrument ...*
> *Today, like every other day, we wake up empty*
> *and frightened. Don't open the door to the study*
> *and begin reading. Take down a musical instrument.*
>
> *Let the beauty we love be what we do.*
> *-- Jalāl al-Dīn Rūmī, translation by Coleman Barks.*
>
> *I am a hole in a flute*
> *That Christ's breath moves through.*
>
> *-Hafiz - 14th Century Persian Poet*

Notes Found on the Dukah "D" Nay

This is the most commonly used nay and should be the first one approached by the beginning student.

The instrument has a range of about three octaves for accomplished musicians. These notes come from 4-5 registers where two of them are difficult to achieve. The Nay is tuned to easily play the Rast scale. In the standard Arabic scale, the two notes E, and B are played a quarter tone lower. This makes playing a regular chromatic scale a bit challenging on the Ney.

Fine tuning pitches can be accomplished by simply changing the movements of your lips, the angle of the nay and the strength of the air. For example, if you play a D you can easily go to D# without changing finger positions and you can even go to E half-flat or E. The thumb hole has 4 notes usually used, if using the Dukah nay then these notes would be A, Bb, B half-flat, and B.

Normal blowing in the Dukah Nay with all the holes covered produces the 'C' note (first register). Underblowing the Nay will produce 'C' in the lower octave (lower "kabá" register). Overblowing in the Nay (second register) produces a note that is a perfect fifth higher (G). Overblowing again (third register) produces 'C' again. An expert player can play a higher (fourth) register which starts again in 'G'.

The Lowest Notes

These first six notes shown on this and the following page represent the lowest notes obtainable on the nay. They sound so soft and weak until the art of mixing them into the notes in the octave above is mastered that they can hardly enhance performance. How to achieve this is covered more in depth on pages 118-119.

They match the pitches of the notes C4 through F#4 on the keyboard. The Arabic names for these lowest notes do not really exist. They are off the chart; lower than where the named notes begin. But I have given them the Arabic note names from the next register above as this would be common practice among musicians who know and use the traditional note names.

The lowest named note in Arabic tradition is Yakah which also happens to be where the nay begins to come to life without the necessity of mixing the pitches by creating the "bridge" from the two lowest registers. The beginning nay student should concentrate on notes beginning with the Yakah G4 but even more especially on the next higher register which begins on C5.

So many correspondences exist between the notes available on the nay and the old traditional Arabic note names that it seems possible that it was from the nay that those note names evolved.

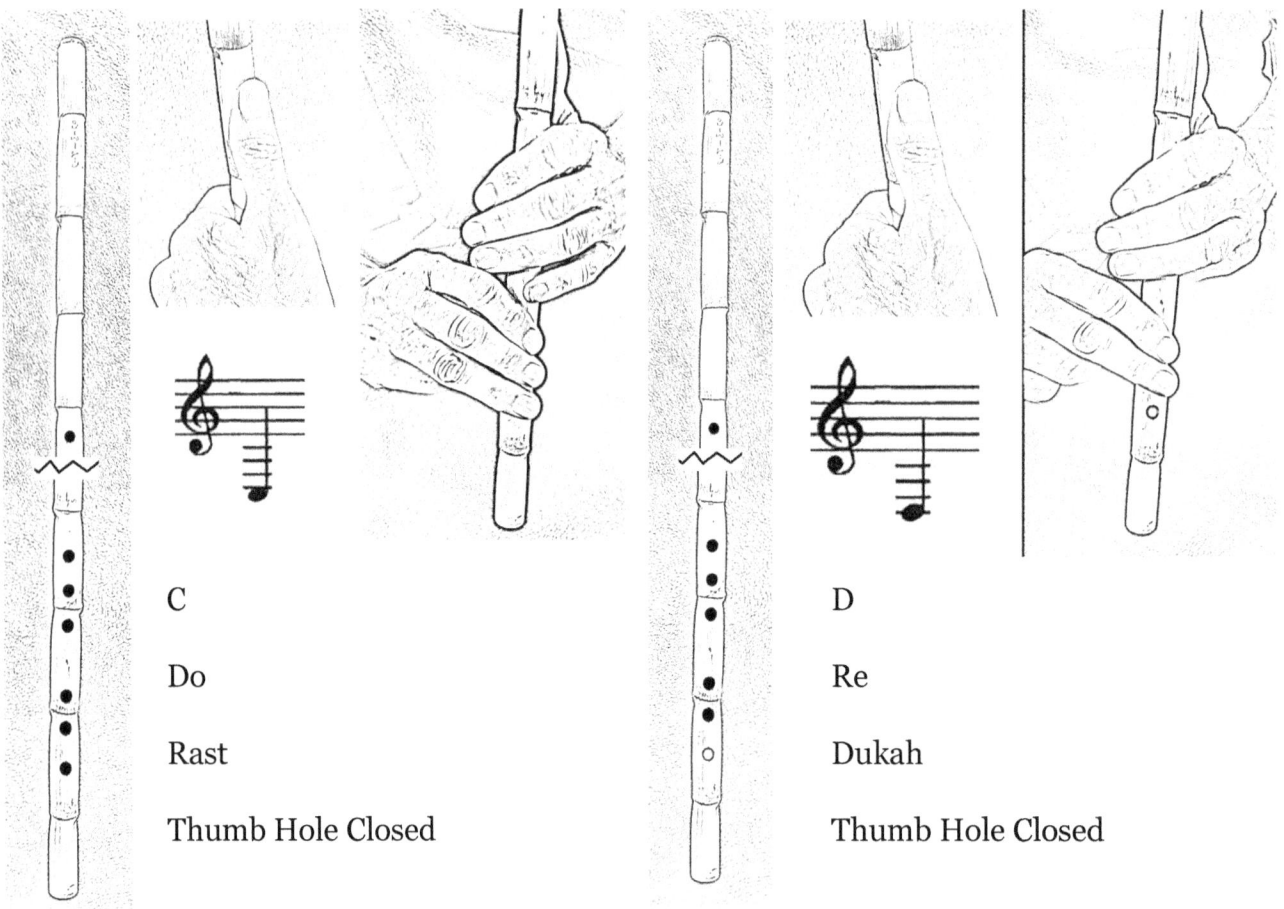

C

Do

Rast

Thumb Hole Closed

D

Re

Dukah

Thumb Hole Closed

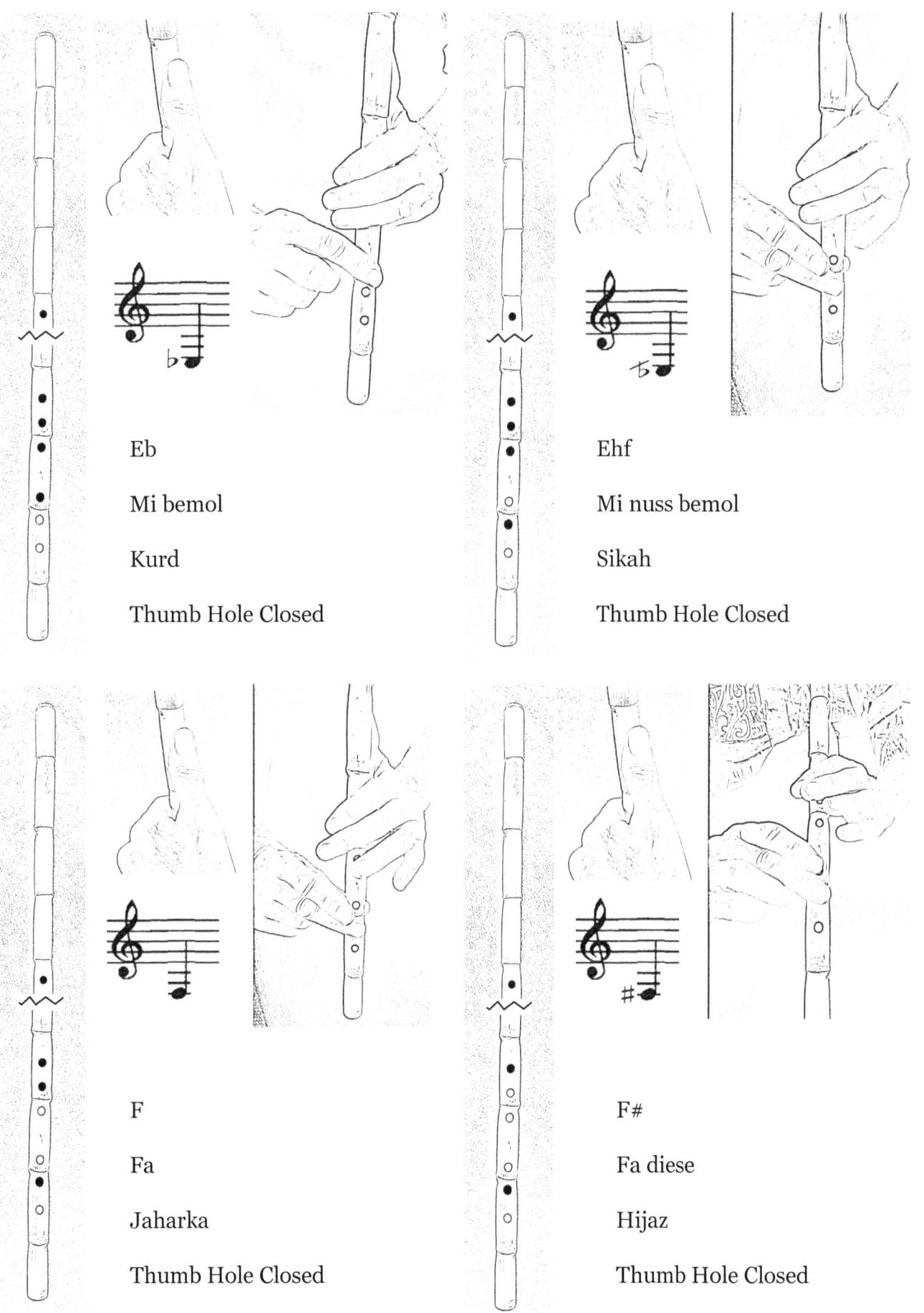

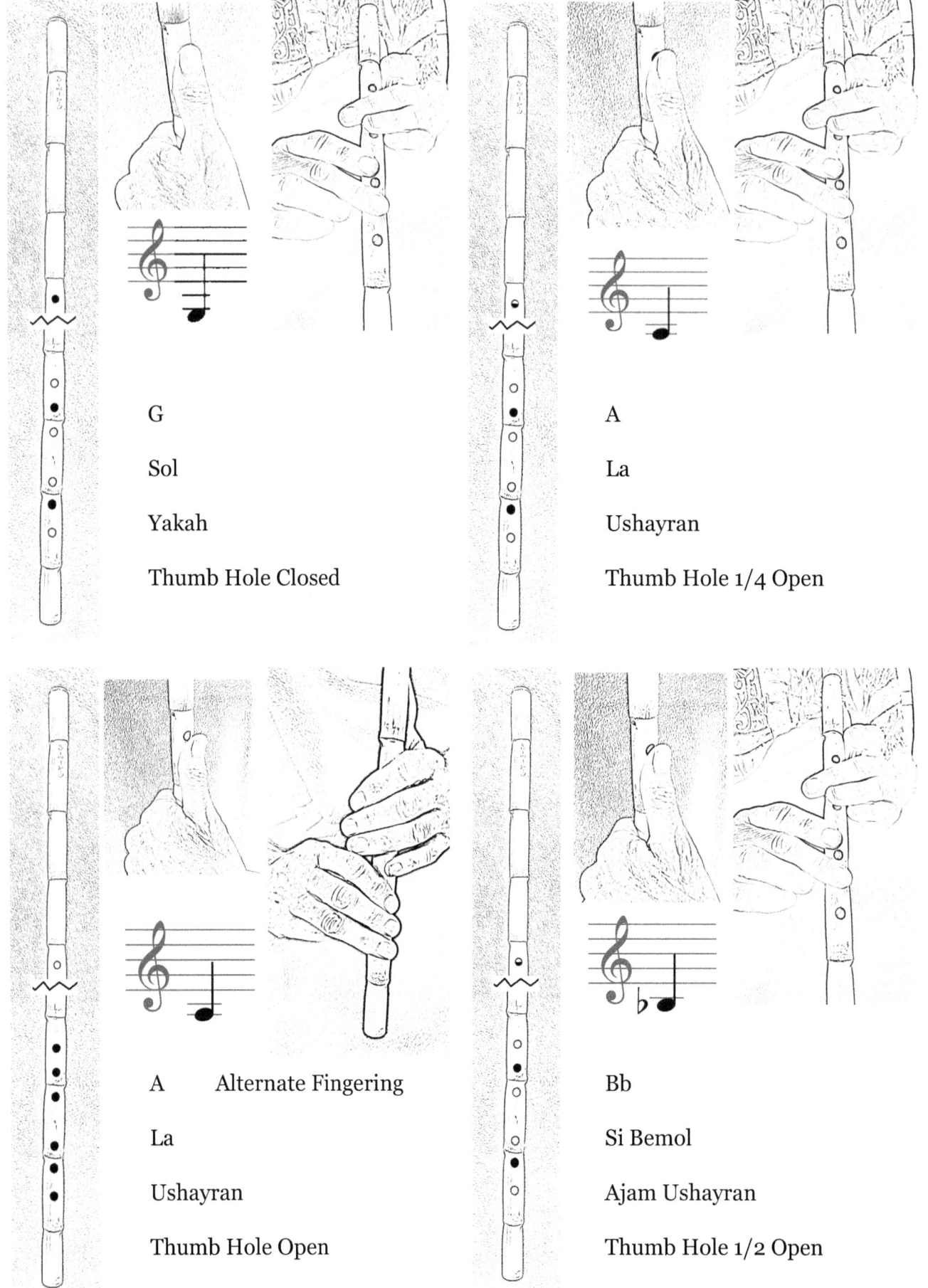

G

Sol

Yakah

Thumb Hole Closed

A

La

Ushayran

Thumb Hole 1/4 Open

A   Alternate Fingering

La

Ushayran

Thumb Hole Open

Bb

Si Bemol

Ajam Ushayran

Thumb Hole 1/2 Open

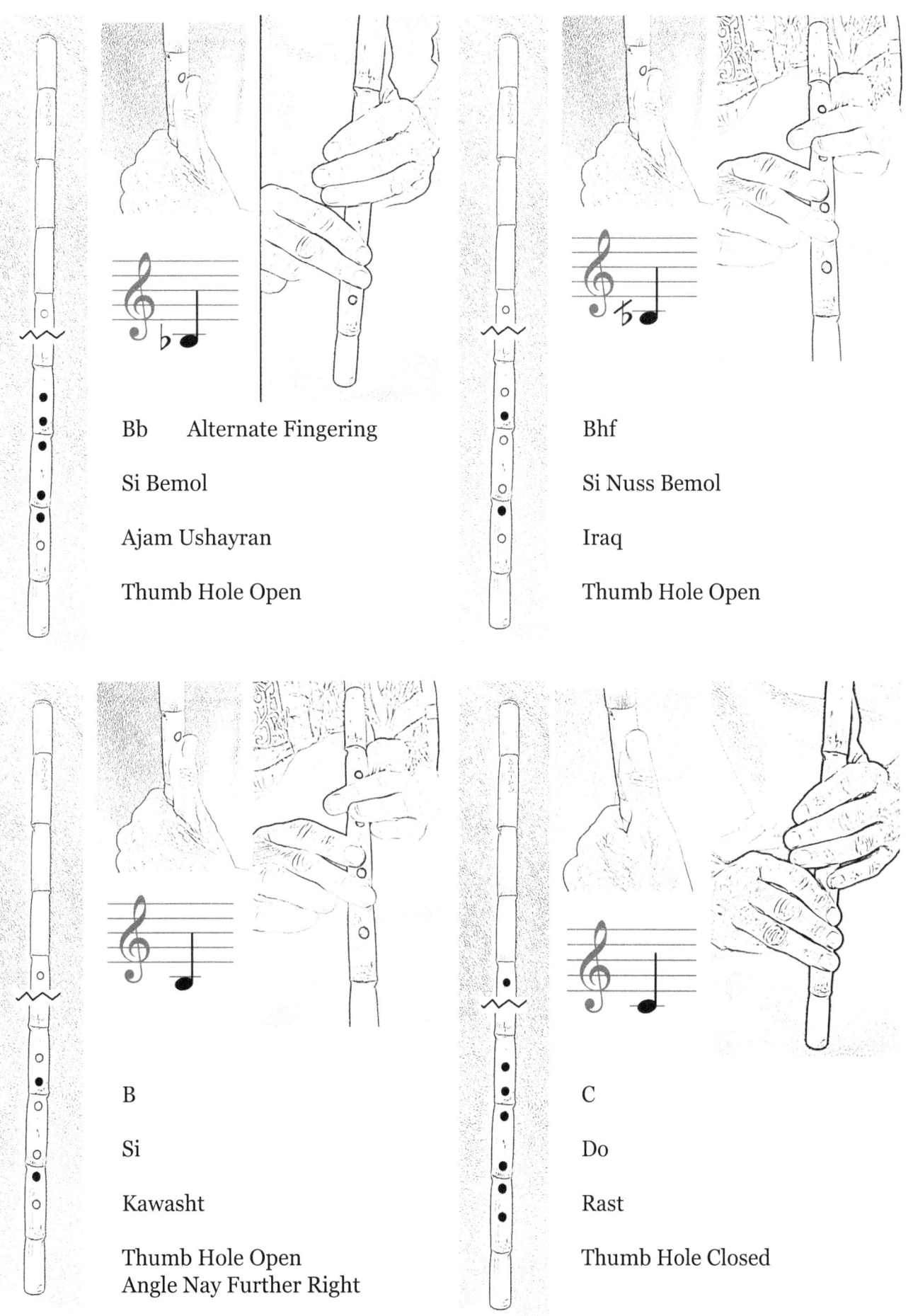

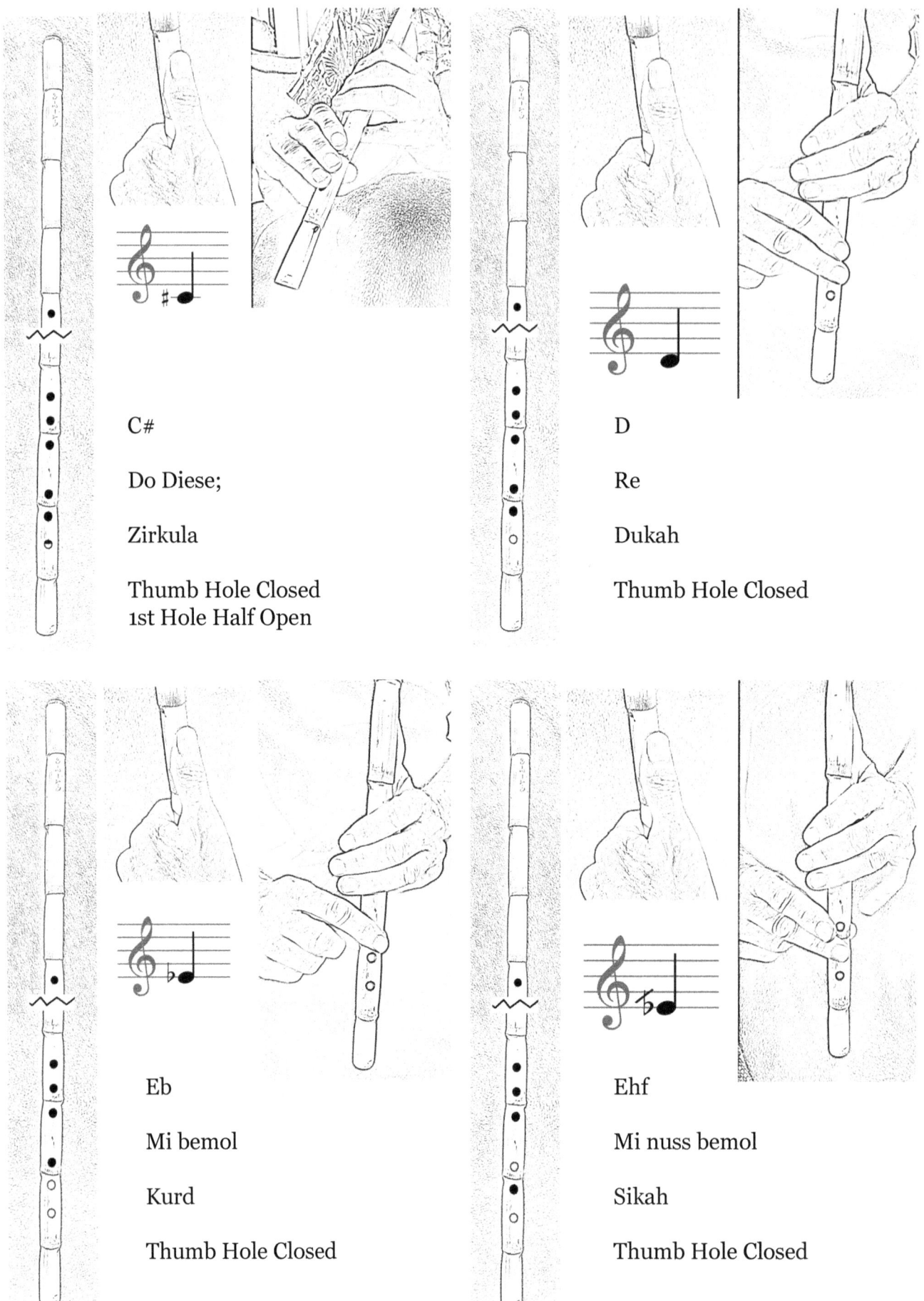

C#

Do Diese;

Zirkula

Thumb Hole Closed
1st Hole Half Open

D

Re

Dukah

Thumb Hole Closed

Eb

Mi bemol

Kurd

Thumb Hole Closed

Ehf

Mi nuss bemol

Sikah

Thumb Hole Closed

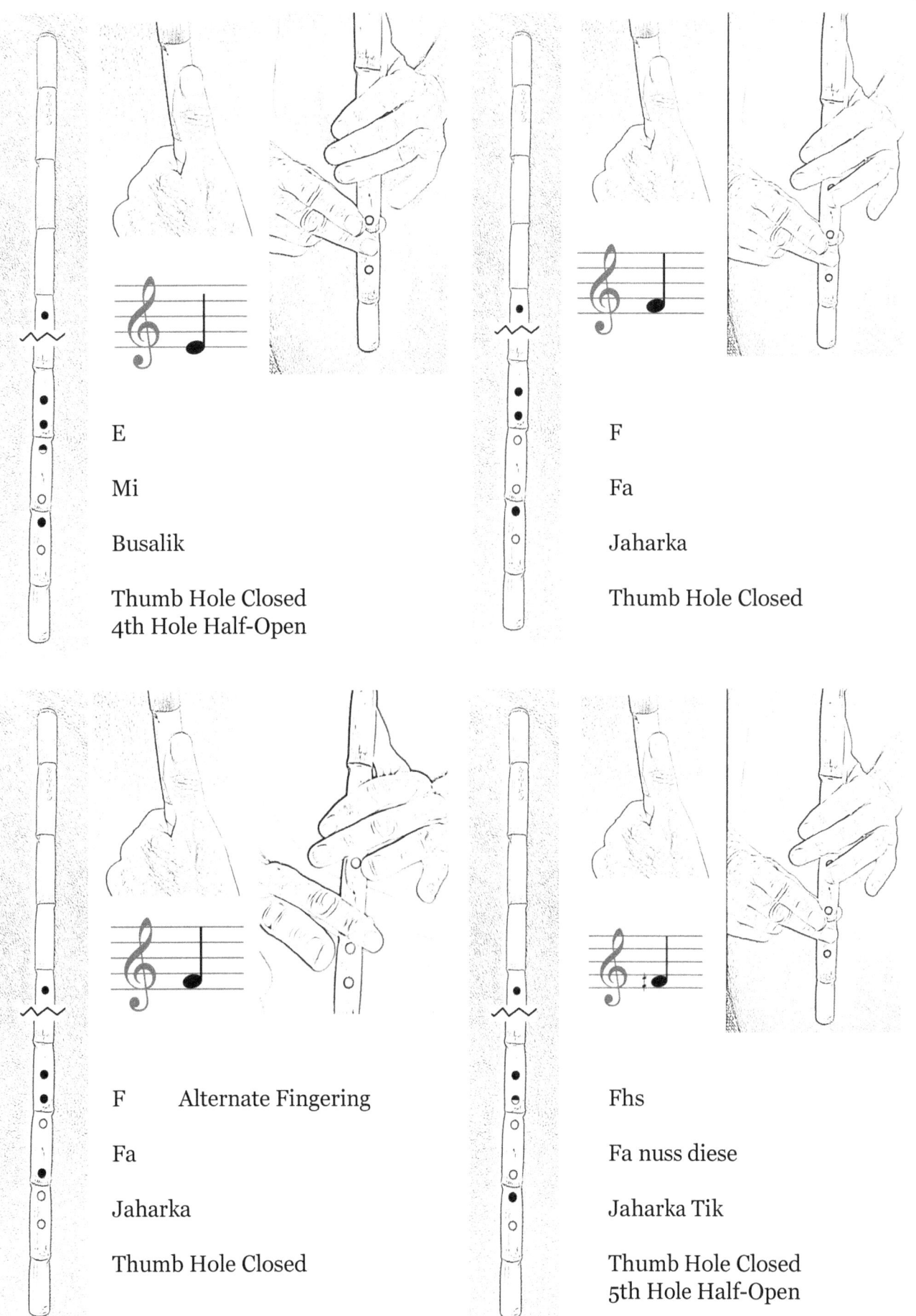

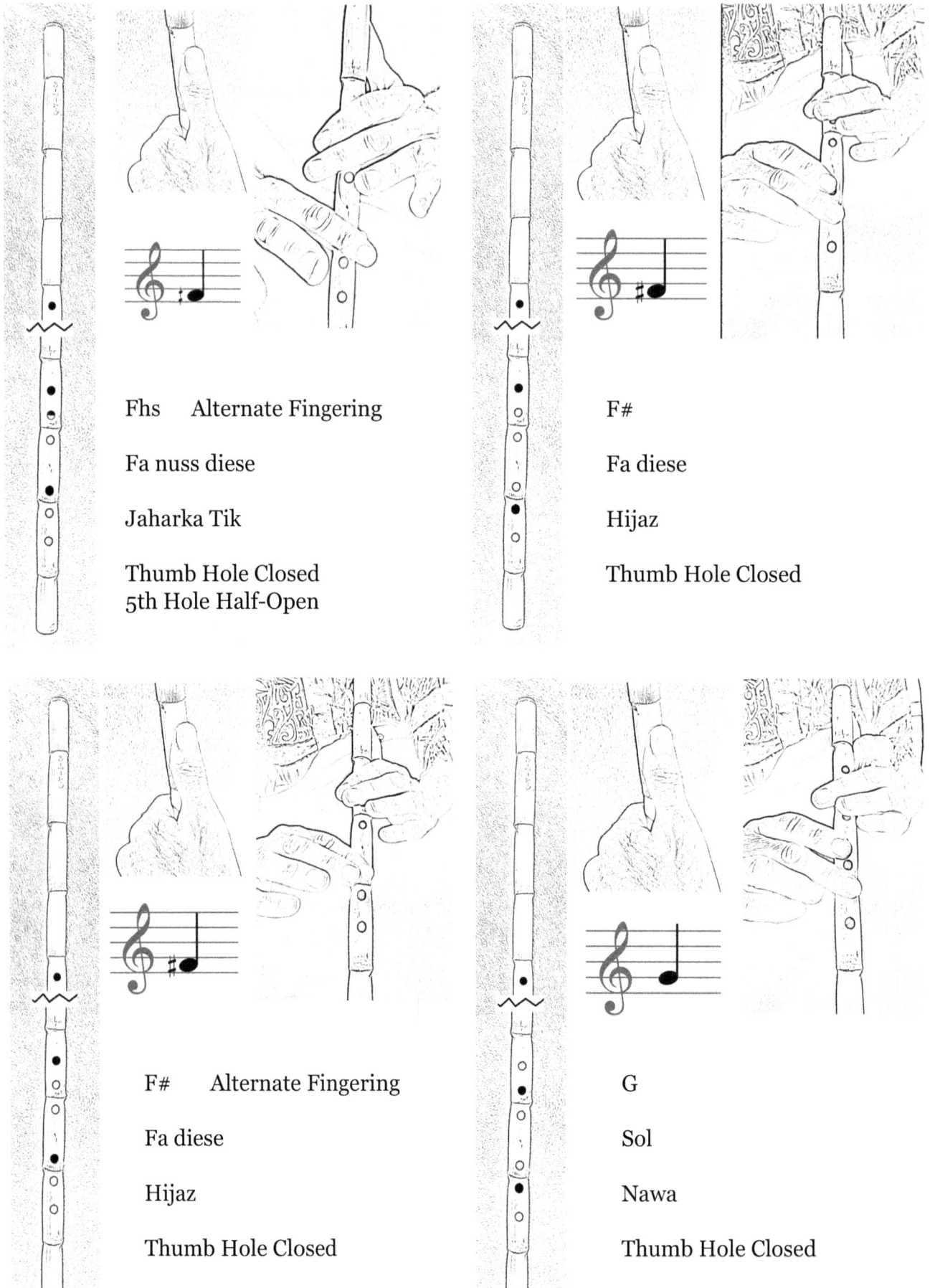

Fhs   Alternate Fingering

Fa nuss diese

Jaharka Tik

Thumb Hole Closed
5th Hole Half-Open

F#

Fa diese

Hijaz

Thumb Hole Closed

F#   Alternate Fingering

Fa diese

Hijaz

Thumb Hole Closed

G

Sol

Nawa

Thumb Hole Closed

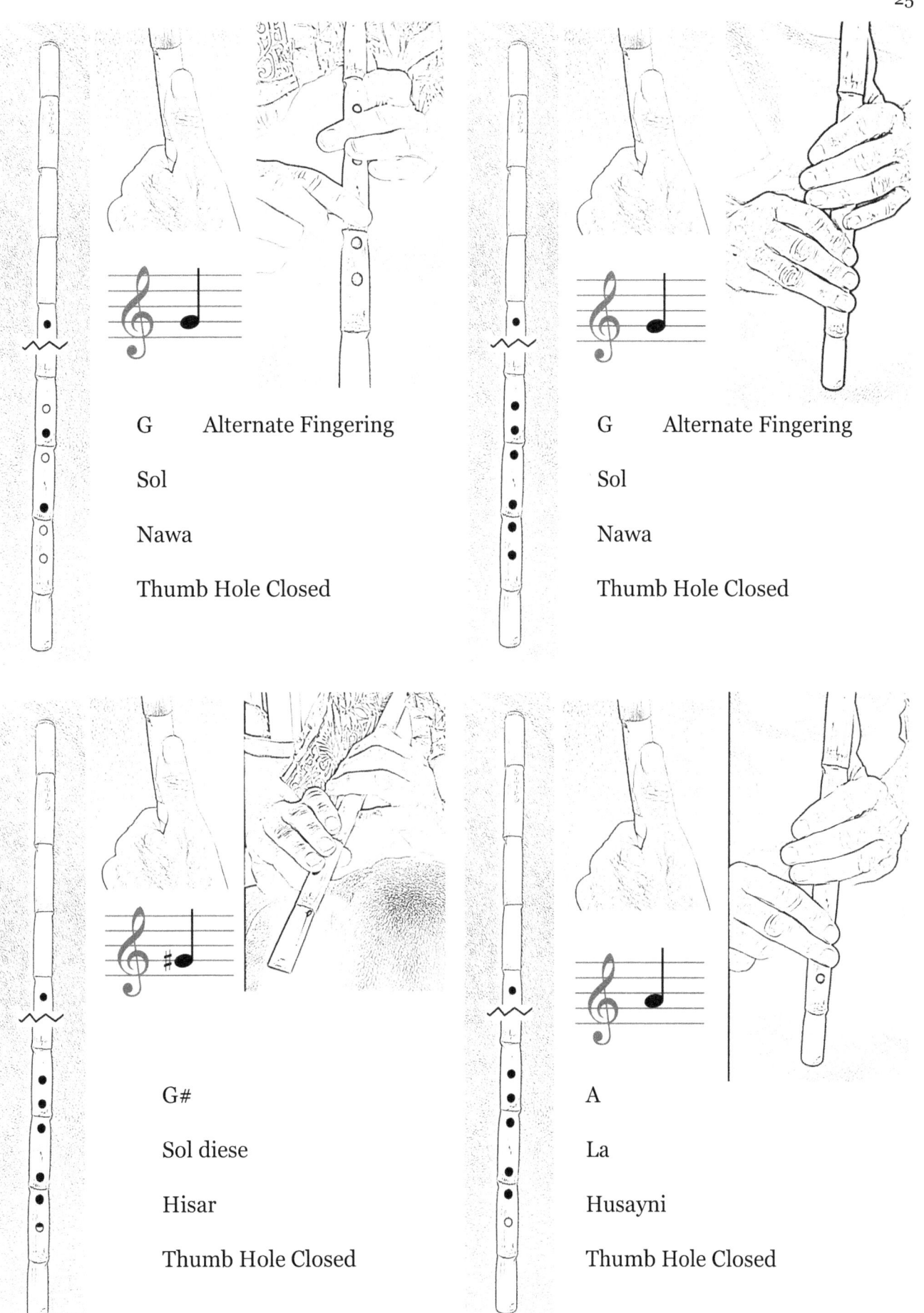

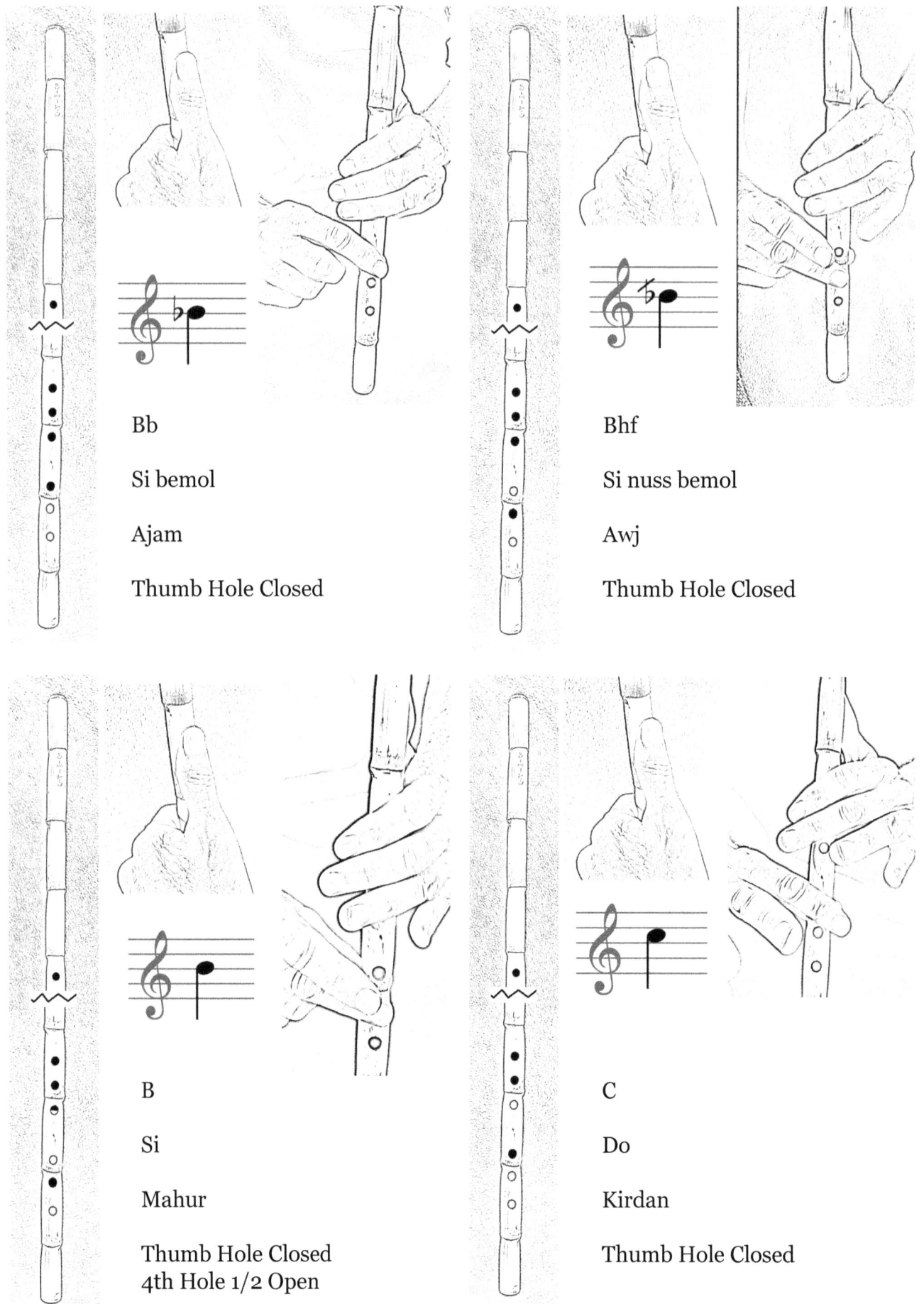

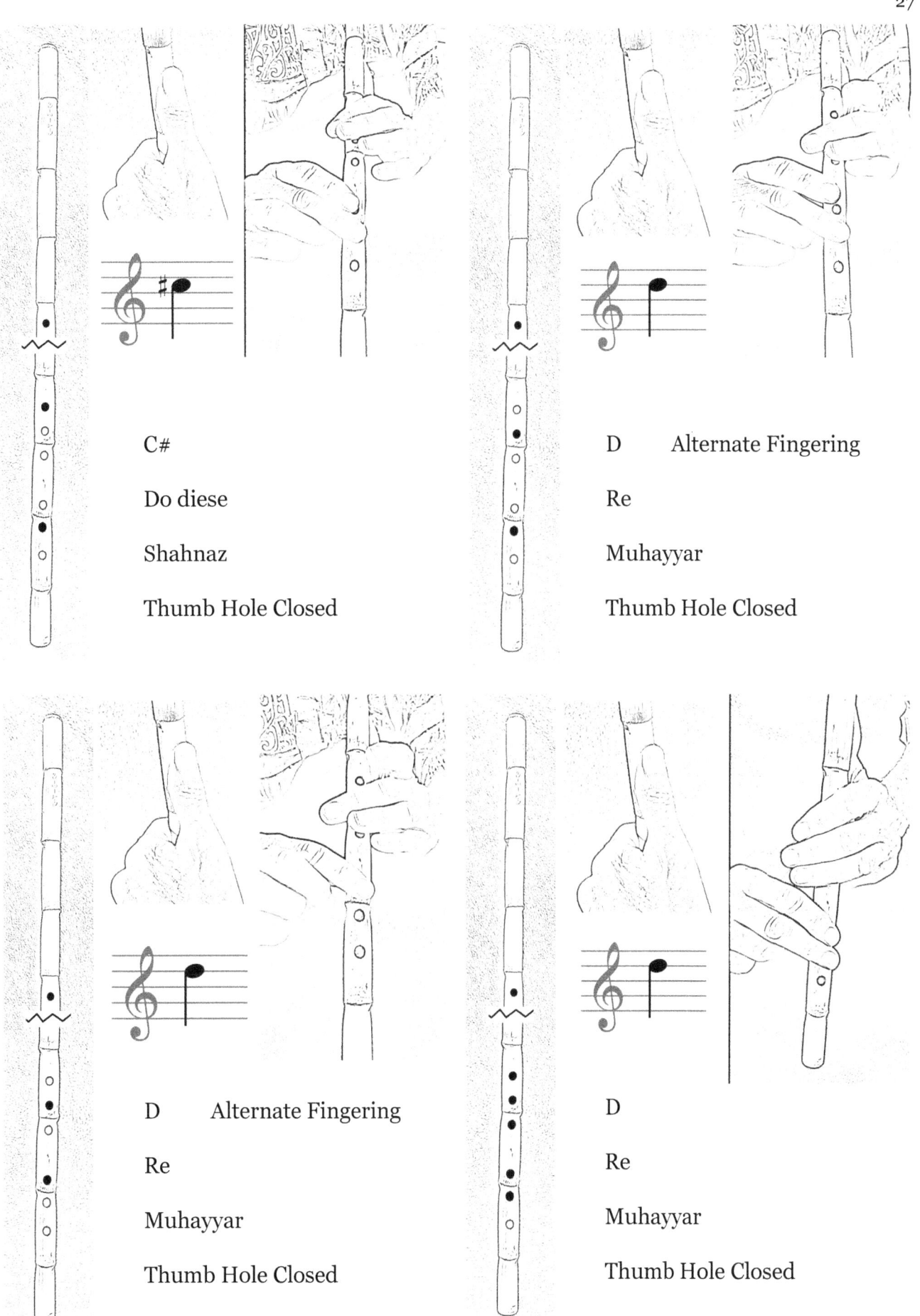

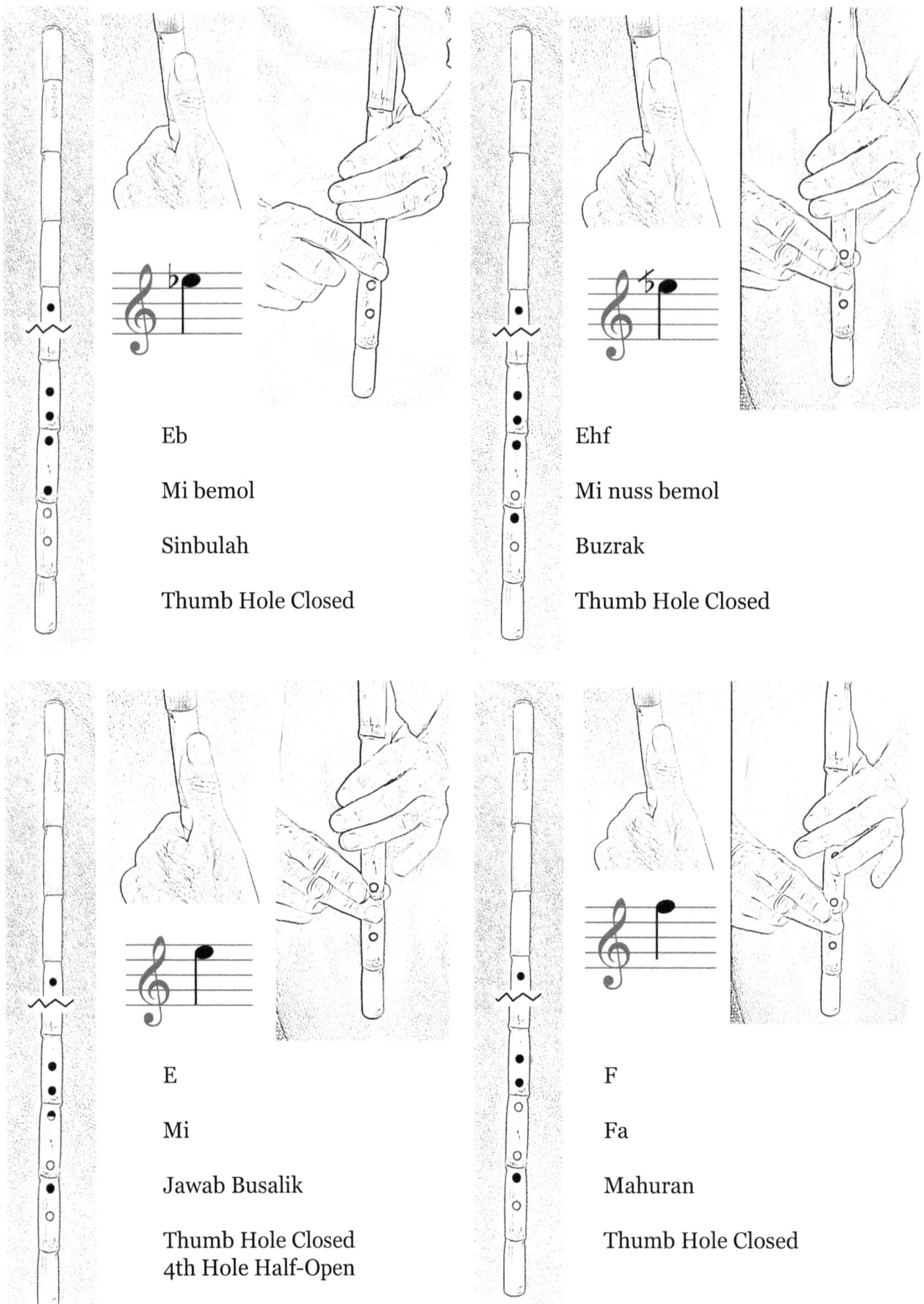

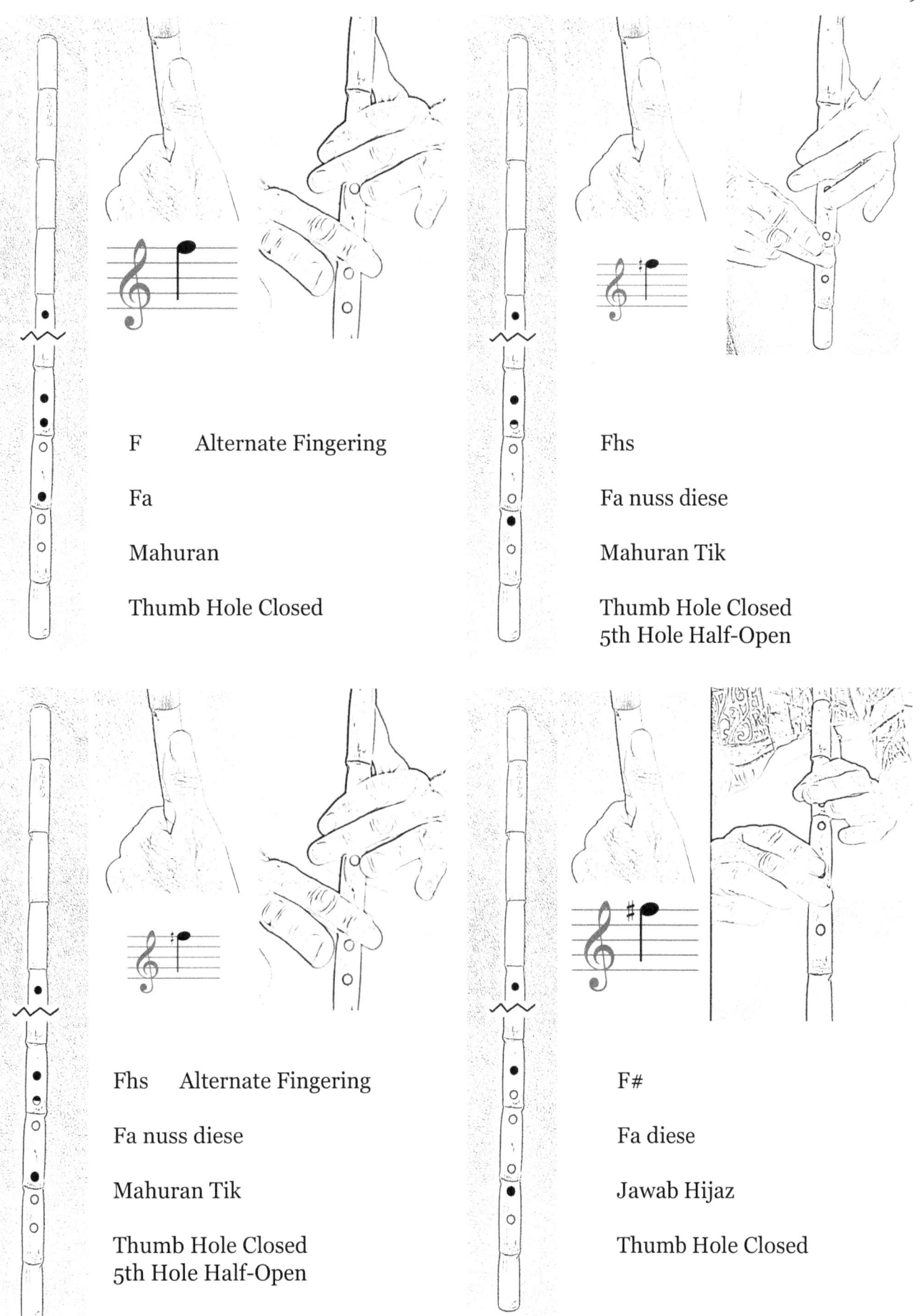

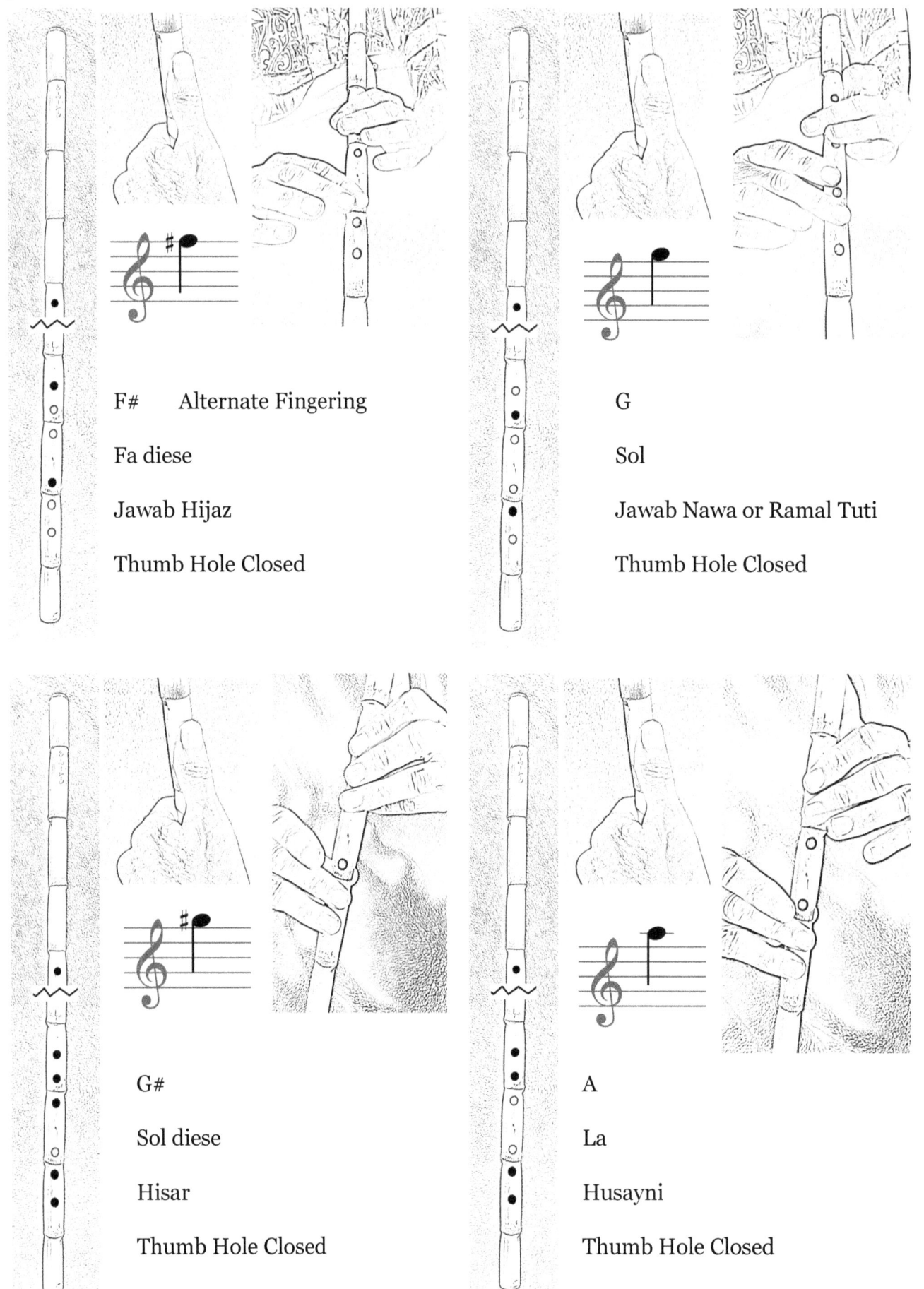

F#   Alternate Fingering

Fa diese

Jawab Hijaz

Thumb Hole Closed

G

Sol

Jawab Nawa or Ramal Tuti

Thumb Hole Closed

G#

Sol diese

Hisar

Thumb Hole Closed

A

La

Husayni

Thumb Hole Closed

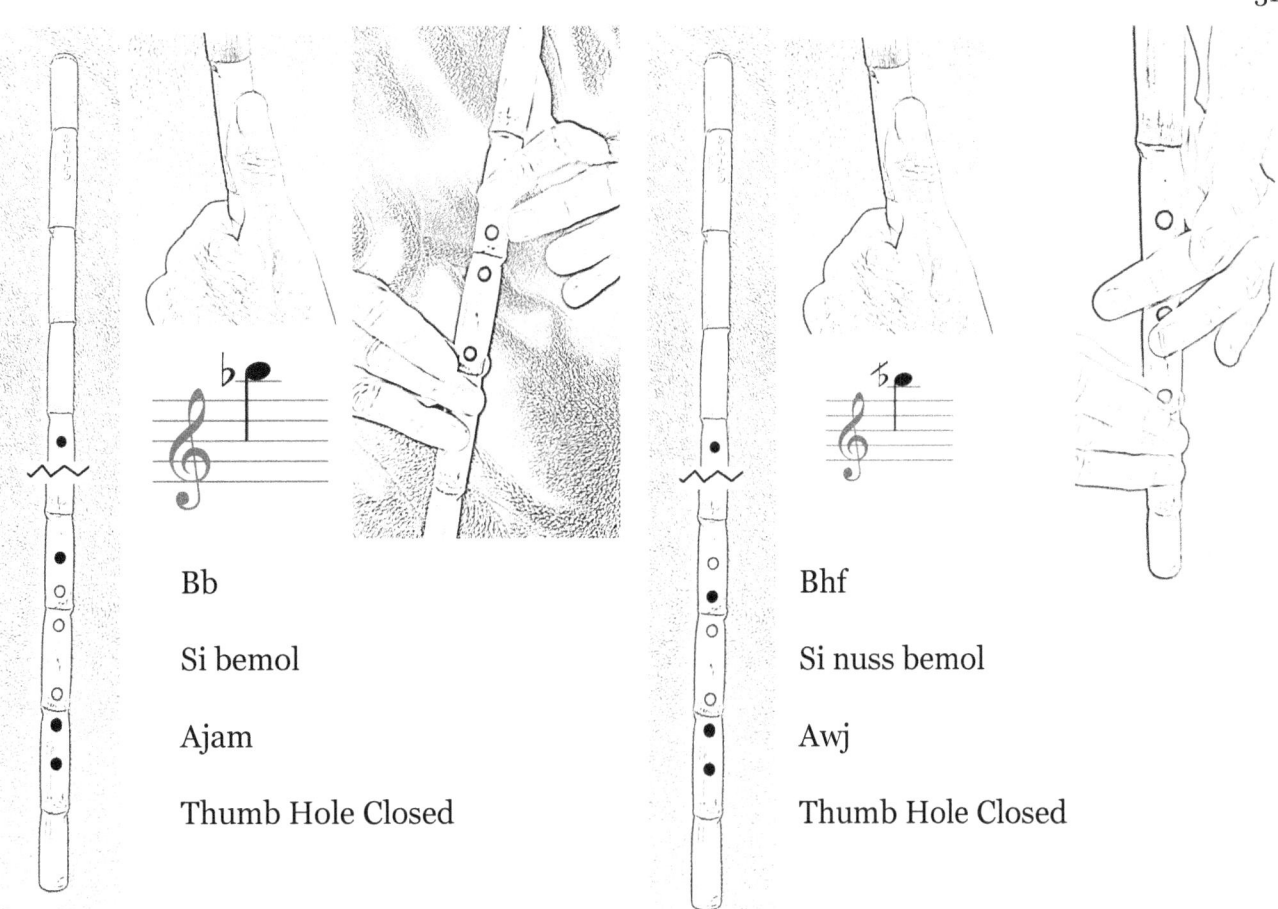

Bb

Si bemol

Ajam

Thumb Hole Closed

Bhf

Si nuss bemol

Awj

Thumb Hole Closed

> *The lament of the Nay is a fire...*
> *He who lacks this fire will perish!*
>
> *Mevlana Rumi*

The Reed Flute's Song

Listen to the story told by the reed,
of being separated.

"Since I was cut from the reedbed,
I have made this crying sound.

Anyone apart from someone he loves
understands what I say.

Anyone pulled from a source
longs to go back.

At any gathering I am there,
mingling in the laughing and grieving,

a friend to each, but few
will hear the secrets hidden

within the notes. No ears for that.
Body flowing out of spirit,

spirit up from body: no concealing
that mixing. But it's not given us

to see the soul. The reed flute
is fire, not wind. Be that empty."

Hear the love fire tangled
in the reed notes, as bewilderment

melts into wine. The reed is a friend
to all who want the fabric torn

and drawn away. The reed is hurt
and salve combining. Intimacy

and longing for intimacy, one
song. A disastrous surrender

and a fine love, together. The one
who secretly hears this is senseless.

A tongue has one customer, the ear.
A sugarcane flute has such effect

because it was able to make sugar
in the reedbed. The sound it makes

is for everyone. Days full of wanting,
let them go by without worrying

that they do. Stay where you are
inside sure a pure, hollow note.

Every thirst gets satisfied except
that of these fish, the mystics,

who swim a vast ocean of grace
still somehow longing for it!

No one lives in that without
being nourished every day.

But if someone doesn't want to hear
the song of the reed flute,

it's best to cut conversation
short, say good-bye, and leave.

The Essential Rumi - translation by Coleman Barks and John Moyne

Mapping the Maqams onto the Dukah Nay

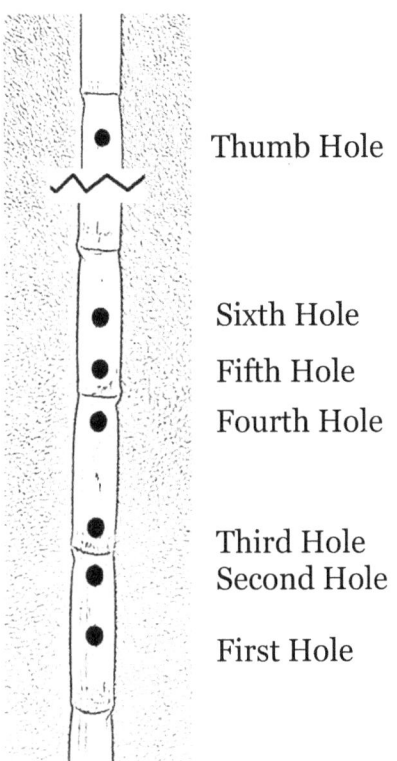

Thumb Hole

Sixth Hole
Fifth Hole
Fourth Hole

Third Hole
Second Hole

First Hole

Jins or Ajnas - Building Blocks

The "Jins" (plural "Ajnas") are the short sequences of 3 or 4 or 5 notes which form the building blocks from which the Maqams (plural "Maqamat") are assembled. They may be placed to begin on the 1st, 3rd, 4th or 5th note of a given scale or "Maqam."

Jins Rast on C

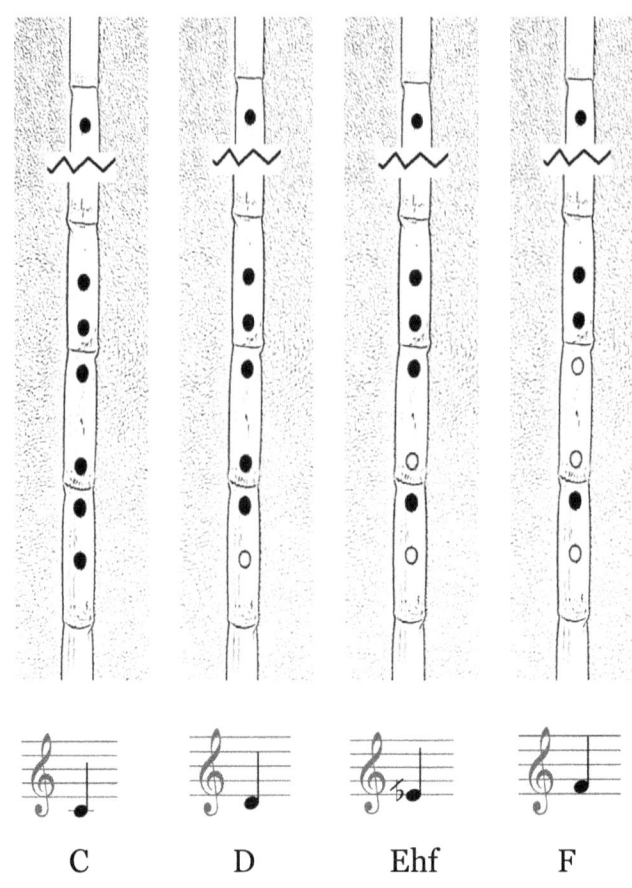

Jins Nahawand on C

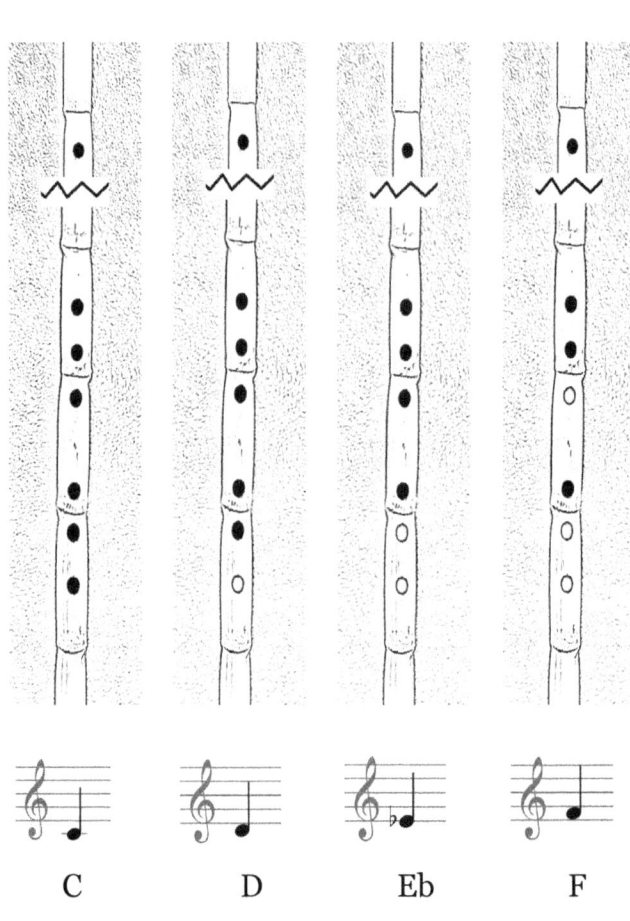

Jins Nawa Athar on C

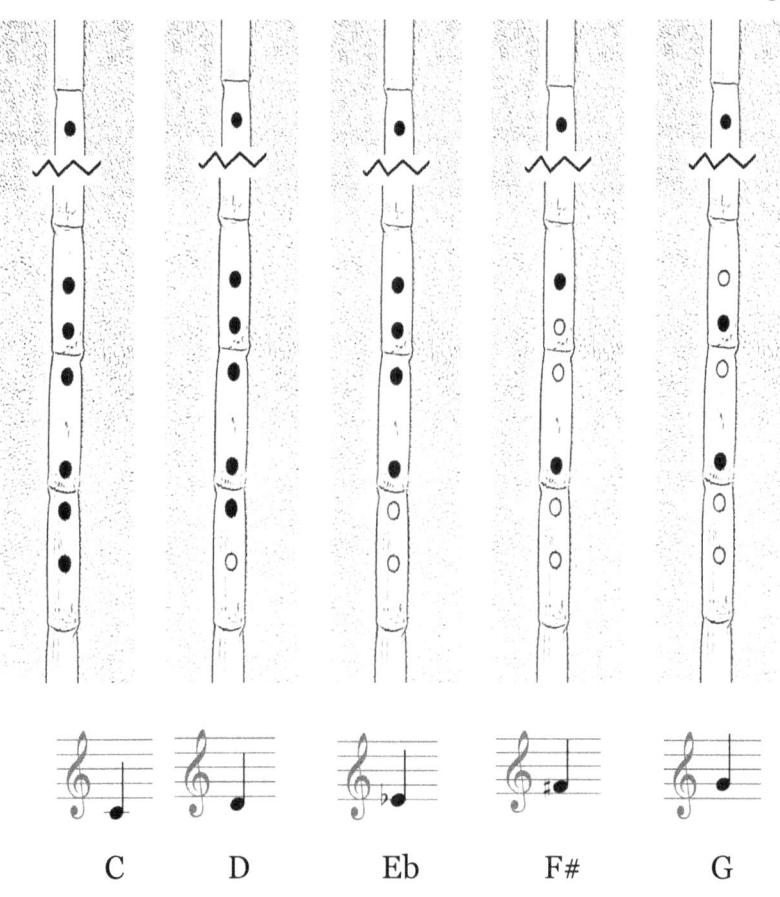

Jins Bayati on D

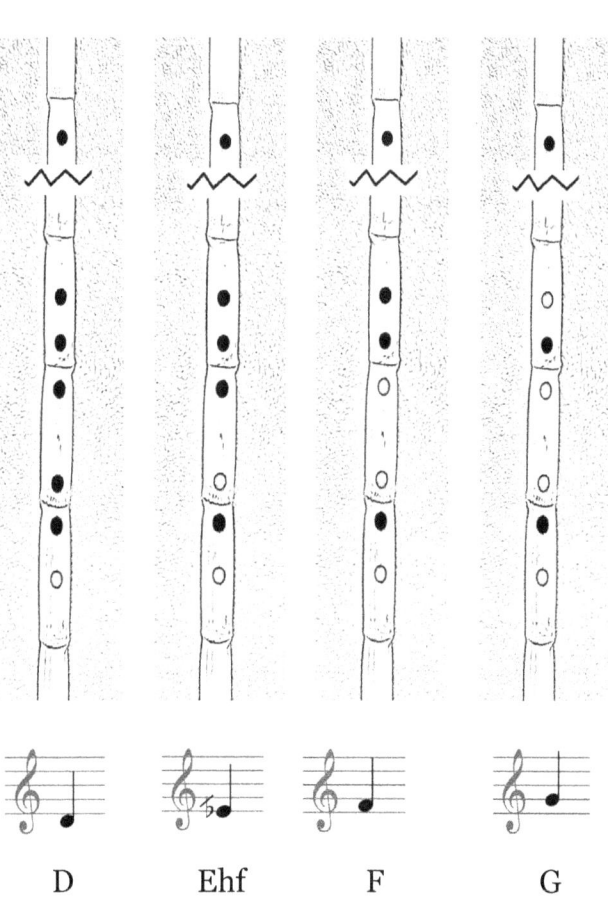

36

Jins Saba on D

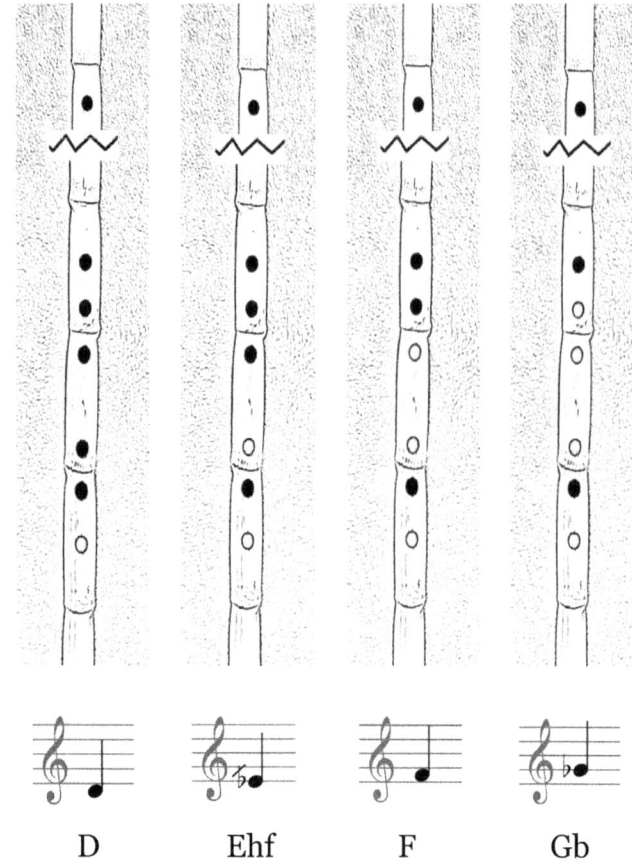

| D | Ehf | F | Gb |

Jins Hijaz on D

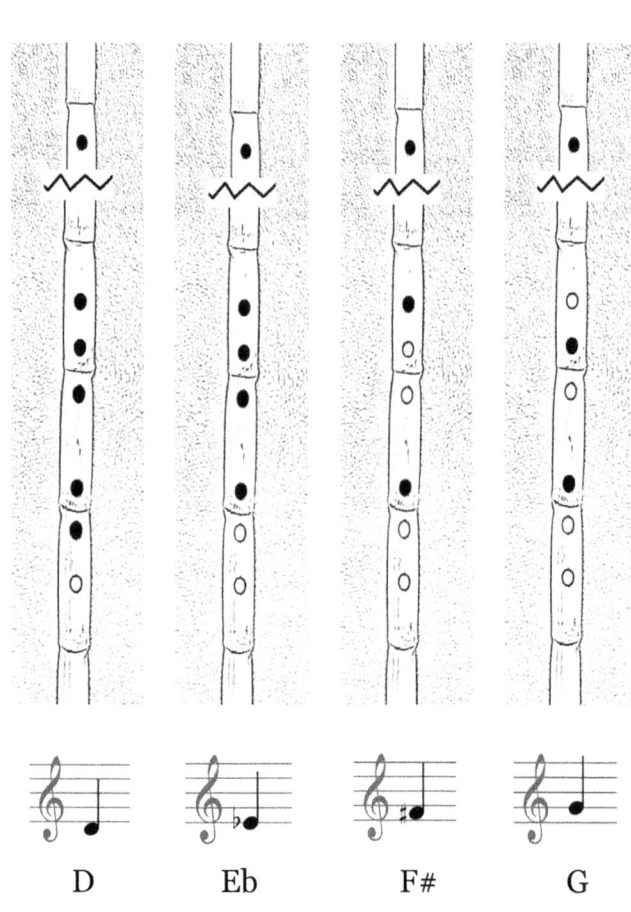

| D | Eb | F# | G |

Jins Kurd on D

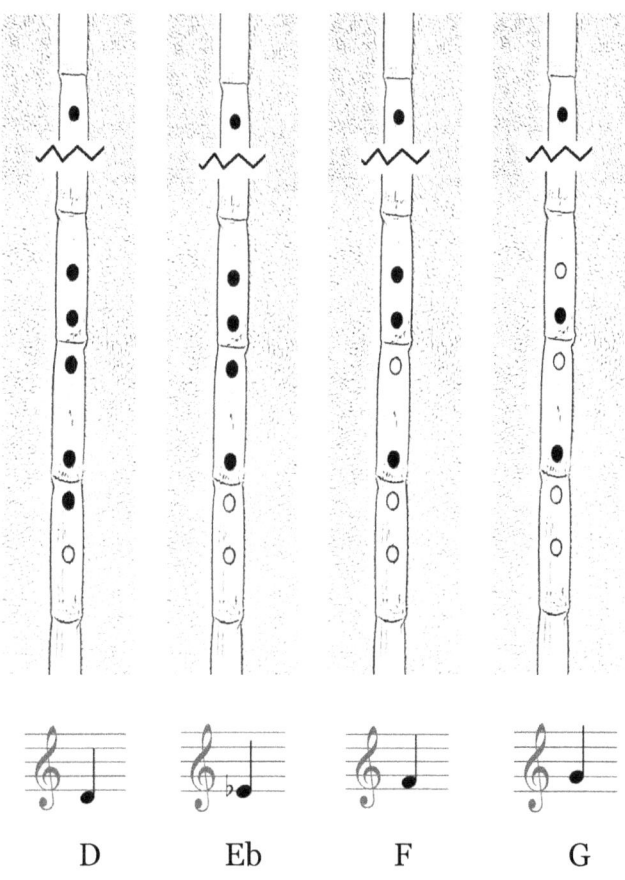

Jins Sikah on E half-flat

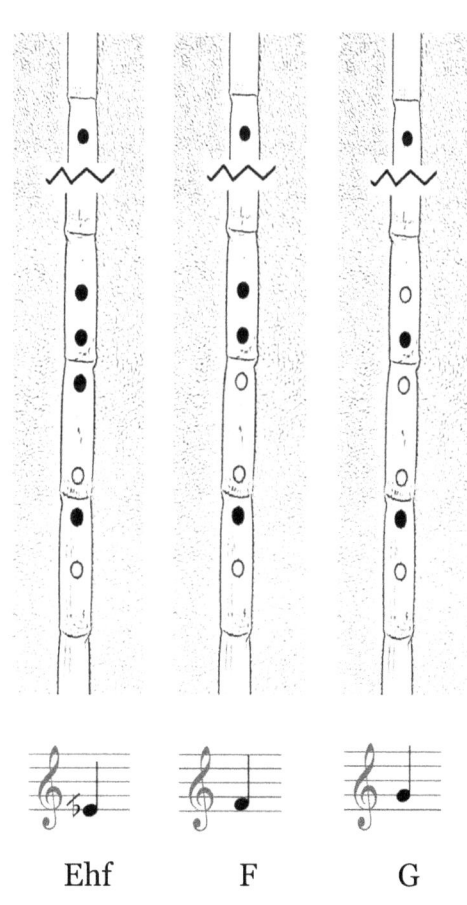

Jins Ajam on Bb

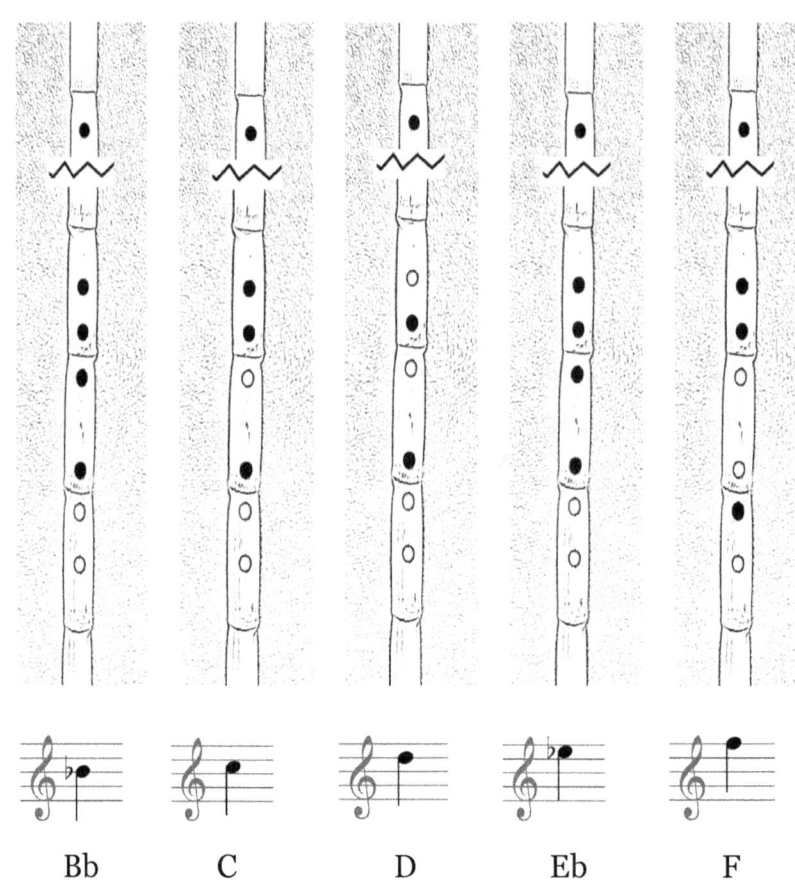

Bb   C   D   Eb   F

Jins Saba Zamzama on D

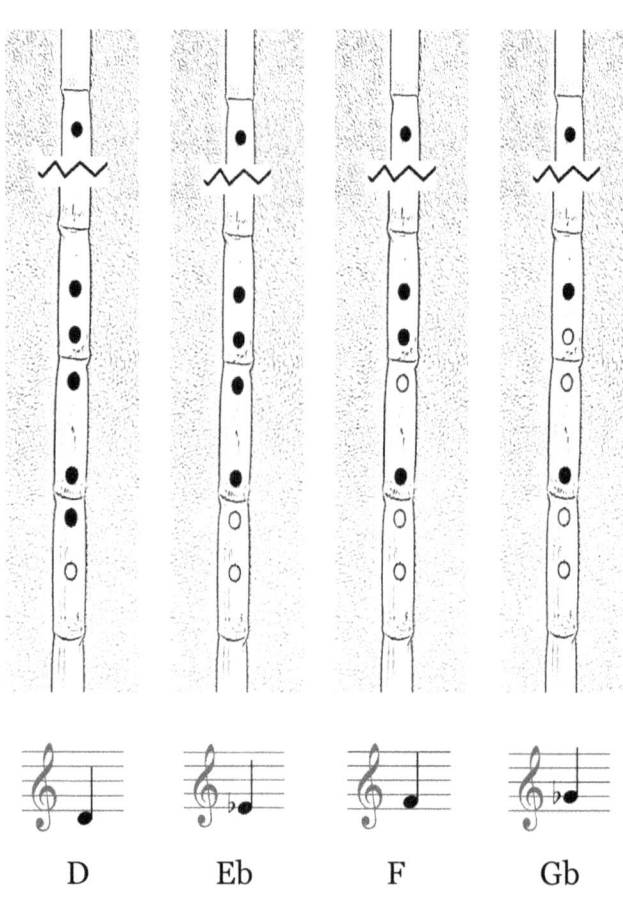

D   Eb   F   Gb

Jins Athar Kurd on C

Difficult on the nay because of the awkward half-holed Db.

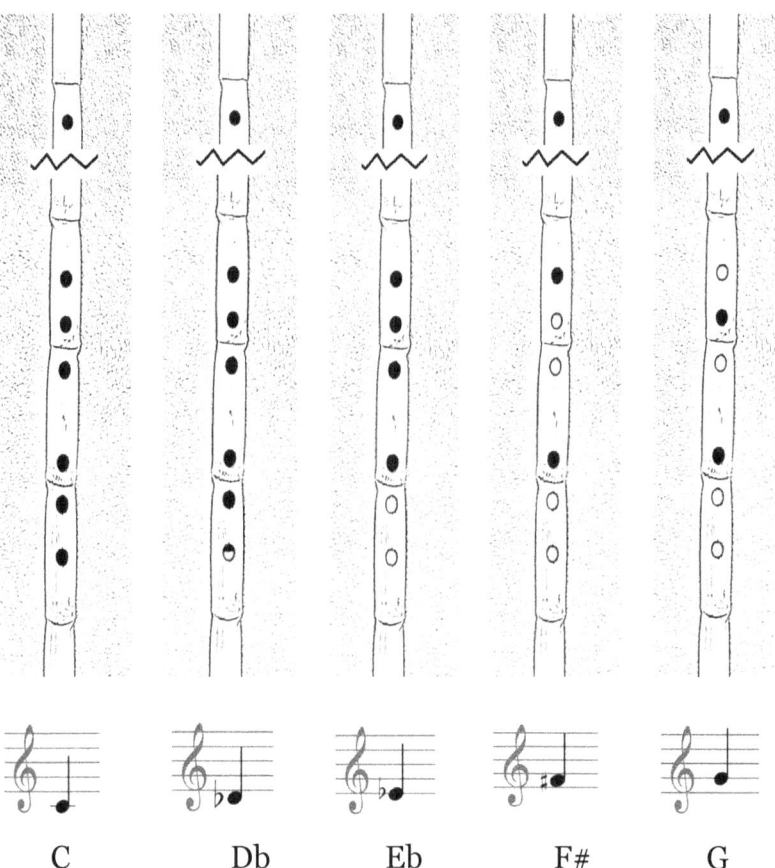

C　　　Db　　　Eb　　　F#　　　G

Leading Low Notes

Oddly, it is possible in indigenous Middle Eastern music to use this same sequence of rising pitches to introduce many different Maqam melodies regardless of their composition or tonic.

A repeating underlying rhythmic bass line which offers a soloist an opportunity for improvisation or "taqasim" may be composed of these four notes and great freedom for modulation remains without requiring the necessity for changing these notes.

Of course the musicians may also choose to modify the notes to match the overlying melodies more precisely.

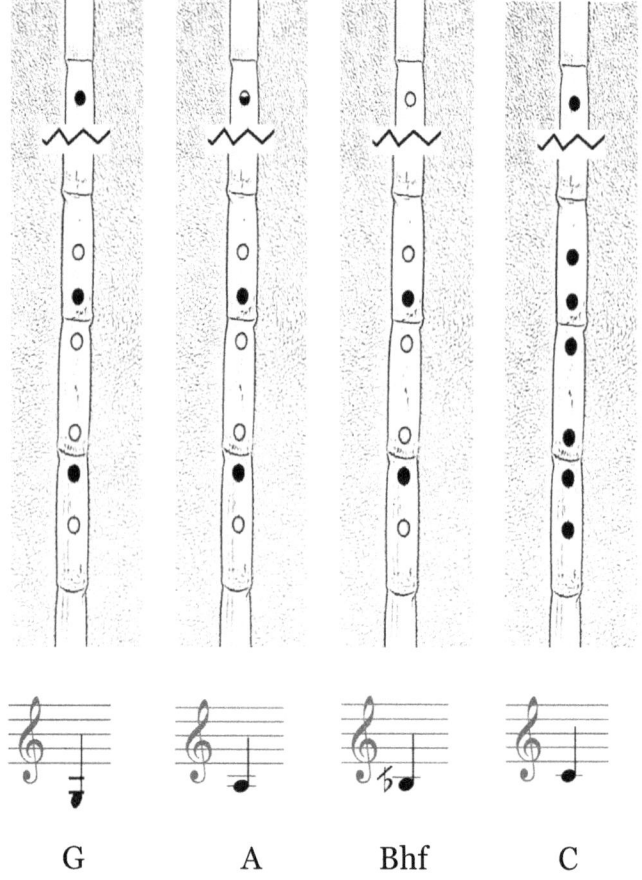

G   A   Bhf   C

Maqam Charts

The following finger position charts are designed for the "Dukah" Nay - Known as best for Key (Tonic or "Qarar") of D (Re).

Charts for other size nays would be the same although the keys of the maqams produced would be of course higher or lower.

I will break with modern tradition and, going back to the old Arabic note names, begin with maqams in G instead of C. If it's true, as I suspect, that the whole maqam system comes from the nay, then it makes sense to begin with maqams based on the G note in the low "Kabá" Register. If you close only the thumb hole and softly blow you will hear the low G which is the note called Yakah. Of course you will probably close the 2nd and 5th holes also with your fingers but this is just to support the instrument. Those hole closures do not actually change the pitch of the note.

List of Maqams for Dukah Nay

Kabá (Low) Register:

Thumb Closed
G Farahfaza (Nahawand 1)
G Sultani Yaka (Nahawand 2)
G Yakah (Yah-Gah or Rast Nawa)

Thumb Quarter Open
A Shawki Tarab (Kurd on A with Saba)
A Busalik Ushayran (Bayati on A)
Maqam Bayati Ushayran (Bayatayn on A)
Maqam Hijazi Ushayran (Shuri on A)

Thumb Half Open
Bb Ajam Ushayran
Bb Shawq Afza

Thumb Open
Bhf Rahat al Arwah (Huzam)
Bhf Irak
Bhf Bastanikar

First Register:

1st Hole
C Rast
C Suznak
C Dalanshin
C Nahawand 1
C Nahawand 2
C Nakriz
C Nawa Athar
C Athar Kurd
C Basandidah

2nd Hole
D Bayati
D Husayni
D Saba
D Saba Zamzama
D Shuri
D Hijaz
D Hijaz Awji
D Shehnaz
D Kurd
D Shehnaz Kurdi

3rd Hole
Eb Ajam on Eb

4th Hole
Ehf Sikah
Ehf Huzam
Ehf Awshar

5th Hole
F Jaharka (Ajam)
F Jaharka Turki (Shehnaz)

6th Hole
F# - Not used as "qarar" or "tonic"

Maqams Basic to the Nay

Of the maqams listed below learn the ones in Bold lettering first. These are the most primary and basic.

It could be that the origin of the maqam system of musical scales is actually nothing more nor less than choosing different holes on the nay as starting points.
These starting points for these various musical scales are called 'qarar' or 'tonic' or 'key' depending on which language or music tradition is referenced.

Although there are laws of acoustic physics which lead to the primacy of an 8-note justly intonated diatonic scale, there is nothing about the structure of string instruments which invites the adoption of various tonics at certain finger positions. It could be that the laws of physics underly the maqam system but it could also be that the notes created by taking a simple stalk of reed and boring 7 holes in it has done the trick.

Kabá Register

Thumb Closed
G Farahfaza (Nahawand 1)
G Sultani Yaka (Nahawand 2)
G Yakah (Yah-Gah or Rast Nawa)

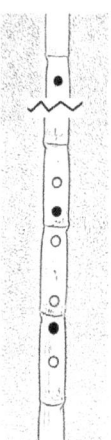

Thumb Quarter Open
A Shawki Tarab (Kurd with Saba)
A Busalik Ushayran (Bayati)
A Bayati Ushayran (Bayatayn)
A Hijazi Ushayran (Shuri)

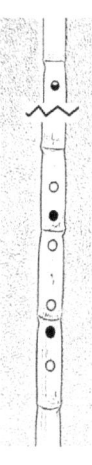

Thumb Half Open
Bb Ajam Ushayran
Bb Shawq Afza

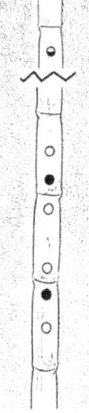

Thumb Open
Bhf Rahat al Arwah (Huzam)
Bhf Irak
Bhf Bastanikar

It is easy to bend the note produced using this hole pattern from Bb to B half-flat by using the lips and breath alone.

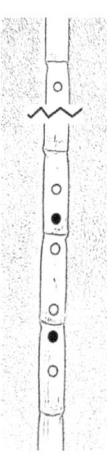

First Register

1st Hole – C

C Rast
C Suznak
C Dalanshin
C Nahawand 1
C Nahawand 2
C Nakriz
C Nawa Athar
C Athar Kurd
C Basandidah

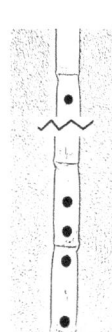

2nd Hole – D

D Bayati
D Husayni
D Saba
D Saba Zamzama
D Shuri
D Hijaz
D Hijaz Awji
D Shehnaz
D Kurd
D Shehnaz Kurdi

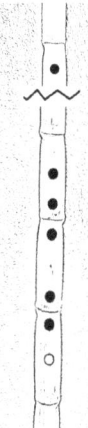

3rd Hole – Eb
Ajam on Eb

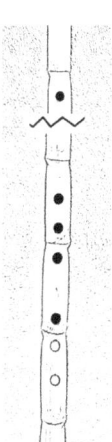

4th Hole – Ehf
4th Hole
Ehf Sikah
Ehf Huzam
Ehf Awshar

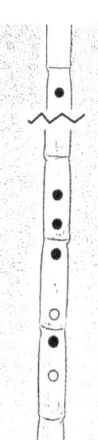

5th Hole – F
5th Hole
F Jaharka (Ajam)
F Jaharka Turki (Shehnaz)

Alternate fingerings are available depending on whether maqam contains Eb or Ehf.

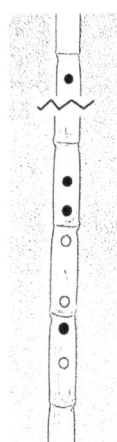

6th Hole
F# - Not used as tonic

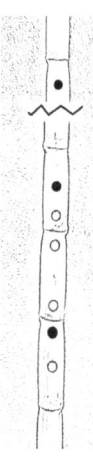

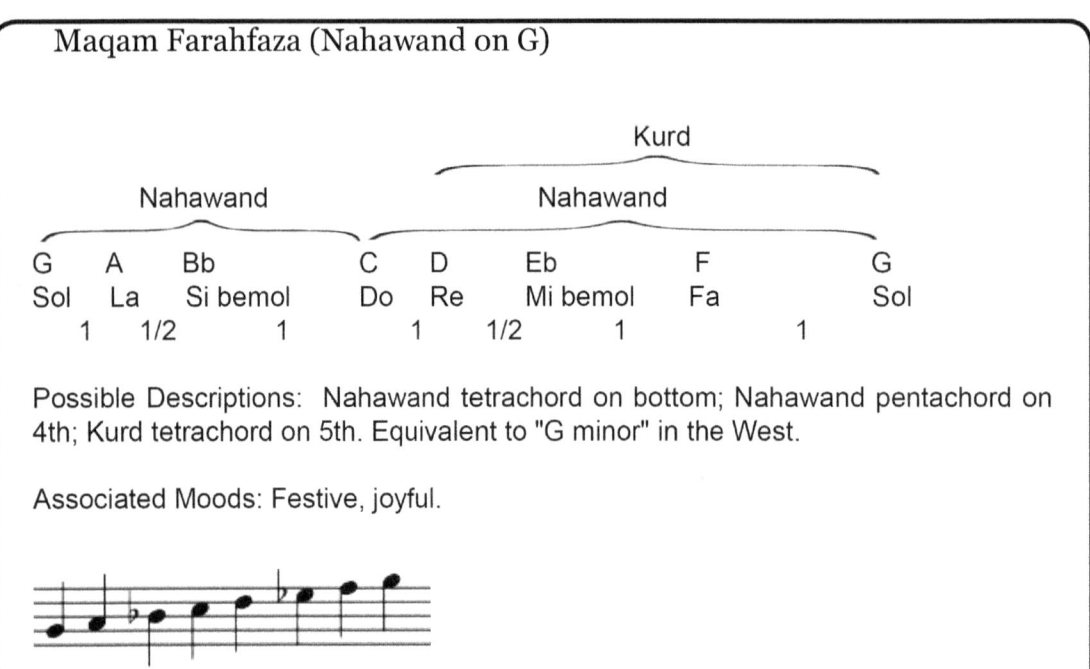

Maqam Farahfaza (Nahawand on G)

Nahawand: G A Bb — Sol La Si bemol — 1 1/2 1
Nahawand: C D Eb F — Do Re Mi bemol Fa — 1 1/2 1
Kurd: C D Eb — (tetrachord on 5th)
... G — Sol — 1

Possible Descriptions: Nahawand tetrachord on bottom; Nahawand pentachord on 4th; Kurd tetrachord on 5th. Equivalent to "G minor" in the West.

Associated Moods: Festive, joyful.

Low Kabá Register:

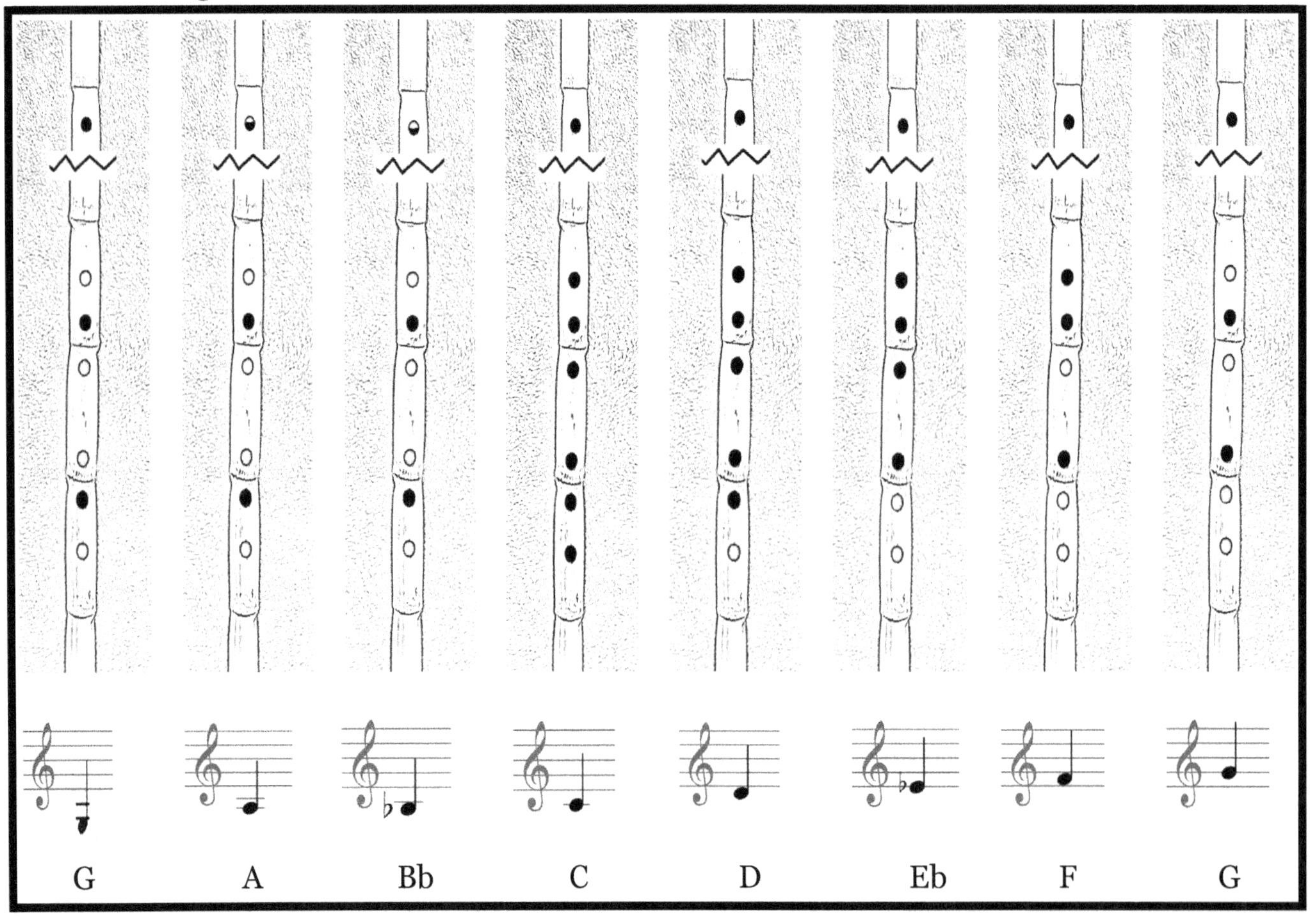

G   A   Bb   C   D   Eb   F   G

Main Register:

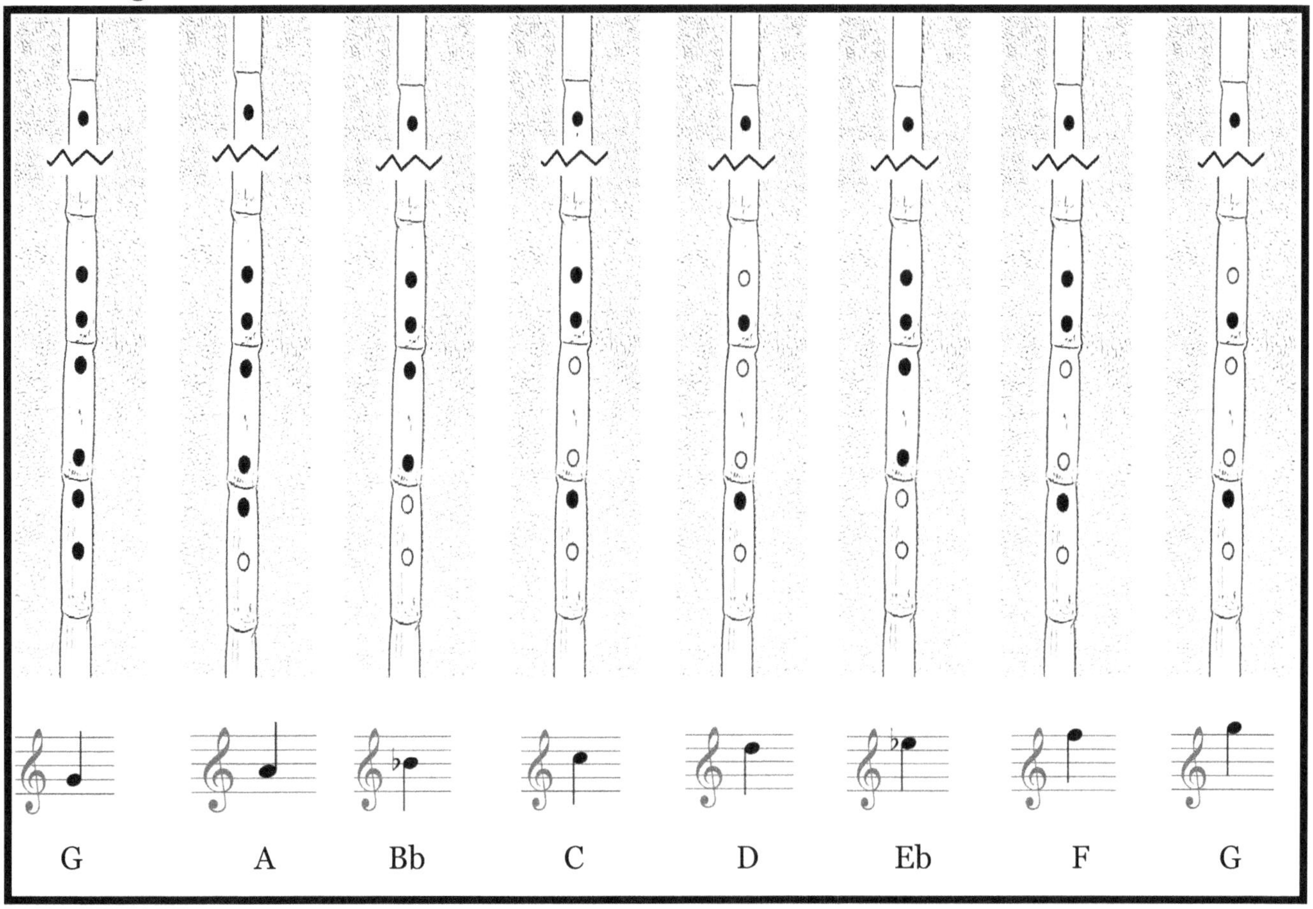

| G | A | Bb | C | D | Eb | F | G |

Second Register:

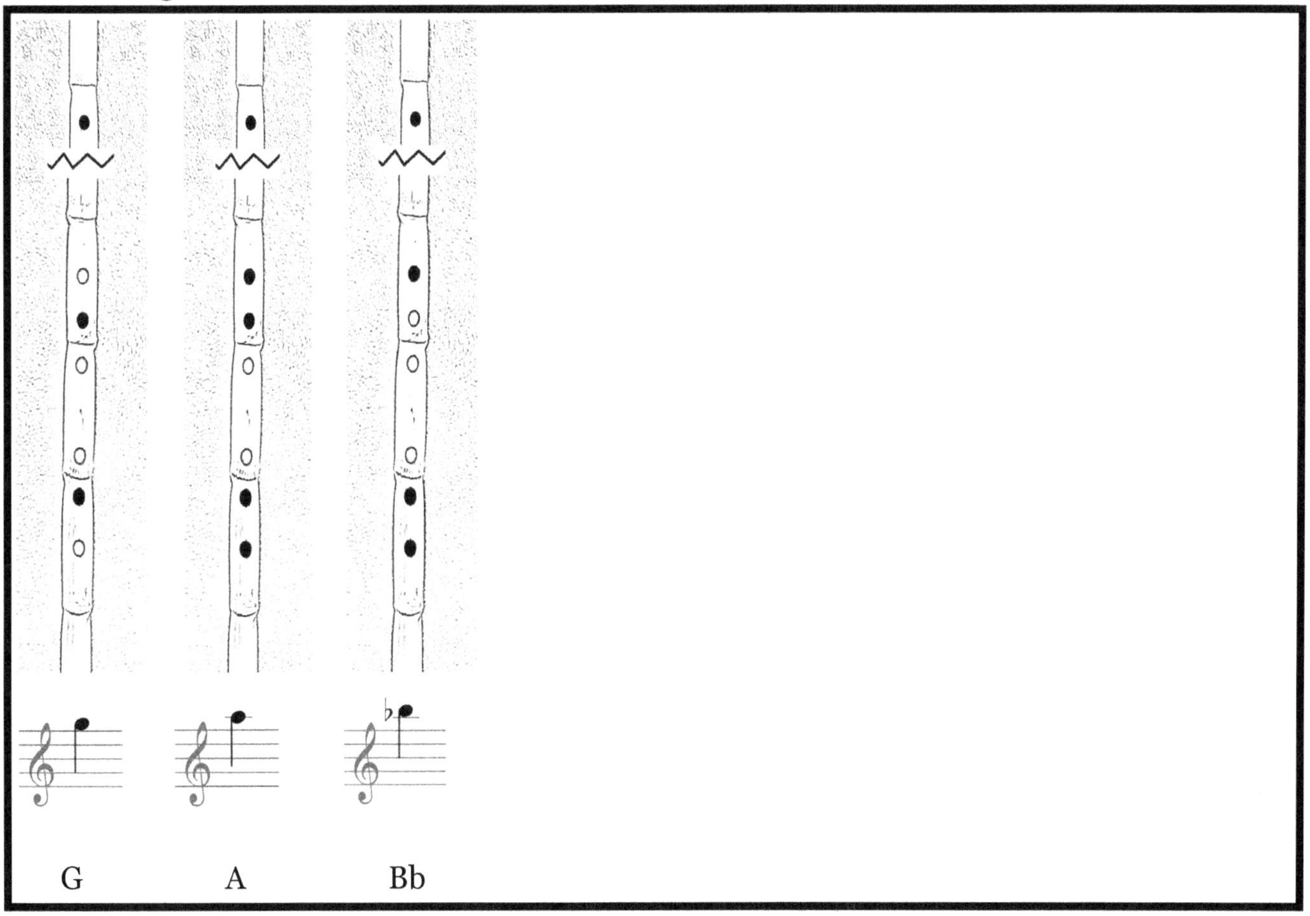

| G | A | Bb |

Maqam Sultani Yaka (Nahawand 2 on G)

Closely Related Maqamat: Rahat Faza

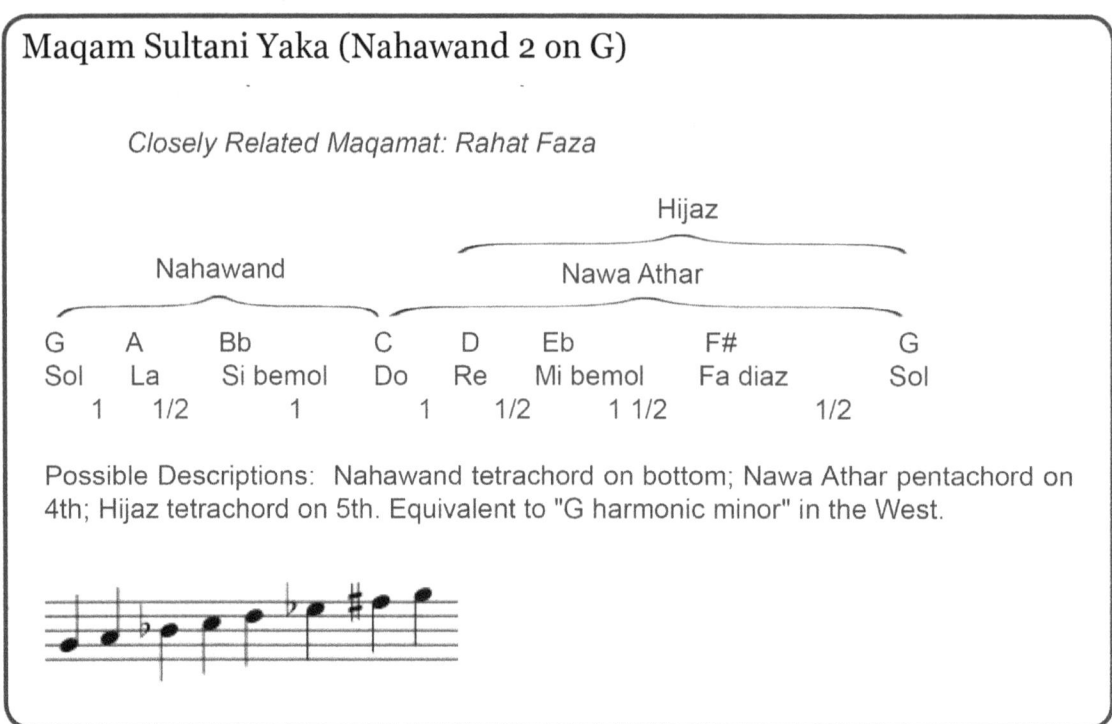

	Nahawand				Nawa Athar		Hijaz	
G	A	Bb	C	D	Eb		F#	G
Sol	La	Si bemol	Do	Re	Mi bemol		Fa diaz	Sol
	1	1/2	1	1	1/2	1 1/2		1/2

Possible Descriptions: Nahawand tetrachord on bottom; Nawa Athar pentachord on 4th; Hijaz tetrachord on 5th. Equivalent to "G harmonic minor" in the West.

Low Kabá Register:

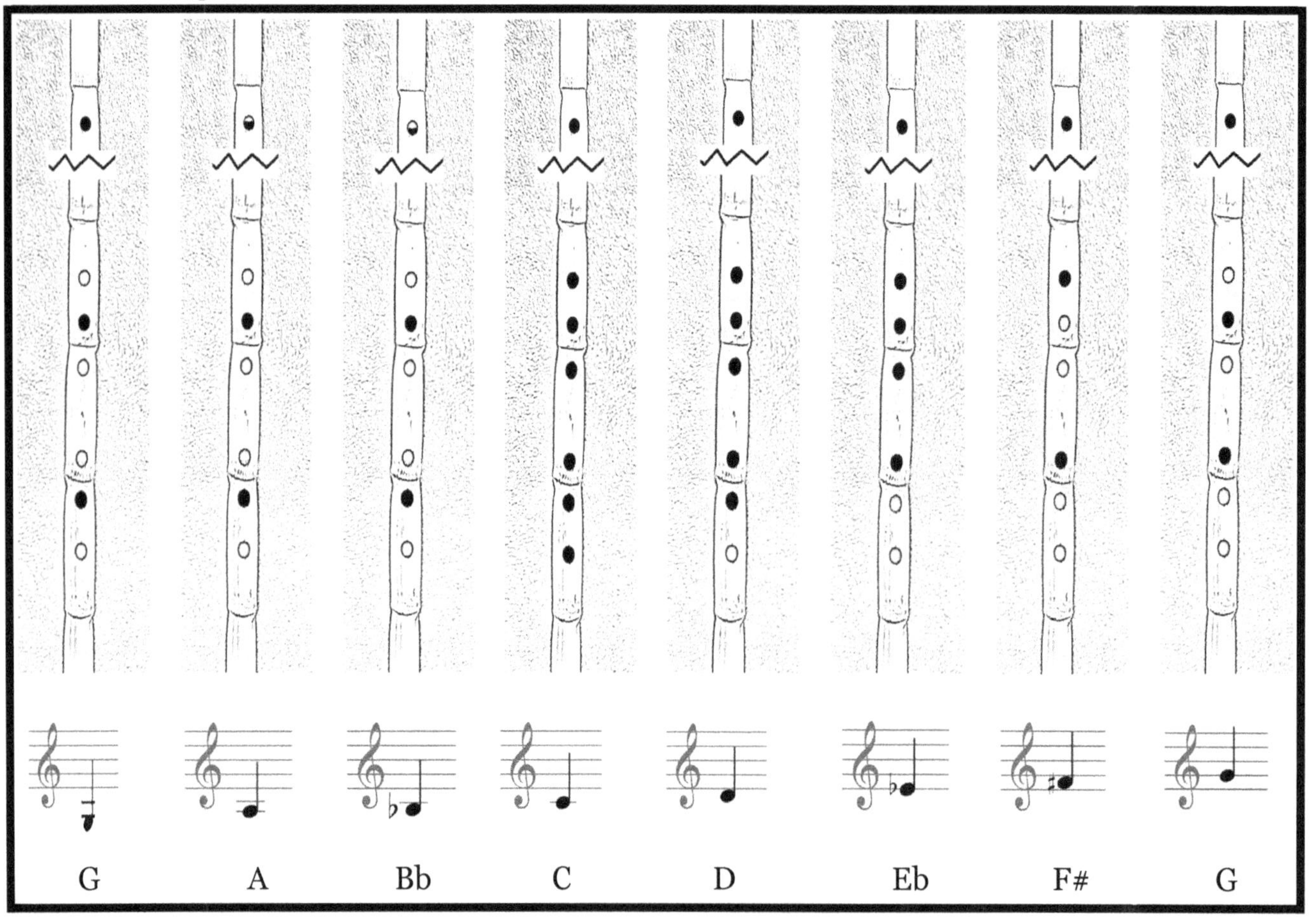

| G | A | Bb | C | D | Eb | F# | G |

Main Register:

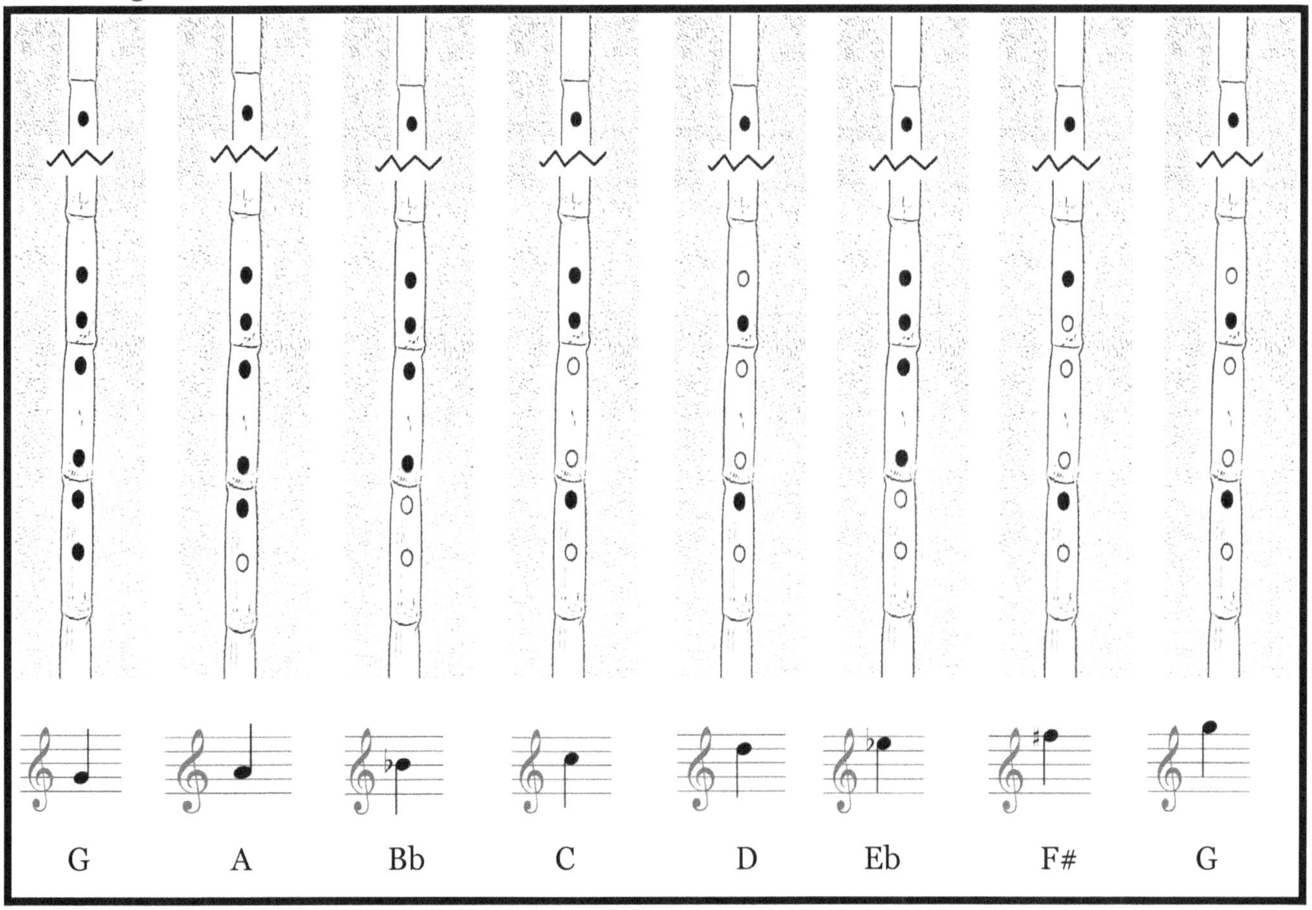

| G | A | Bb | C | D | Eb | F# | G |

Second Register:

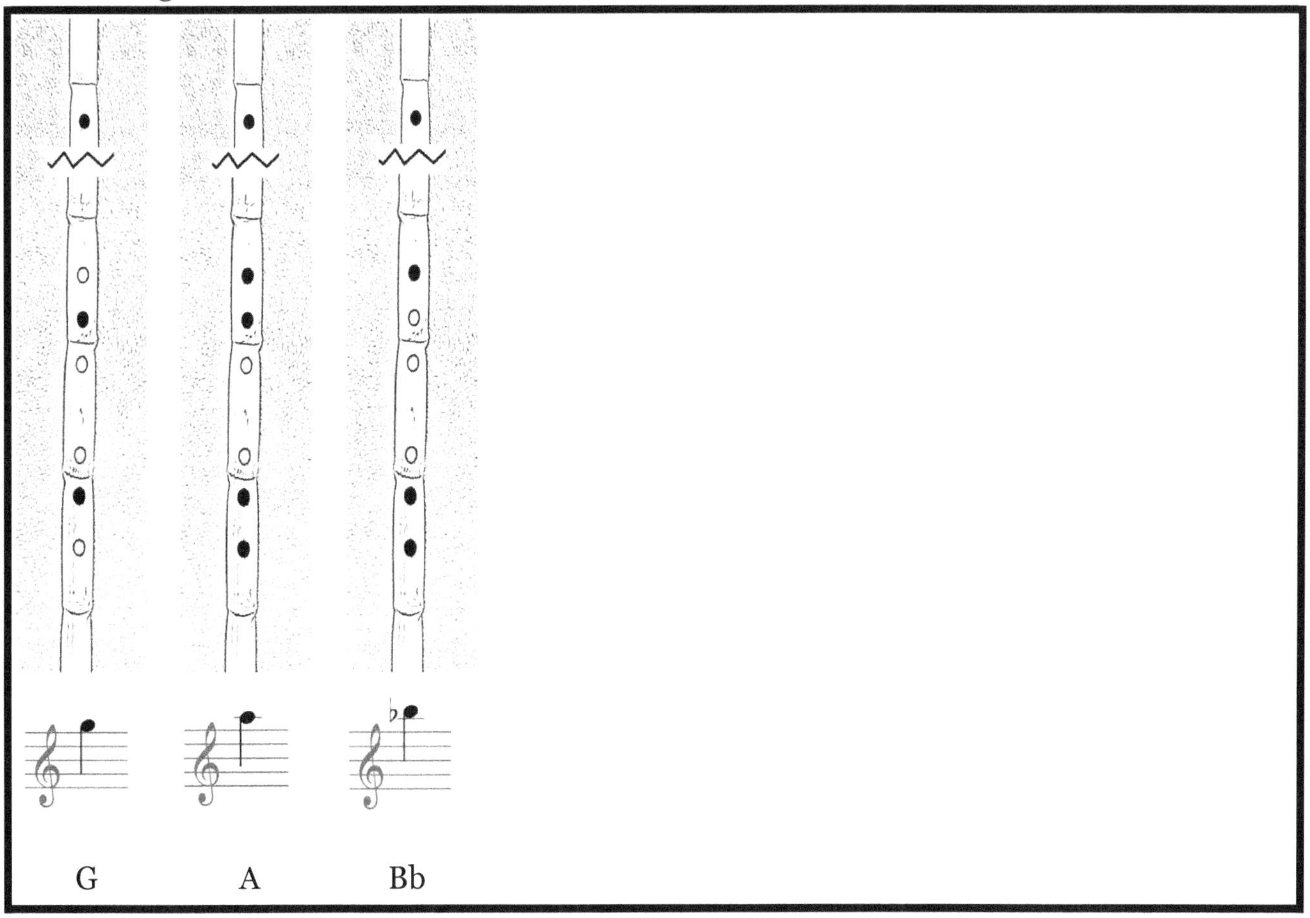

| G | A | Bb |

47

48

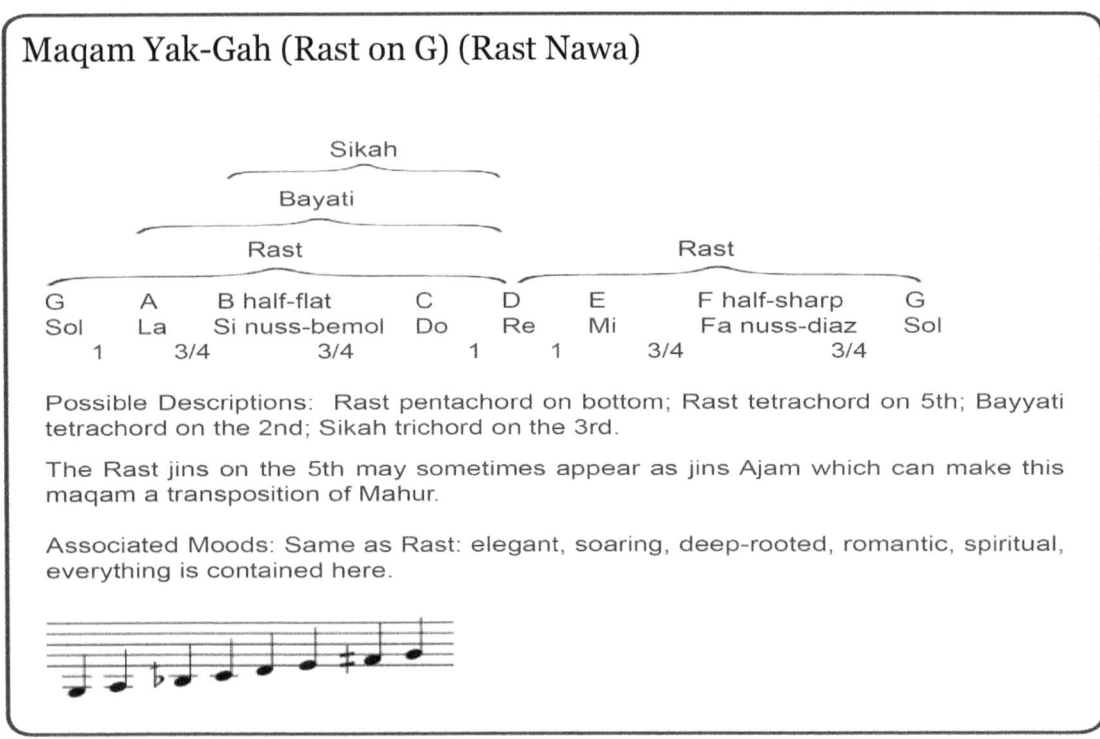

Maqam Yak-Gah (Rast on G) (Rast Nawa)

```
                    Sikah
              Bayati
         Rast                          Rast
G     A    B half-flat   C      D    E    F half-sharp   G
Sol   La   Si nuss-bemol Do     Re   Mi   Fa nuss-diaz   Sol
  1    3/4      3/4       1      1    3/4       3/4
```

Possible Descriptions: Rast pentachord on bottom; Rast tetrachord on 5th; Bayyati tetrachord on the 2nd; Sikah trichord on the 3rd.

The Rast jins on the 5th may sometimes appear as jins Ajam which can make this maqam a transposition of Mahur.

Associated Moods: Same as Rast: elegant, soaring, deep-rooted, romantic, spiritual, everything is contained here.

Due to the awkwardness of playing some of these low notes and also the F half-sharp on the nay, it would be easiest to play this maqam on the A Husayni Nay or on the low A Mansur Nay.

Low Kabá Register:

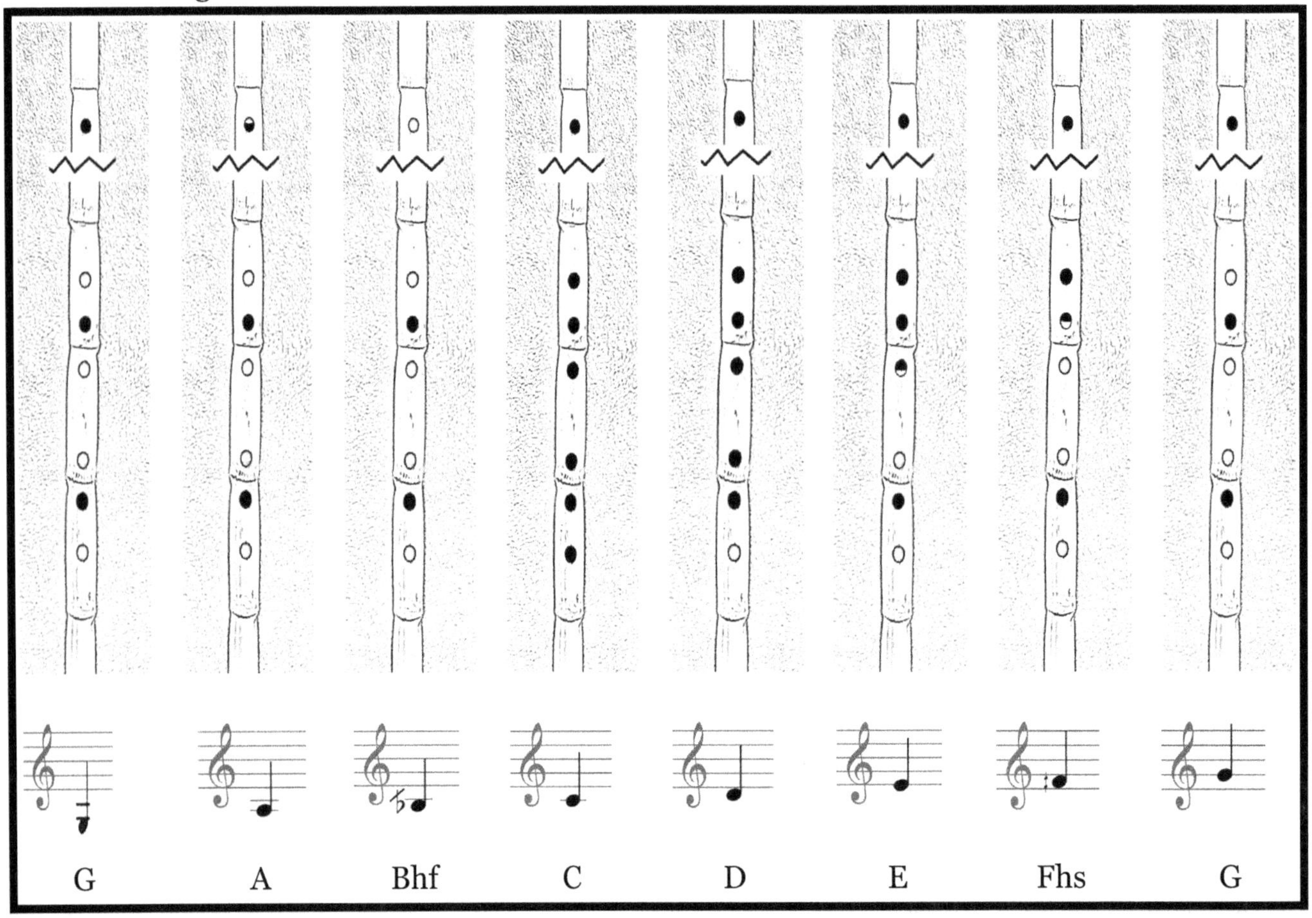

G   A   Bhf   C   D   E   Fhs   G

Main Register:

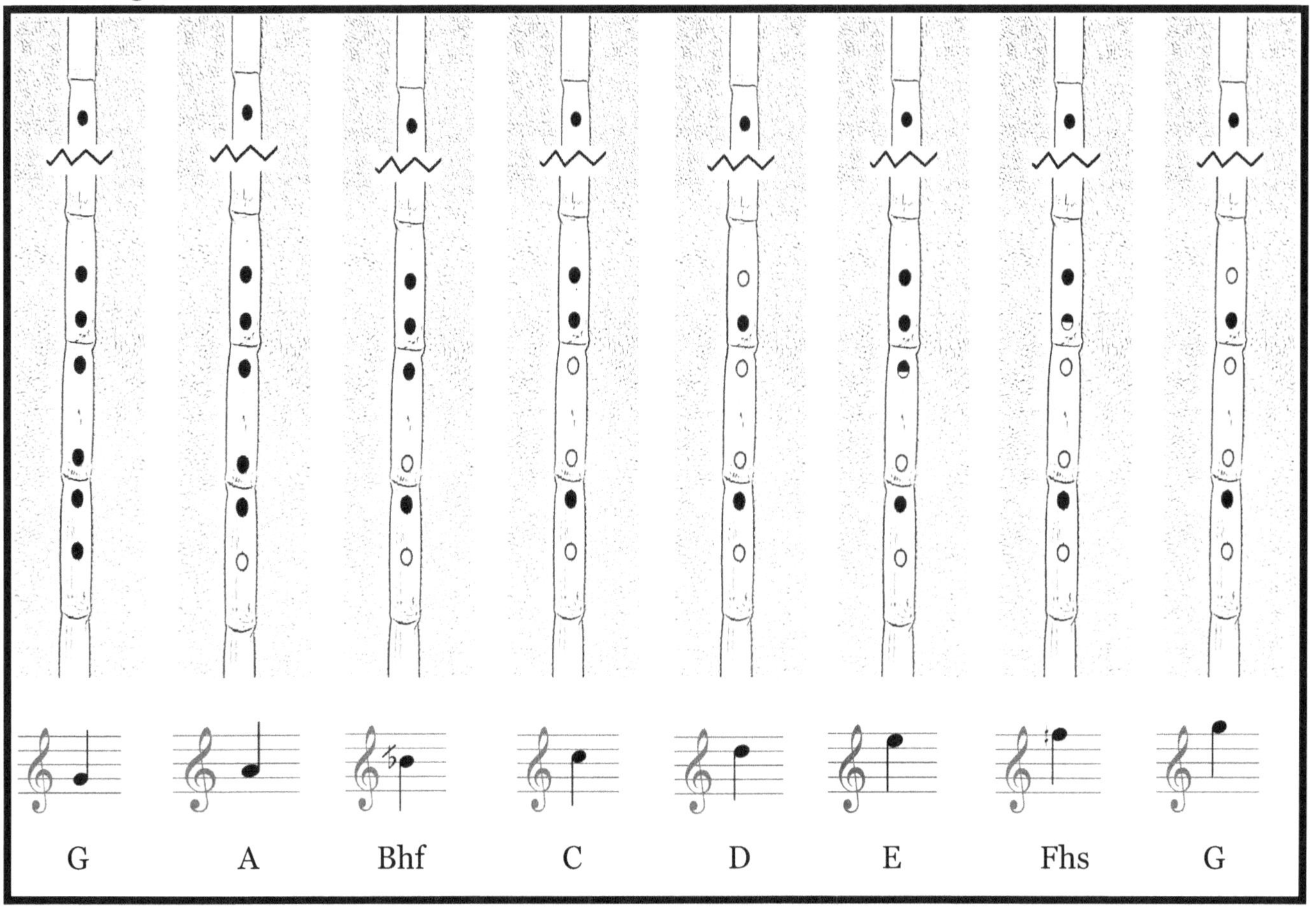

| G | A | Bhf | C | D | E | Fhs | G |

Second Register:

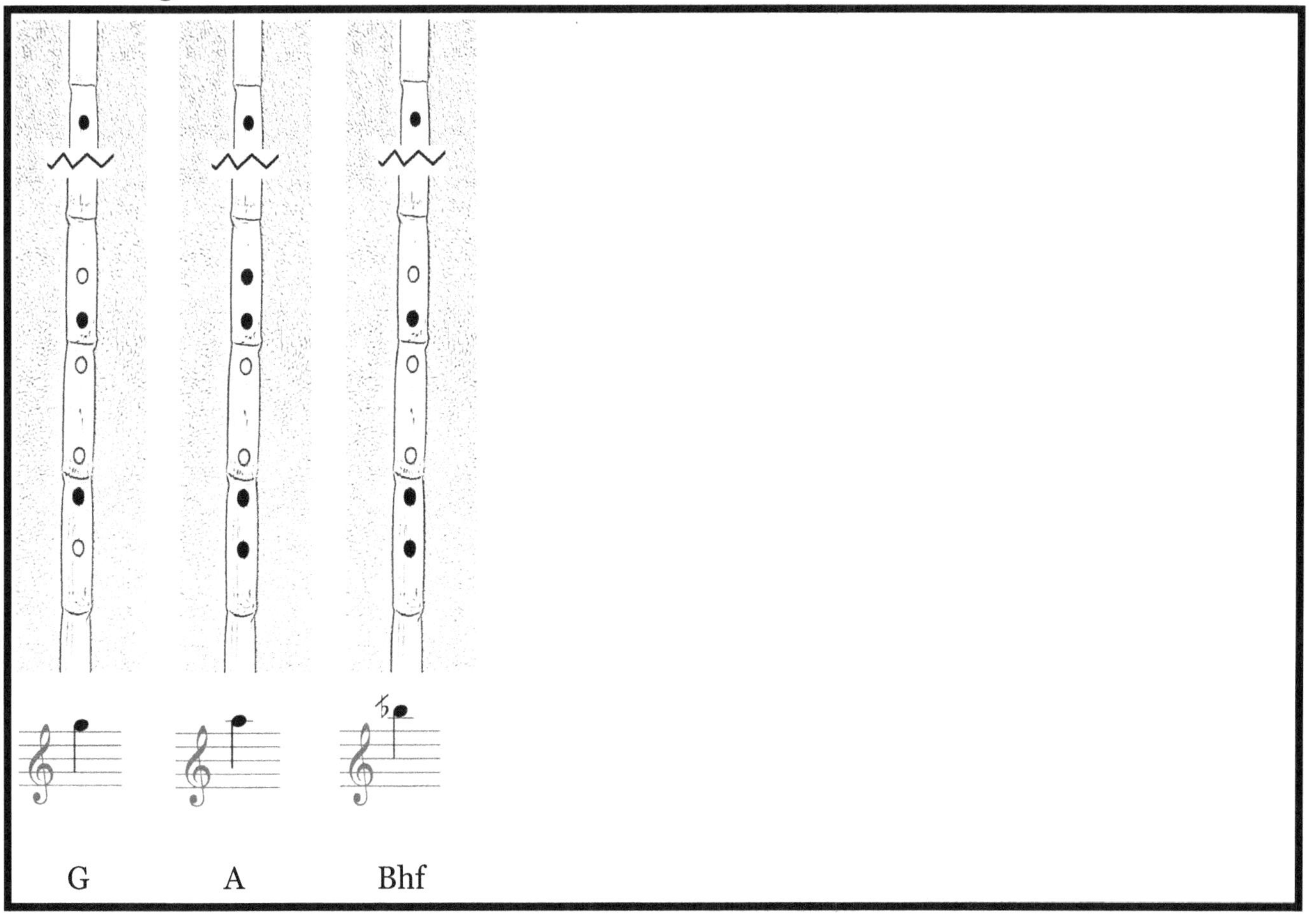

| G | A | Bhf |

Maqam Shawki Tarab (Kurd on A with Saba)

	Kurd				Saba		
A	Bb	C	D	E half-flat	F	Gb
La	Si bemol	Do	Re	Mi nuss-bemol	Fa	Sol
	1/2	1	1	3/4	3/4	1/2

Possible Descriptions: Kurd tetrachord on bottom; Saba tetrachord on 4th.

Low Kabá Register:

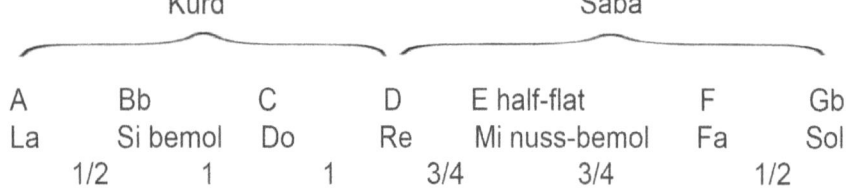

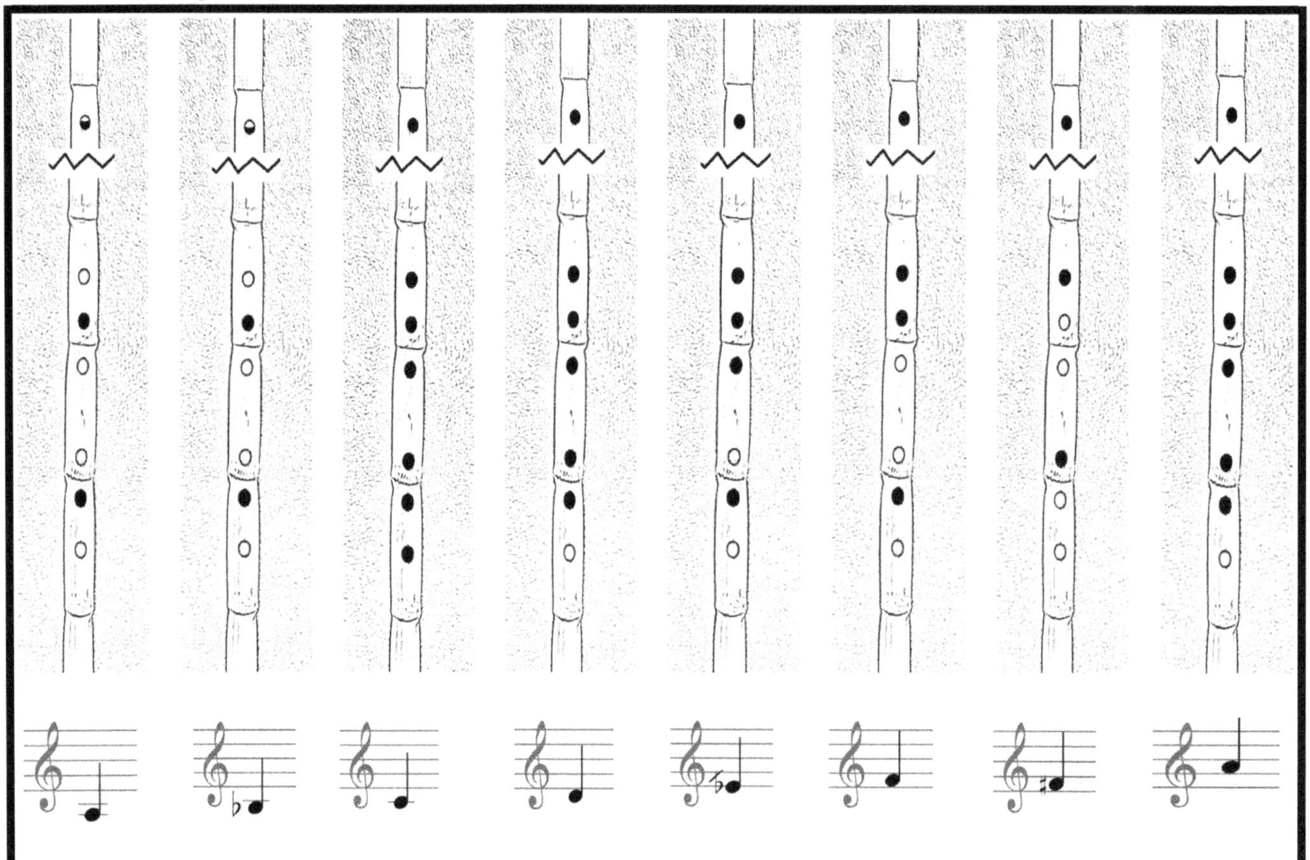

| A | Bb | C | D | Ehf | F | F# | A |

Main Register:

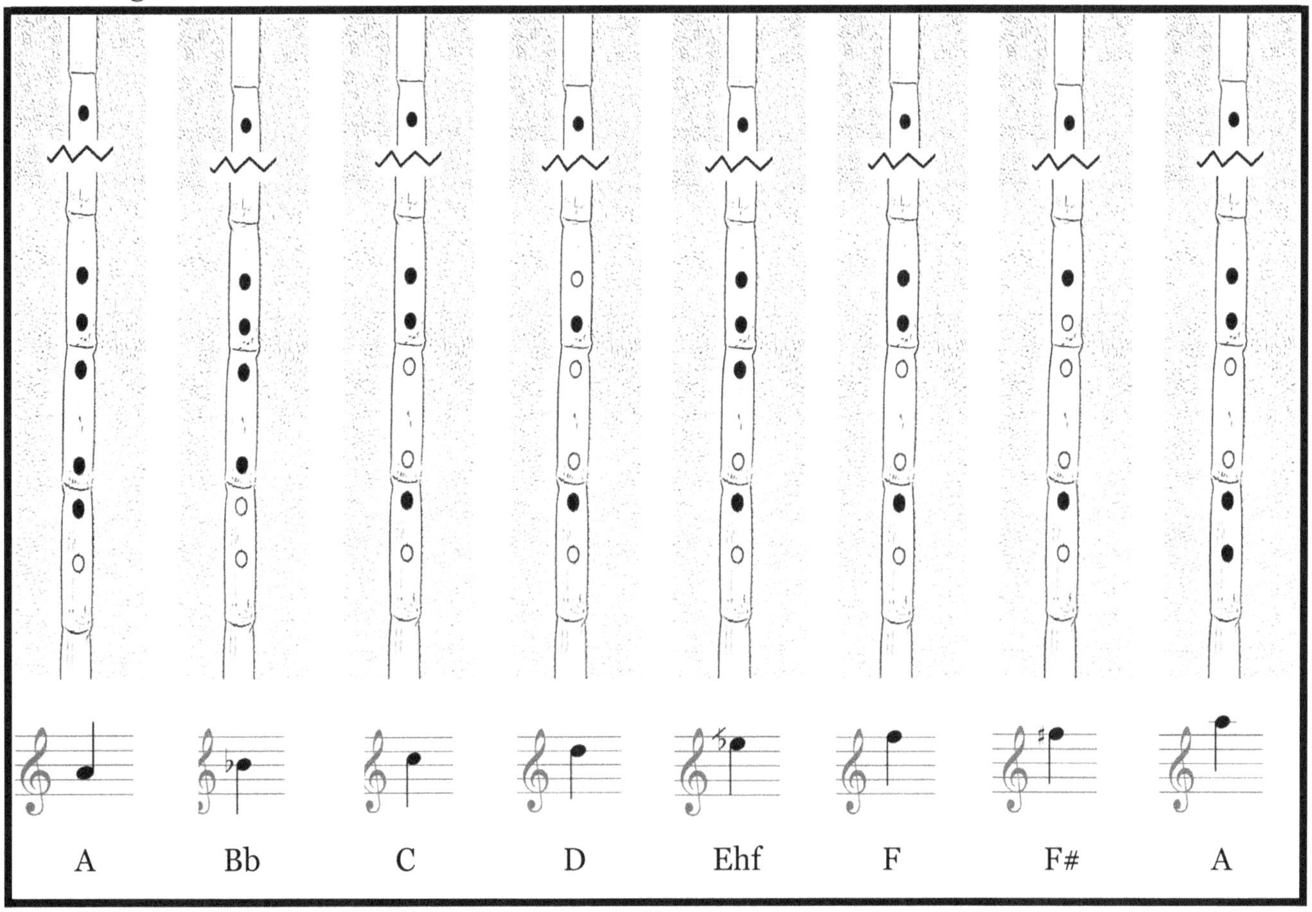

A	Bb	C	D	Ehf	F	F#	A

Second Register:

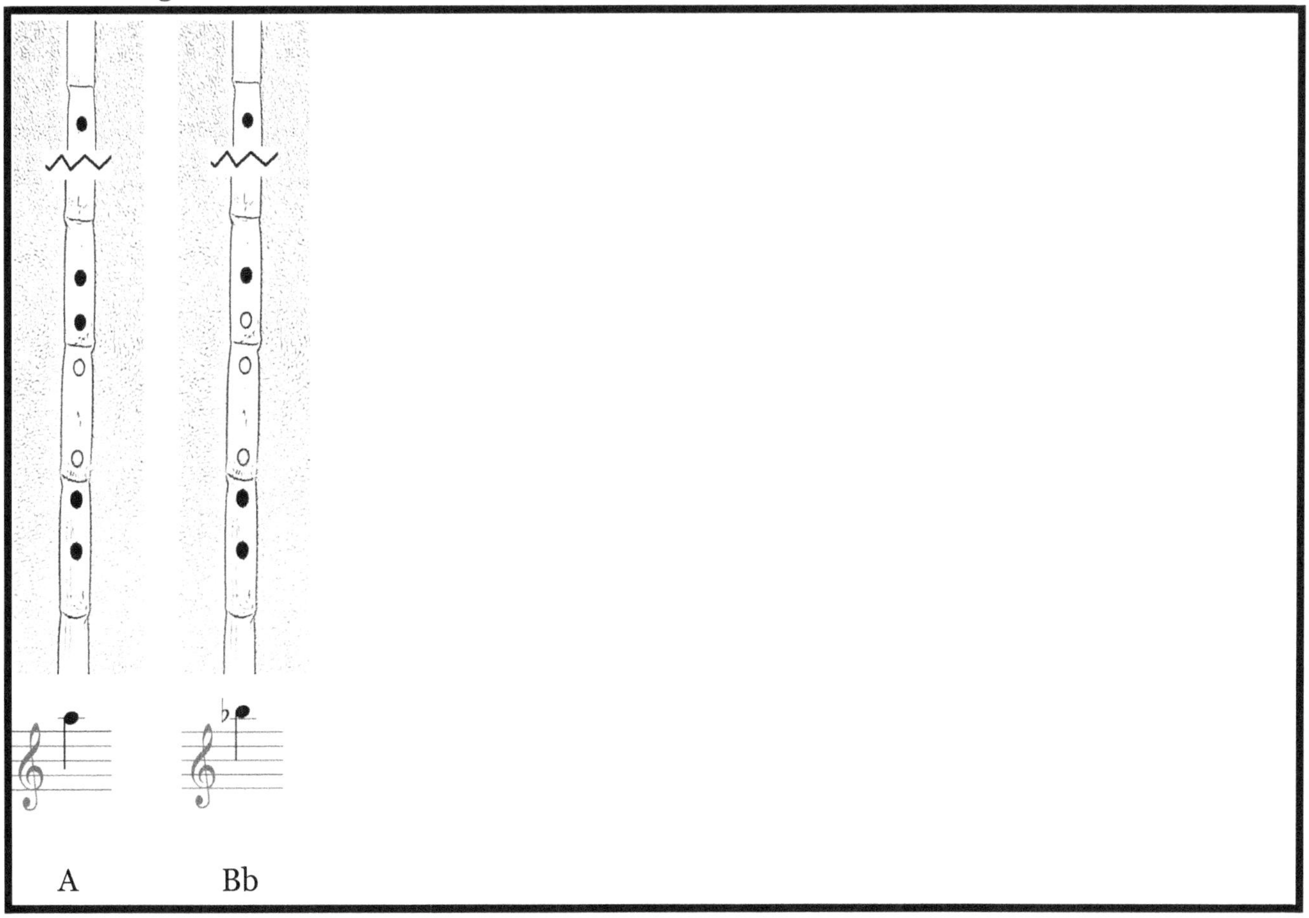

A	Bb

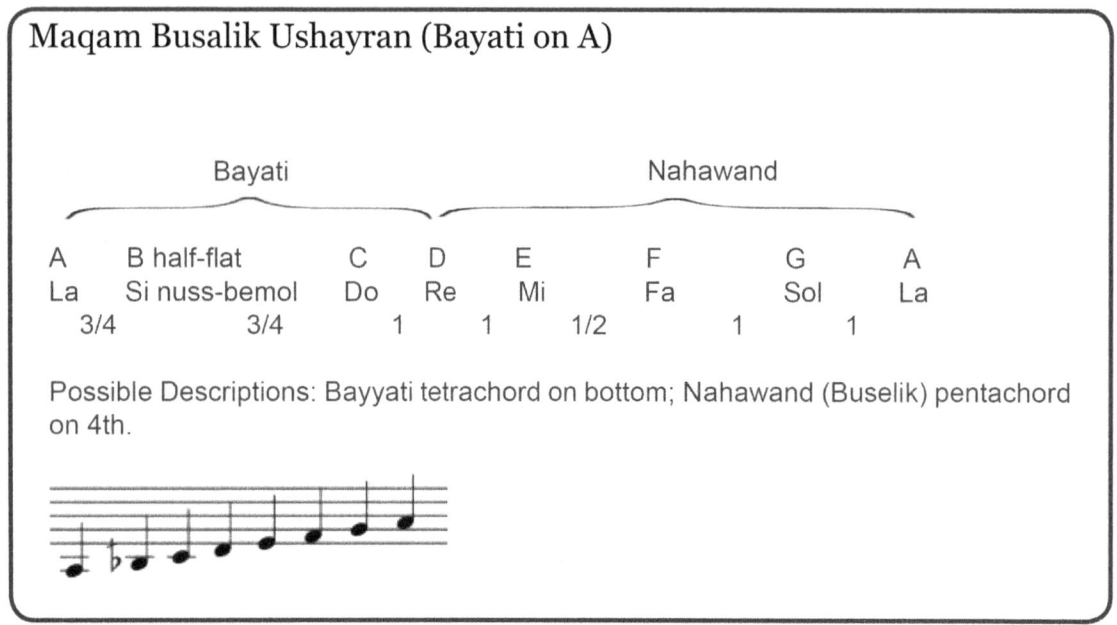

Maqam Busalik Ushayran (Bayati on A)

Bayati				Nahawand			
A	B half-flat	C	D	E	F	G	A
La	Si nuss-bemol	Do	Re	Mi	Fa	Sol	La
3/4	3/4	1	1	1/2	1	1	

Possible Descriptions: Bayyati tetrachord on bottom; Nahawand (Buselik) pentachord on 4th.

The E natural makes this maqam a little difficult for the nay.

Low Kabá Register:

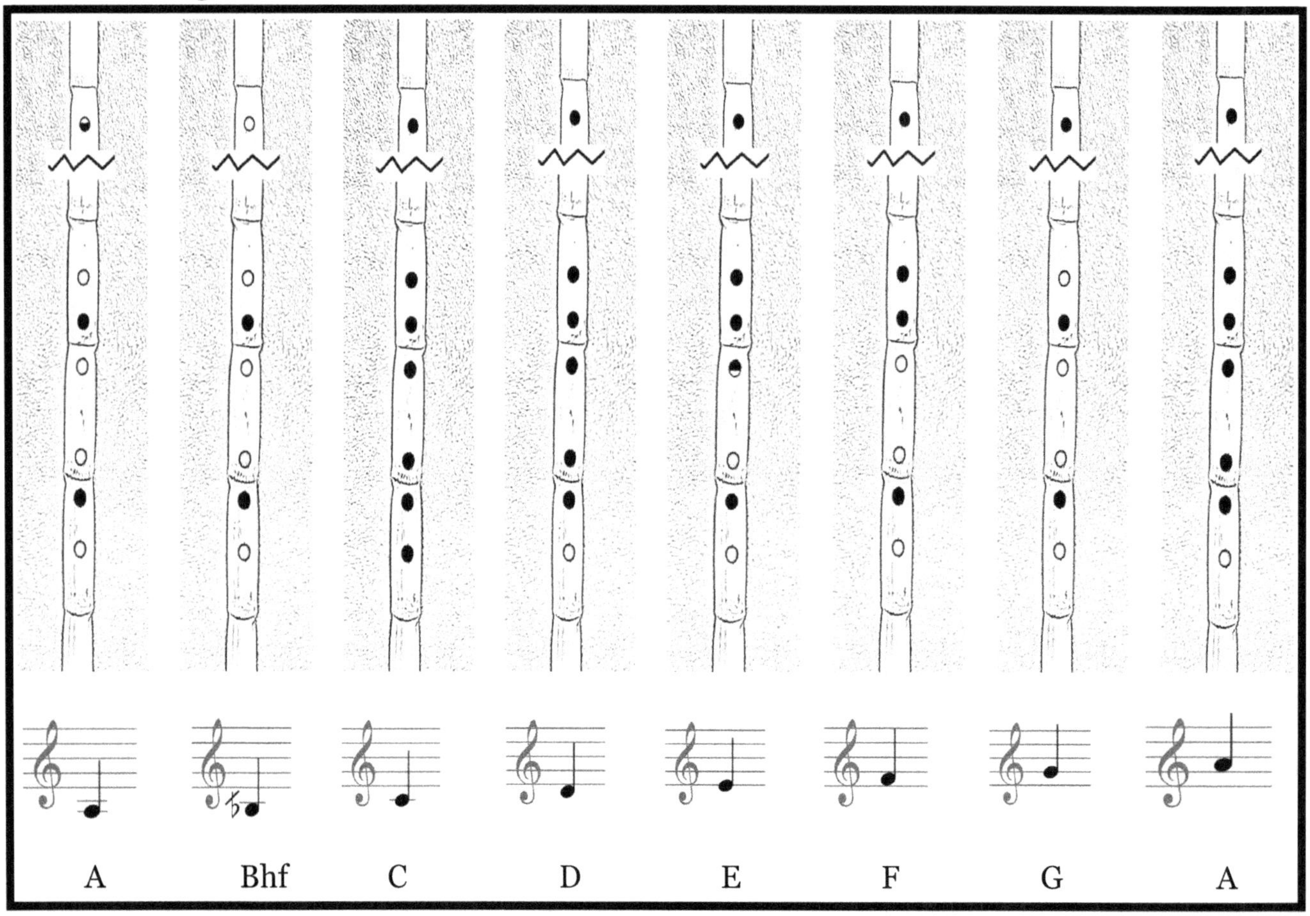

| A | Bhf | C | D | E | F | G | A |

Main Register:

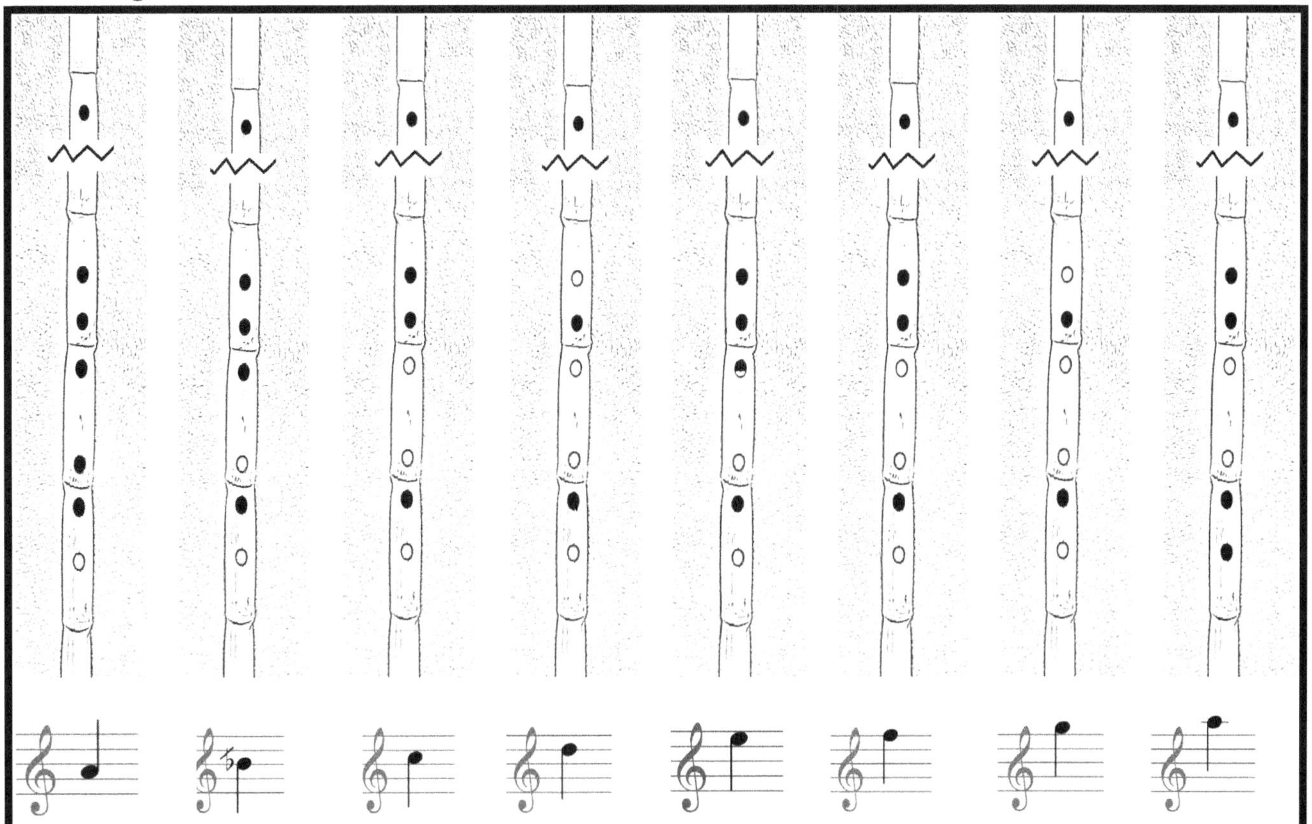

A	Bhf	C	D	E	F	G	A

Second Register:

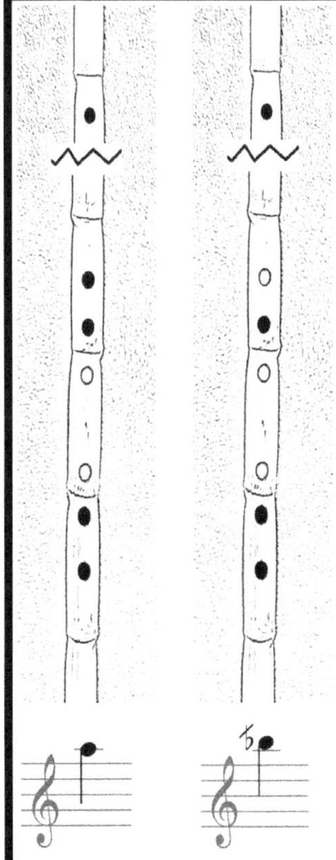

A	Bhf

Maqam Bayati Ushayran (Bayatayn on A)

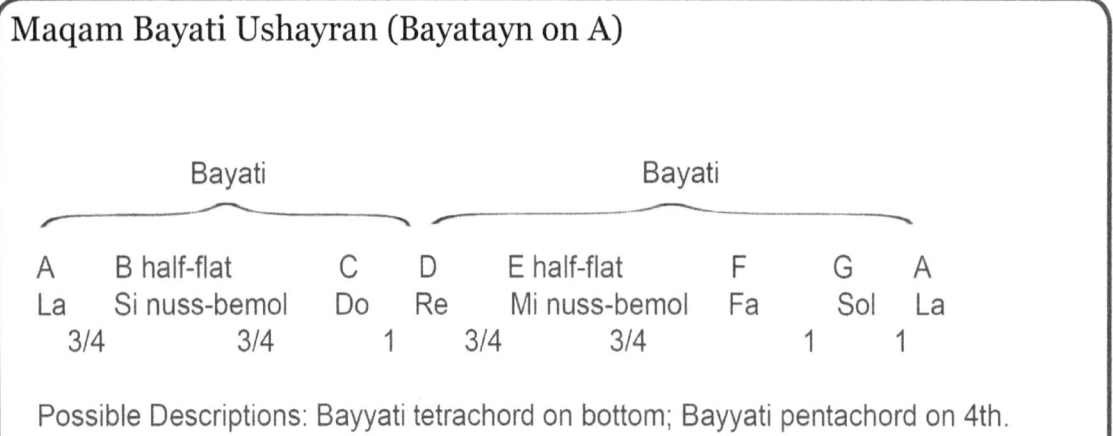

	Bayati				Bayati			
A	B half-flat		C	D	E half-flat		F	G	A
La	Si nuss-bemol		Do	Re	Mi nuss-bemol		Fa	Sol	La
	3/4	3/4		1	3/4	3/4		1	1

Possible Descriptions: Bayyati tetrachord on bottom; Bayyati pentachord on 4th.

Low Kabá Register:

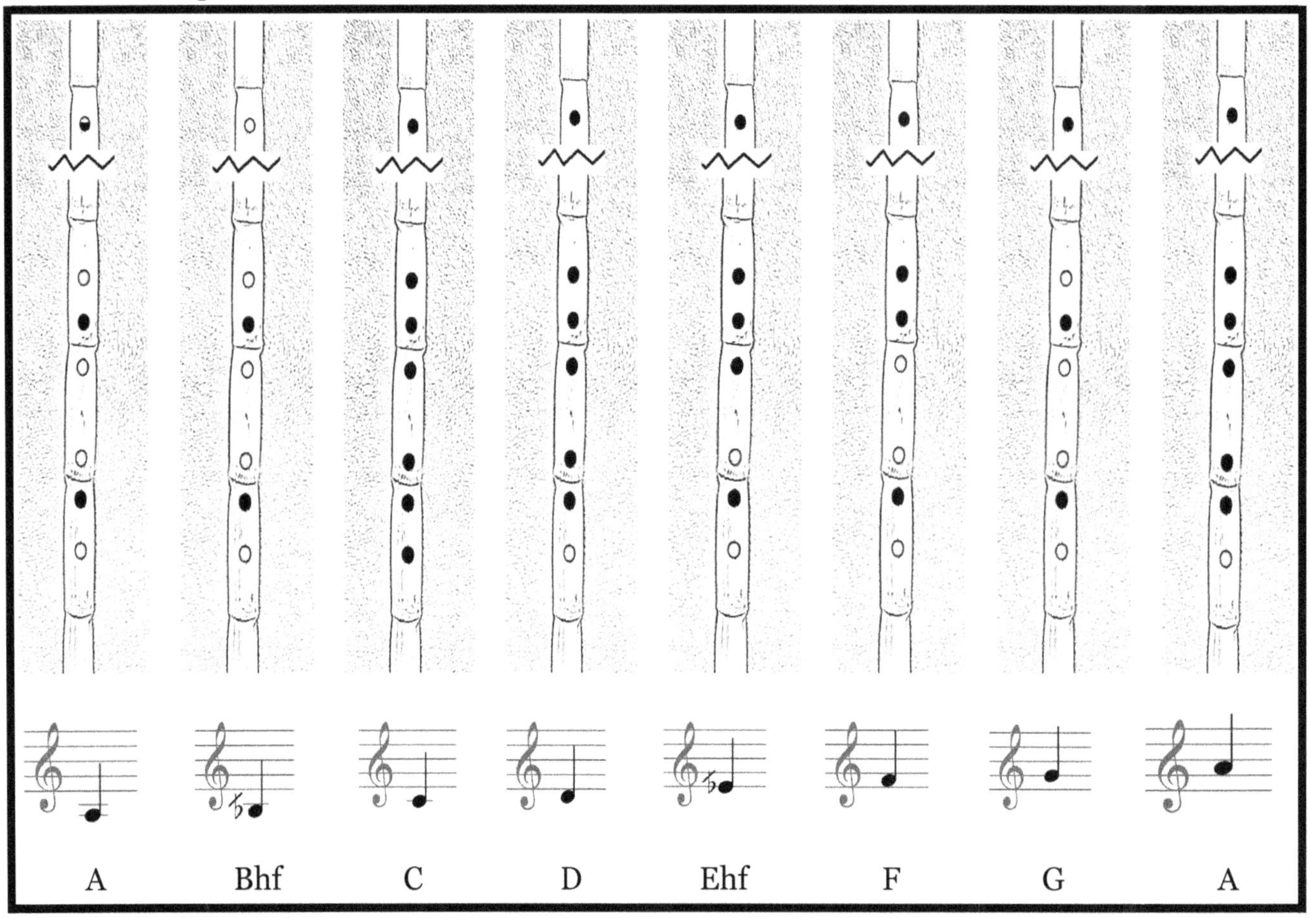

| A | Bhf | C | D | Ehf | F | G | A |

Main Register:

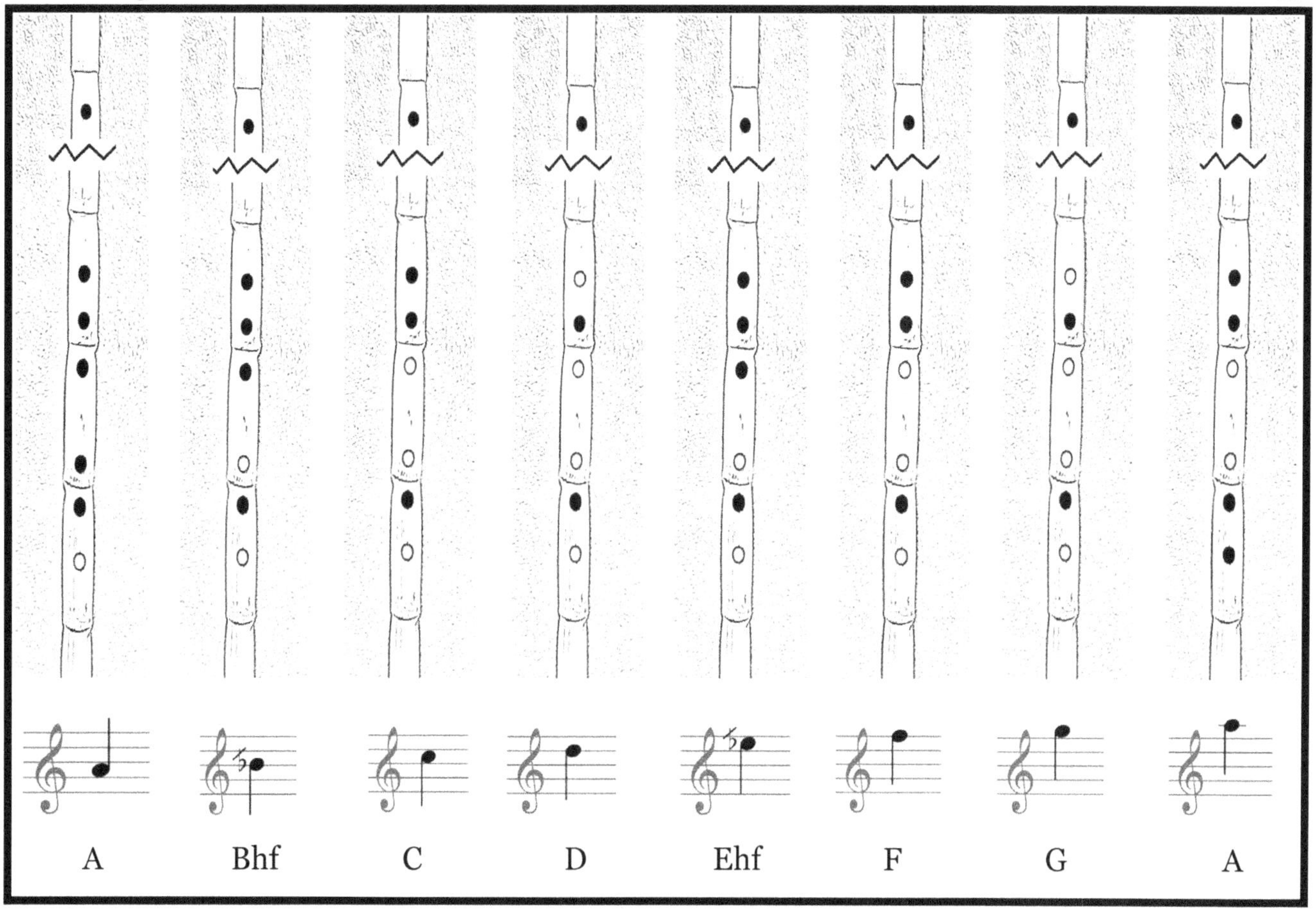

A	Bhf	C	D	Ehf	F	G	A

Second Register:

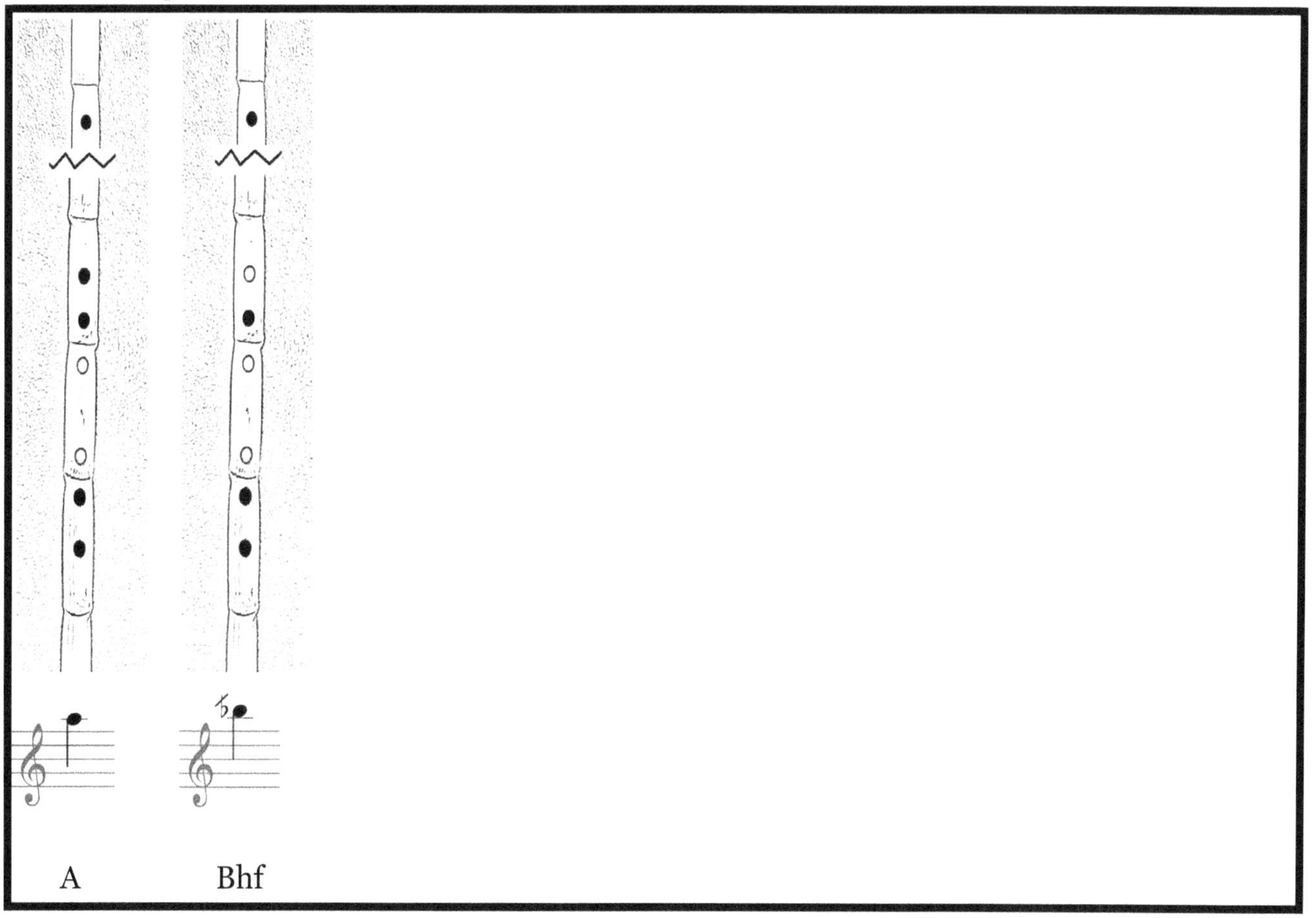

A	Bhf

Maqam Hijazi Ushayran (Shuri on A)

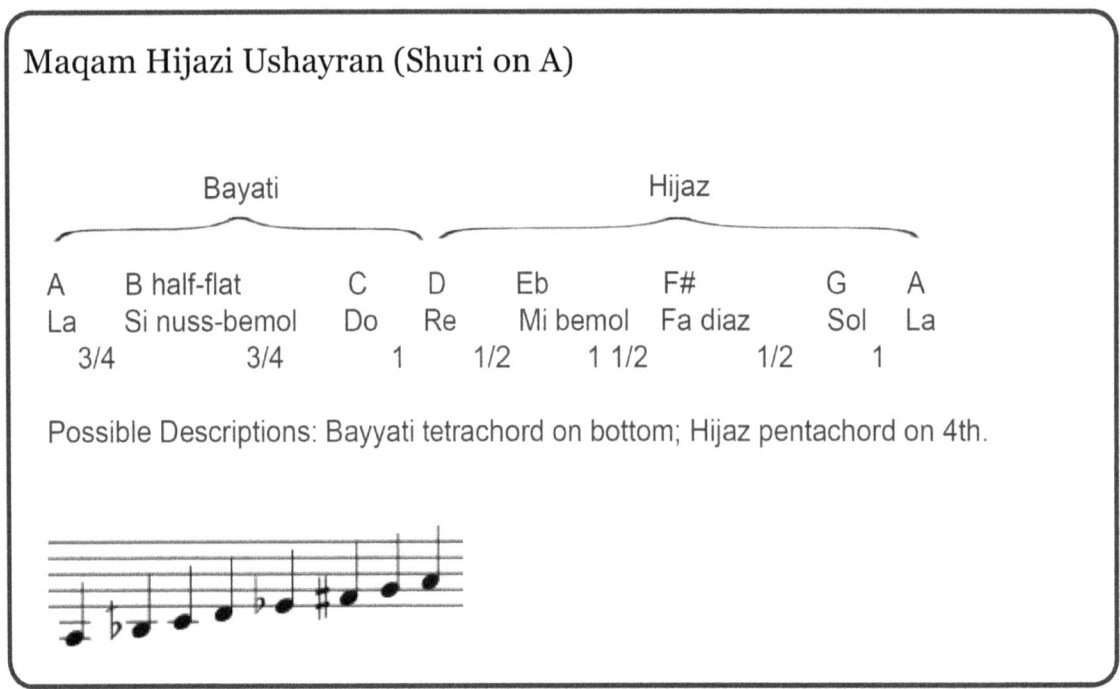

Bayati — A, B half-flat, C, D
Hijaz — Eb, F#, G, A

A	B half-flat	C	D	Eb	F#	G	A
La	Si nuss-bemol	Do	Re	Mi bemol	Fa diaz	Sol	La
3/4	3/4	1	1/2	1 1/2	1/2	1	

Possible Descriptions: Bayyati tetrachord on bottom; Hijaz pentachord on 4th.

Low Kabá Register:

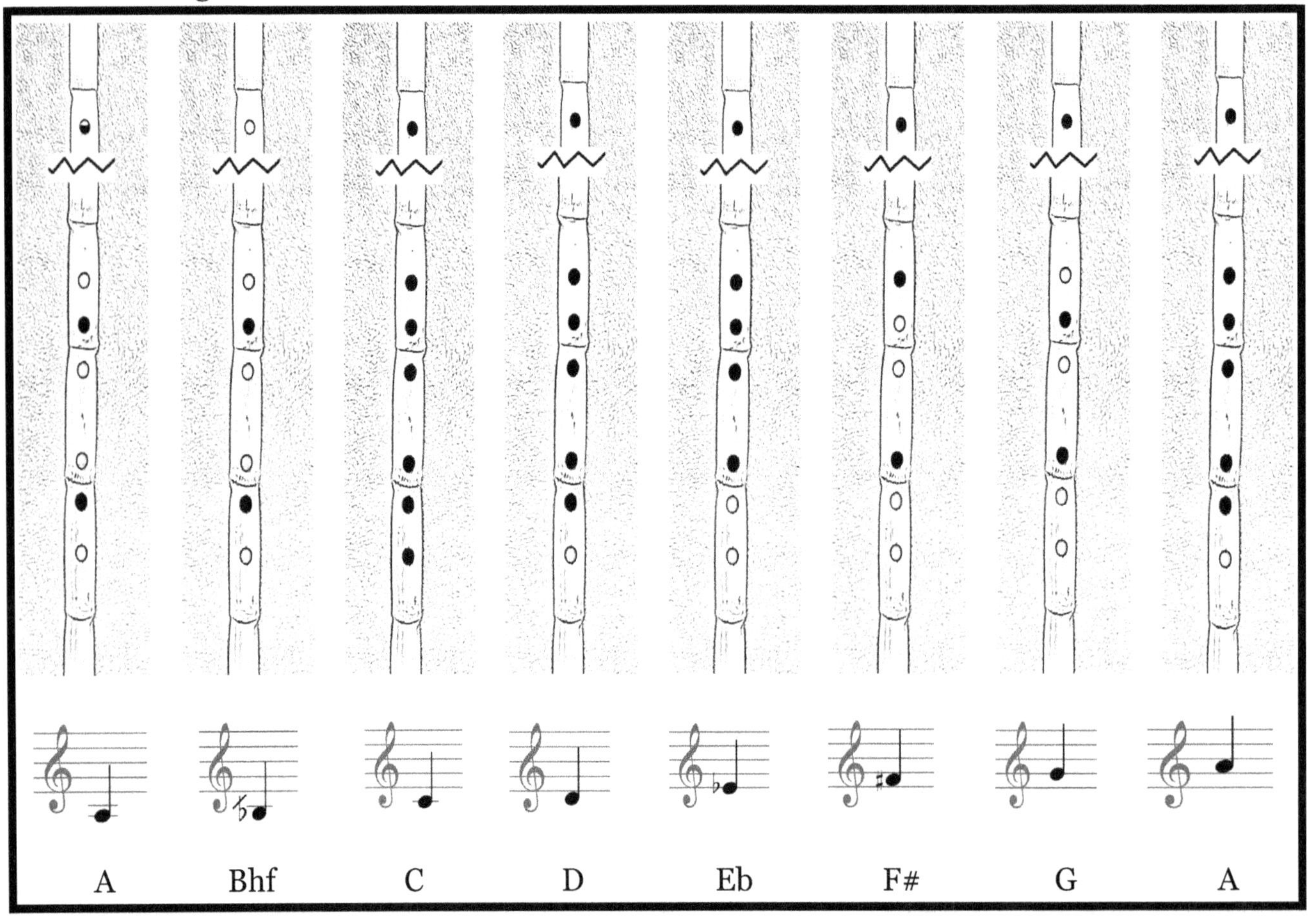

| A | Bhf | C | D | Eb | F# | G | A |

Main Register:

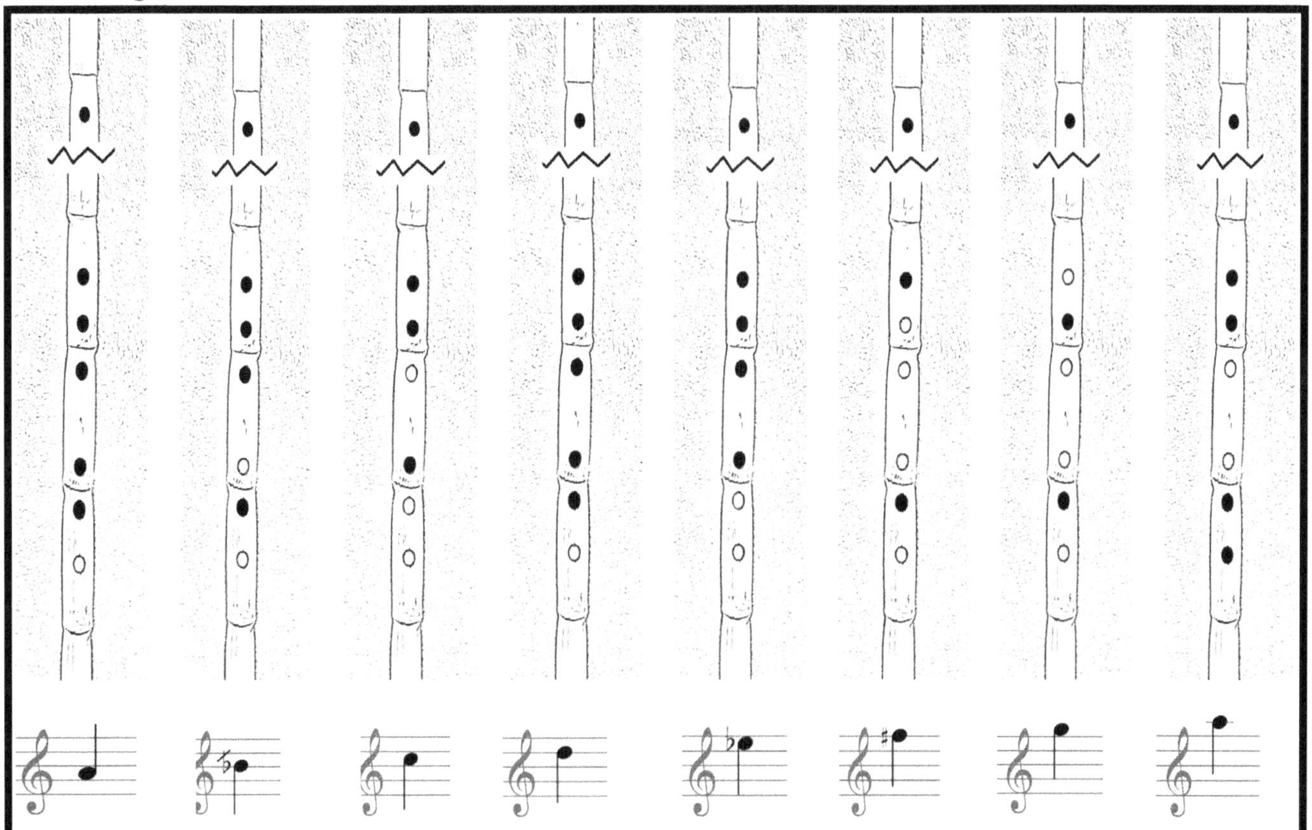

| A | Bhf | C | D | Eb | F# | G | A |

Second Register:

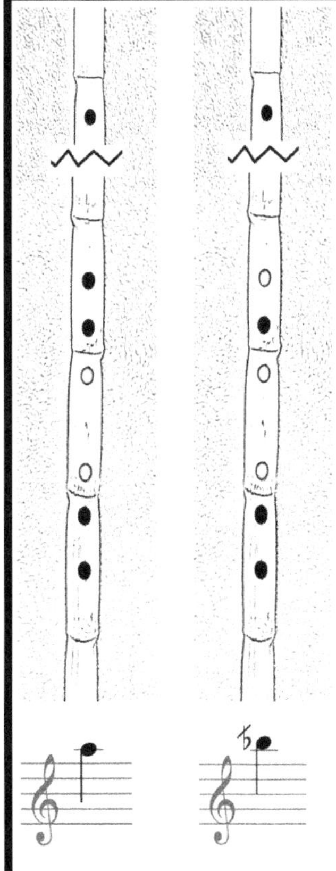

| A | Bhf |

Maqam Ajam Ushayran (Bb Major)

Closely Related: Huezawi (Iraqi), Ionian Mode

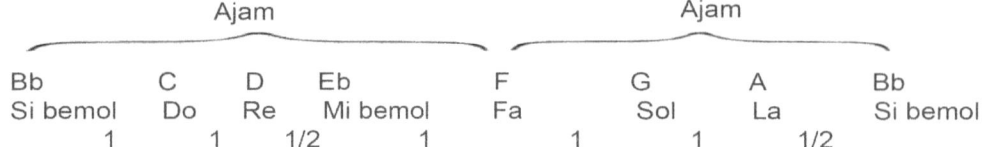

Ajam				Ajam			
Bb	C	D	Eb	F	G	A	Bb
Si bemol	Do	Re	Mi bemol	Fa	Sol	La	Si bemol
1	1	1/2		1	1	1/2	

Possible Descriptions: Ajam or "Jaharka" pentachord on bottom; Ajam or "Jaharka" tetrachord on 5th; Farahfaza maqam on 6th; Ajam Ushayran is "relative major" to Farahfaza (G minor scale).

It is common to show a brief interlude into Ajam during taqasims based in Saba or Bayyati. This is accomplished by first emphasizing the 6th note in one of those maqams which is, of course, Bb, then descending the Ajam scale and re-ascending it back to the Bb. Once this has been shown, the maqam usually returns to Saba or Bayati.

Low Kabá Register:

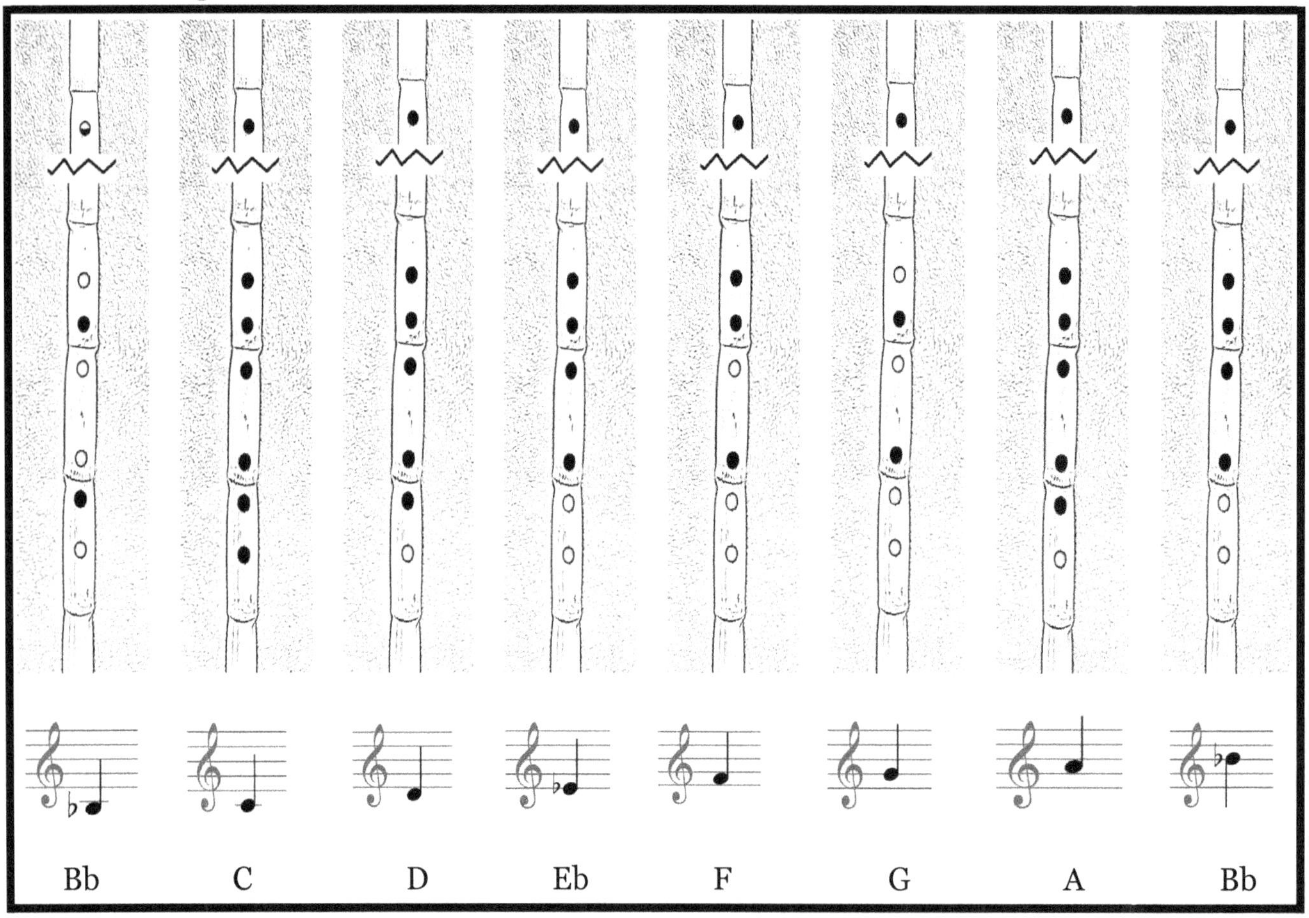

Bb	C	D	Eb	F	G	A	Bb

Main Register: 59

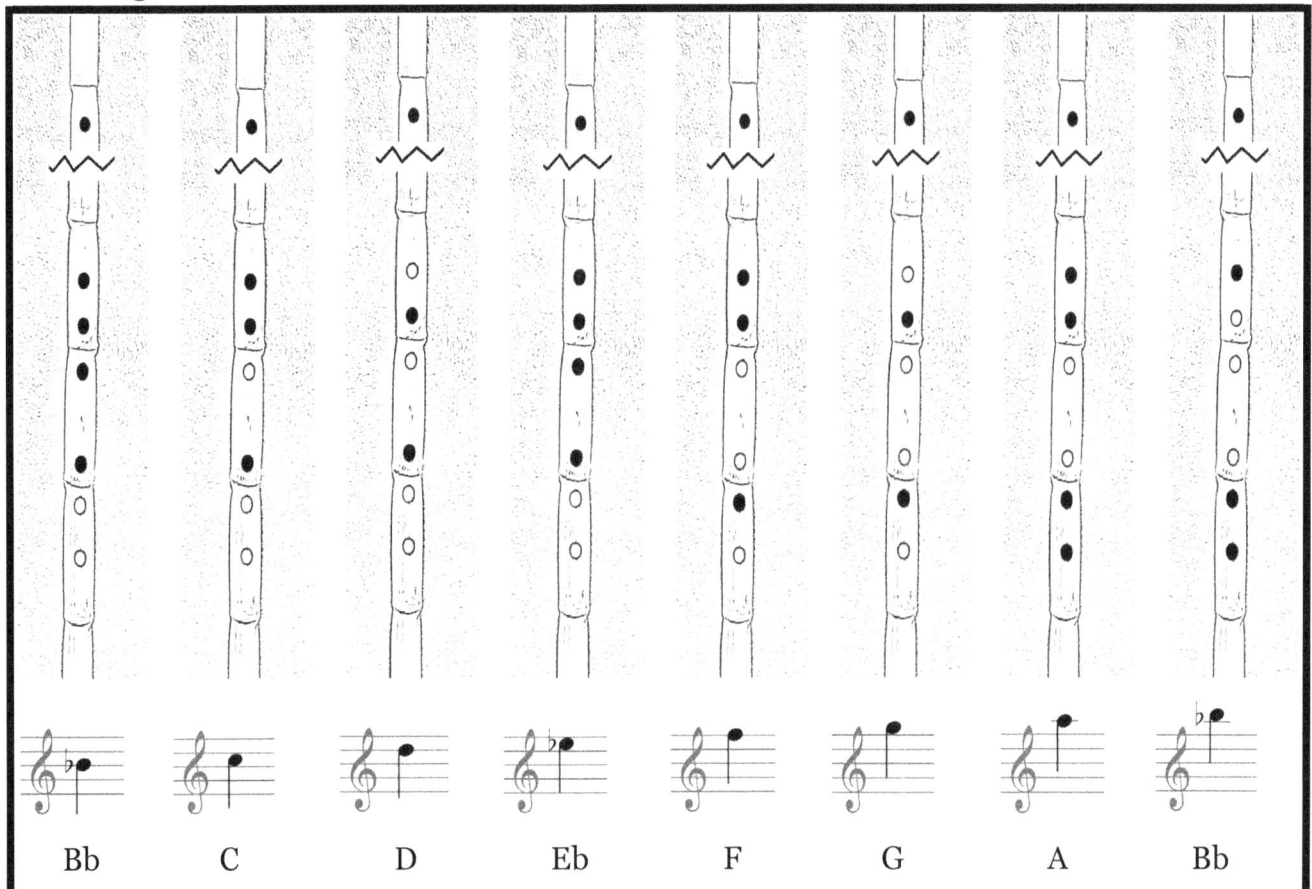

Maqam Shawq Afza

Nawa Athar

Saba Zamzama

Ajam | Hijaz

Bb	C	D	Eb	F	Gb	A	Bb
Si bemol	Do	Re	Mi bemol	Fa	Sol bemol	La	Si bemol

1 1 1/2 1 1/2 1 1/2 1/2

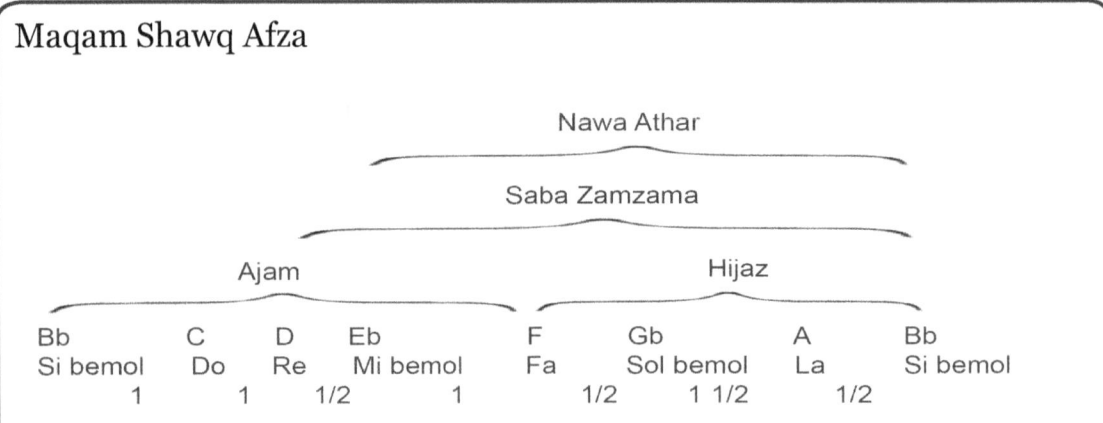

Possible Descriptions: Ajam or "Jaharka" pentachord on bottom; Hijaz tetrachord on 5th; Nawa Athar pentachord on 4th; maqam Saba Zamzama on 3rd. And if the Eb is raised to E half-flat then maqam Saba appears on the 3rd. This is an acceptable substitution within Shawq Afza.

The option of using jins hijaz on the 5th is a common pattern. Rast becomes Suznak with this change and Nahawand 1 becomes Nahawand 2 with this same change.

Low Kabá Register:

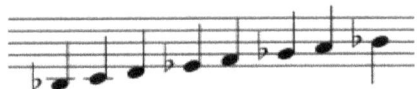

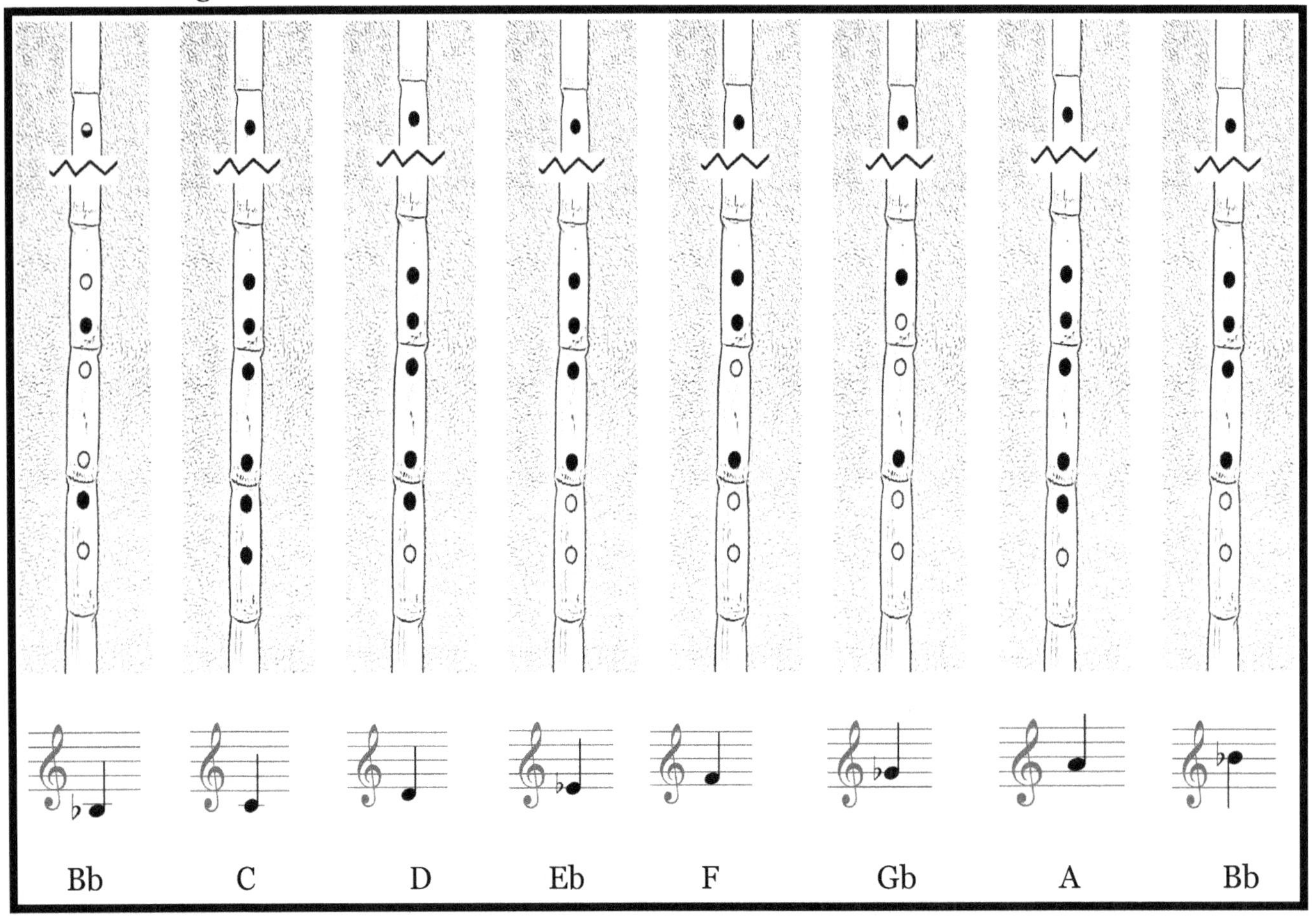

Main Register:

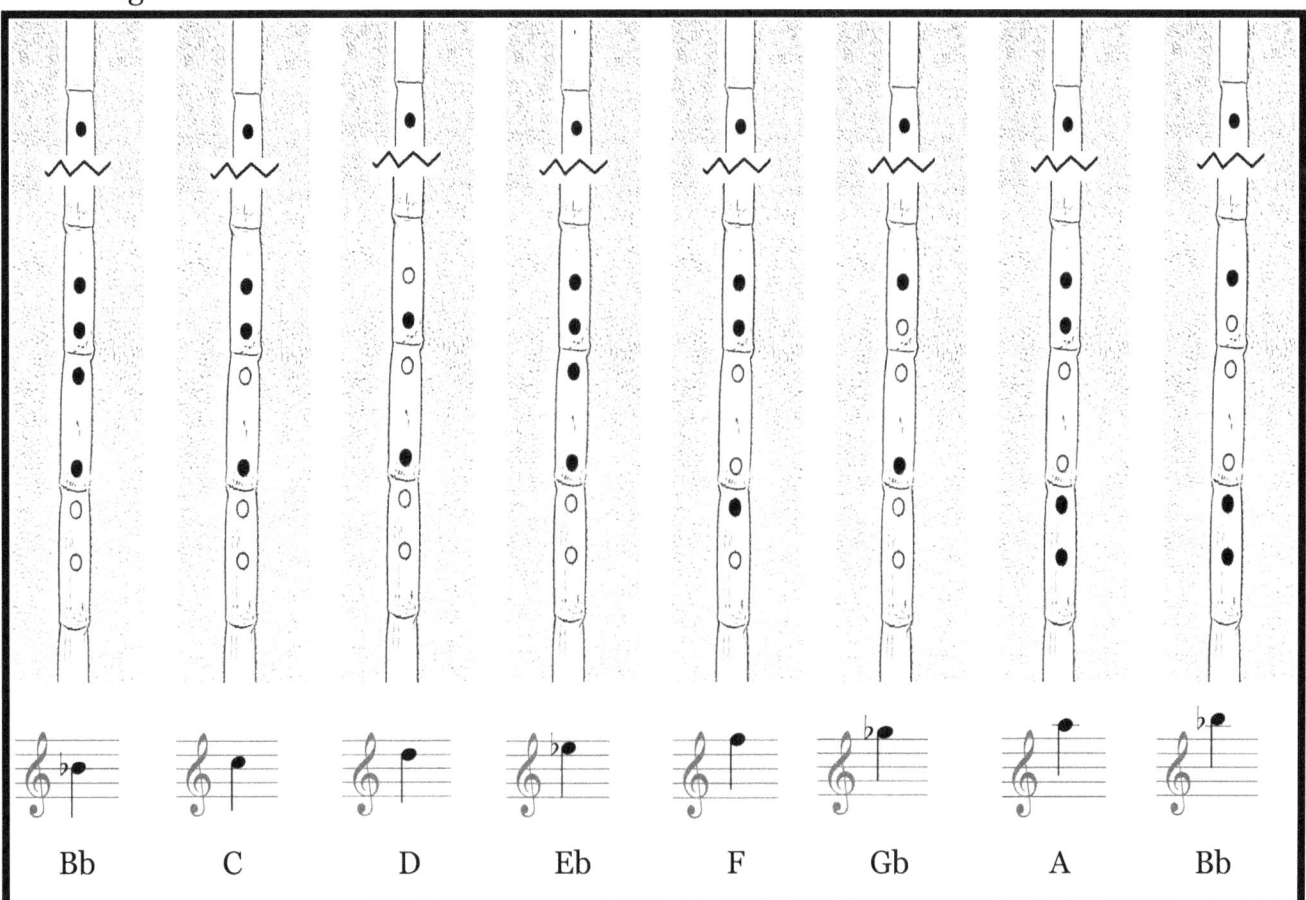

Maqam Rahat el Arwah (Huzam on B half-flat)

Sikah			Hijaz			Rast		
B half-flat	C	D	Eb	F#	G	A	B half-flat	
Si nuss-bemol	Do	Re	Mi bemol	Fa diaz	Sol	La	Si nuss-bemol	
3/4	1	1/2	1 1/2	1/2	1	3/4		

Possible Descriptions: Sikah trichord on bottom; Hijaz pentachord on 3rd; Rast trichord on 6th; Suznak maqam on 6th.

This maqam is very extensively used. It is very common at the end of a D hijaz composition to move down and rest on the B half-flat. For Westerners it may feel like moving from a major scale to its relative minor. There is some kind of similarity in feeling.

The maqam Rahat el Arwah is extremely rich in justly intonated harmonic possibilities which are found extensively in Arabic music of many kinds. Holding the B half-flat tonic while moving to either the D or the G creates a deep magic. For a Westerner to learn to sing these approximately 1 3/4 step intervals with precision in just intonation takes some practice but is deeply rewarding. One enters a harmonic realm unknown in Western music.

And modulation from B half-flat to either G or D maqamat is an entryway into a huge musical playground of possibilities.

Low Kabá Register:

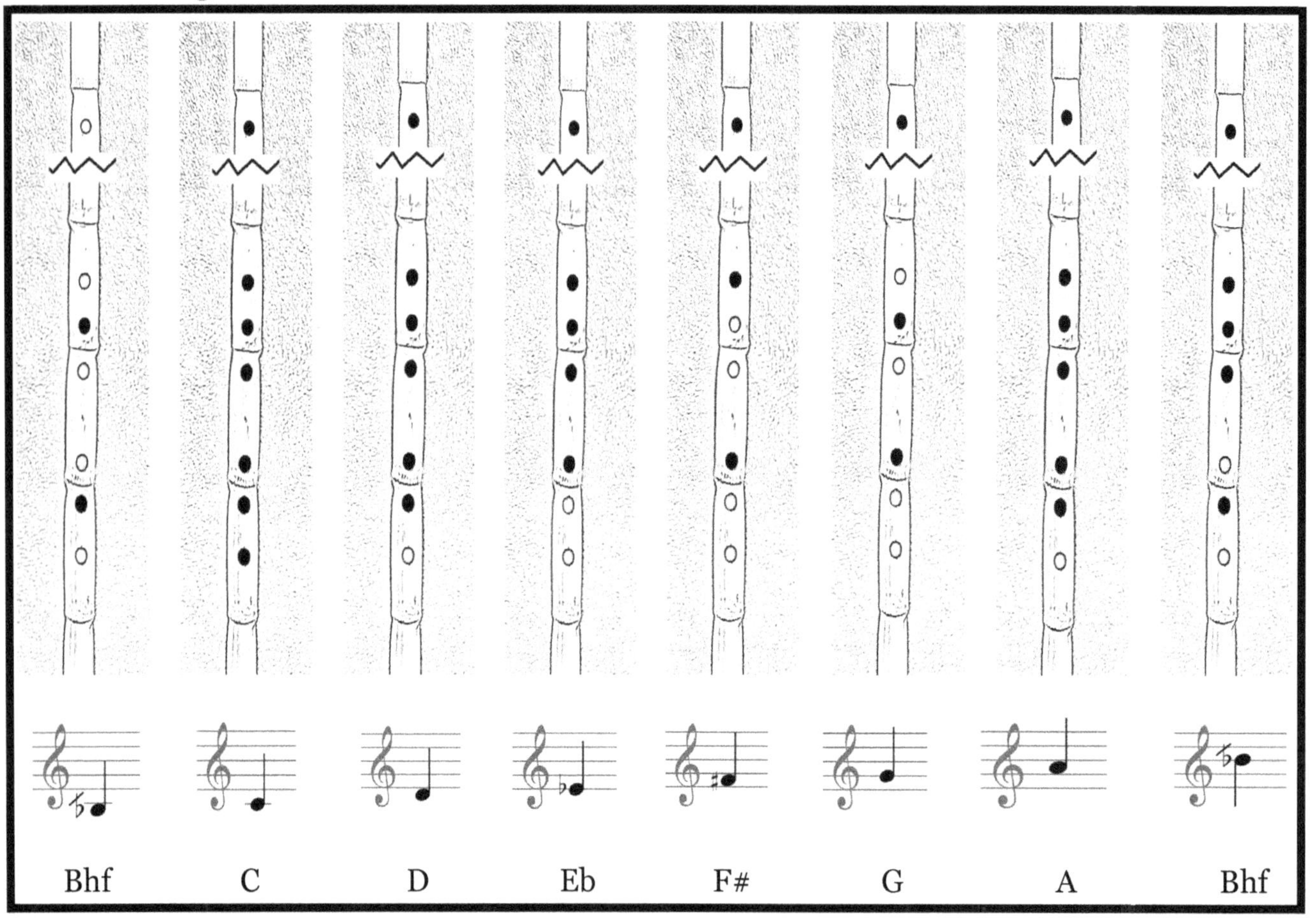

| Bhf | C | D | Eb | F# | G | A | Bhf |

Main Register:

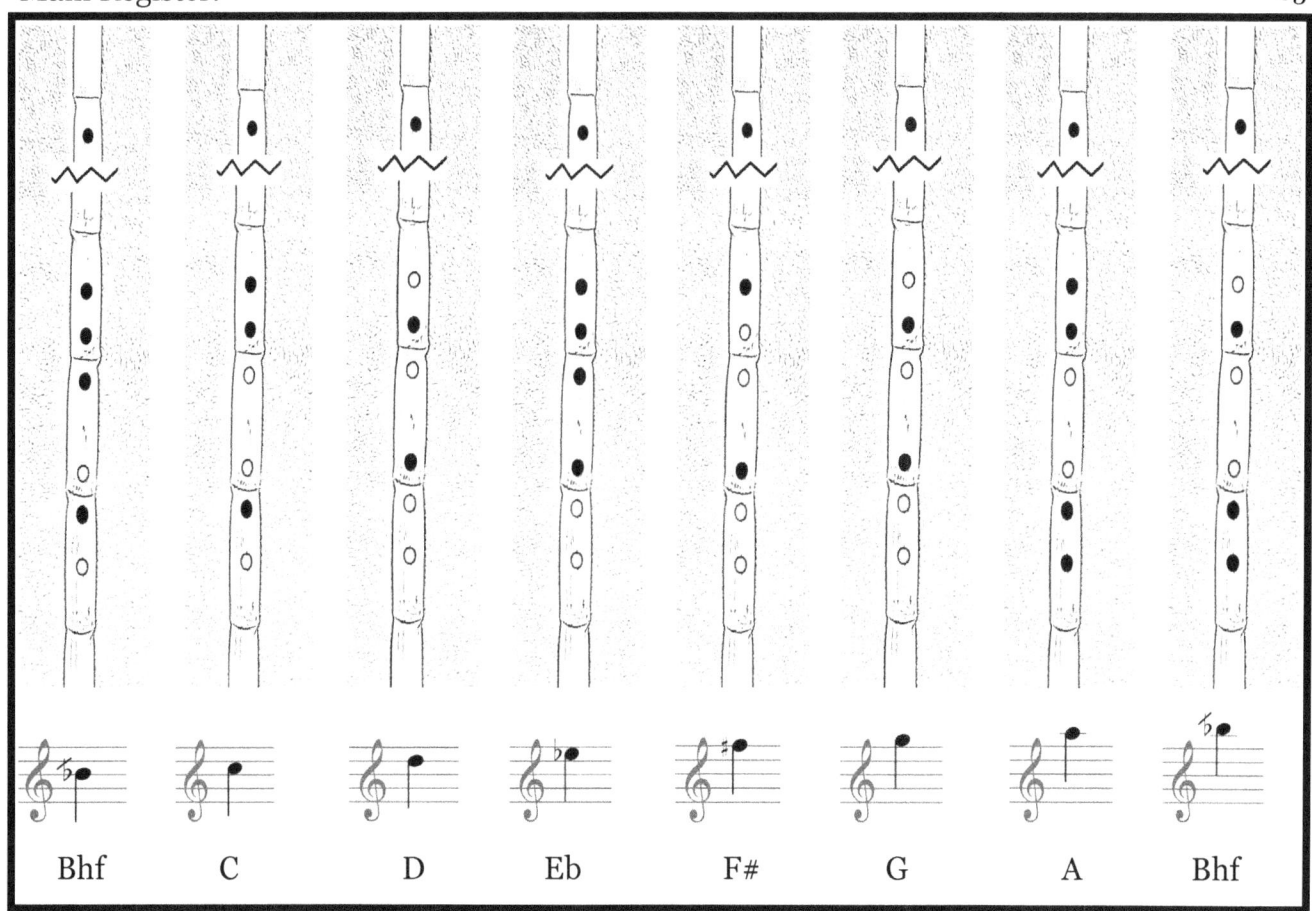

Maqam Irak (Huzam on B half-flat with Bayati)

Sikah: B half-flat, C, D
Bayati: E half-flat, F, G, A, B half-flat

	B half-flat	C	D	E half-flat	F	G	A	B half-flat
	Si nuss-bemol	Do	Re	Mi nuss-bemol	Fa	Sol	La	Si nuss-bemol
	3/4	1	3/4	3/4	1	1	3/4	

Possible Descriptions: Sikah trichord on bottom. Bayyati pentachord on 3rd.

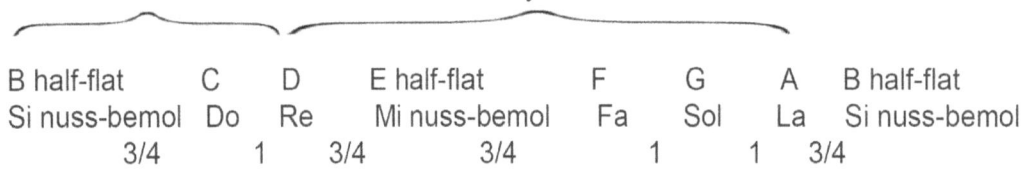

Low Kabá Register:

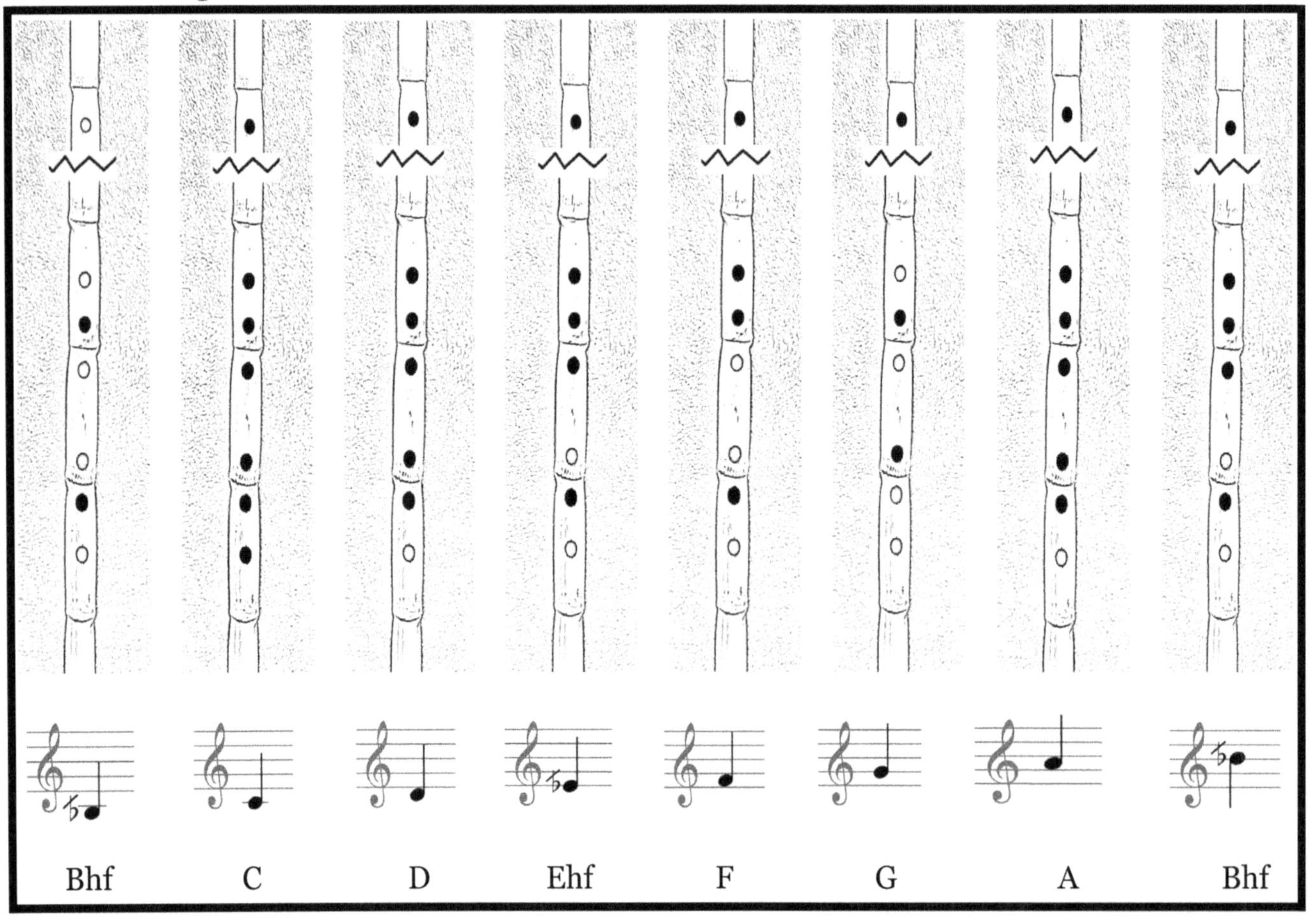

| Bhf | C | D | Ehf | F | G | A | Bhf |

Main Register:

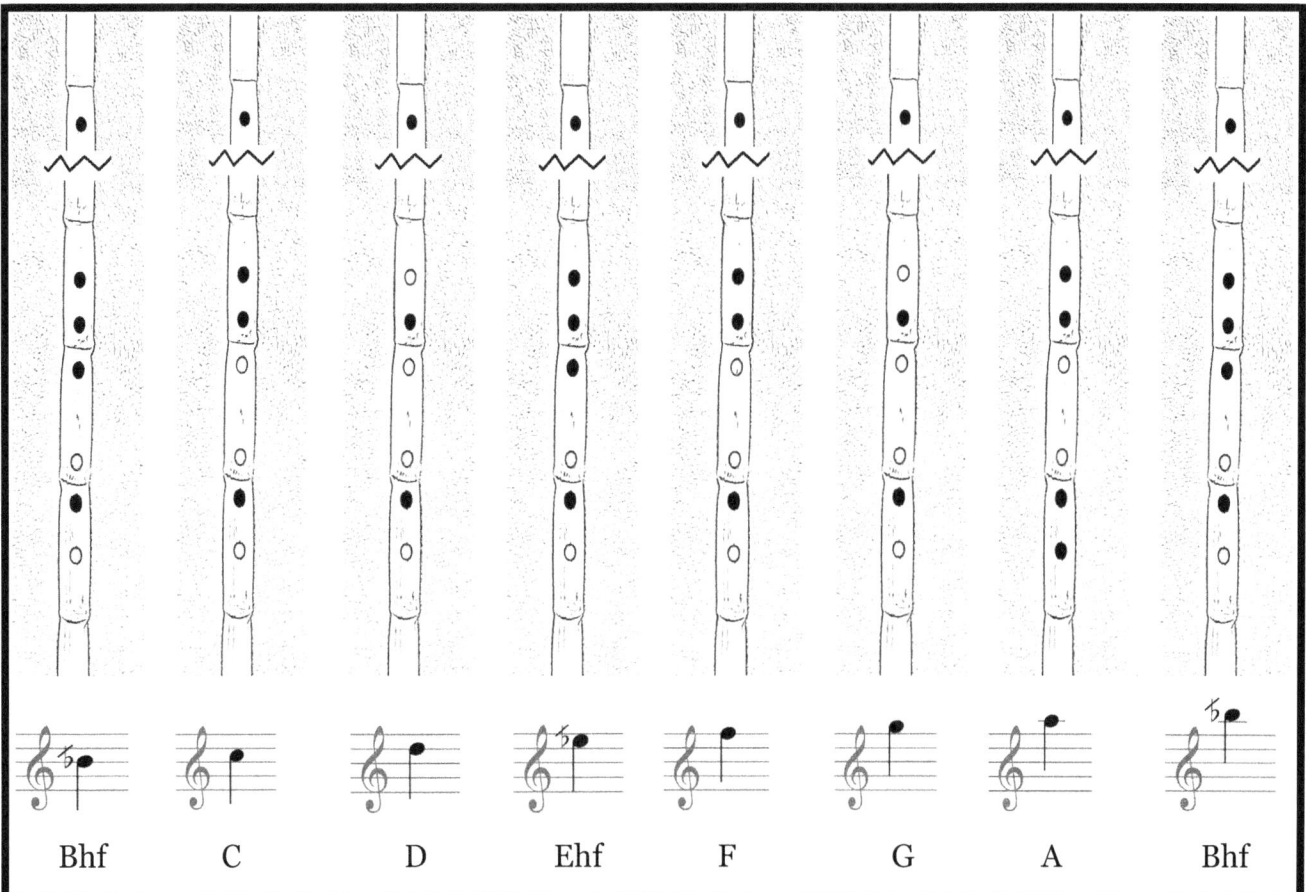

Maqam Bastanikar (Huzam on B half-flat with Saba)

Closely Related Maqamat: Taz Nuin

Sikah			Saba				
B half-flat	C	D	E half-flat	F	Gb	A	B half-flat
Si nuss-bemol	Do	Re	Mi nuss-bemol	Fa	Sol bemol	La	Si nuss-bemol
3/4	1	3/4	3/4	1/2	1	1/2	3/4

Possible Descriptions: Sikah trichord on bottom; Saba pentachord on 3rd.

The quartertone mystique of numerous 3/4 step intervals is exquisitely available in this maqam.

Low Kabá Register:

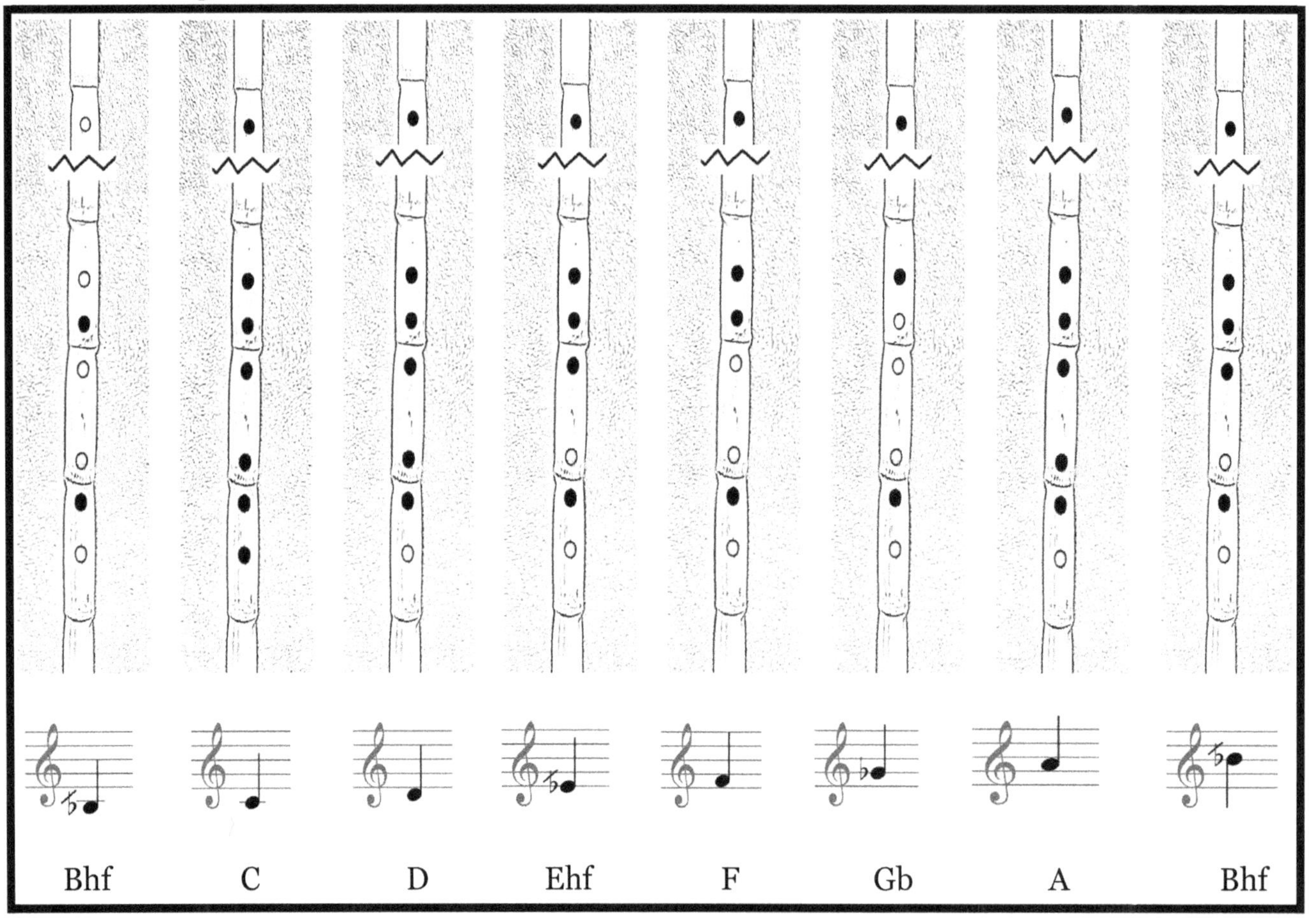

| Bhf | C | D | Ehf | F | Gb | A | Bhf |

Main Register:

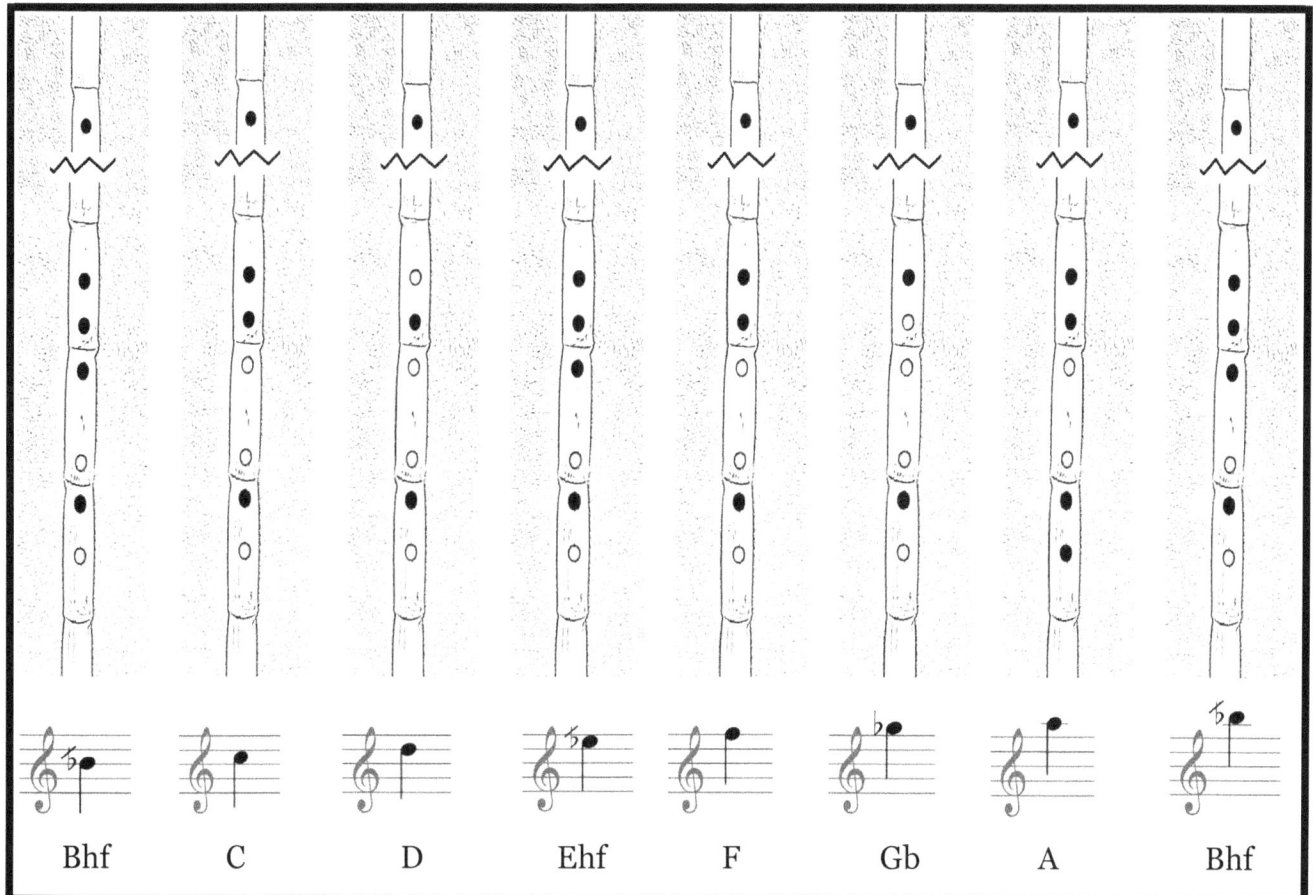

Maqam Rast

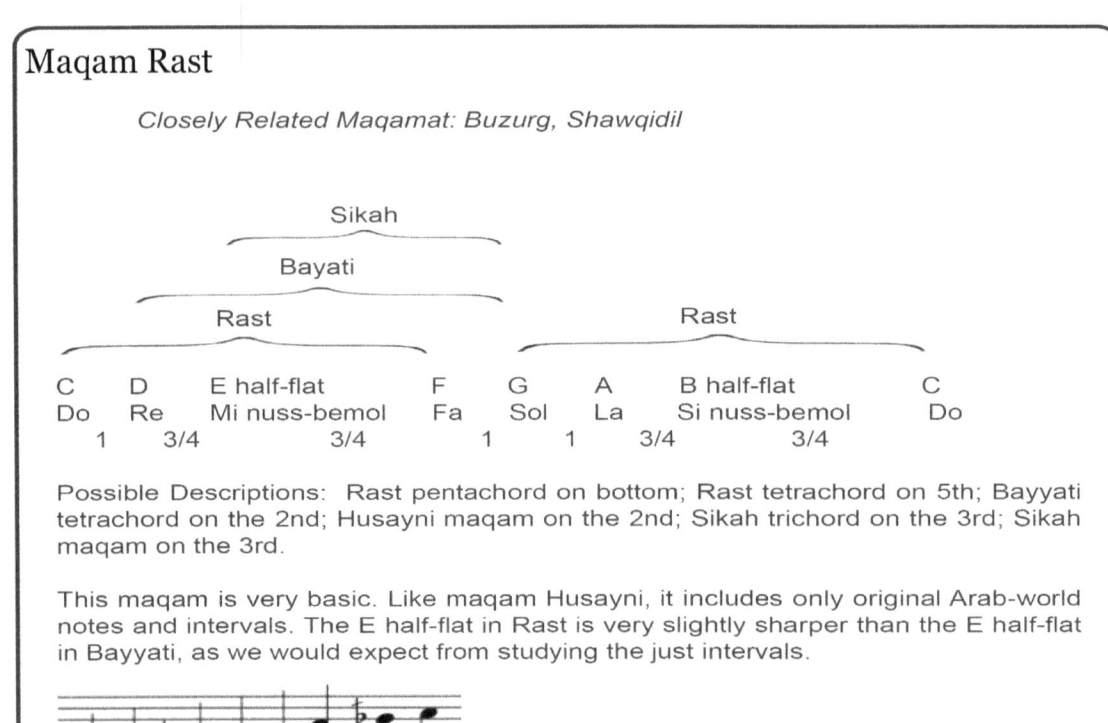

Closely Related Maqamat: Buzurg, Shawqidil

Possible Descriptions: Rast pentachord on bottom; Rast tetrachord on 5th; Bayyati tetrachord on the 2nd; Husayni maqam on the 2nd; Sikah trichord on the 3rd; Sikah maqam on the 3rd.

This maqam is very basic. Like maqam Husayni, it includes only original Arab-world notes and intervals. The E half-flat in Rast is very slightly sharper than the E half-flat in Bayyati, as we would expect from studying the just intervals.

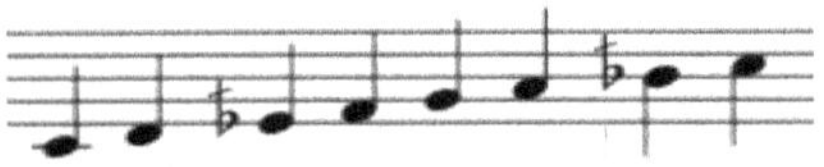

Low Kabá Register:

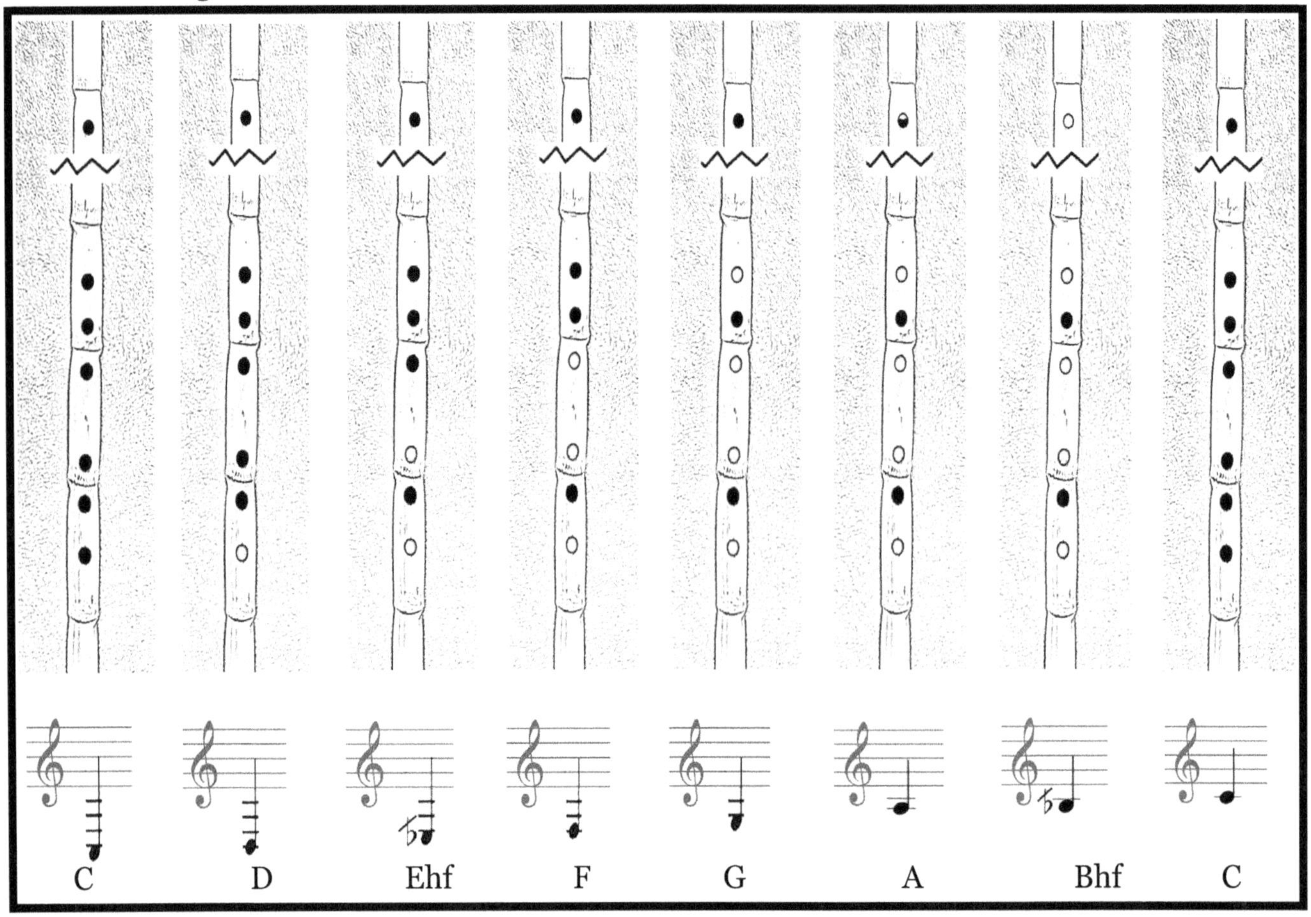

| C | D | Ehf | F | G | A | Bhf | C |

Main Register:

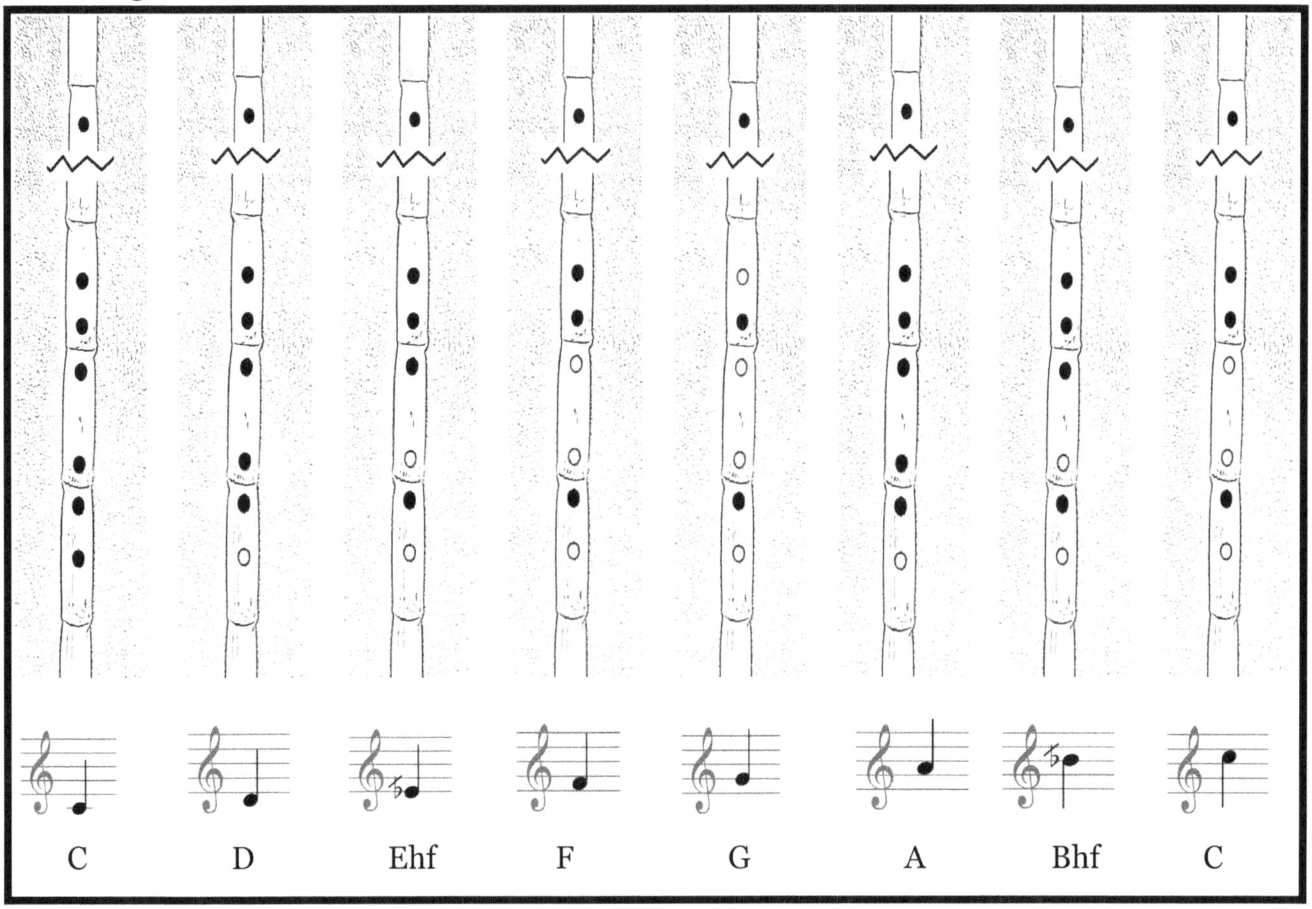

| C | D | Ehf | F | G | A | Bhf | C |

Second Register:

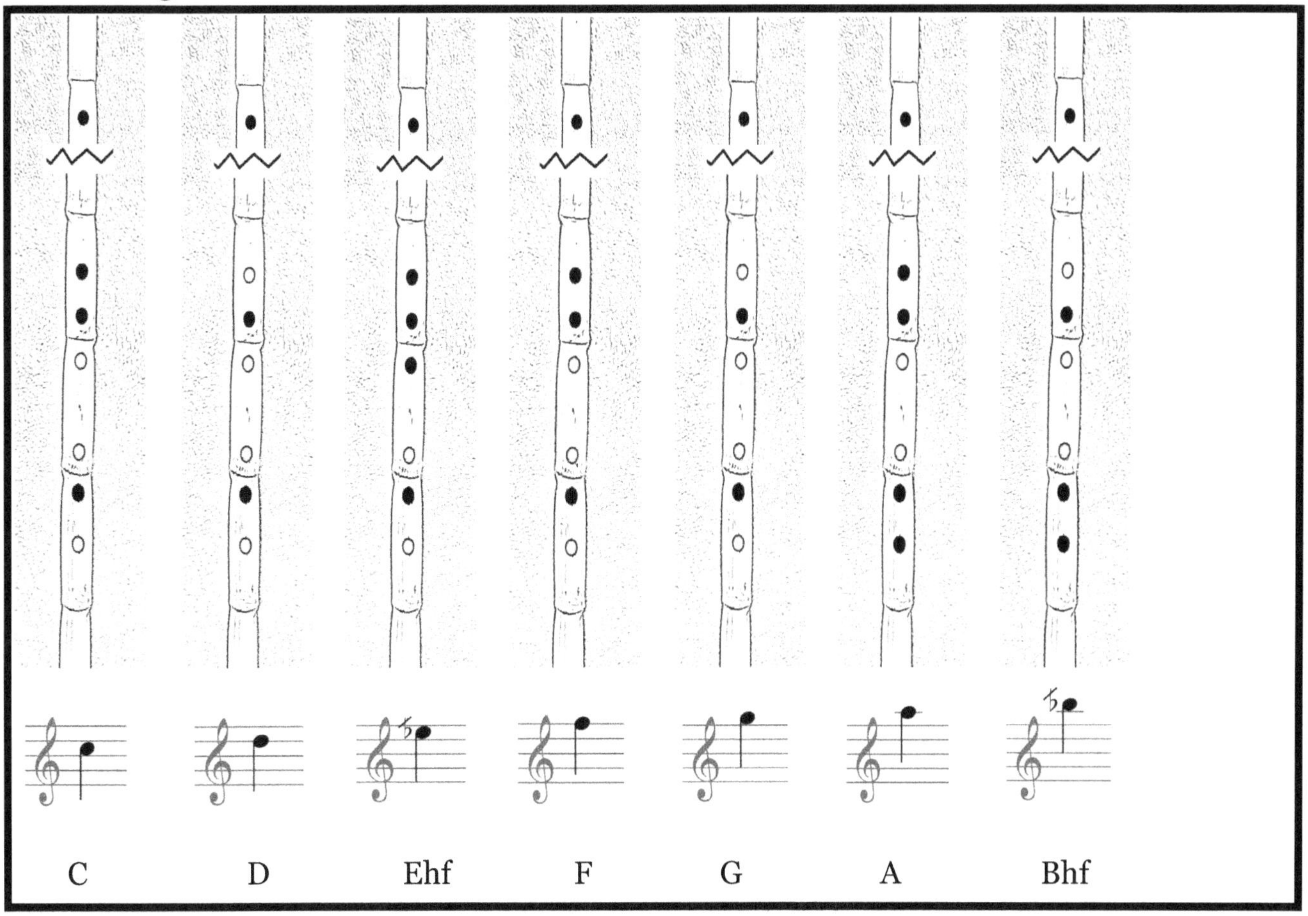

| C | D | Ehf | F | G | A | Bhf |

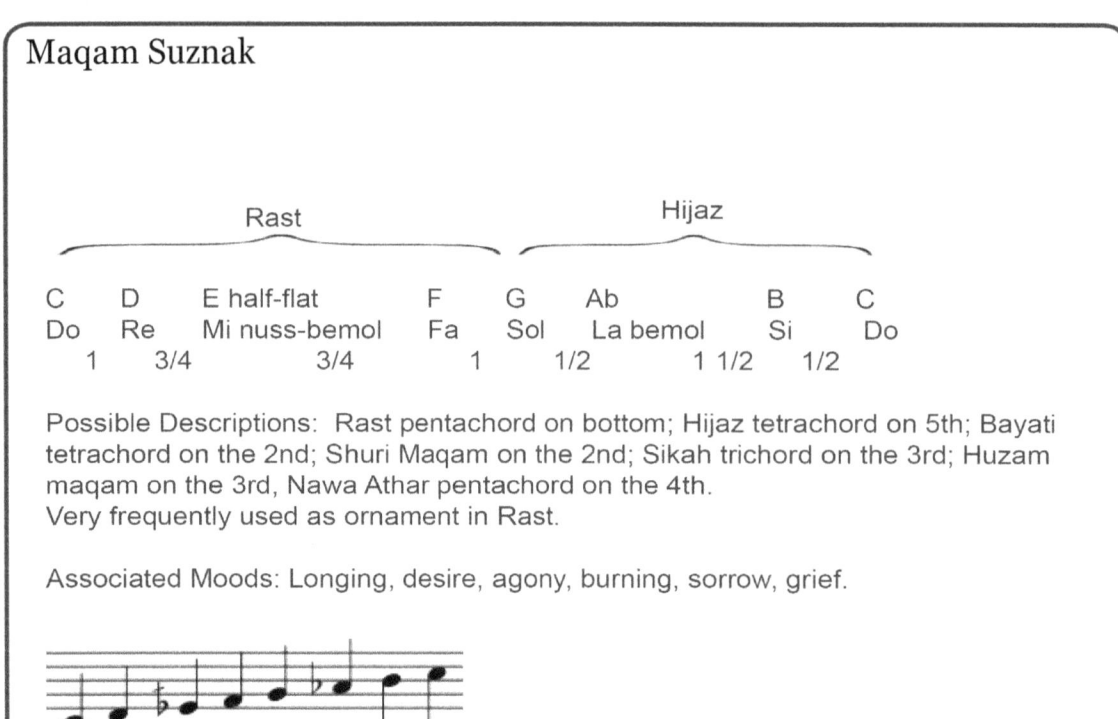

Maqam Suznak

Rast: C (Do) 1 — D (Re) 3/4 — E half-flat (Mi nuss-bemol) 3/4 — F (Fa) 1

Hijaz: G (Sol) 1/2 — Ab (La bemol) 1 1/2 — B (Si) 1/2 — C (Do)

Possible Descriptions: Rast pentachord on bottom; Hijaz tetrachord on 5th; Bayati tetrachord on the 2nd; Shuri Maqam on the 2nd; Sikah trichord on the 3rd; Huzam maqam on the 3rd, Nawa Athar pentachord on the 4th.
Very frequently used as ornament in Rast.

Associated Moods: Longing, desire, agony, burning, sorrow, grief.

With its Hijaz tetrachord on the top, Suznak is to Rast what Nahawand 2 is to Nahawand 1.

Low Kabá Register:

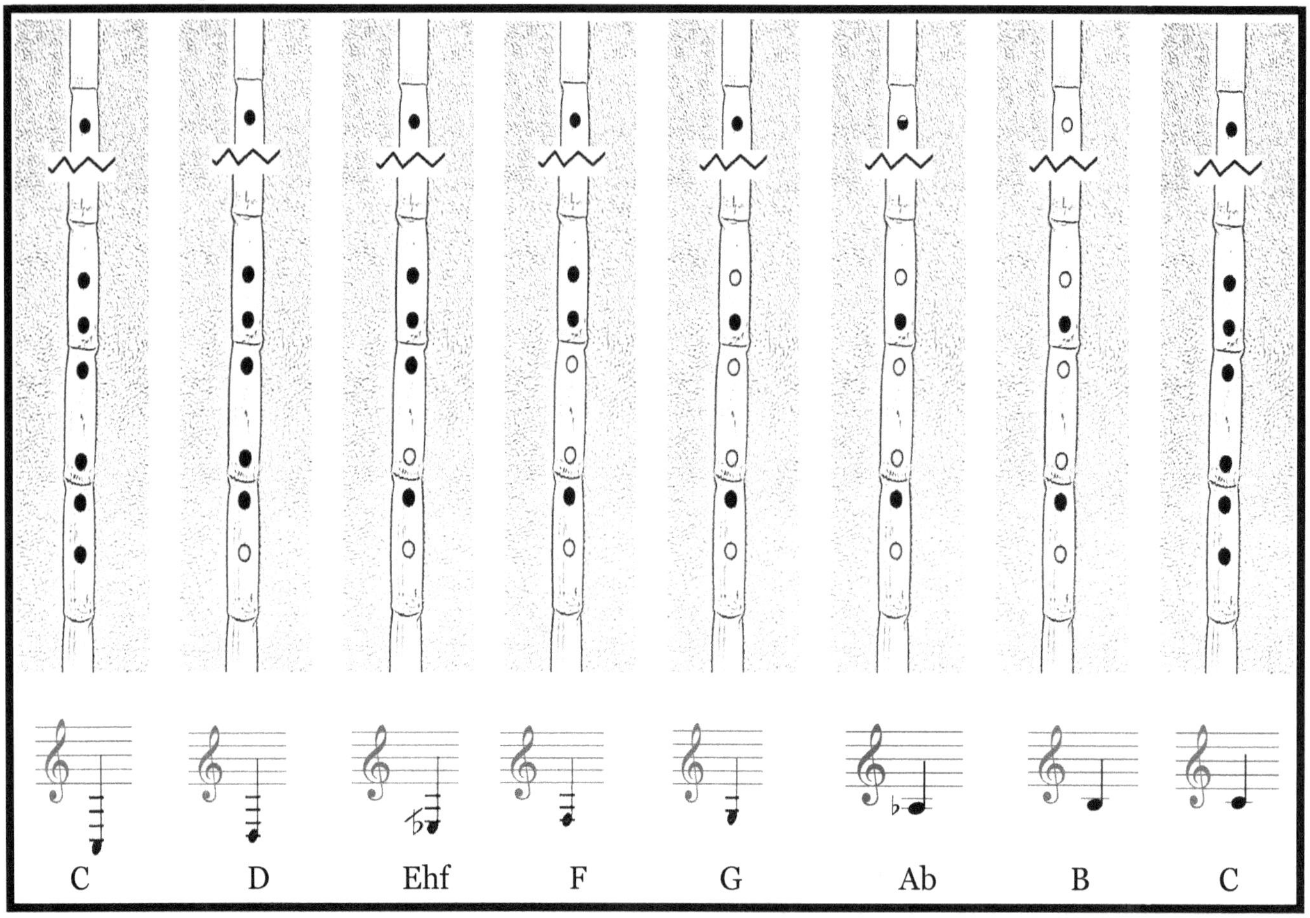

C   D   Ehf   F   G   Ab   B   C

Main Register:

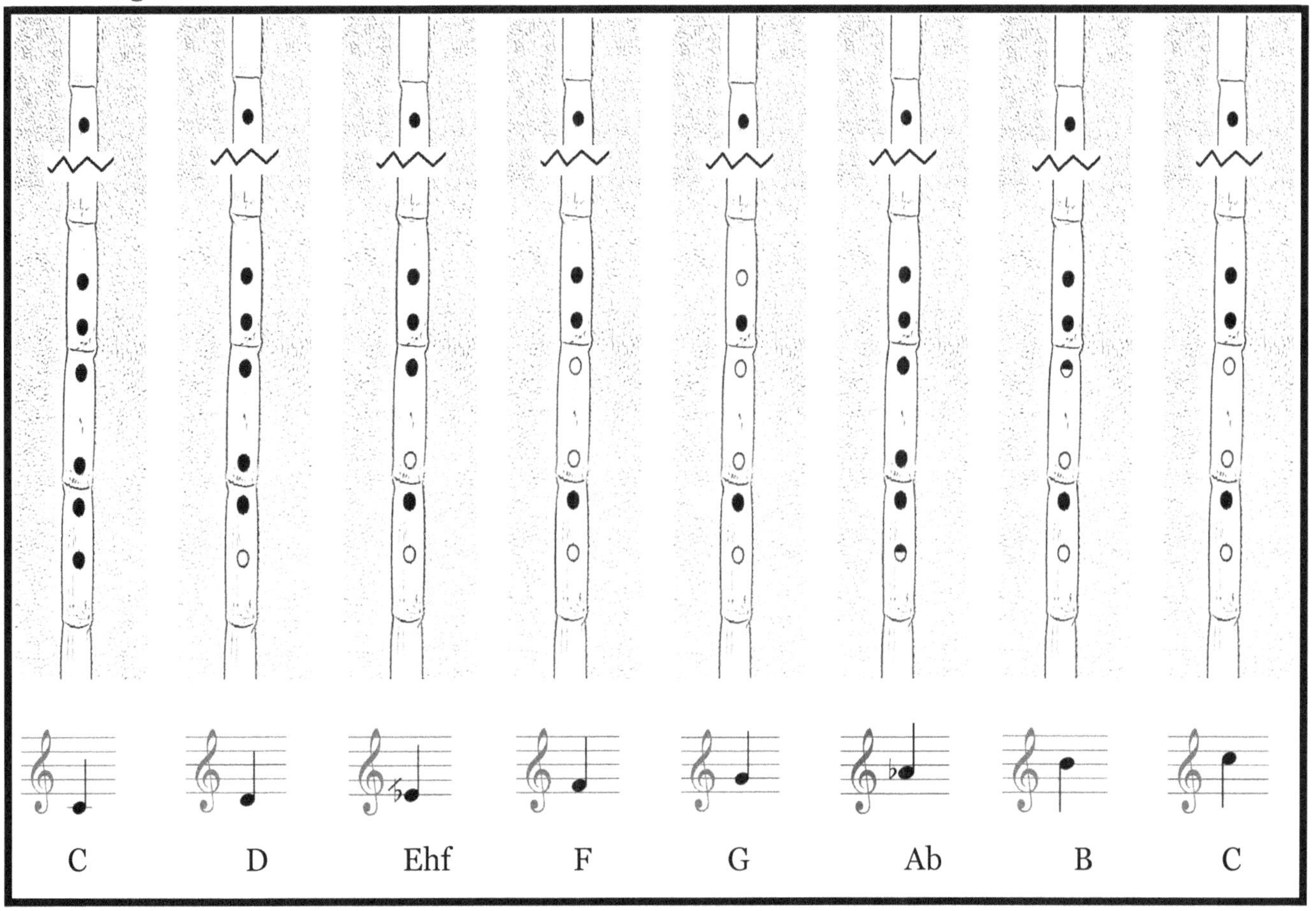

| C | D | Ehf | F | G | Ab | B | C |

Second Register:

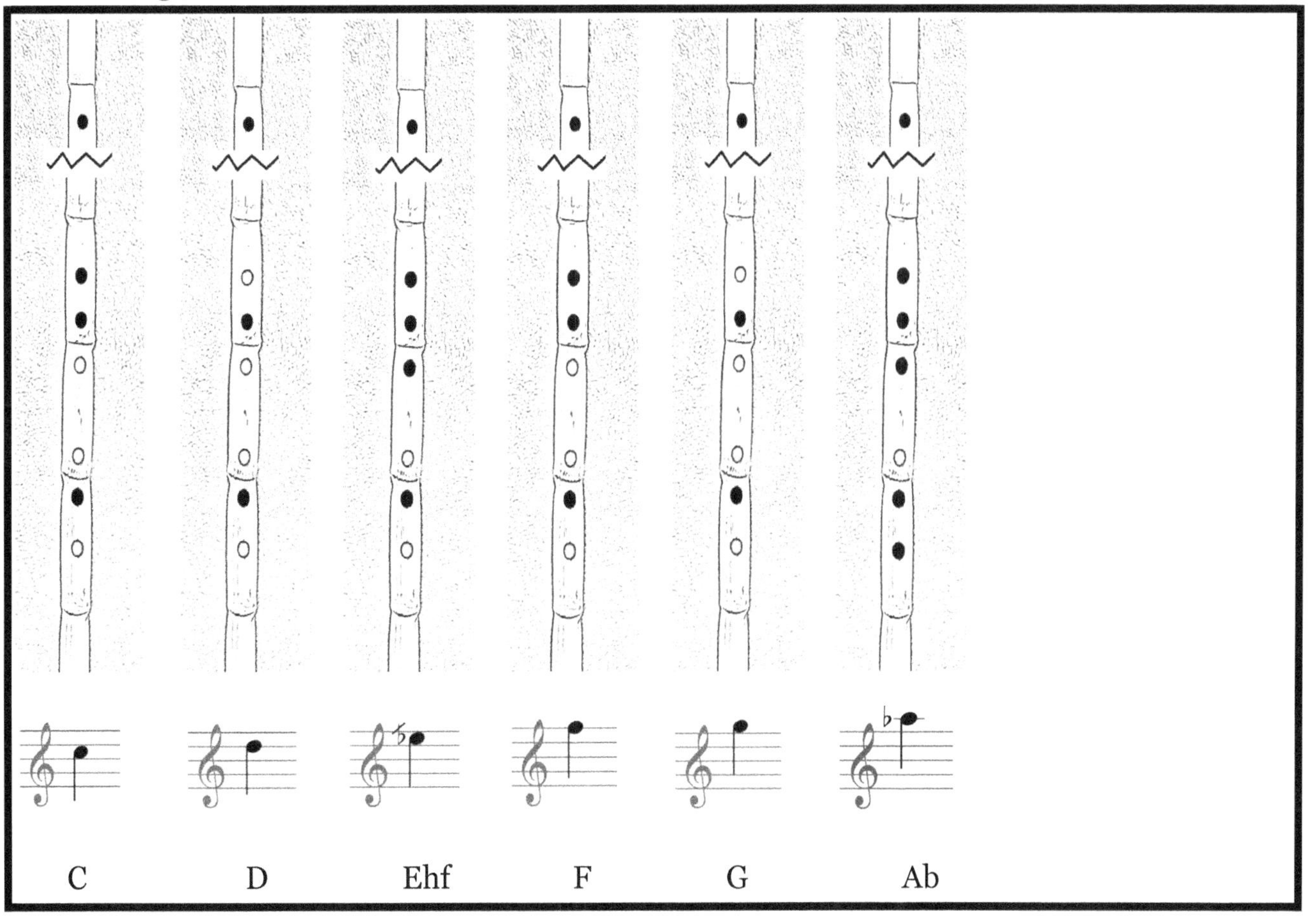

| C | D | Ehf | F | G | Ab |

Maqam Dalanshin

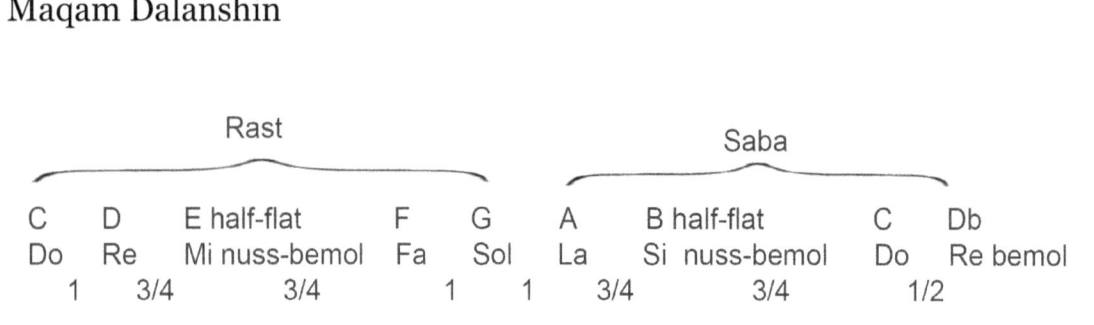

	Rast					Saba			
C	D	E half-flat		F	G	A	B half-flat		C	Db
Do	Re	Mi nuss-bemol		Fa	Sol	La	Si nuss-bemol		Do	Re bemol
1	3/4	3/4		1	1	3/4	3/4		1/2

Possible Descriptions: Rast pentachord on bottom; Saba tetrachord on 6th. Ghammaz on 6th. Modulate into this by moving from the high C to the Db and then down to the A. Improvise in A Saba for a while and then move back to Rast by starting on the G and walking up through A, B half-flat to C.
Used as very exotic ornament in Rast.

Low Kabá Register:

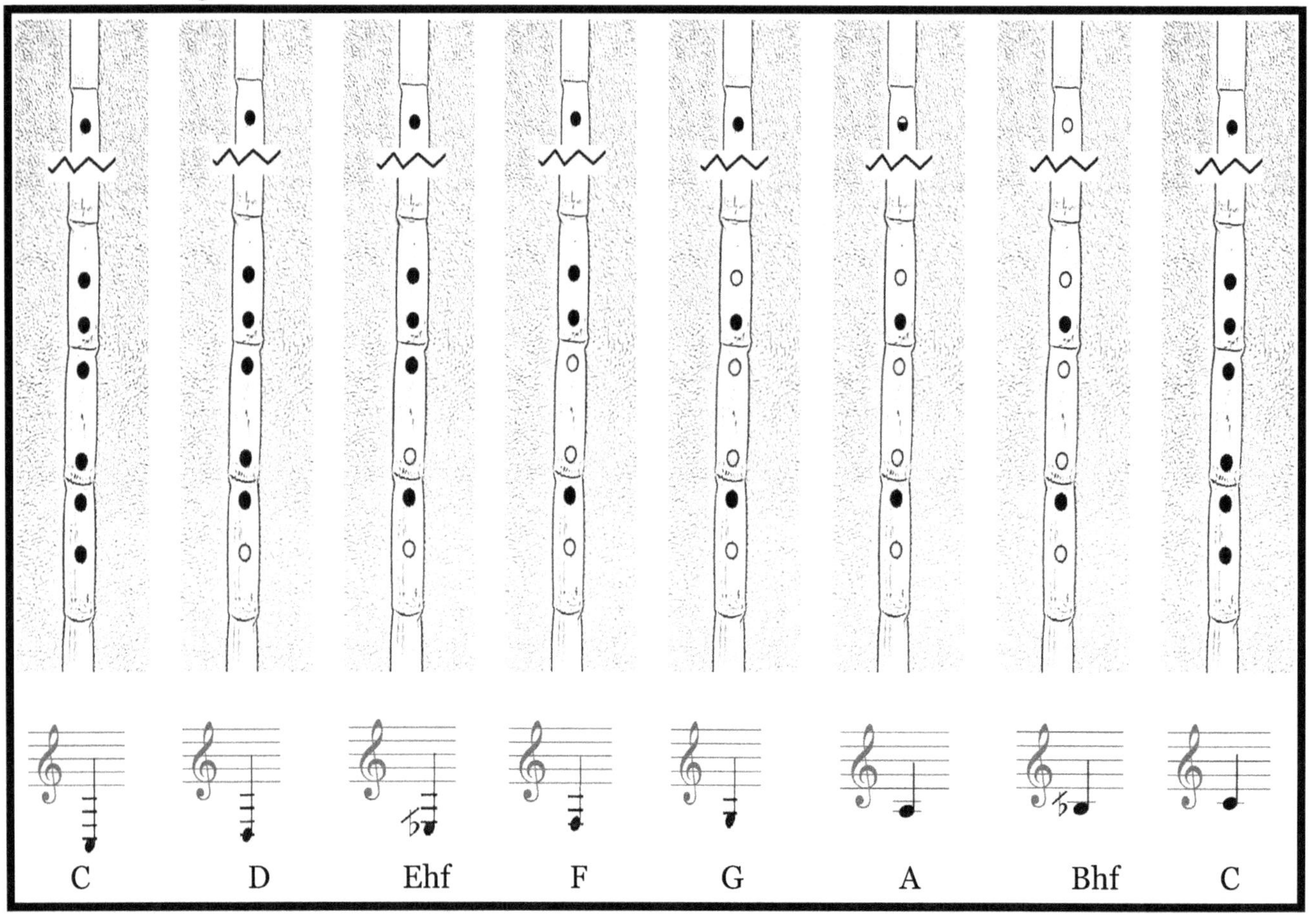

| C | D | Ehf | F | G | A | Bhf | C |

Main Register:

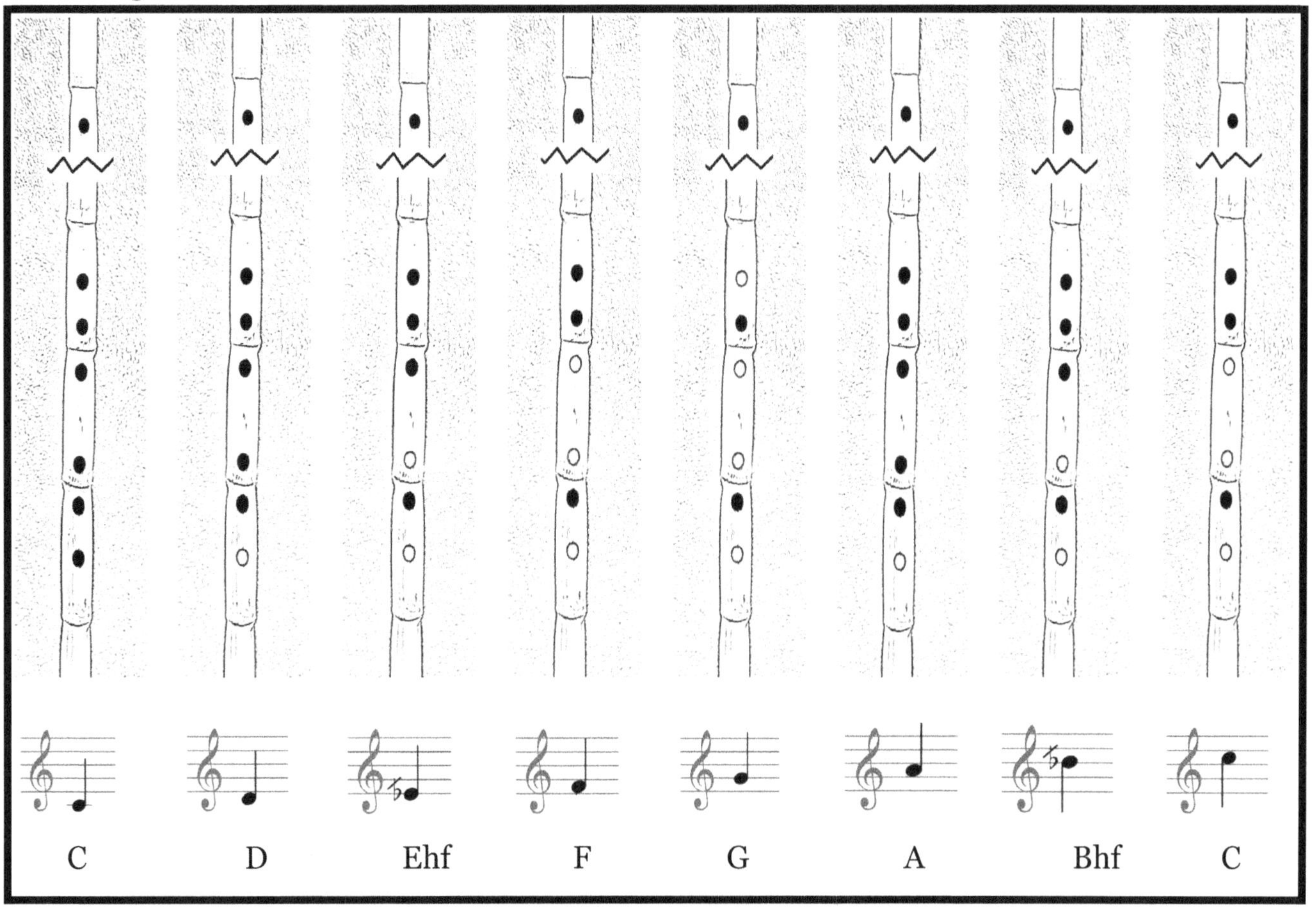

| C | D | Ehf | F | G | A | Bhf | C |

Second Register:

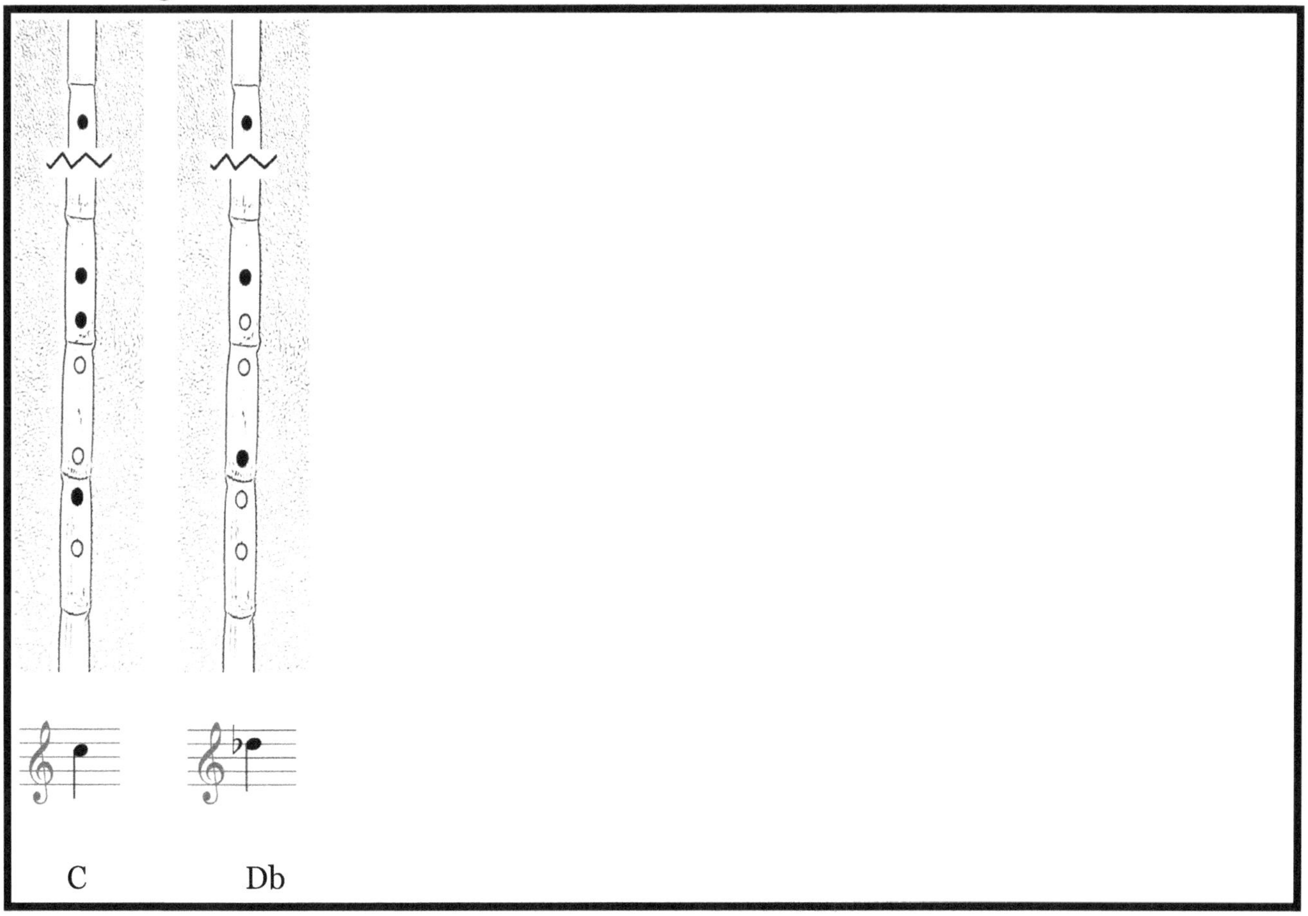

| C | Db |

Maqam Nahawand 1

Closely Related Maqamat and Modes: Nihavent (Turkey), Buselik (Turkey), Natural Minor, Harmonic Minor, Aeolian Mode, Rahawi or Sahili (Algeria), Muhayar Sikah (Tunisia), Isfahan (Persia)

There are two variants of Nahawand which differ only by the position of the 7th. We will call them Nahawand 1 and Nahawand 2.

Possible Descriptions of Nahawand 1: Nahawand tetrachord on bottom; Nahawand pentachord on 4th; Kurd tetrachord on 5th.

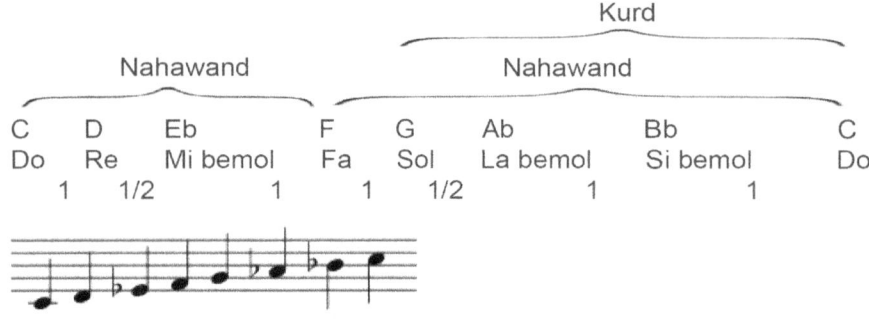

Nahawand in the key of C is difficult to perform on the Dukah nay because of the awkward half-holed G#.

It is much easier to use the G Nawa nay and play from the second register which begins on C.

Low Kabá Register:

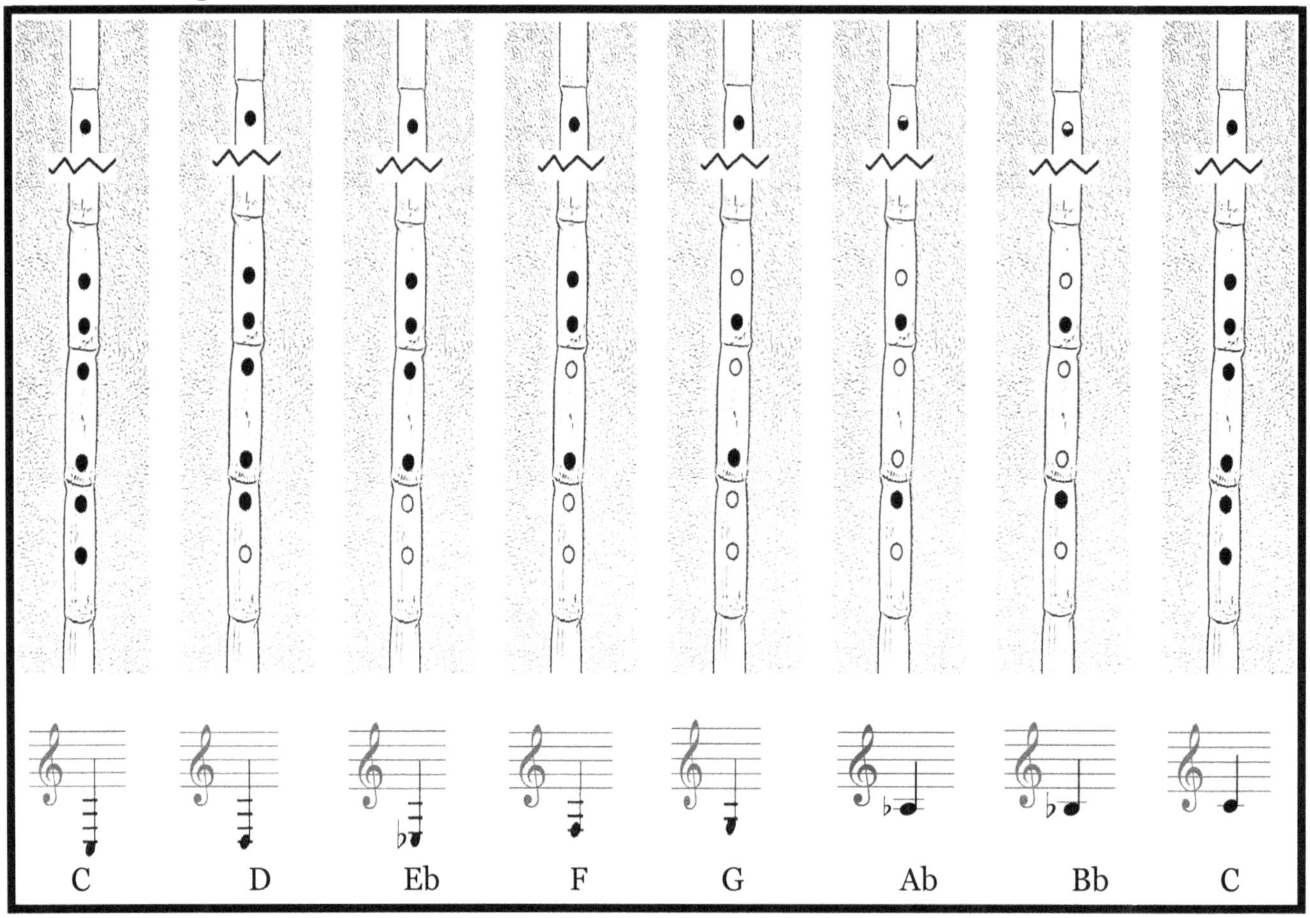

| C | D | Eb | F | G | Ab | Bb | C |

Main Register: 75

| C | D | Eb | F | G | Ab | Bb | C |

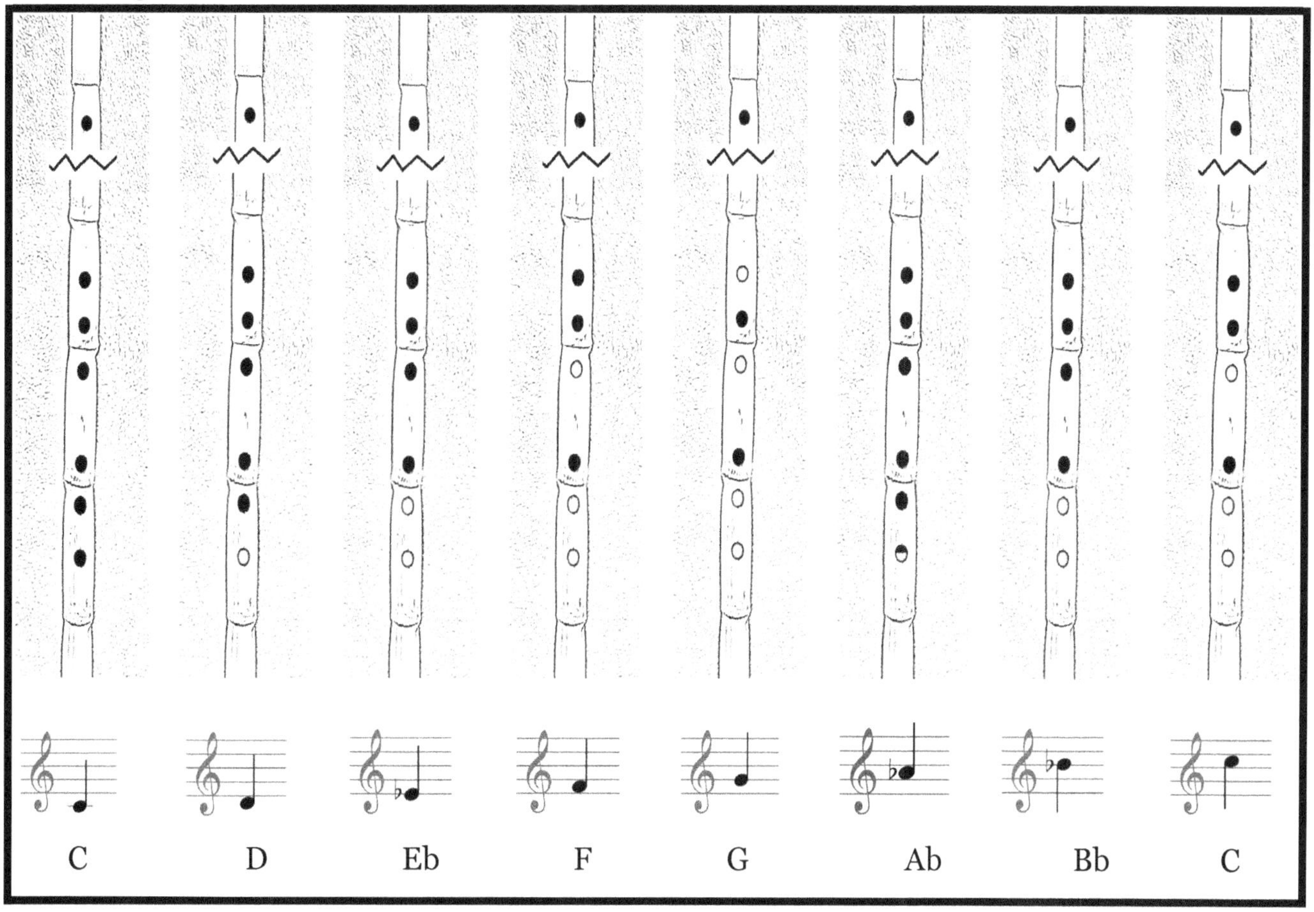

Second Register:

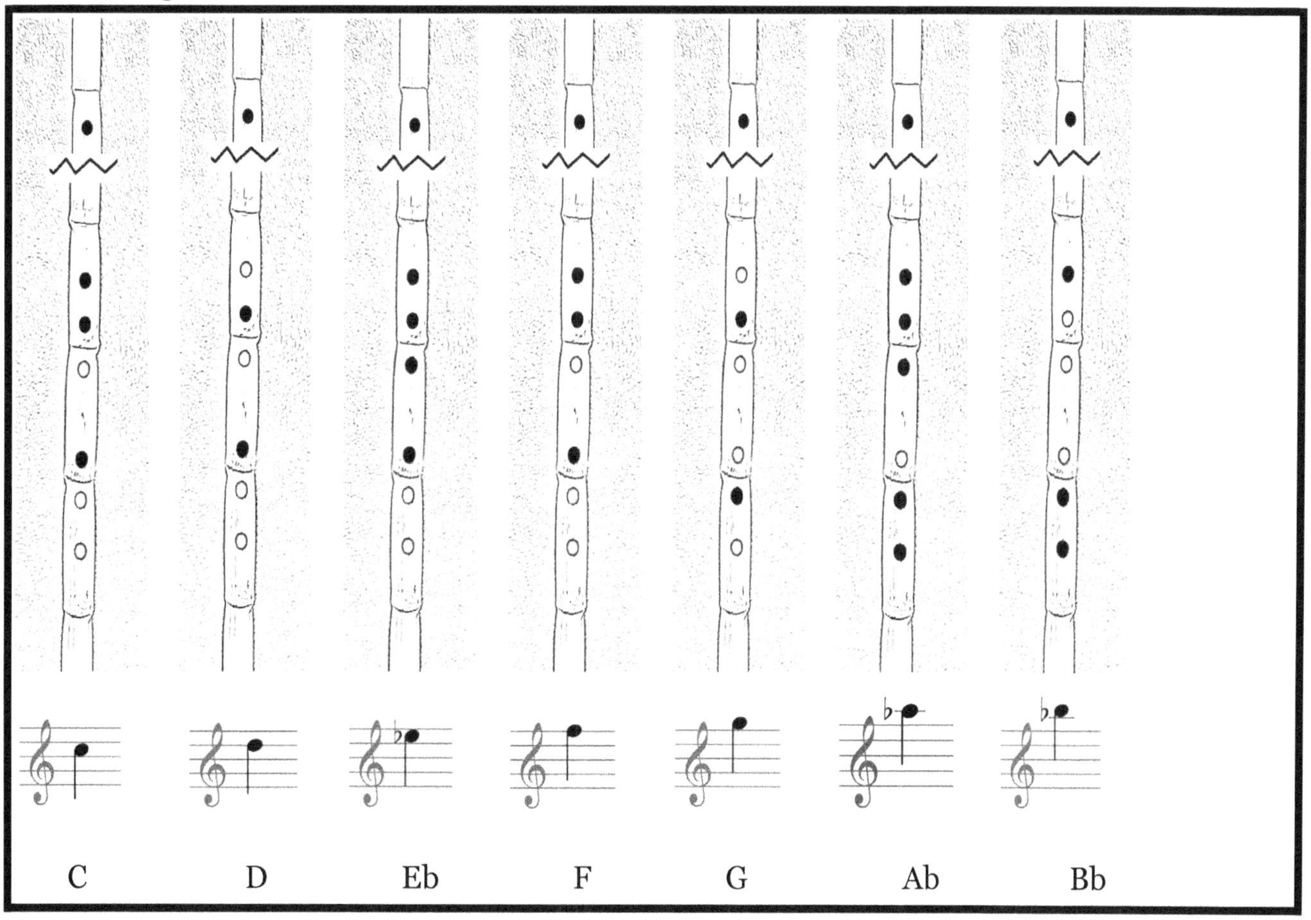

| C | D | Eb | F | G | Ab | Bb |

Maqam Nahawand 2

Closely Related Maqamat and Modes: Nihavent (Turkey), Buselik (Turkey), Natural Minor, Harmonic Minor, Aeolian Mode, Rahawi or Sahili (Algeria), Muhayar Sikah (Tunisia), Isfahan (Persia)

There are two variants of Nahawand which differ only by the position of the 7th. We will call them Nahawand 1 and Nahawand 2.

Possible Descriptions of Nahawand 2: Nahawand tetrachord on bottom; Nawa Athar pentachord on 4th; Hijaz tetrachord on 5th.

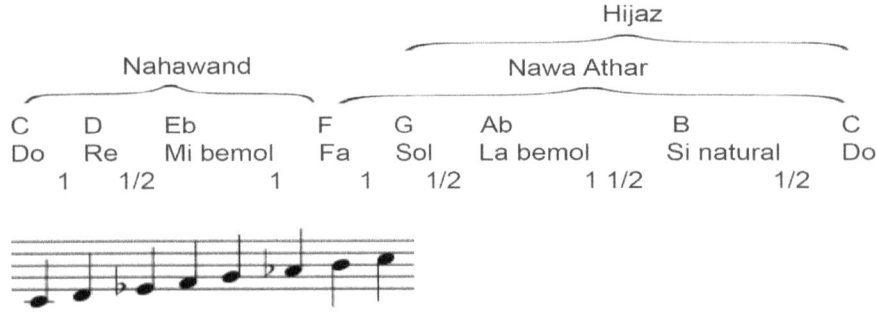

Nahawand in the key of C is difficult to perform on the Dukah nay because of the awkward half-holed G#.

It is much easier to use the G Nawa nay and play from the second register which begins on C.

Low Kabá Register:

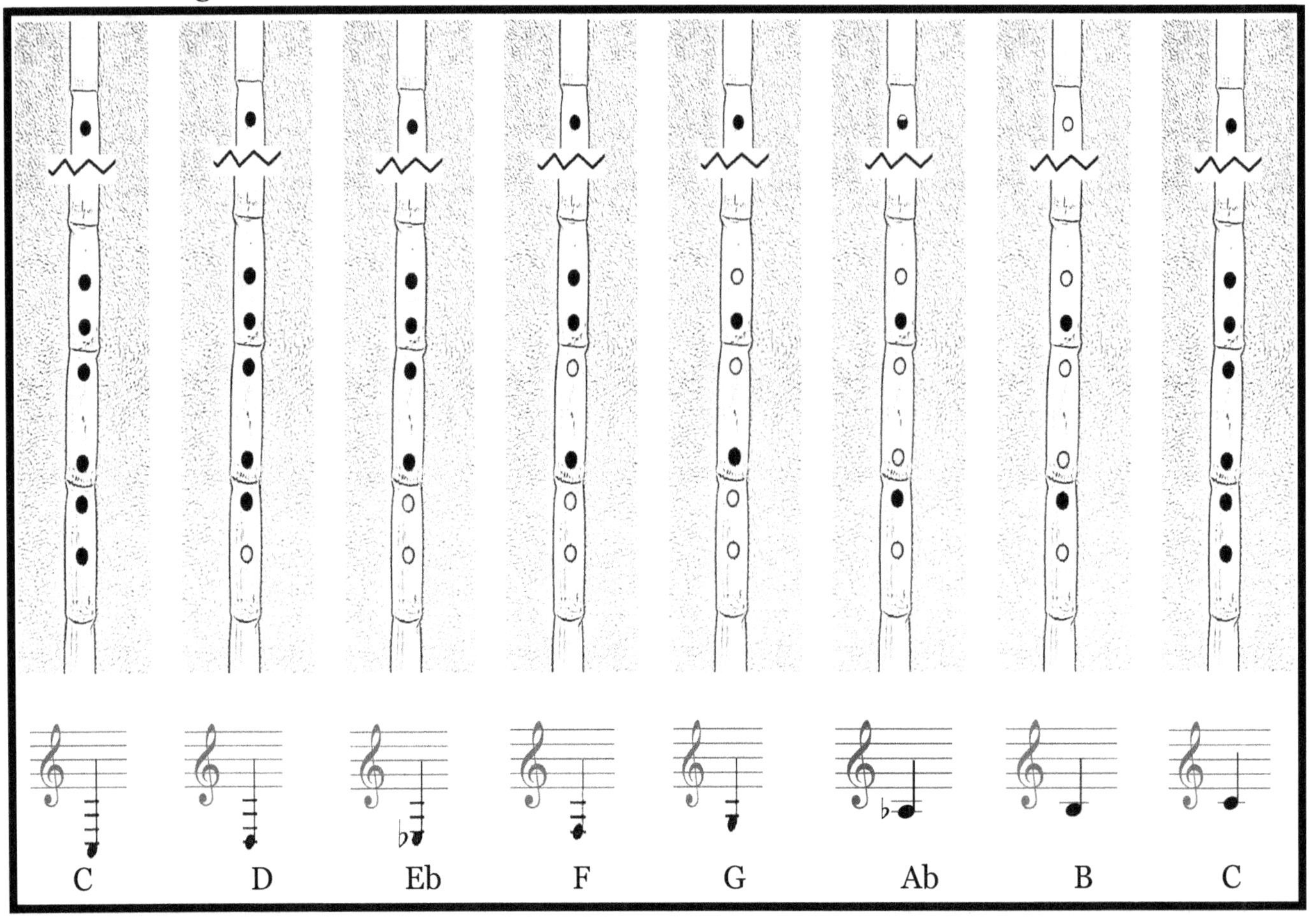

Main Register:

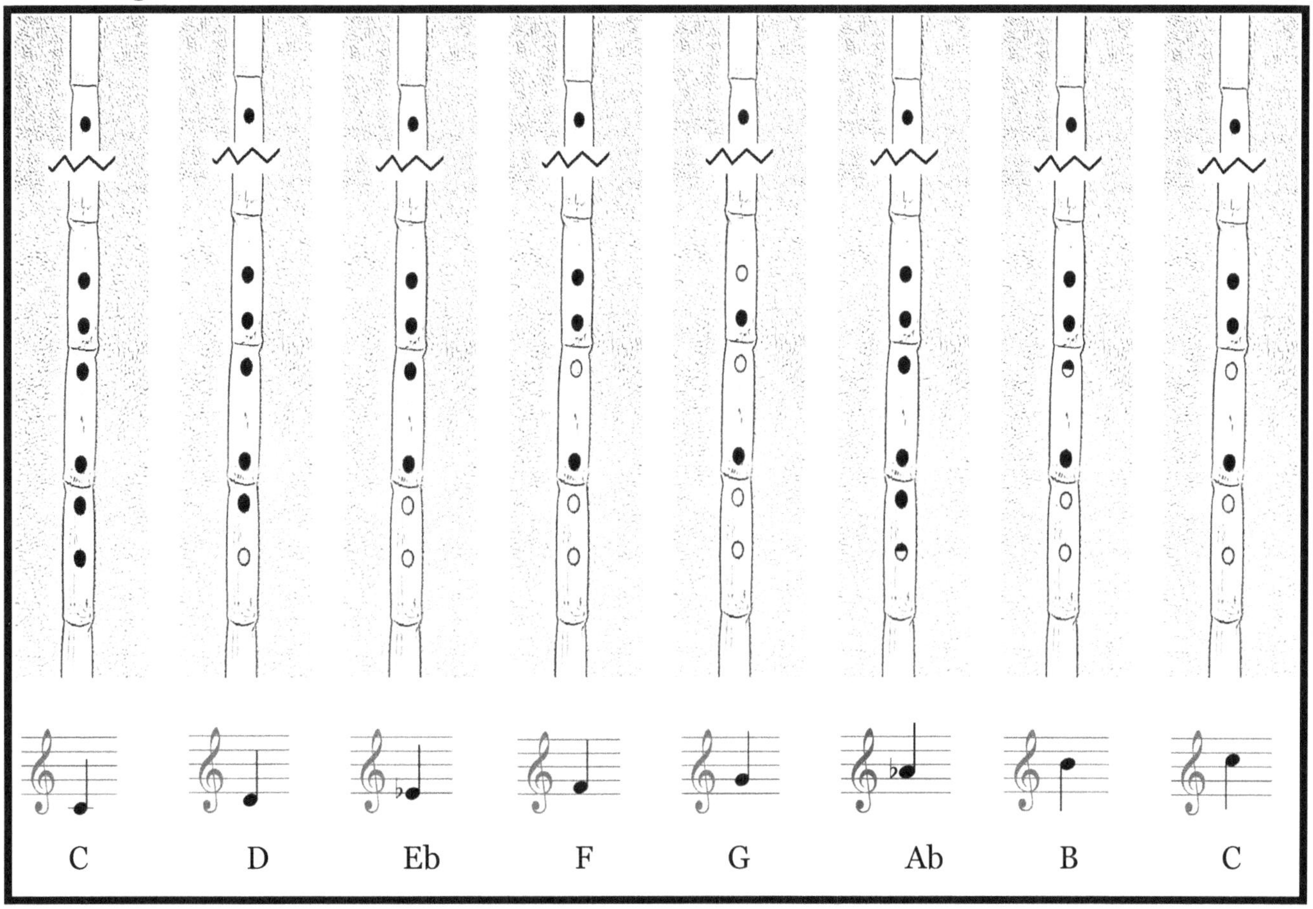

| C | D | Eb | F | G | Ab | B | C |

Second Register:

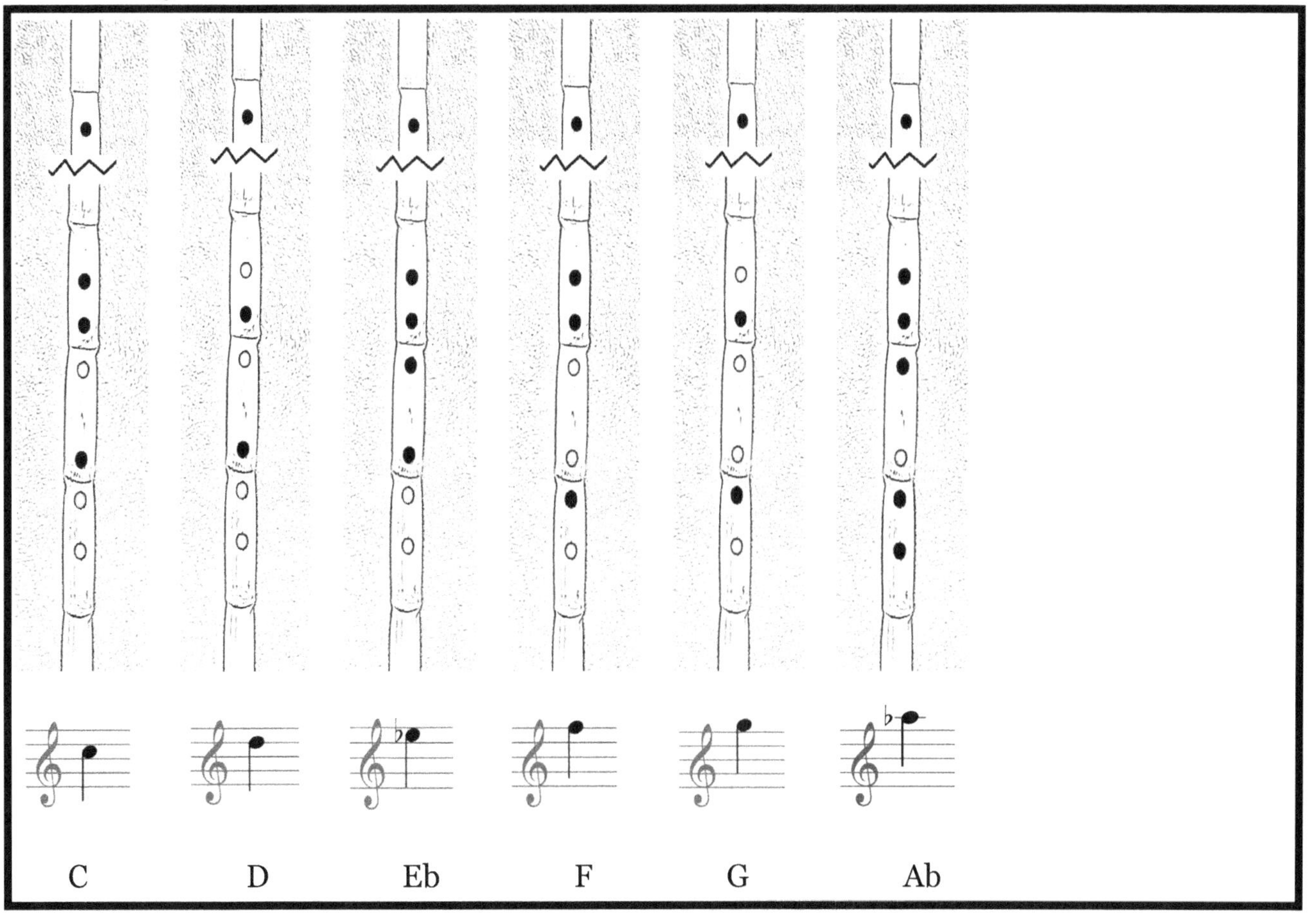

| C | D | Eb | F | G | Ab |

Maqam Nakriz

```
            ┌─────── Hijaz ───────┐
    ┌──── Nawa Athar ────┐              ┌──── Nahawand ────┐
    C    D    Eb       F#       G    A    Bb       C
    Do   Re   Mi bemol Fa diaz  Sol  La   Si bemol Do
       1   1/2    1 1/2    1/2     1   1/2    1
```

Possible Descriptions: Nawa Athar pentachord on bottom; Hijaz tetrachord on 2nd; Nahawand tetrachord on 5nd.

Common in central mountain Greek tsamika-style dance music with clarinet lead. 2nd (Re) is heard as sub-dominant or ghammaz. It is frequently used in melodies as if it were the tonic. This turns out to be temporary as the tune finally resolves back to the 1st (Do).

Low Kabá Register:

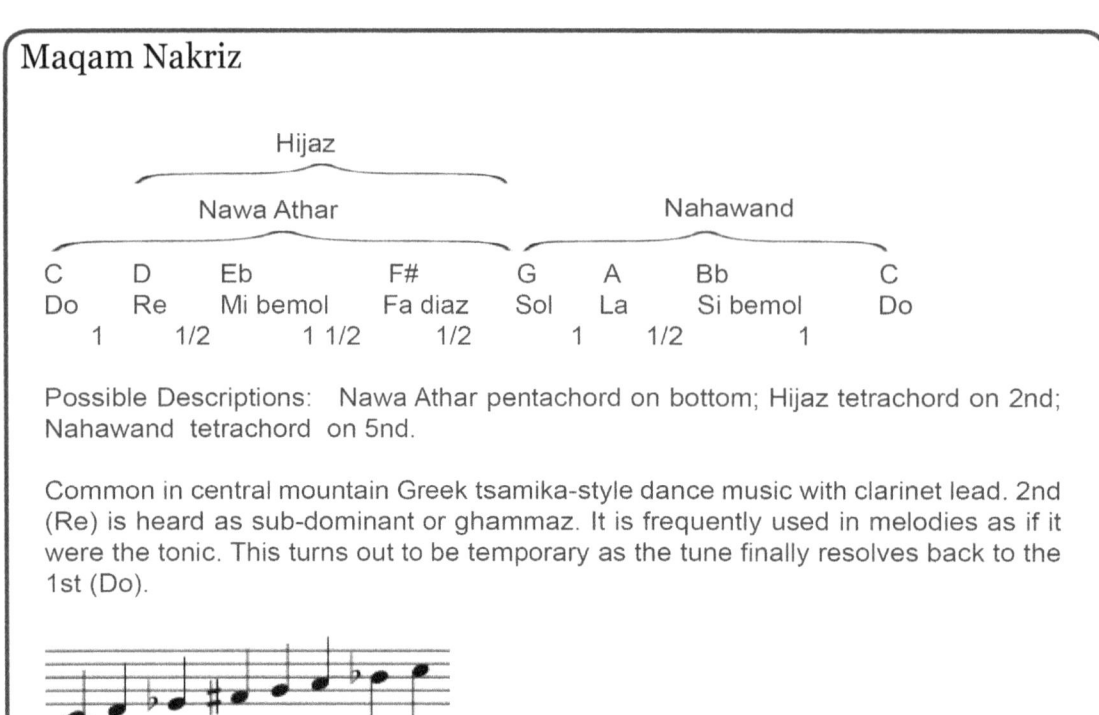

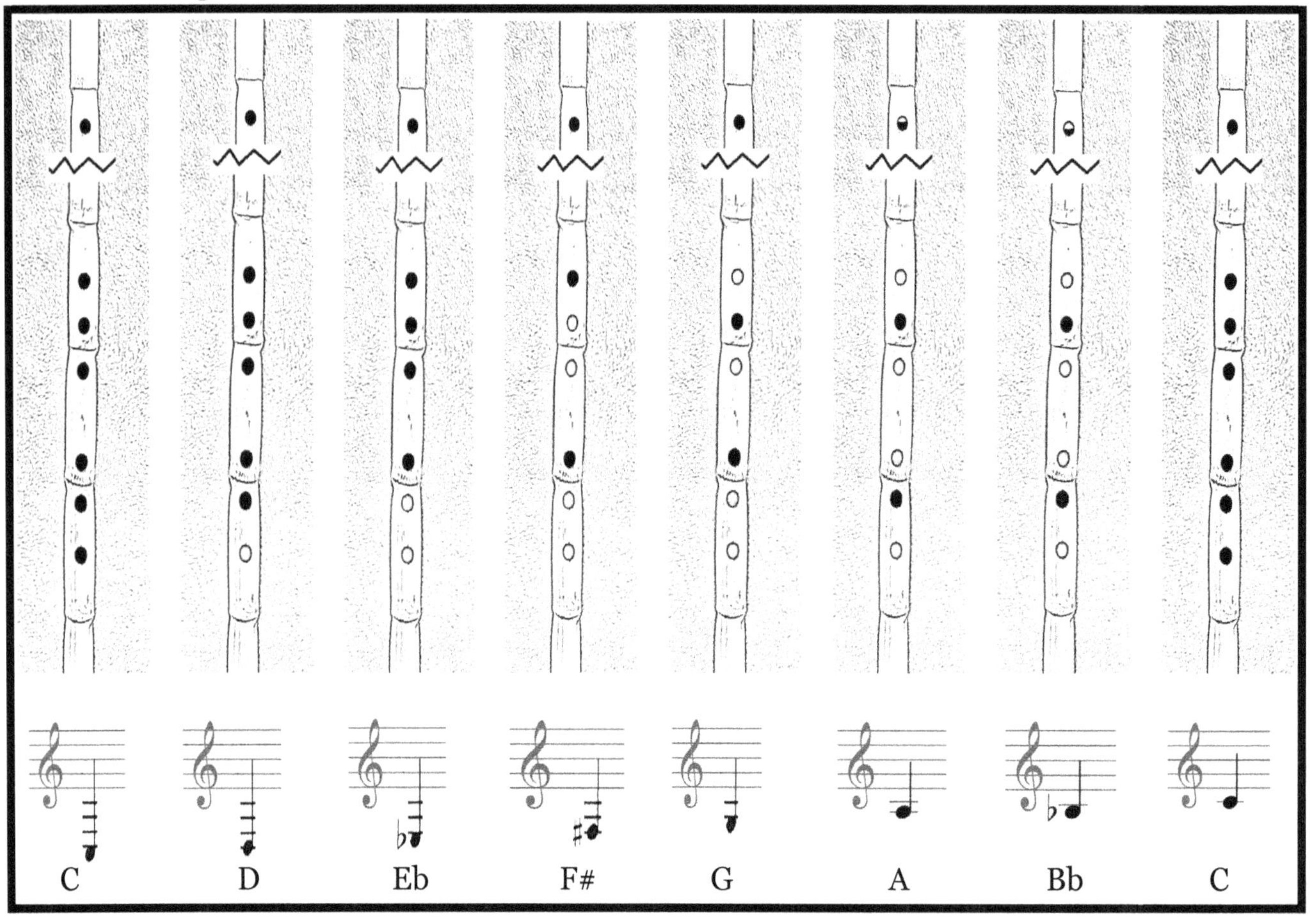

C   D   Eb   F#   G   A   Bb   C

Main Register: 79

| C | D | Eb | F# | G | A | Bb | C |

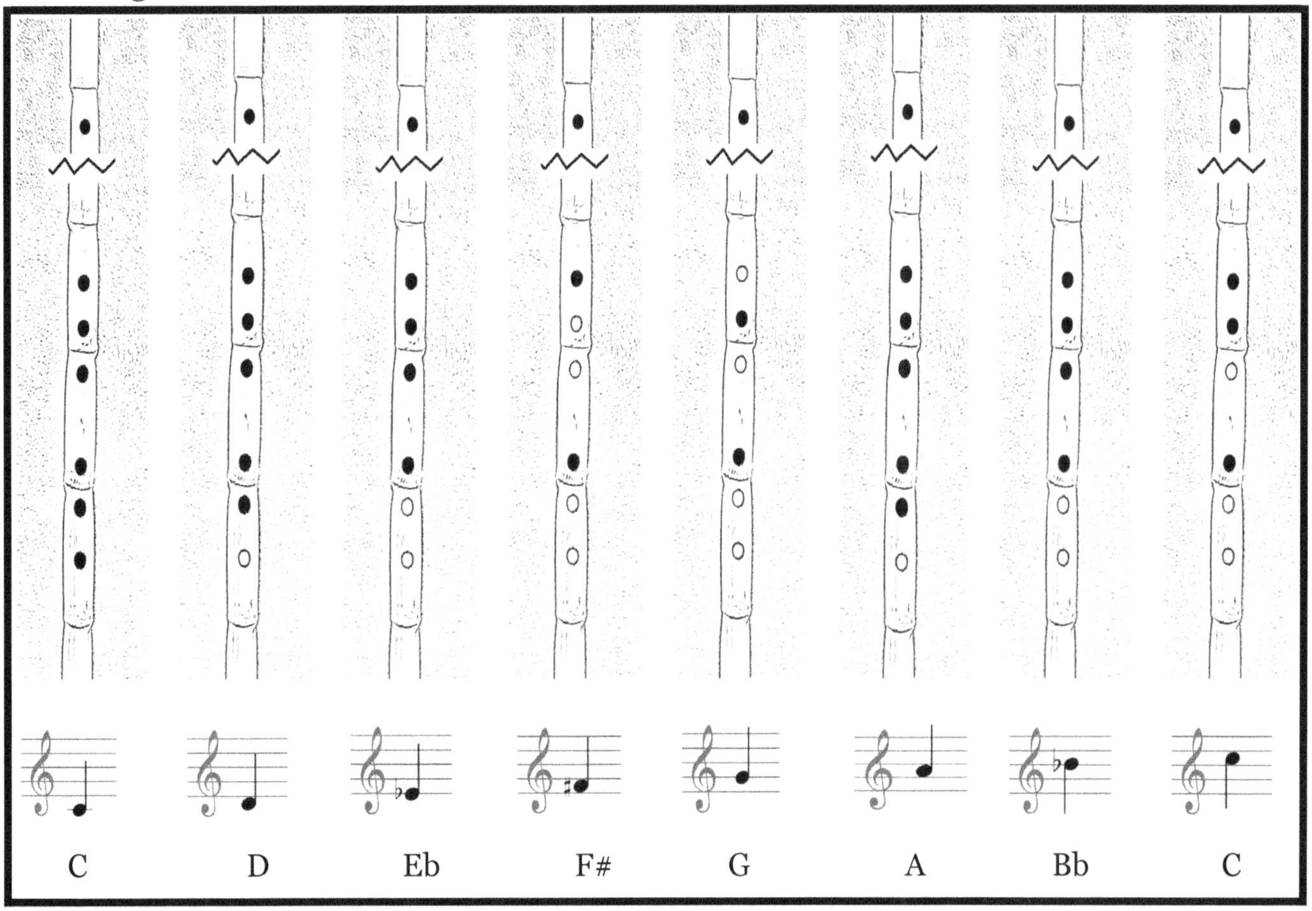

Second Register:

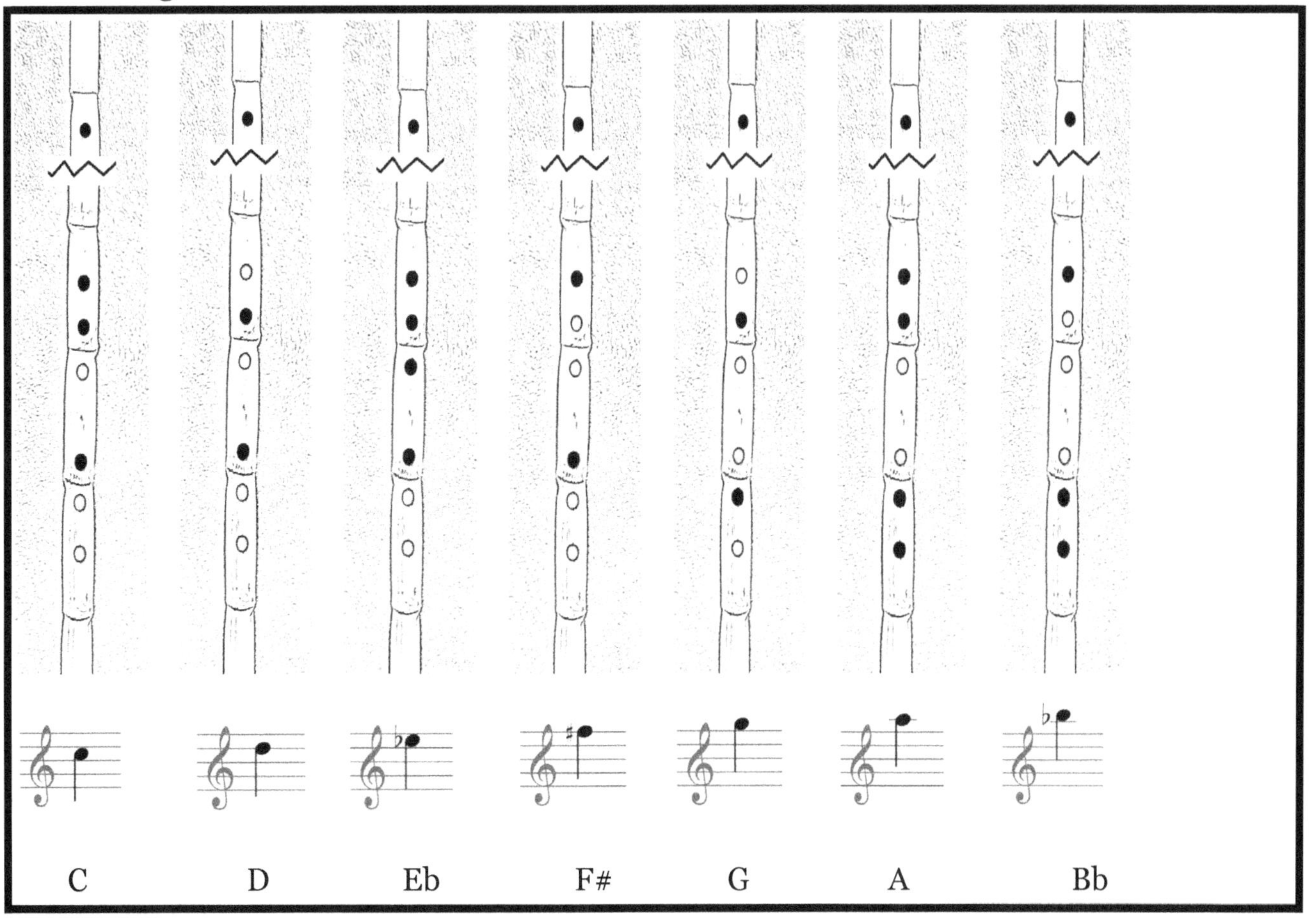

| C | D | Eb | F# | G | A | Bb |

Maqam Nawa Athar

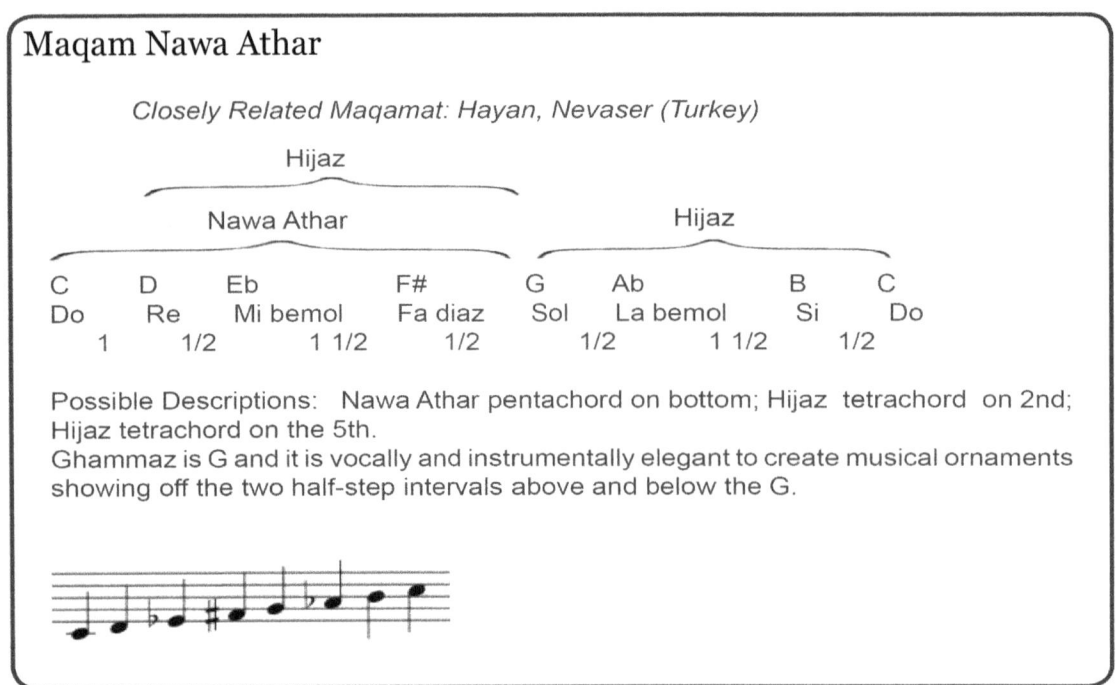

Closely Related Maqamat: Hayan, Nevaser (Turkey)

```
              Hijaz
       ⌢⎯⎯⎯⎯⎯⎯⎯⎯⎯⎯⌢
      Nawa Athar                Hijaz
⌢⎯⎯⎯⎯⎯⎯⎯⎯⎯⎯⎯⎯⎯⎯⌢    ⌢⎯⎯⎯⎯⎯⎯⎯⎯⎯⎯⎯⎯⌢
C    D    Eb        F#    G    Ab        B    C
Do   Re   Mi bemol  Fa diaz Sol La bemol  Si   Do
   1    1/2    1 1/2   1/2   1/2   1 1/2   1/2
```

Possible Descriptions: Nawa Athar pentachord on bottom; Hijaz tetrachord on 2nd; Hijaz tetrachord on the 5th.
Ghammaz is G and it is vocally and instrumentally elegant to create musical ornaments showing off the two half-step intervals above and below the G.

Nawa Athar in the key of C is difficult to perform on the Dukah nay because of the awkward half-holed Ab and B.

This maqam requires awkward half-holing no matter which size nay is used..

Low Kabá Register:

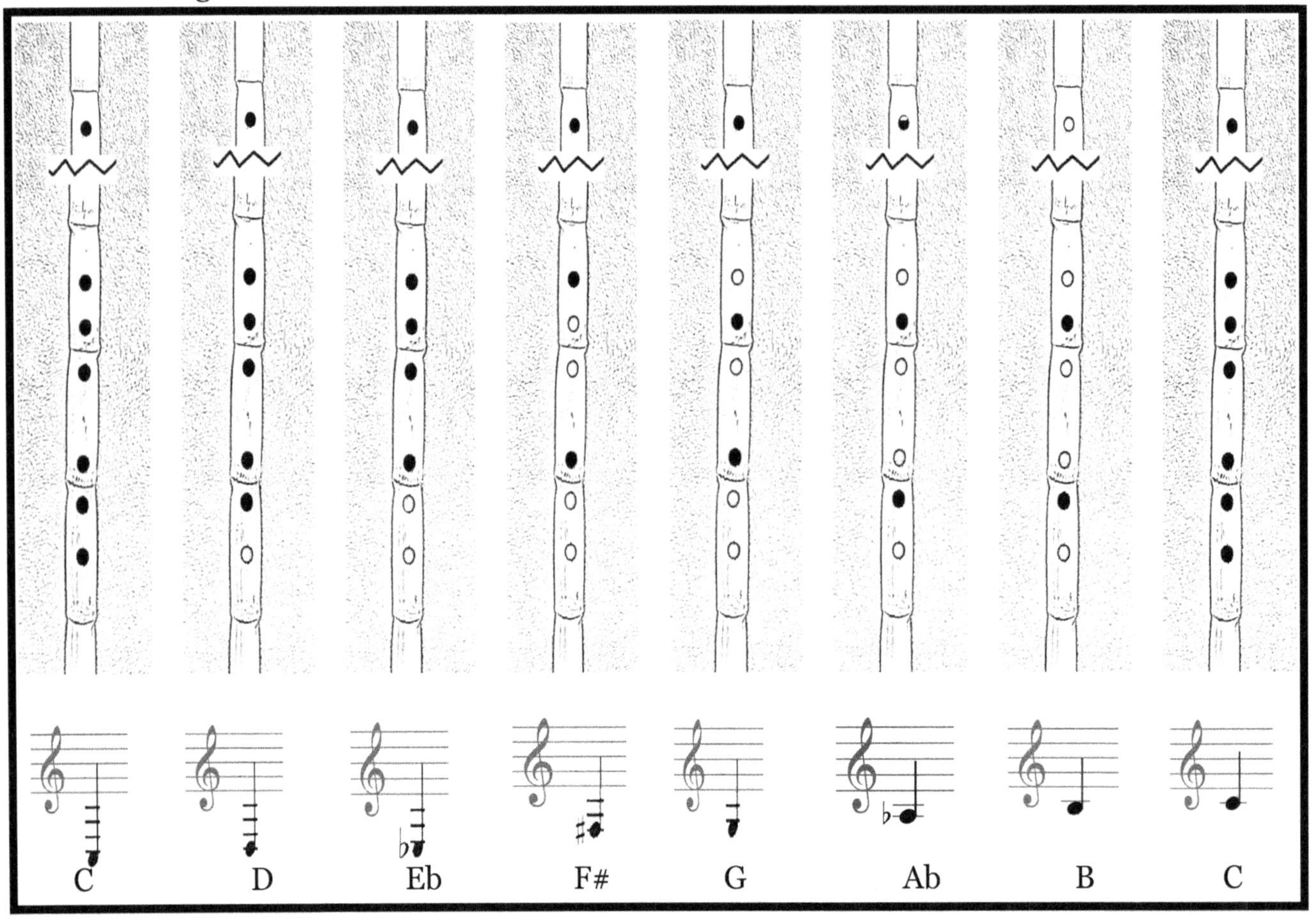

| C | D | Eb | F# | G | Ab | B | C |

Main Register:

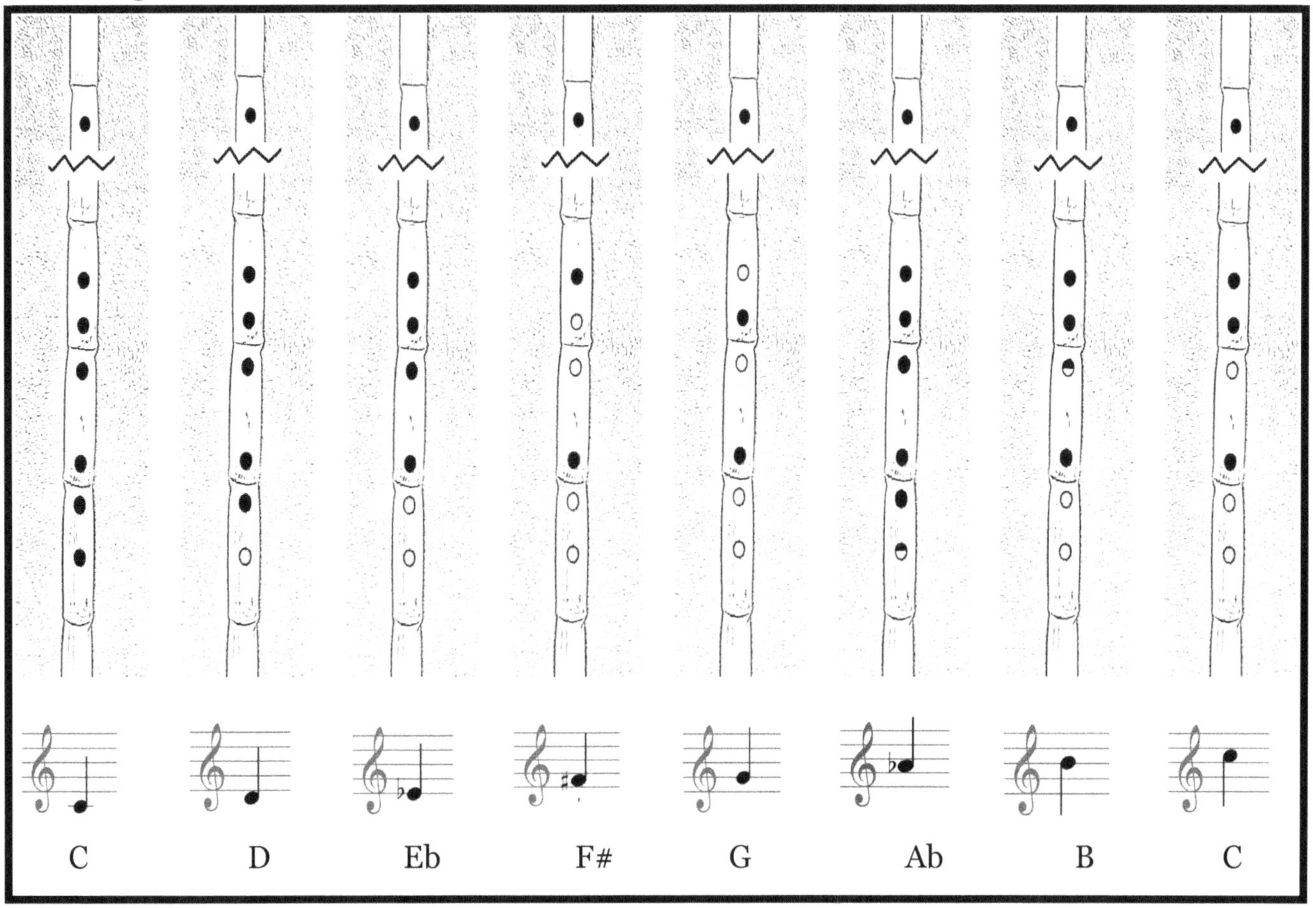

| C | D | Eb | F# | G | Ab | B | C |

Second Register:

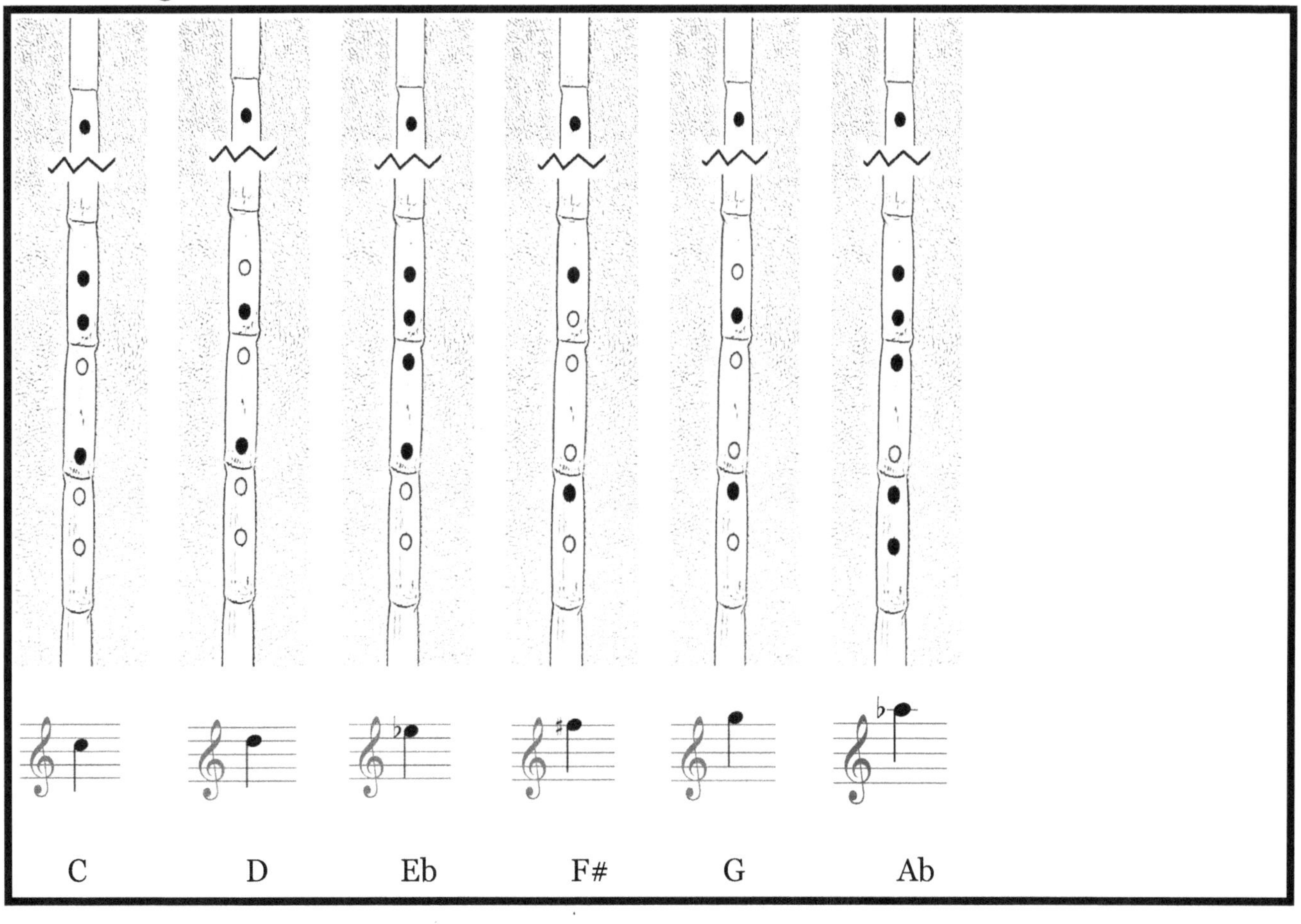

| C | D | Eb | F# | G | Ab |

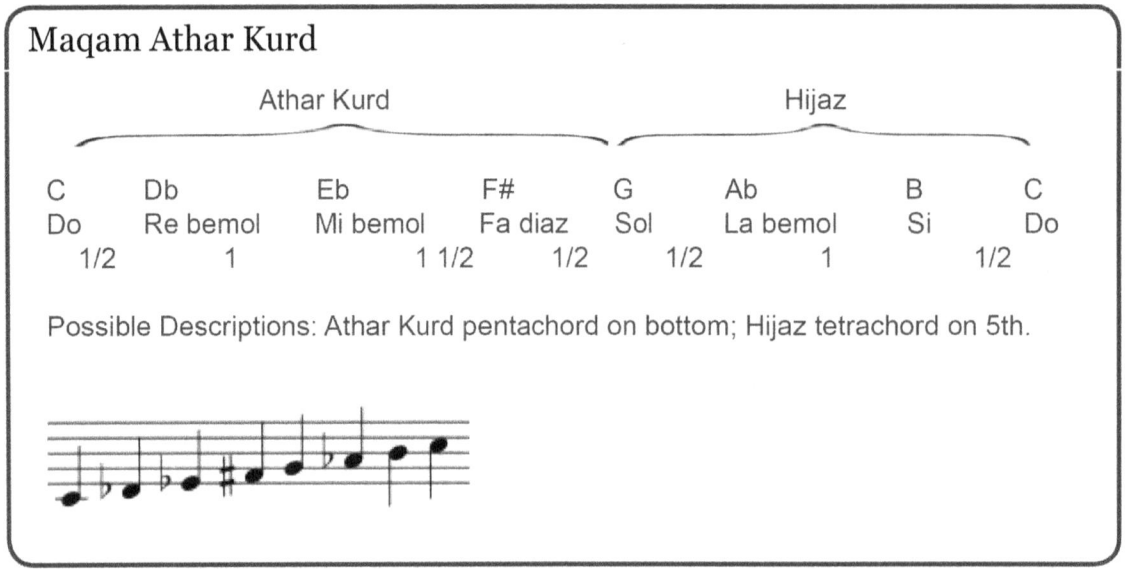

Athar Kurd in the key of C is difficult to perform on the Dukah nay because of the awkward half-holed Db and Ab and B.

This maqam requires awkward half-holing no matter which size nay is used..

Low Kabá Register:

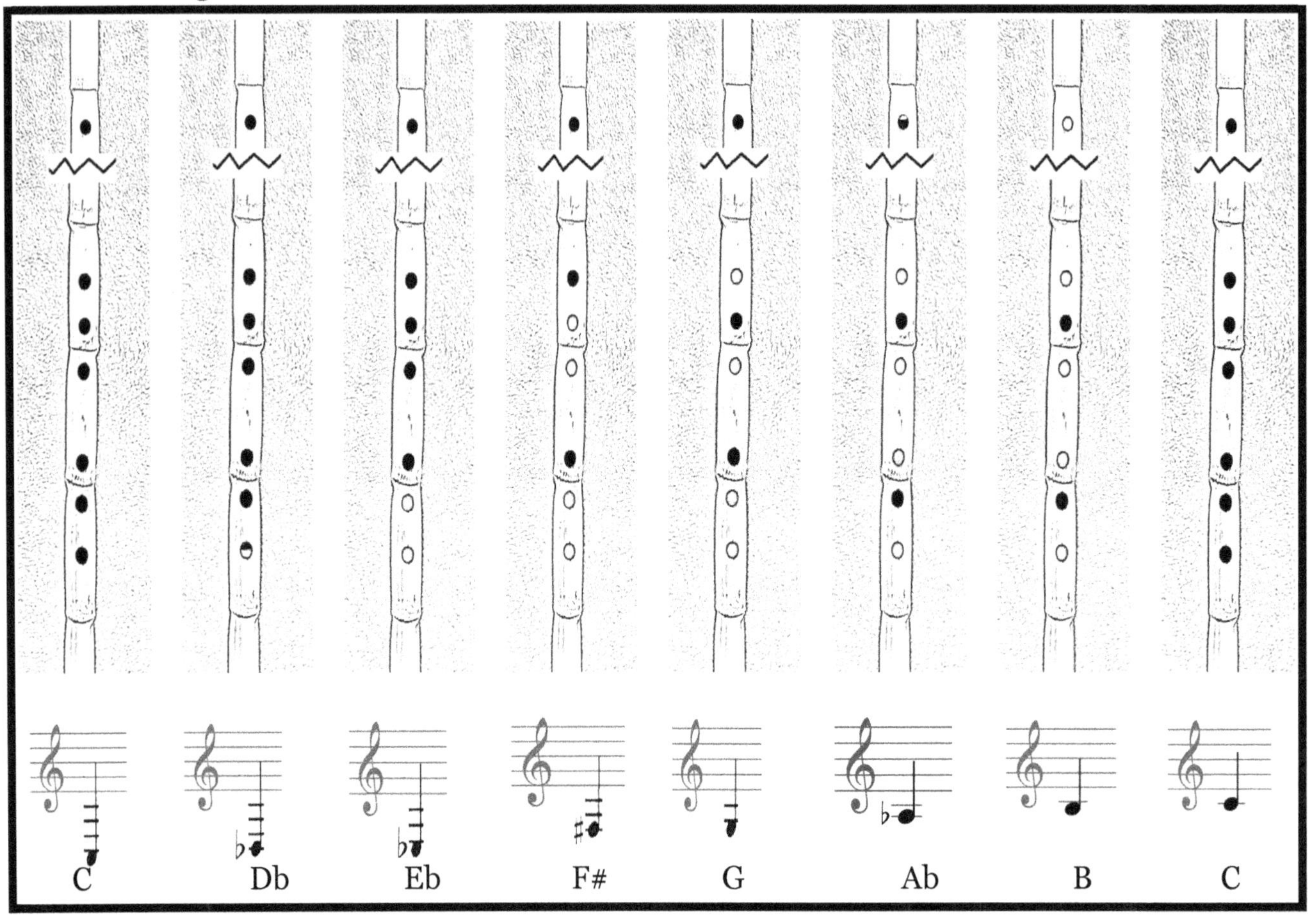

Main Register:

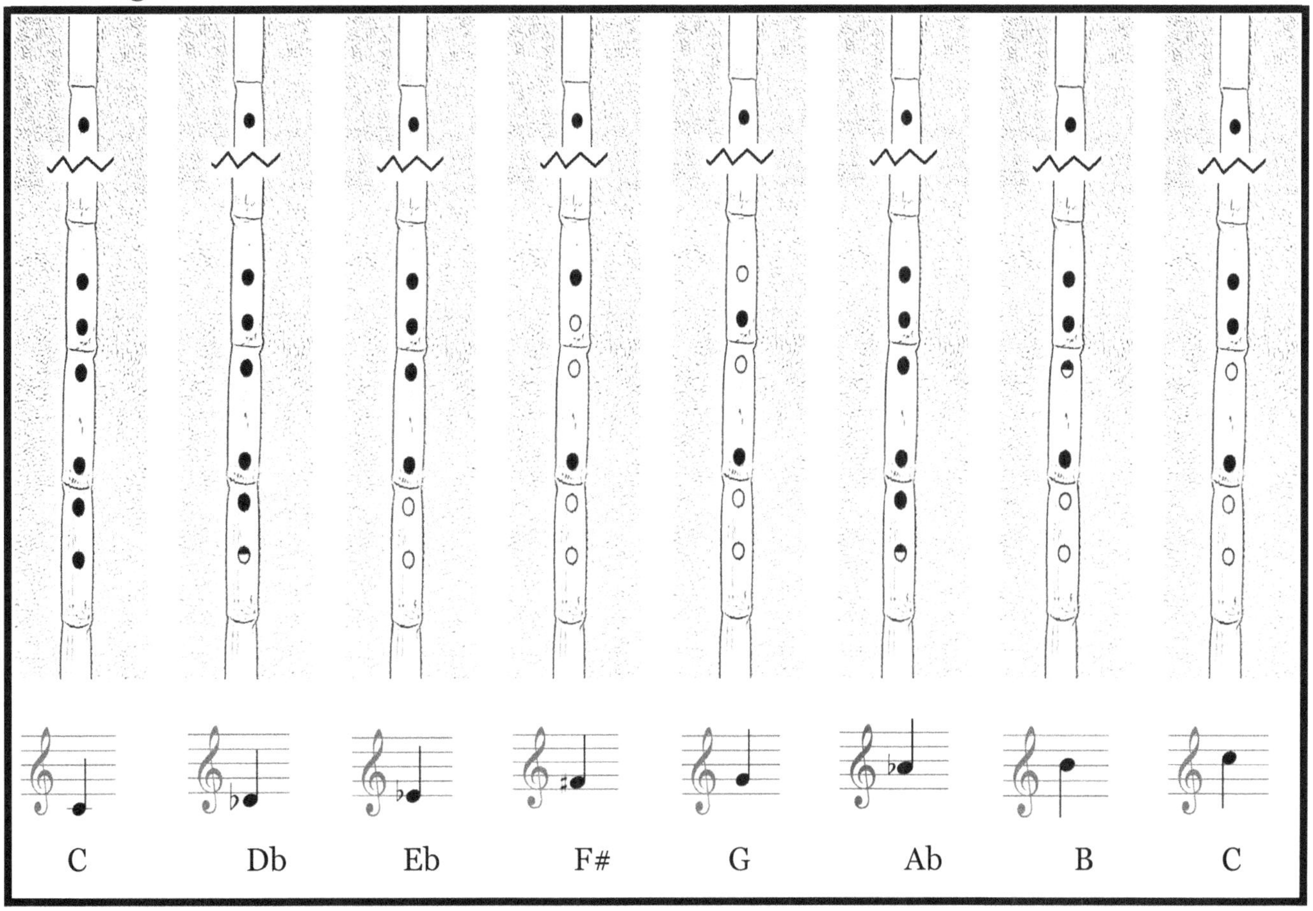

| C | Db | Eb | F# | G | Ab | B | C |

Second Register:

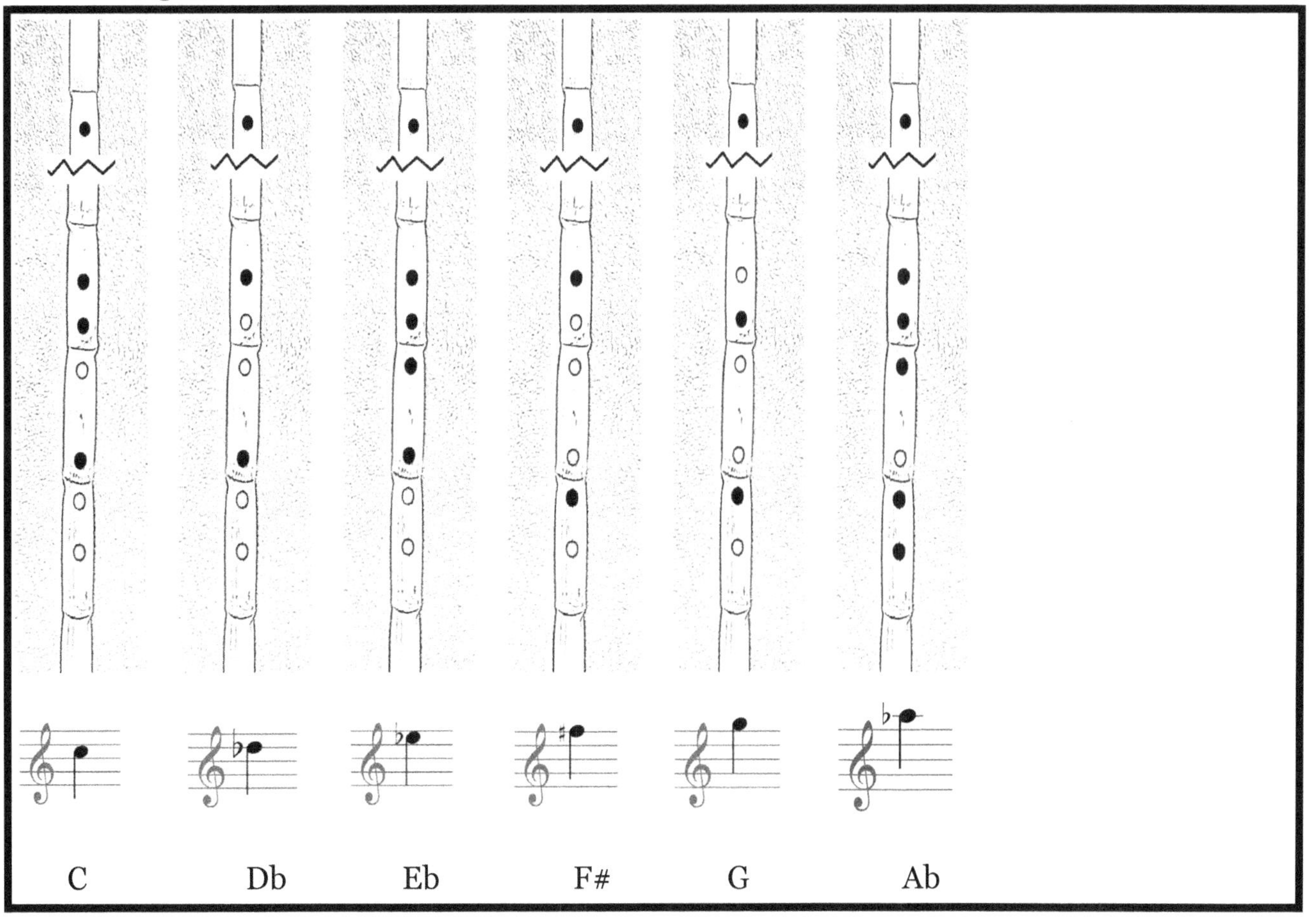

| C | Db | Eb | F# | G | Ab |

Maqam Basandidah

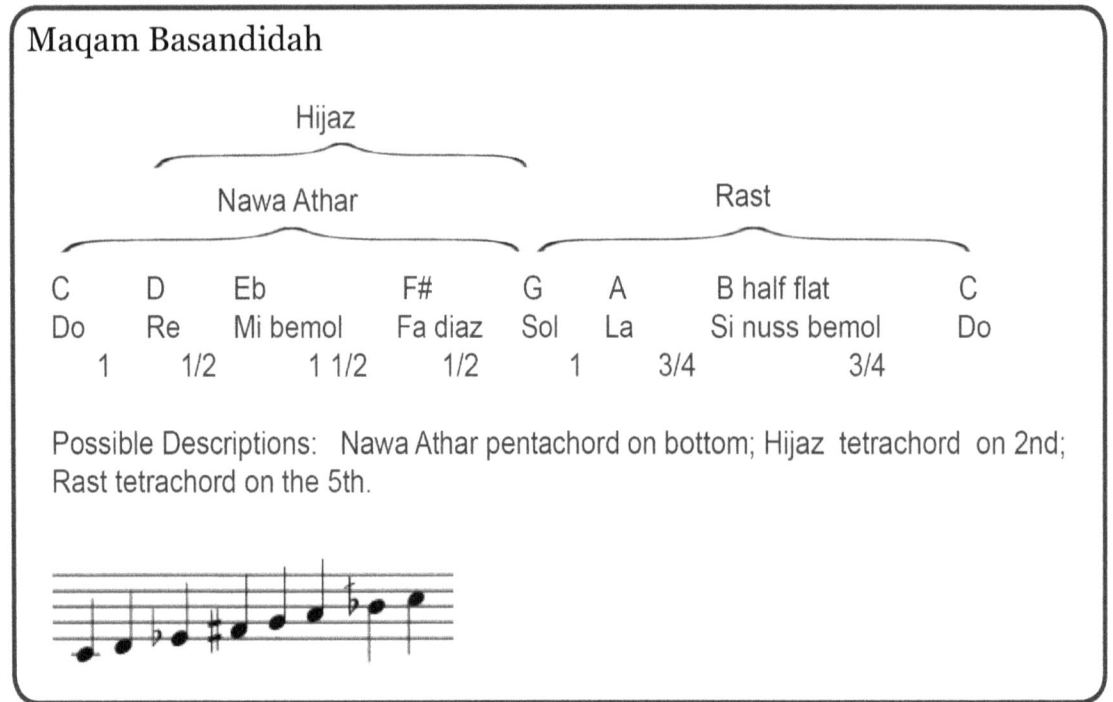

Possible Descriptions: Nawa Athar pentachord on bottom; Hijaz tetrachord on 2nd; Rast tetrachord on the 5th.

Low Kabá Register:

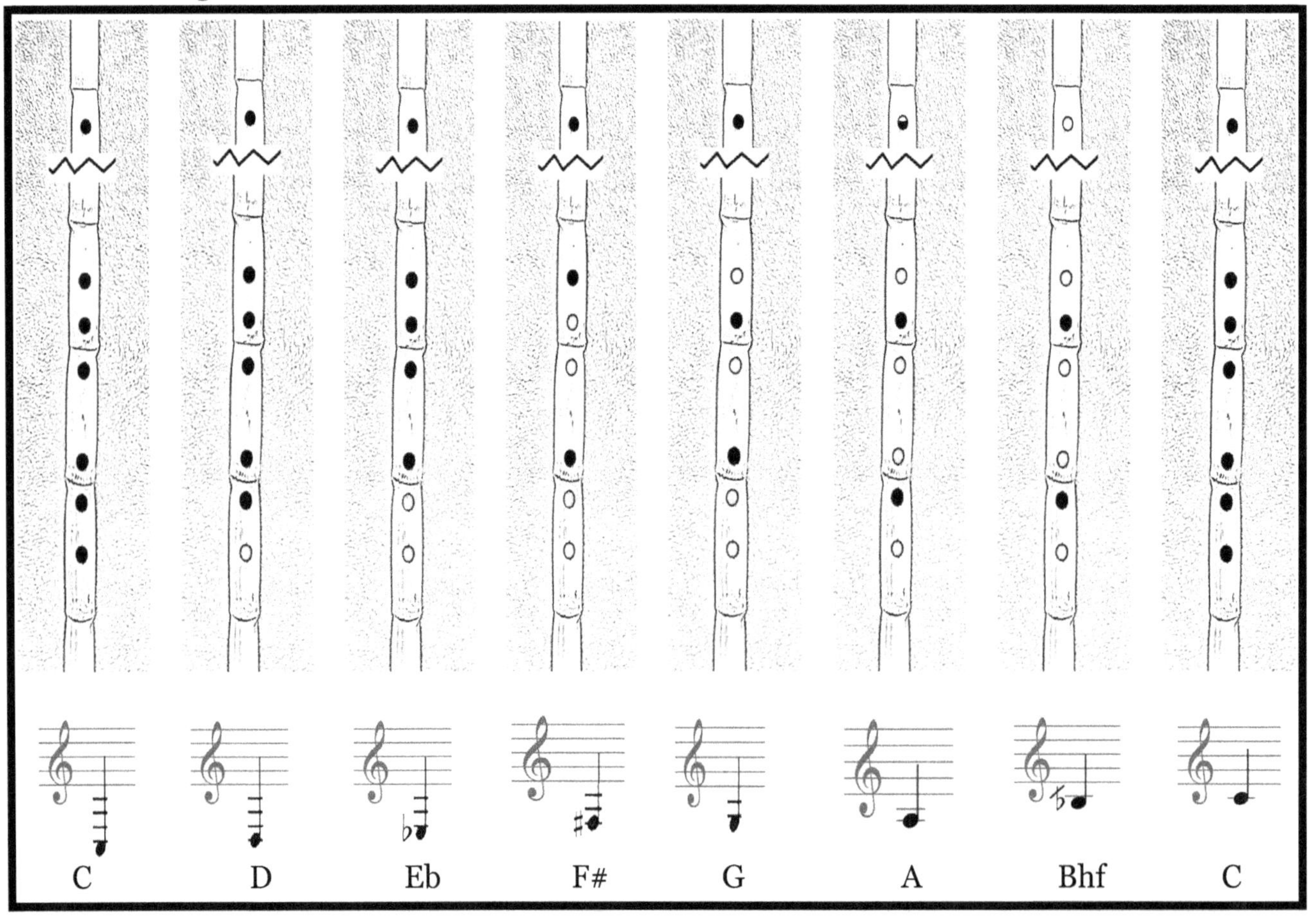

| C | D | Eb | F# | G | A | Bhf | C |

Main Register:

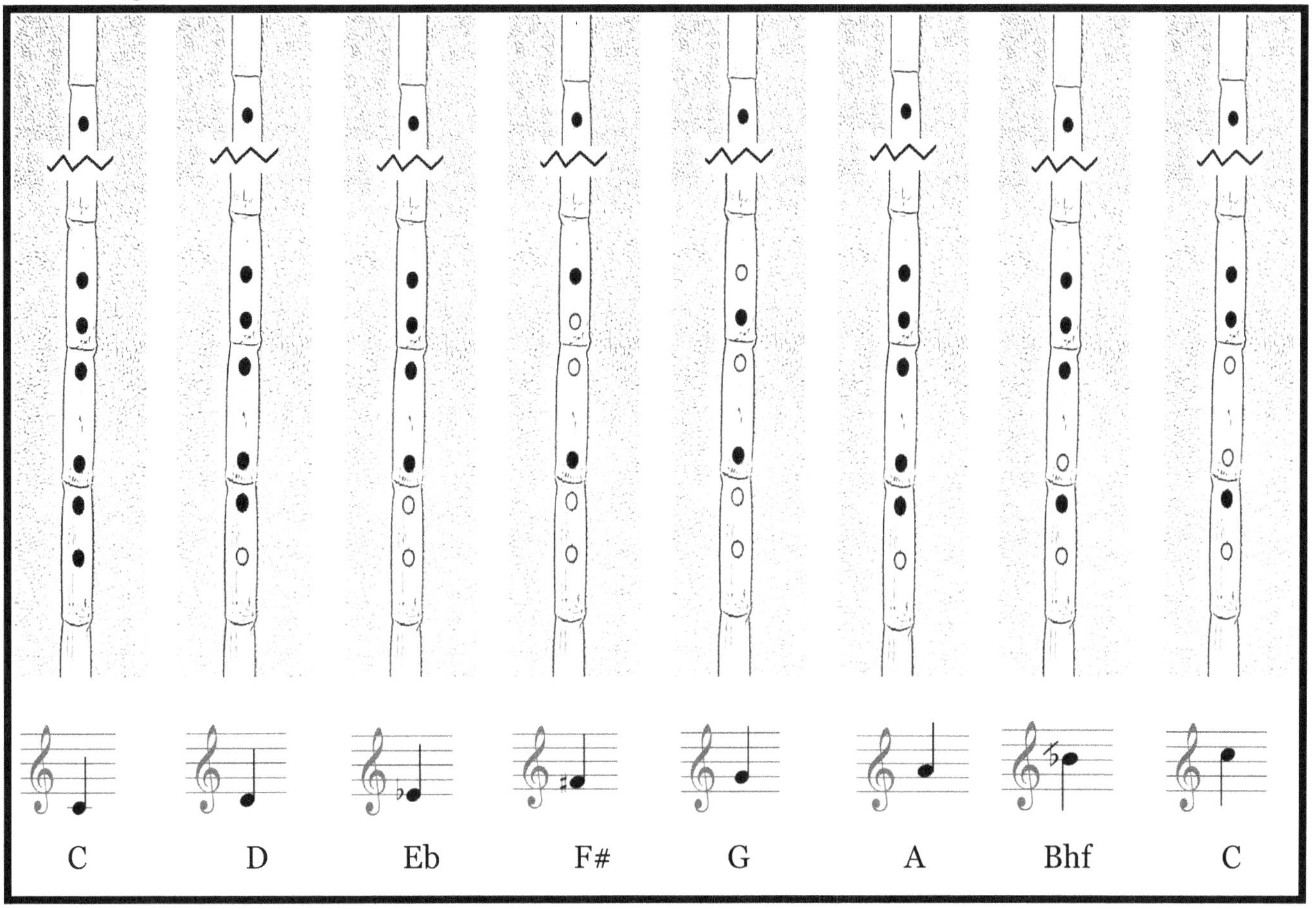

| C | D | Eb | F# | G | A | Bhf | C |

Second Register:

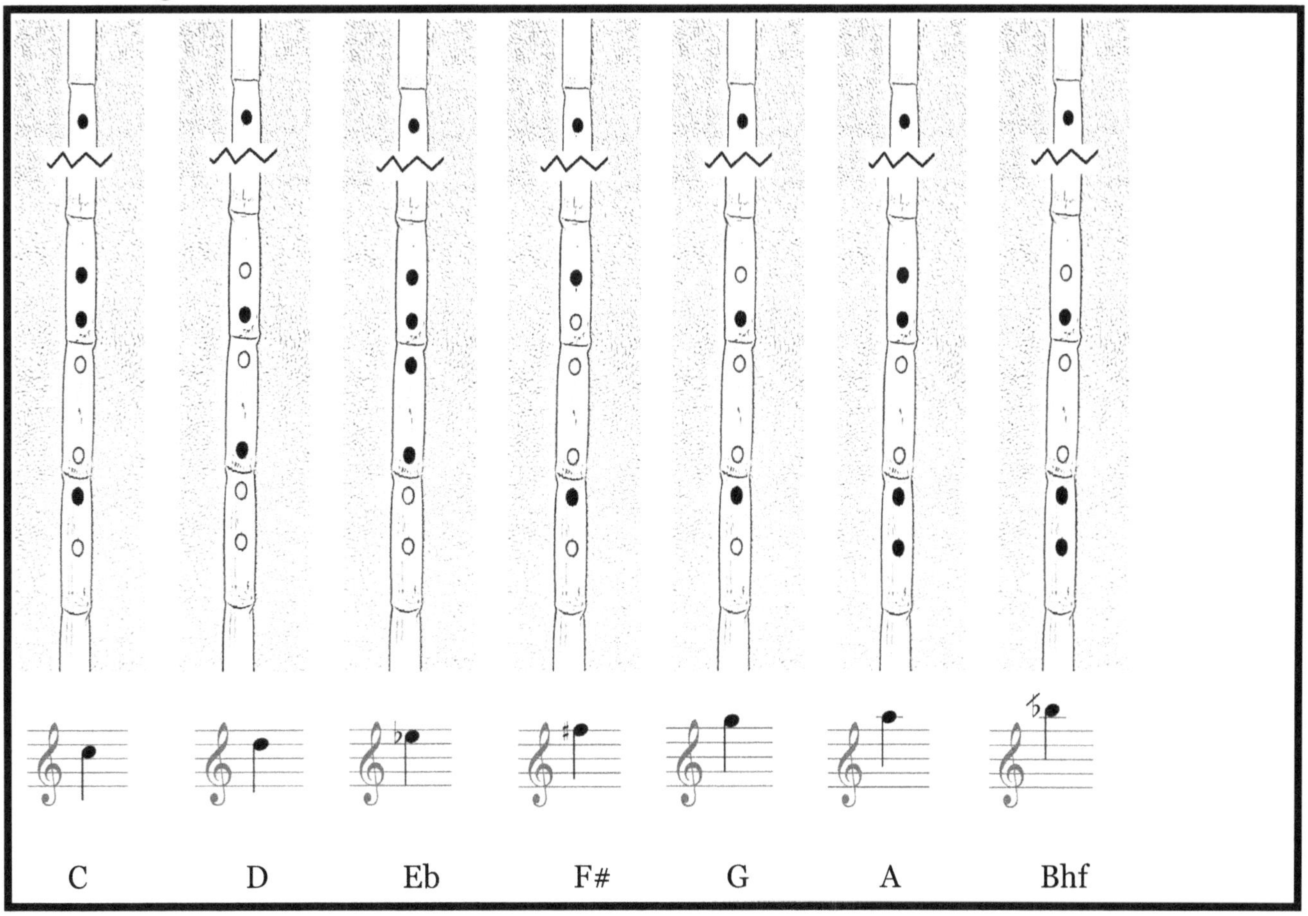

| C | D | Eb | F# | G | A | Bhf |

85

Maqam Bayati

Closely Related Maqamat: Ushaq (Turkey), Bayati Sultani, Ardibar, Isfahan

	Bayati			Nahawand			Kurd	
D	E half-flat		F	G	A	Bb	C	D
Re	Mi nuss-bemol		Fa	Sol	La	Si bemol	Do	Re
3/4		3/4	1	1	1/2		1	1

Possible Descriptions: Bayyati tetrachord on bottom; Kurd tetrachord on 5th; Nahawand pentachord on 4th.

Traditionally it is taught that the E half-flat in Bayyati is very slightly lower than the E half-flat in Rast and Sikah.

The Ghammaz in maqam Bayati falls on G where the Nahawand jins begins. It is common for musicians to emphasize this G very strongly almost immediately upon opening a Bayati taqasim.

Low Kabá Register:

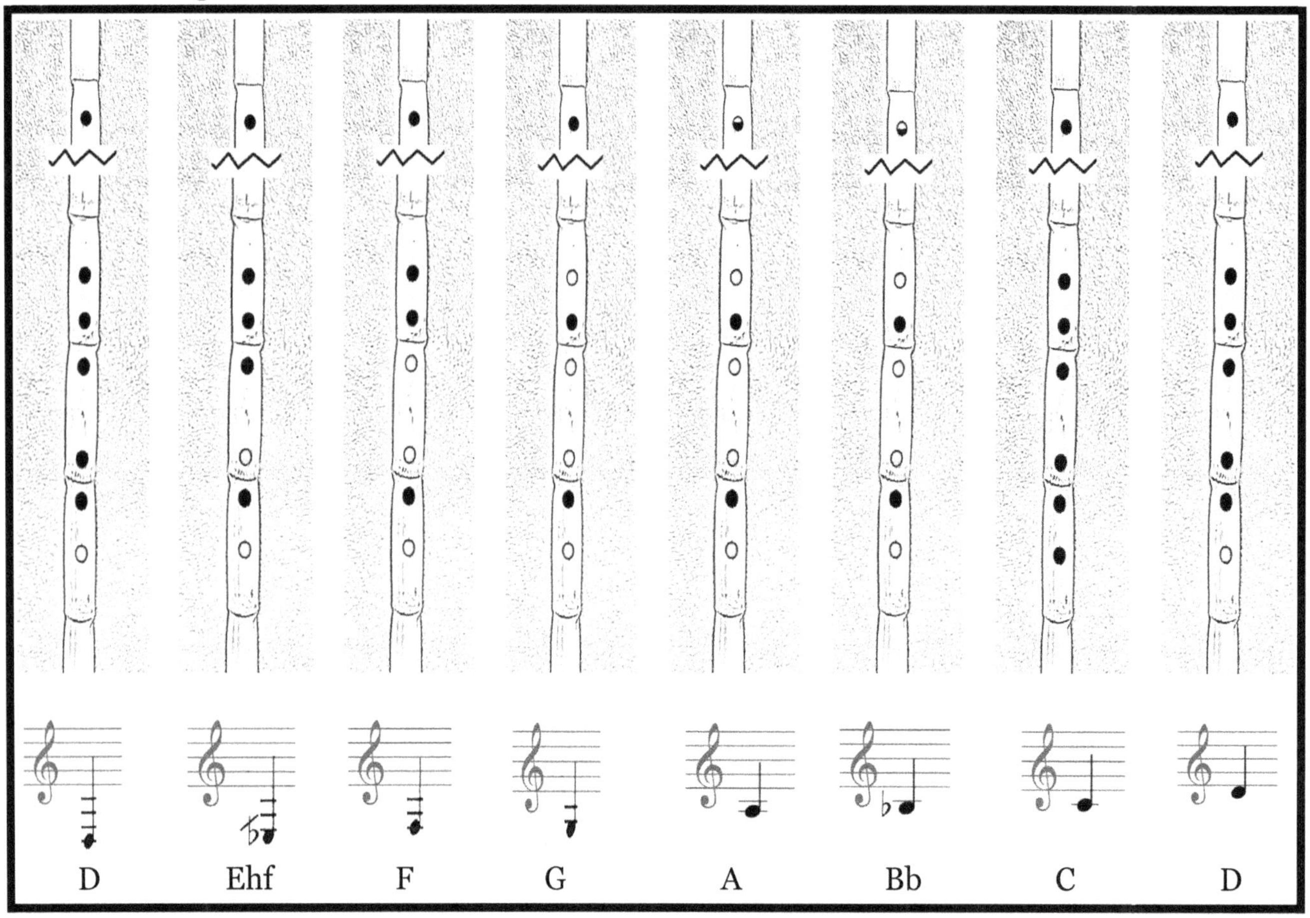

| D | Ehf | F | G | A | Bb | C | D |

Main Register: 87

| D | Ehf | F | G | A | Bb | C | D |

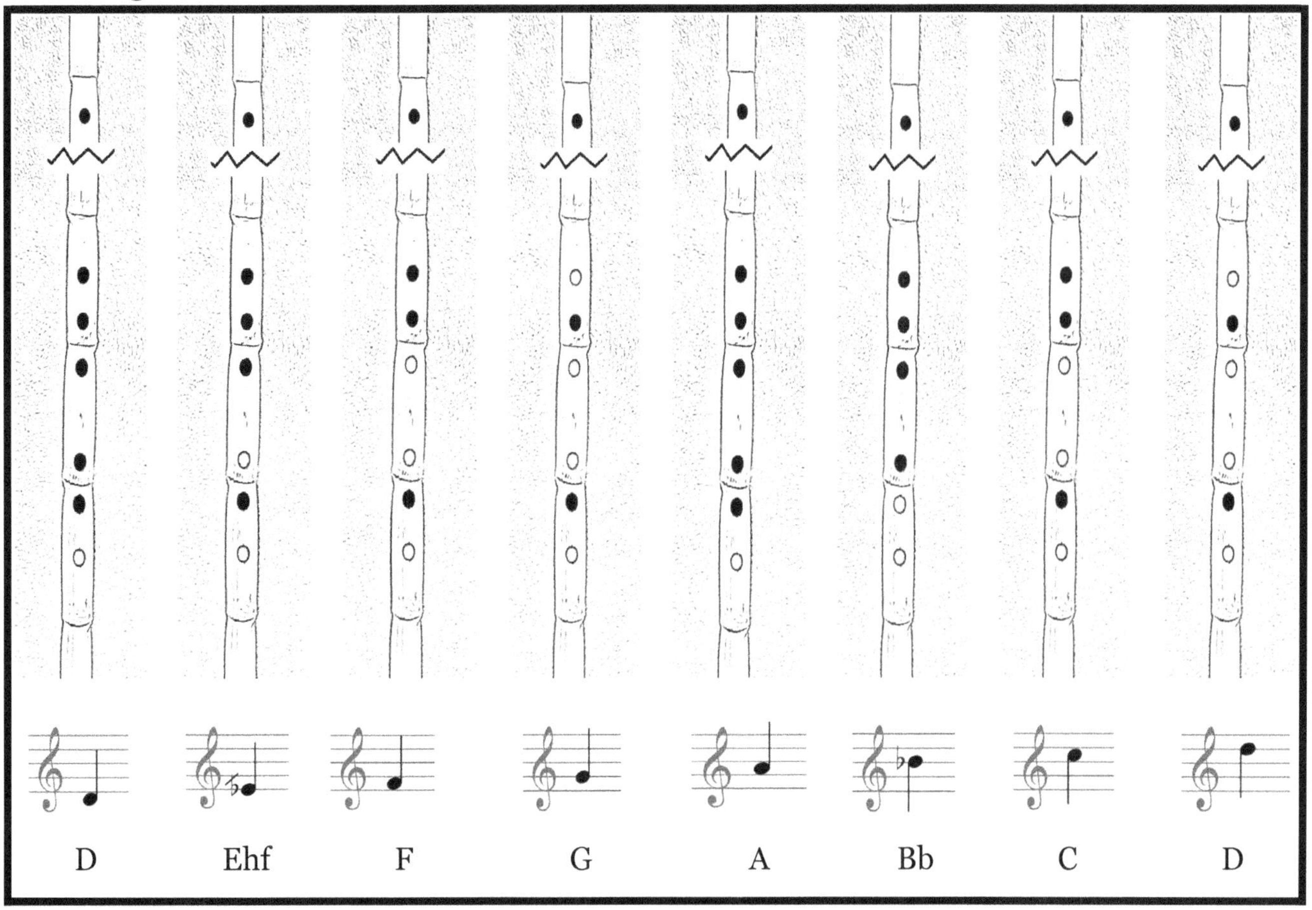

Second Register:

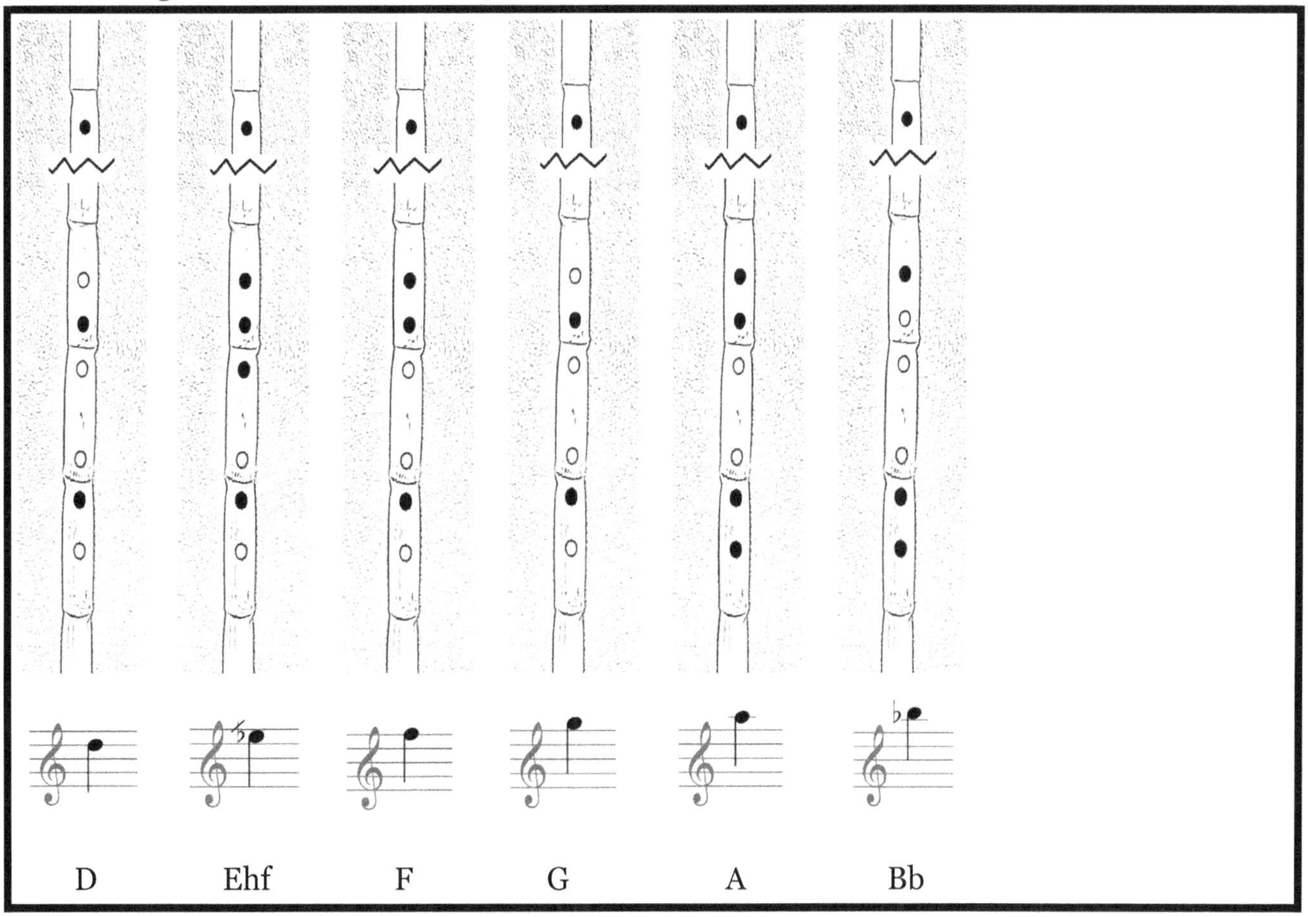

| D | Ehf | F | G | A | Bb |

Maqam Husayni

Closely Related Maqamat: Tahir, Hawzi, Nawa, Kutshuk, Sultani Iraq, Gulizar, Kardan

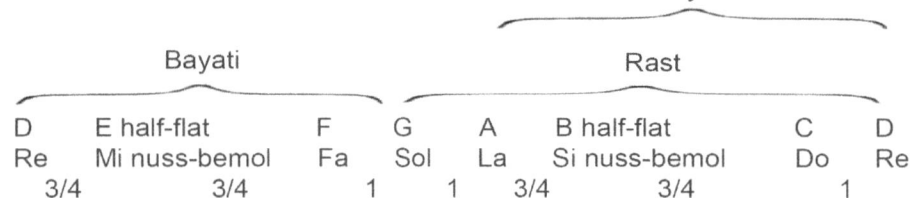

D	E half-flat	F	G	A	B half-flat	C	D
Re	Mi nuss-bemol	Fa	Sol	La	Si nuss-bemol	Do	Re
	3/4	3/4	1	1	3/4	3/4	1

Possible Descriptions: Bayyati tetrachord on bottom; bayyati tetrachord on 5th; rast pentachord on 4th. Ghammaz on A.

This maqam is very basic. Like maqam Rast, it includes only original Arab-world notes and intervals.

Low Kabá Register:

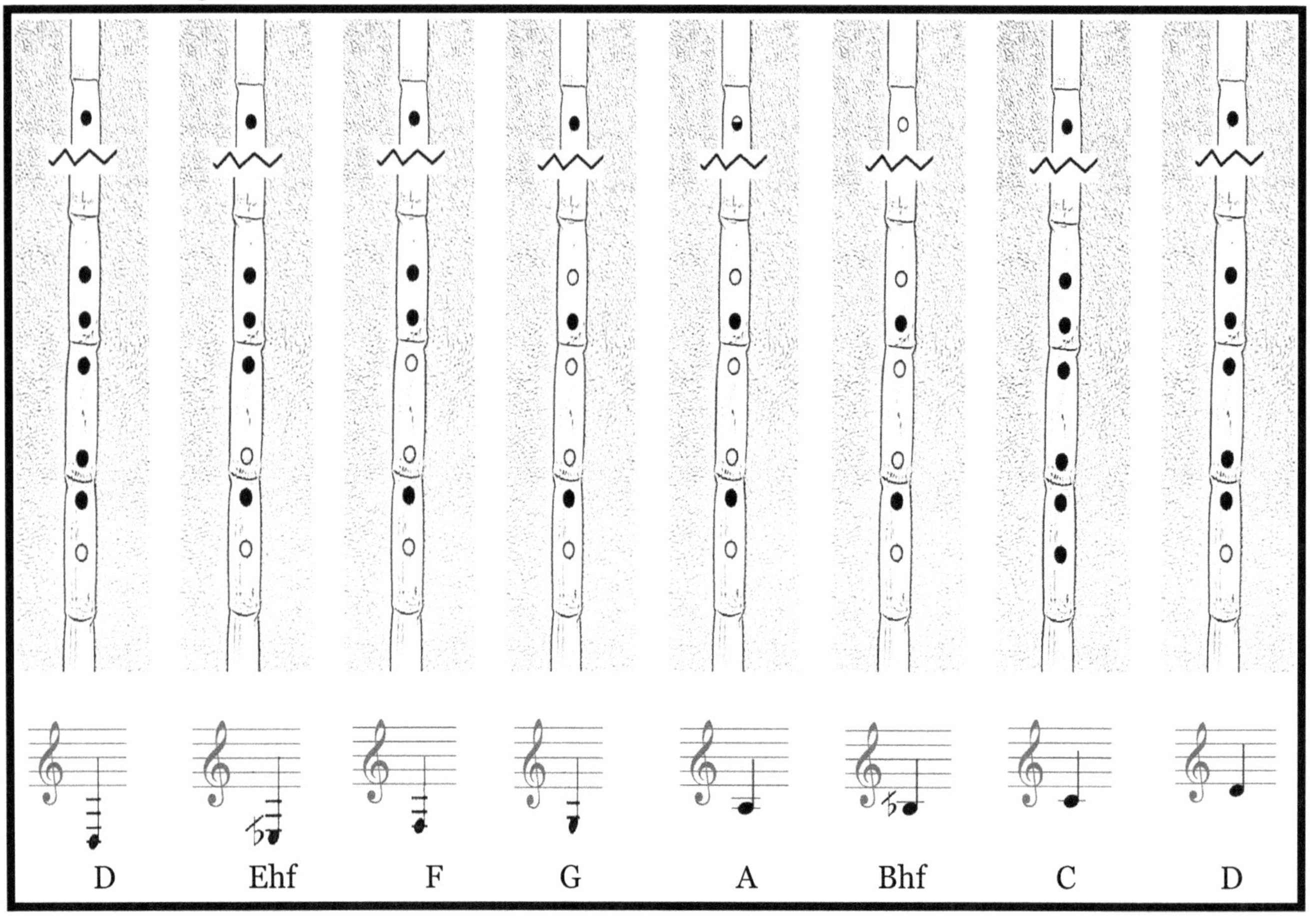

| D | Ehf | F | G | A | Bhf | C | D |

Main Register:

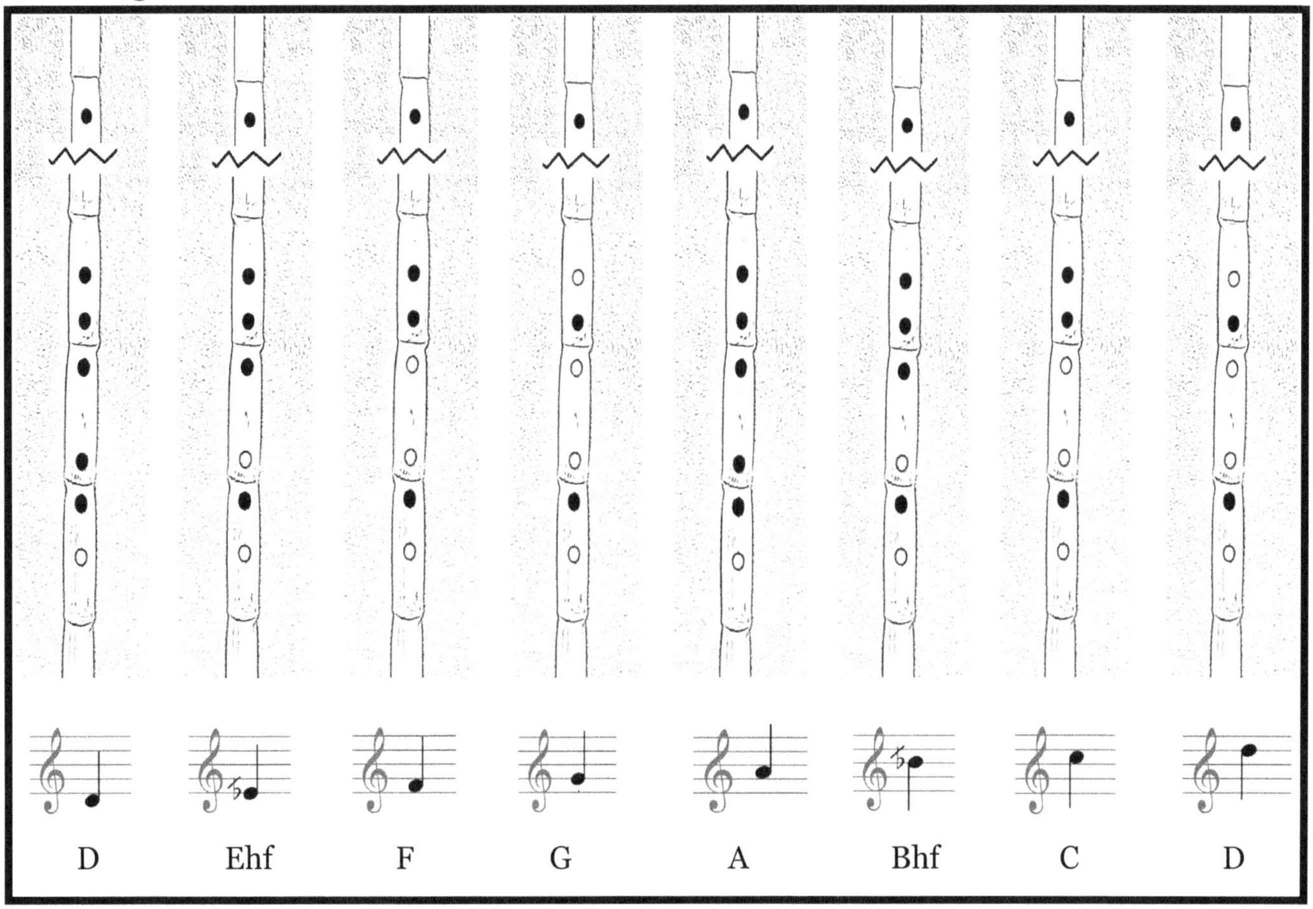

| D | Ehf | F | G | A | Bhf | C | D |

Second Register:

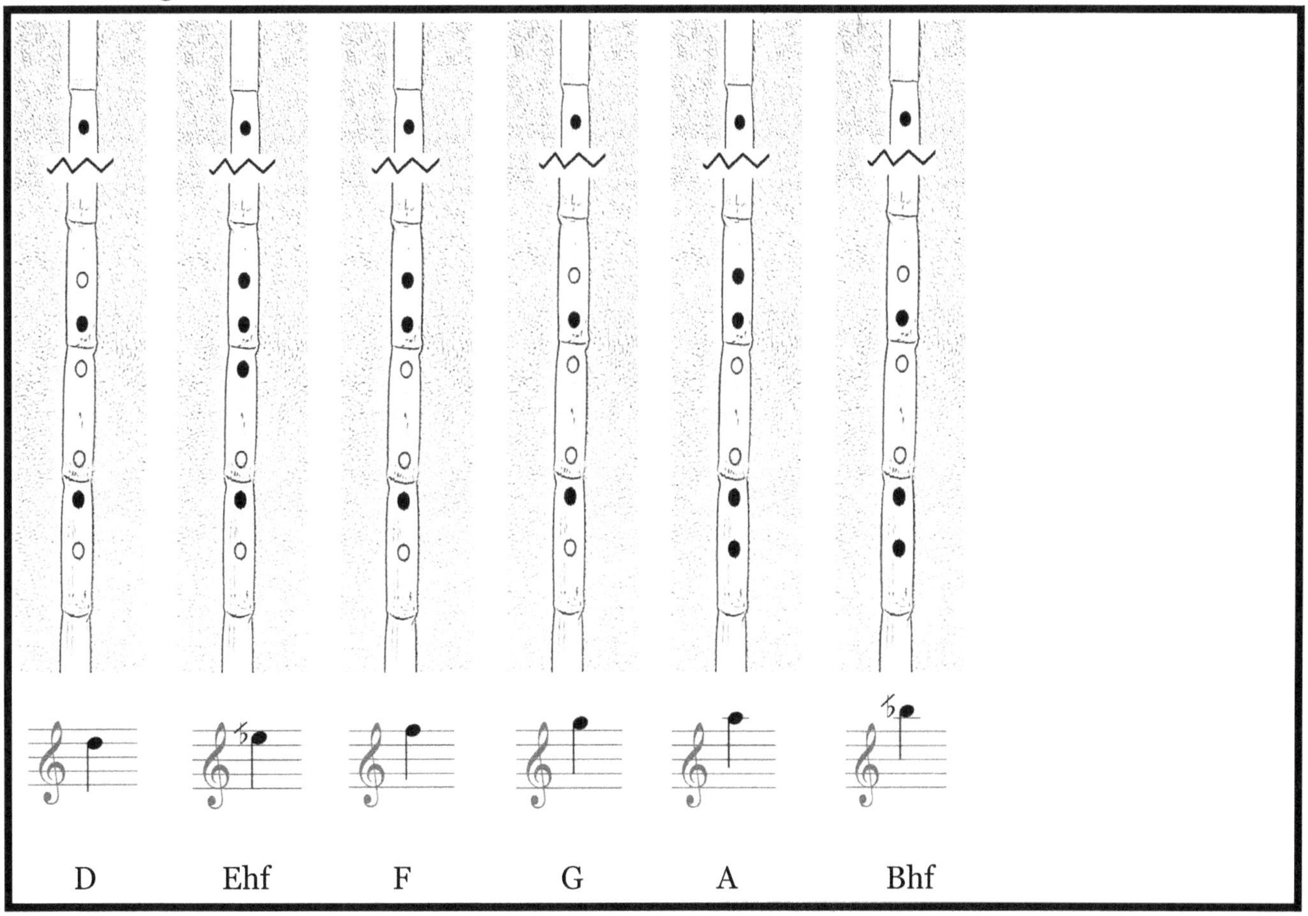

| D | Ehf | F | G | A | Bhf |

Maqam Saba

Associated Moods:
Very powerfully mystical mood. Very different from Western scales. Used extensively in Sufi music. Sad, moving, sincere, tender. Common in folk music about unrequited love.

Closely Related Maqamat: Isfanak, Dugah, Sipahr, Naziniyaz

Hijaz

Saba — Saba Zamzama

D	E half-flat	F	Gb	A	Bb	C	Db
Re	Mi nuss-bemol	Fa	Sol bemol	La	Si bemol	Do	Re bemol

3/4 3/4 1/2 1 1/2 1/2 1 1/2

Possible Descriptions: Bayyati trichord on bottom; Saba tetrachord on bottom; Hijaz tetrachord on 3rd; Shehnaz maqam on 3rd; Saba Zamzama tetrachord on 5th.

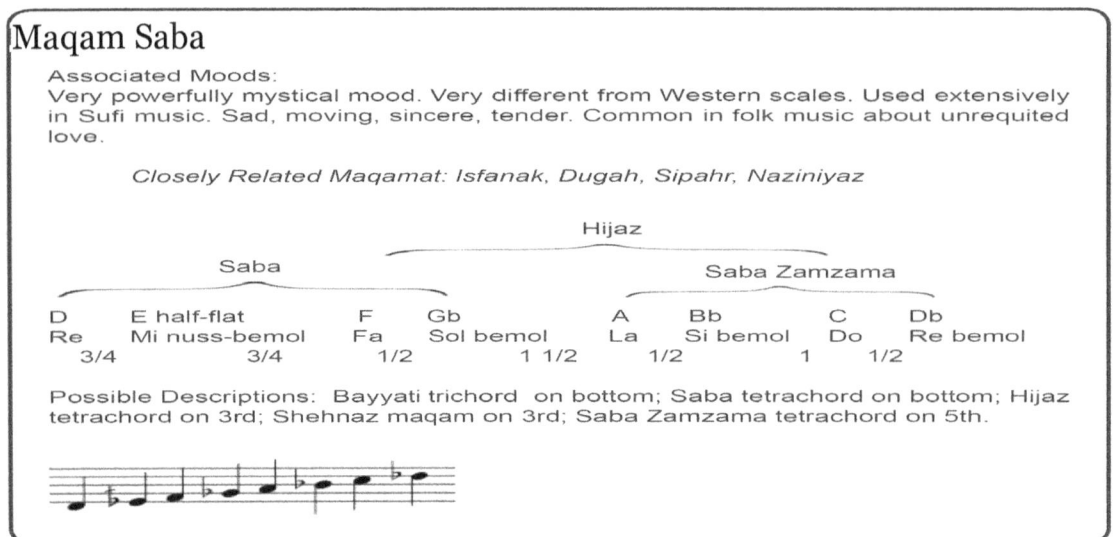

Ghammaz on F. Staying in maqam shehnaz on F for extended periods is common before resolving back down through the saba jins to the D.

The notes above Db are E, F, Gb. (The E half-flat doesn't necessarily repeat in the high part of the maqam.)

Can be used as an ornamentation inside bayyati. Brief modulation to ajem ushayran common.

Since this scale has both a minor 3rd and a major 3rd it become possible to create a very unique mood with this maqam. Musicians find ways to play the F and the Gb in highly repetitive ways to emphasize the magic which they can produce together.

Low Kabá Register:

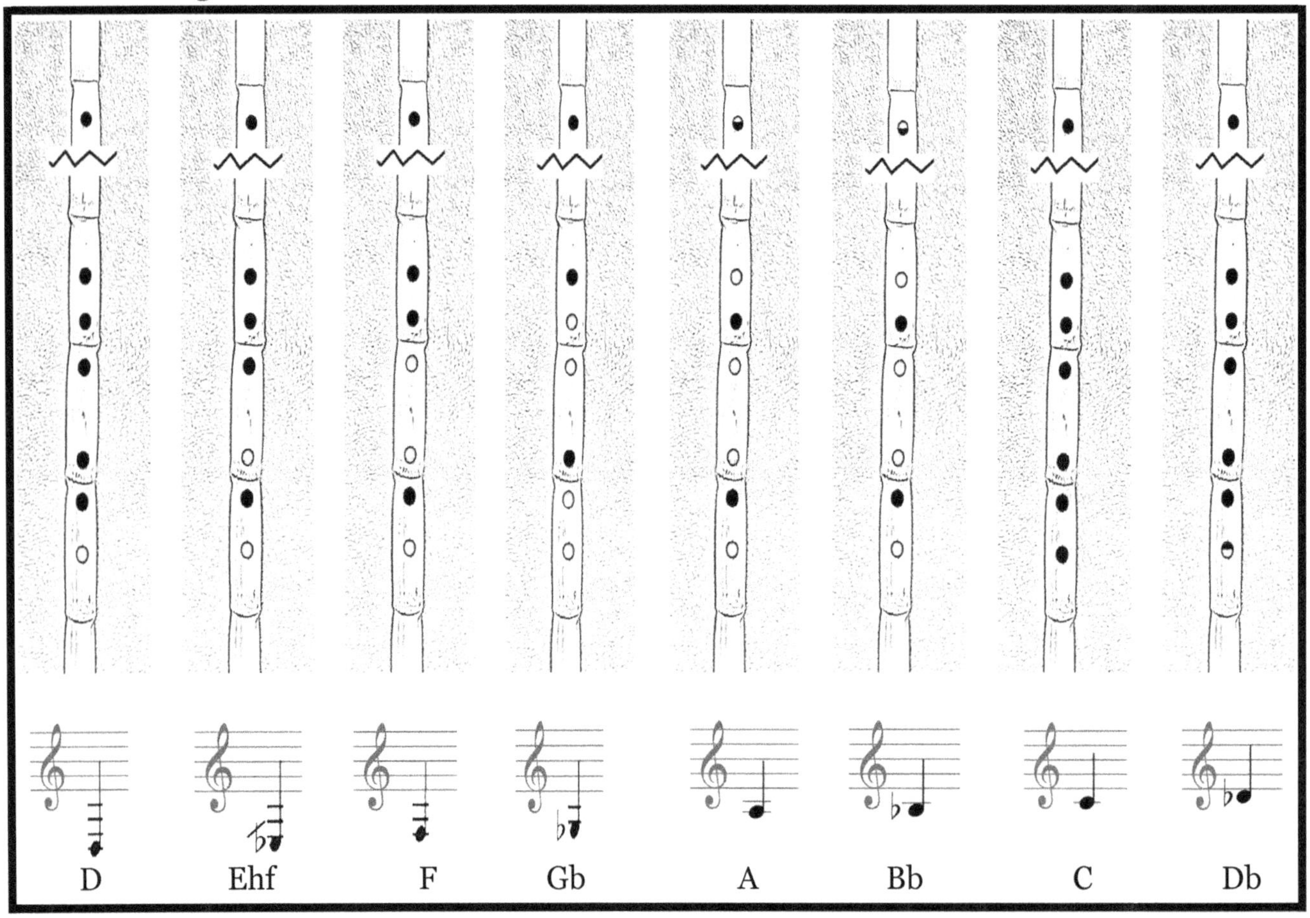

Main Register: 91

| D | Ehf | F | Gb | A | Bb | C | Db |

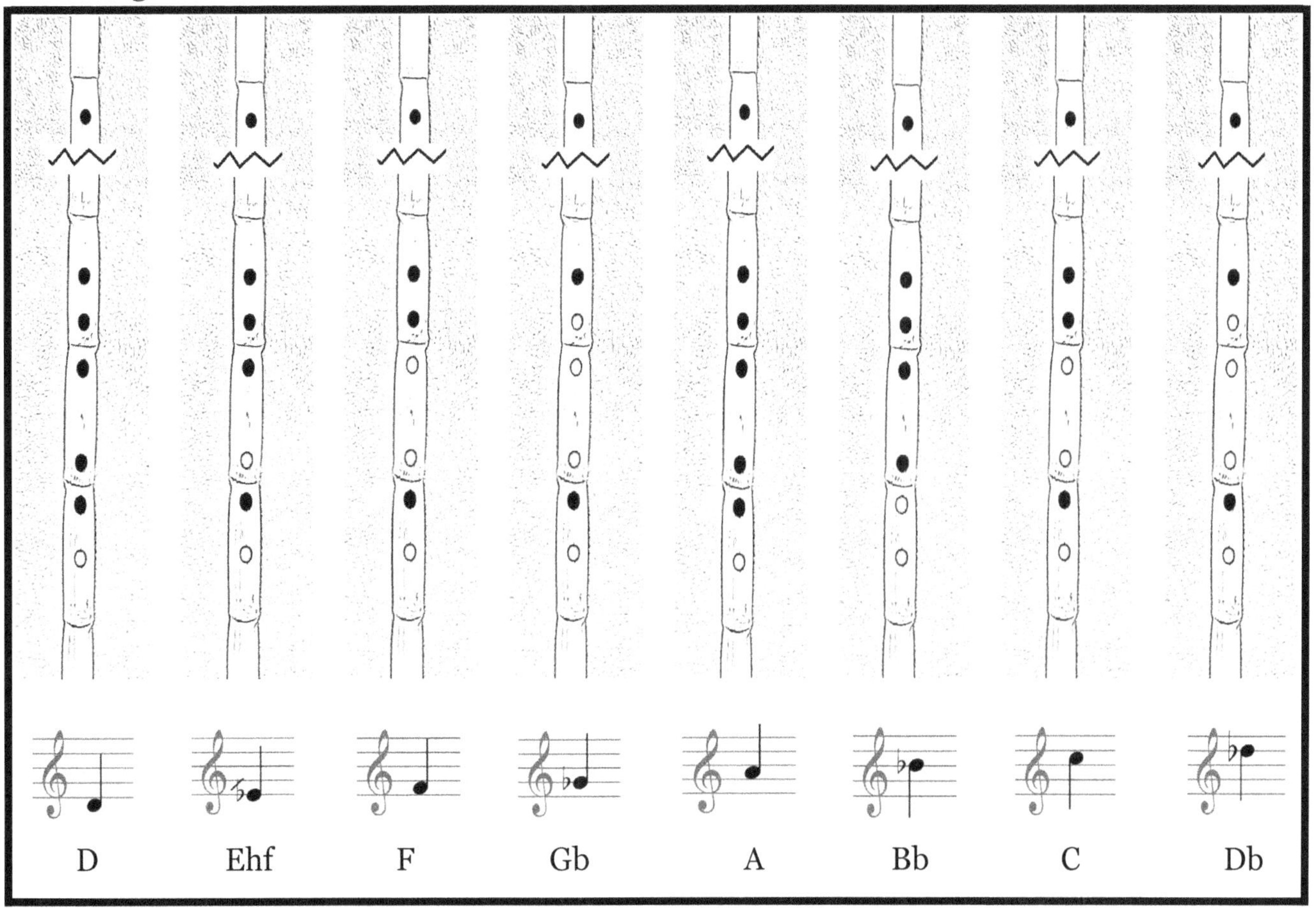

Second Register:

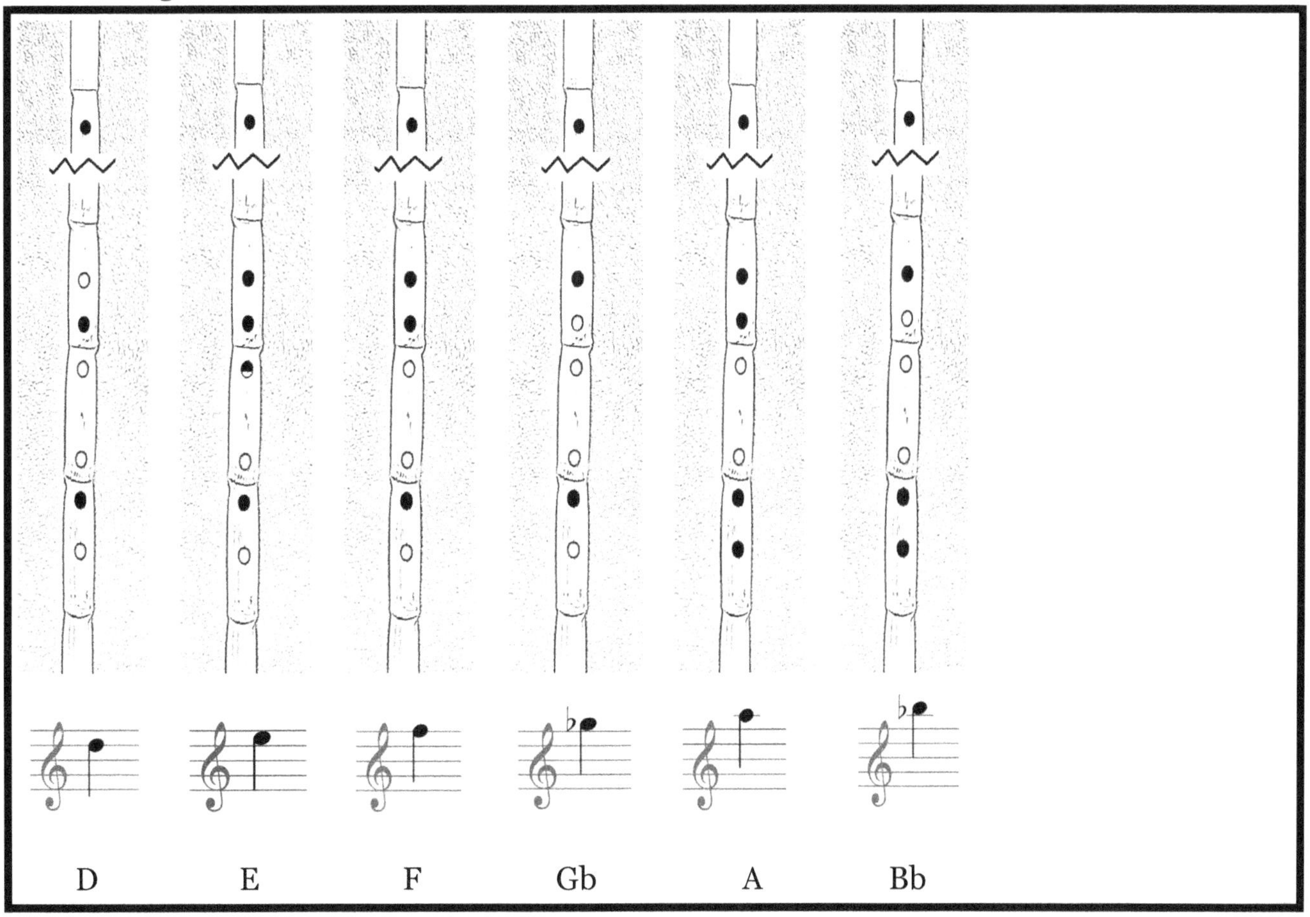

| D | E | F | Gb | A | Bb |

Maqam Saba Zamzama

Closely Related Maqamat: Saba Kurdi

```
                            Hijaz
                        ⌢‾‾‾‾‾‾‾‾‾‾‾⌢
          Saba Zamzama                    Saba Zamzama
        ⌢‾‾‾‾‾‾‾‾‾‾‾⌢                  ⌢‾‾‾‾‾‾‾‾‾‾‾⌢
```

D	Eb	F	Gb	A	Bb	C	Db
Re	Mi bemol	Fa	Sol bemol	La	Si bemol	Do	Re bemol
1/2		1	1/2	1 1/2	1/2	1	1/2

Possible Descriptions: Kurd trichord on bottom; Saba Zamzama tetrachord on bottom; Hijaz tetrachord on 3rd; Shehnaz maqam on 3rd; Saba Zamzama tetrachord on 5th.

This version of Saba can be played on equal-tempered instruments.

Low Kabá Register:

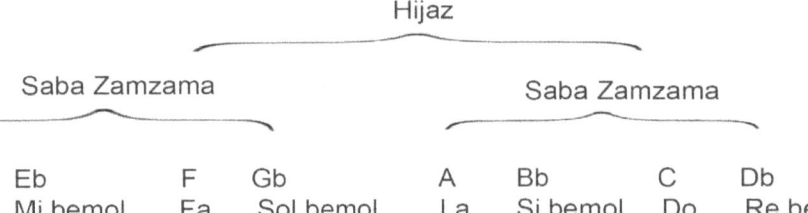

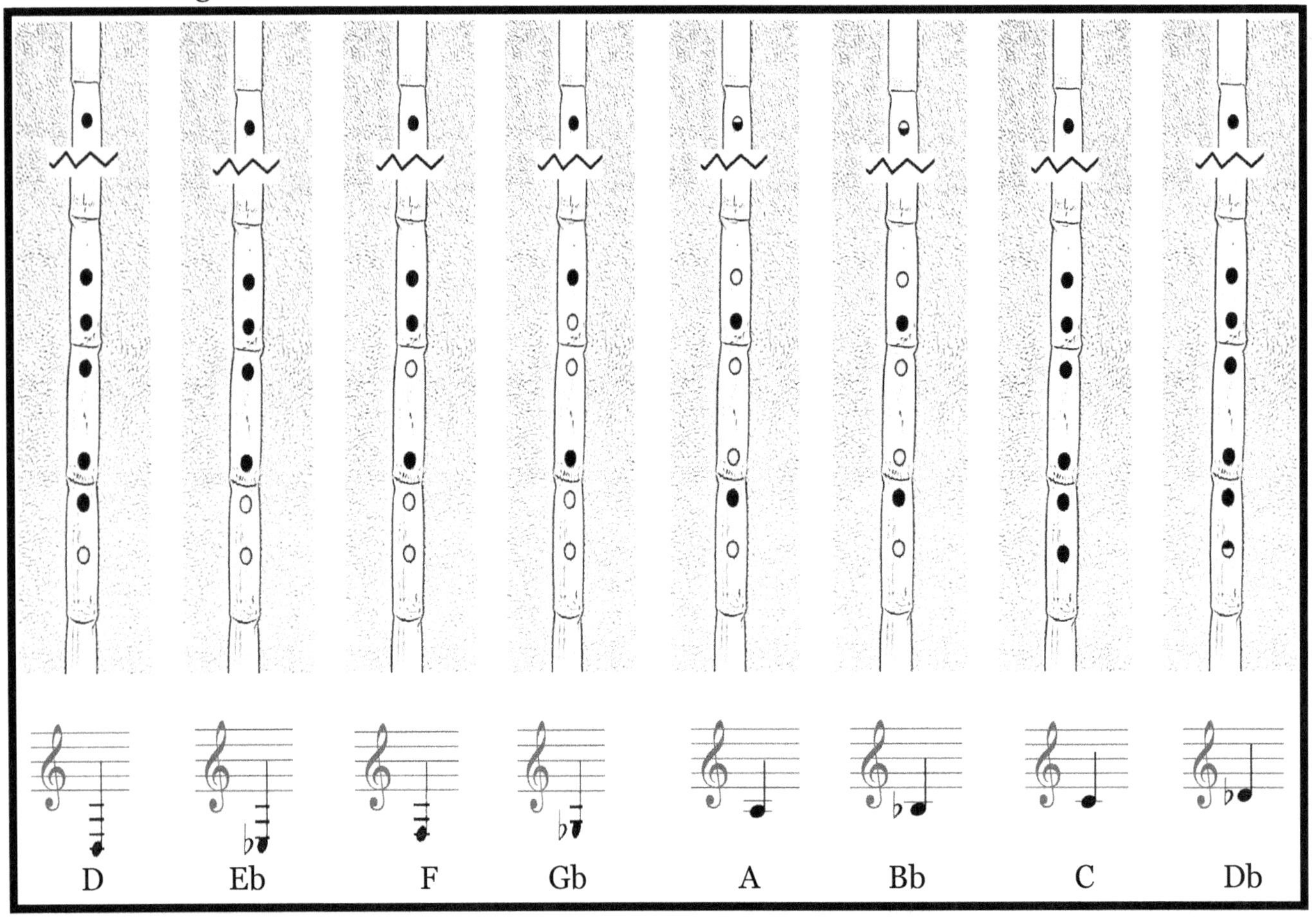

| D | Eb | F | Gb | A | Bb | C | Db |

Main Register:

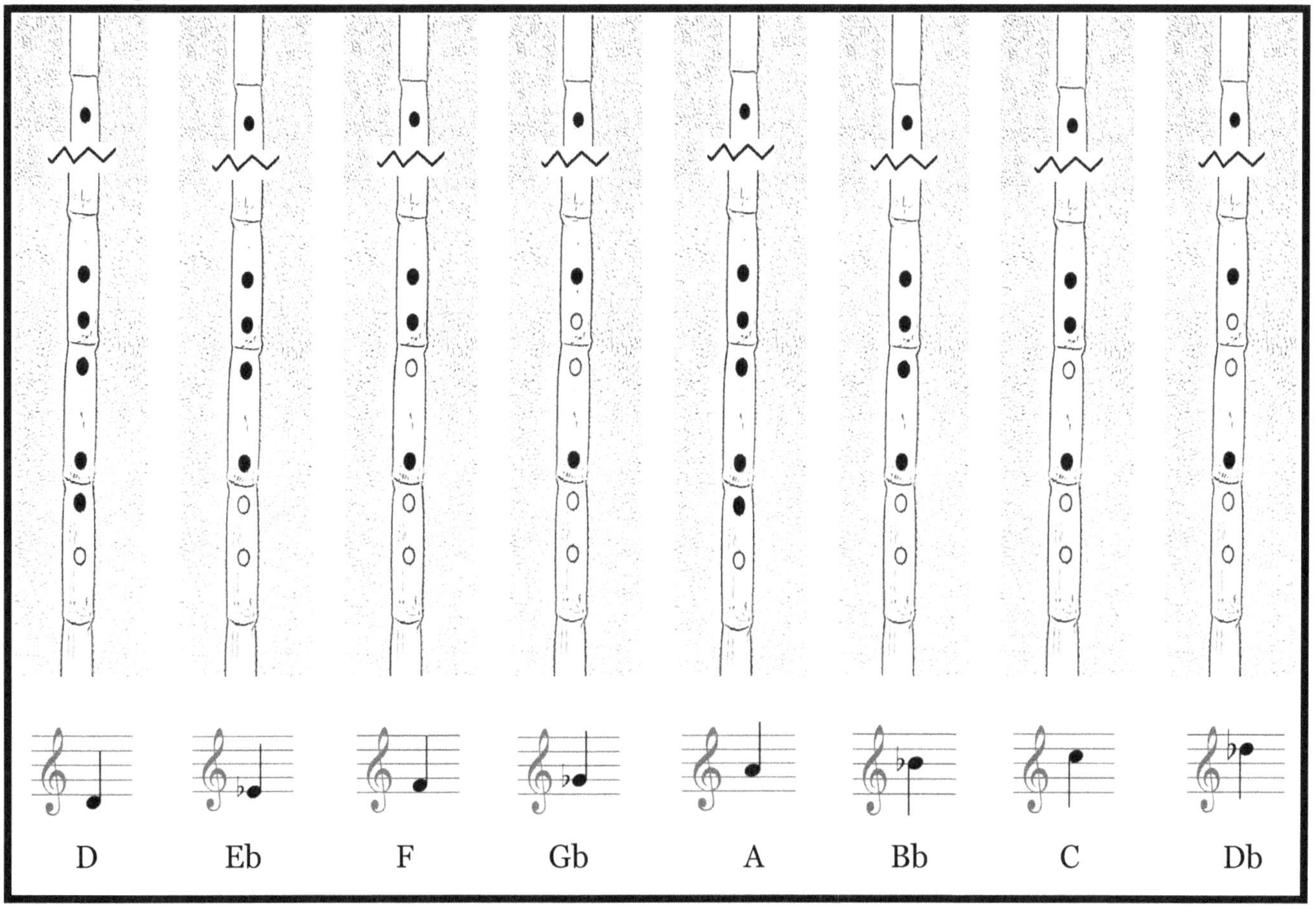

| D | Eb | F | Gb | A | Bb | C | Db |

Second Register:

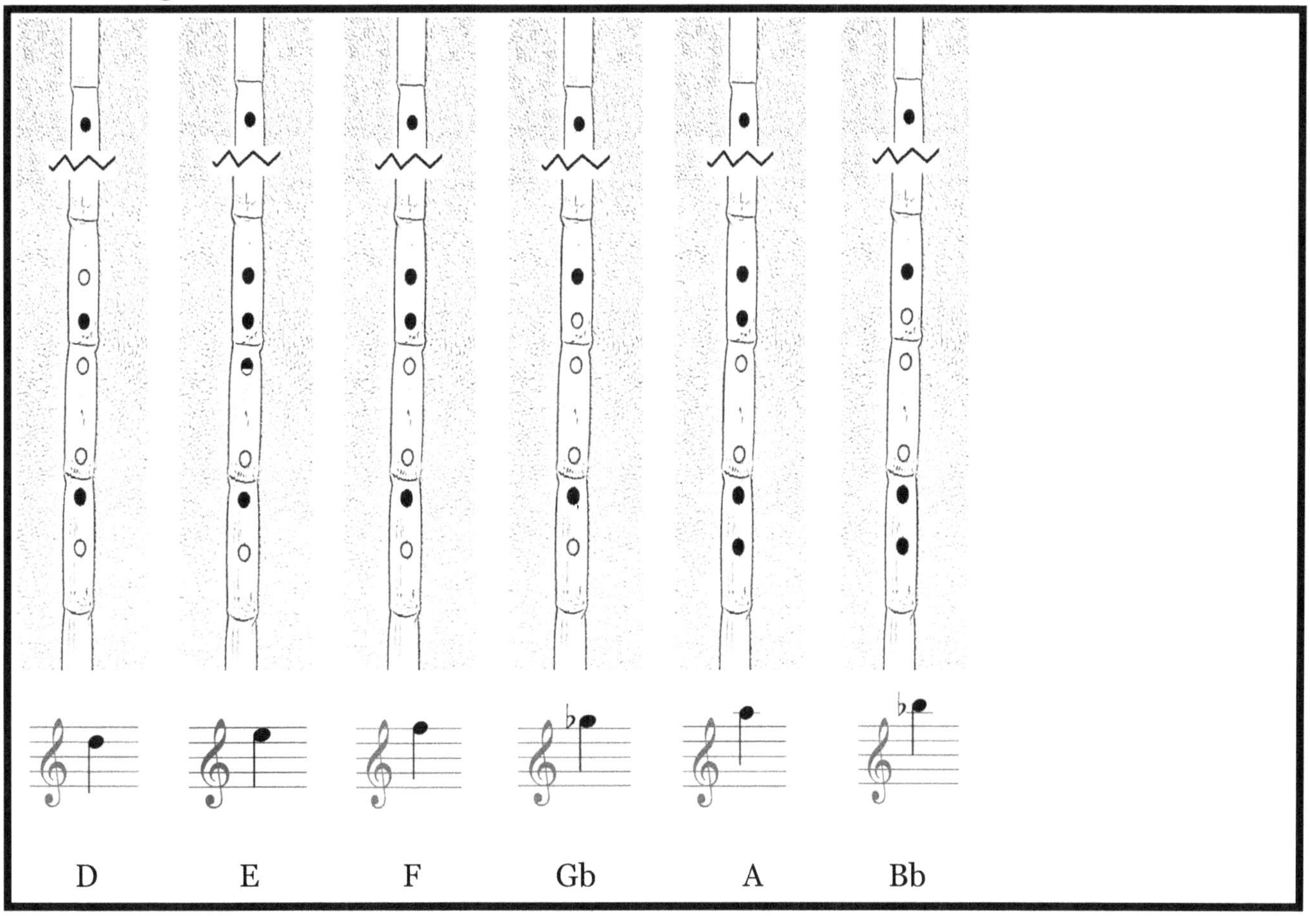

| D | E | F | Gb | A | Bb |

Maqam Shuri

Closely Related Maqamat: Bayati Araban, Ajem Murassa, Karjigar (Turkish)

	Bayati			Hijaz			
D	E half-flat	F	G	Ab	B	C	D
Re	Mi nuss-bemol	Fa	Sol	La bemol	Si	Do	Re
3/4	3/4	1	1/2	1 1/2	1/2	1	

Possible Descriptions: Bayyati tetrachord on bottom; Hijaz pentachord on 4th. Used as a modulation and ornament inside of Bayyati.

Low Kabá Register:

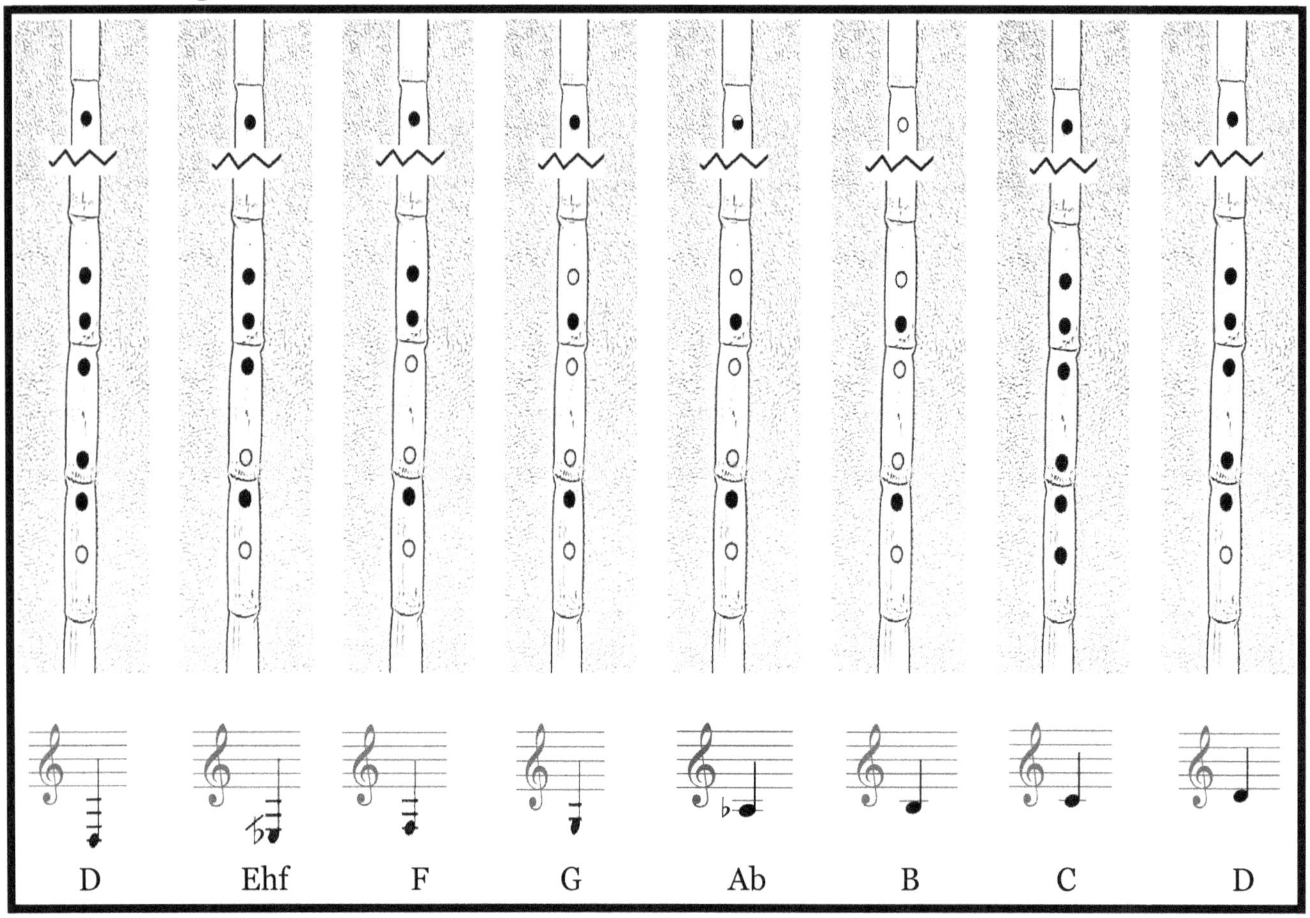

| D | Ehf | F | G | Ab | B | C | D |

Main Register:

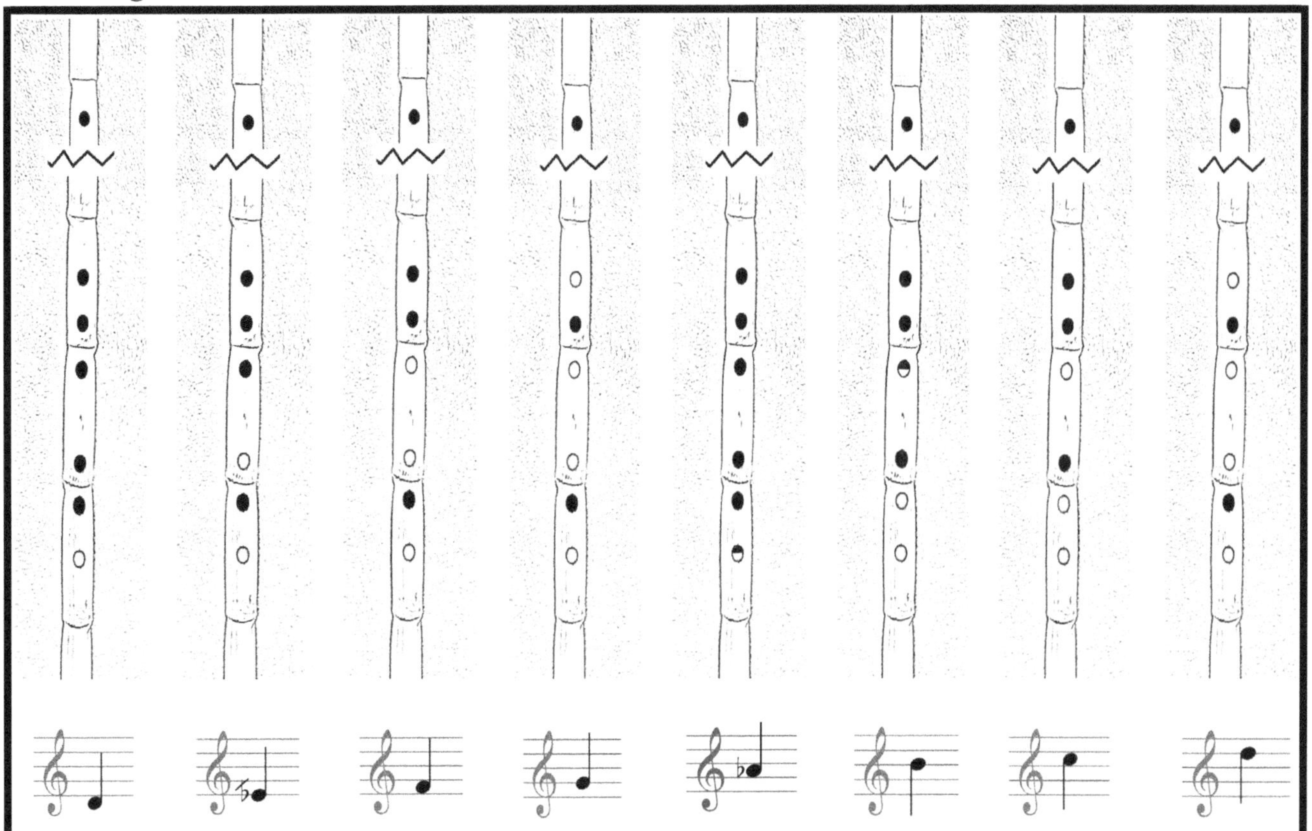

| D | Ehf | F | G | Ab | B | C | D |

Second Register:

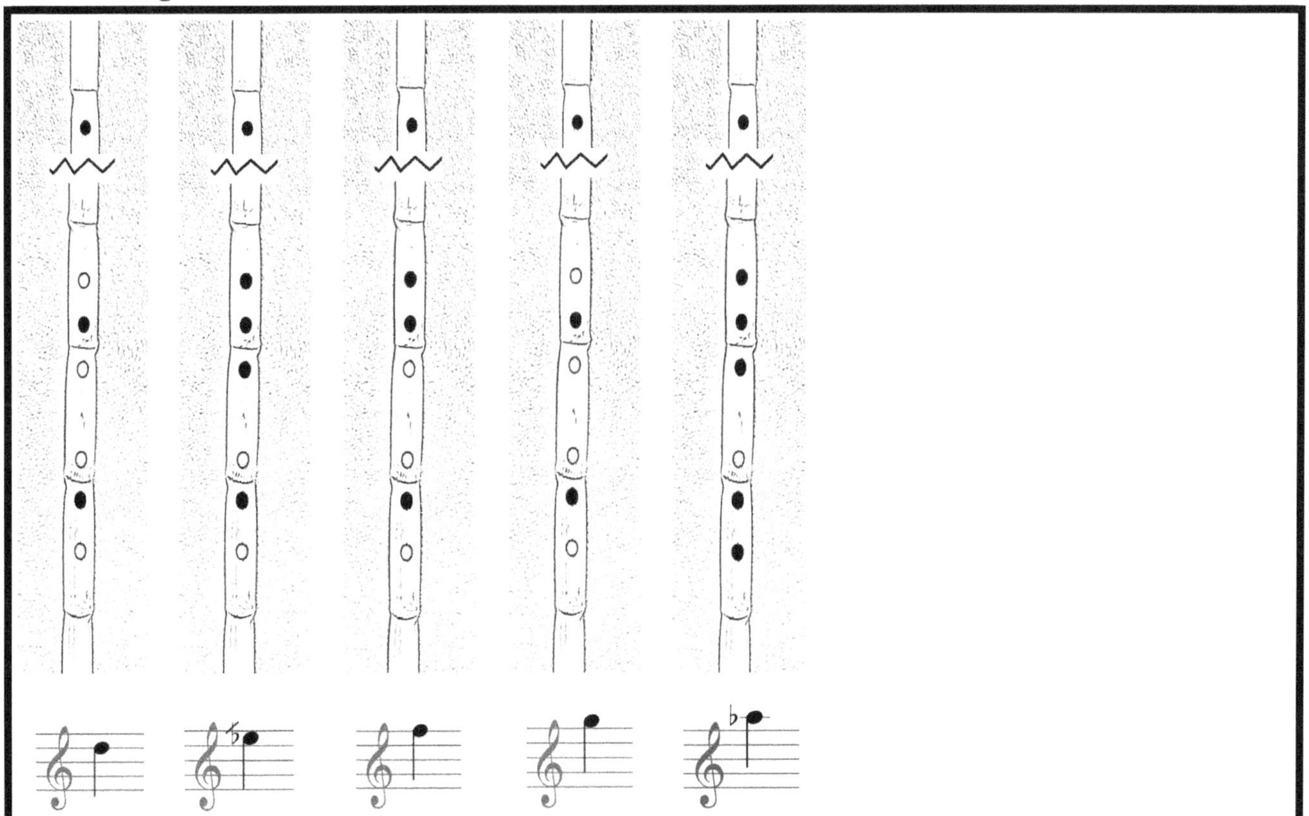

| D | Ehf | F | G | Ab |

Maqam Hijaz

Closely Related Maqamat: Hijaz Humayun, Ajami, al-Isba'ayn (Tunisia), al-Zayyidan (Algeria), Hijaz al-kabir (Morocco), al-Mathnawi (Iraq).

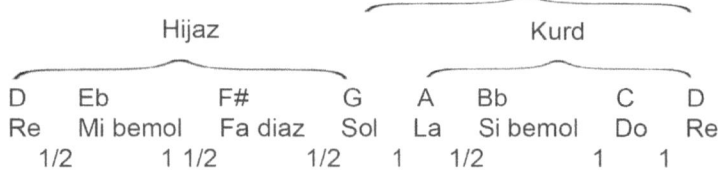

D	Eb	F#	G	A	Bb	C	D
Re	Mi bemol	Fa diaz	Sol	La	Si bemol	Do	Re
1/2		1 1/2	1/2	1	1/2	1	1

Possible Descriptions: Hijaz tetrachord on bottom; nahawand pentachord on 4th; kurd tetrachord on 5th.

It is common practice in the West where keyboards and fretboards are dominant, to play the equal-tempered versions of these notes. There is another more highly tuned option, however, as we shall see on the next page with Hijaz Gharib!

Low Kabá Register:

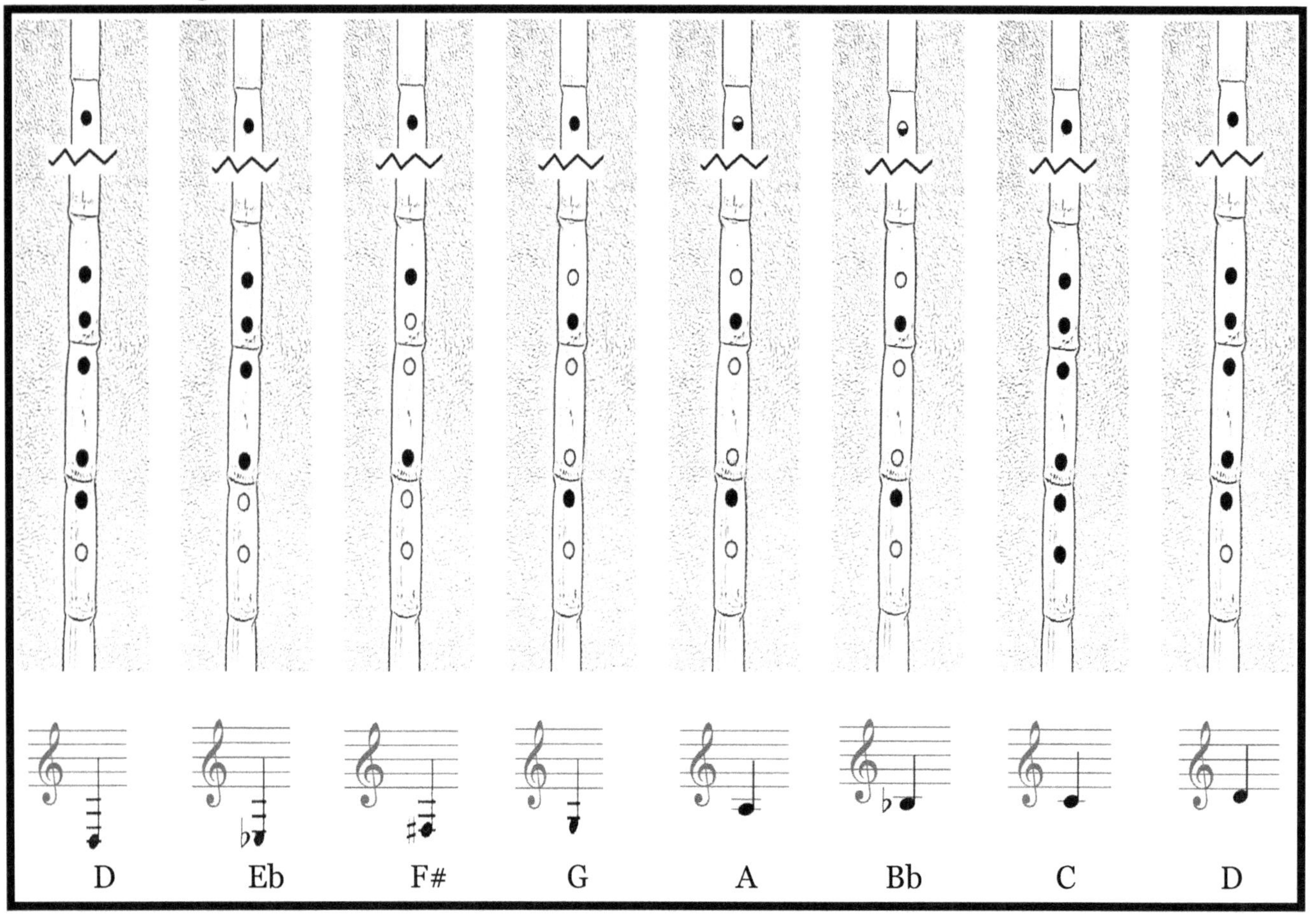

| D | Eb | F# | G | A | Bb | C | D |

Main Register:

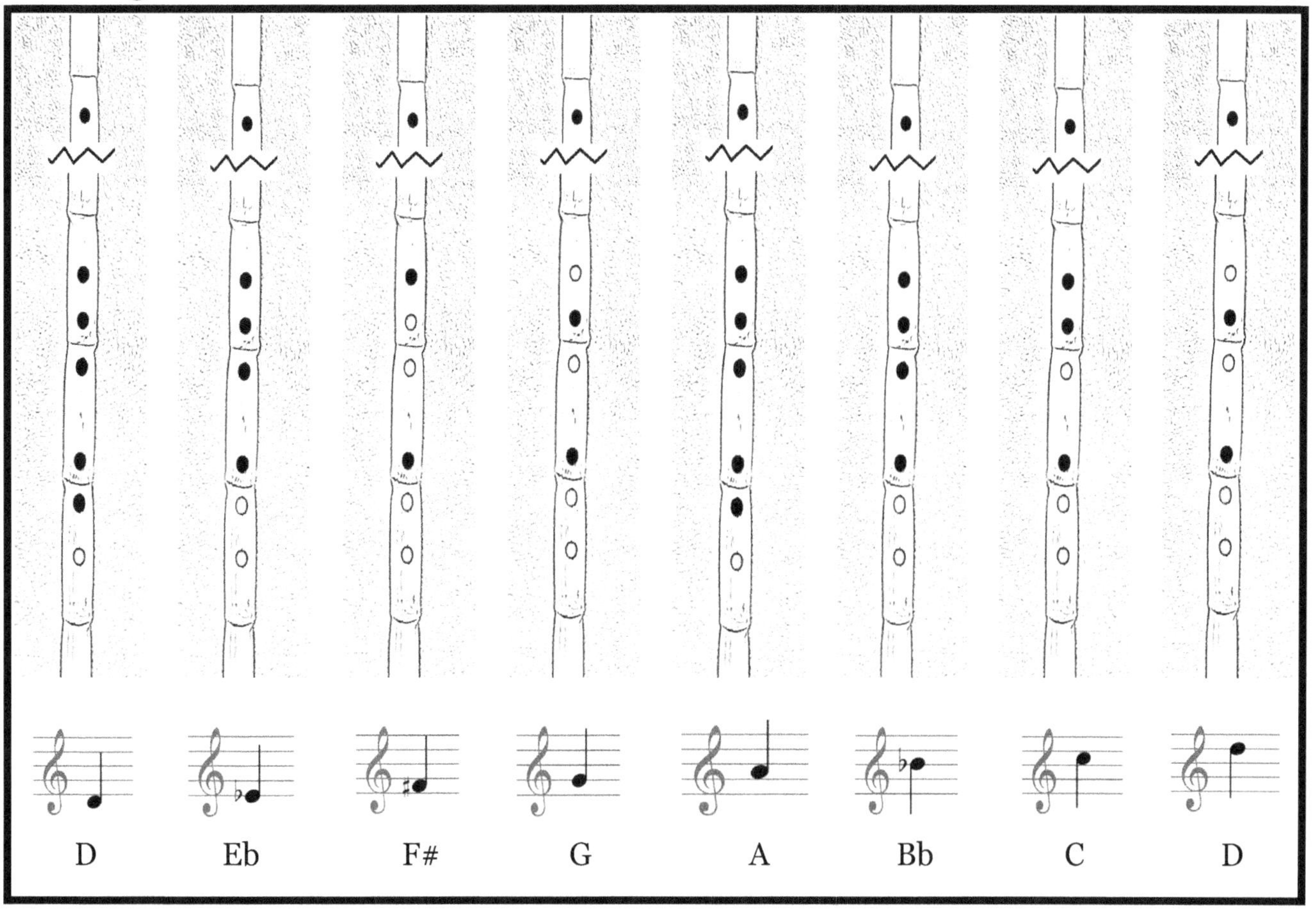

D	Eb	F#	G	A	Bb	C	D

Second Register:

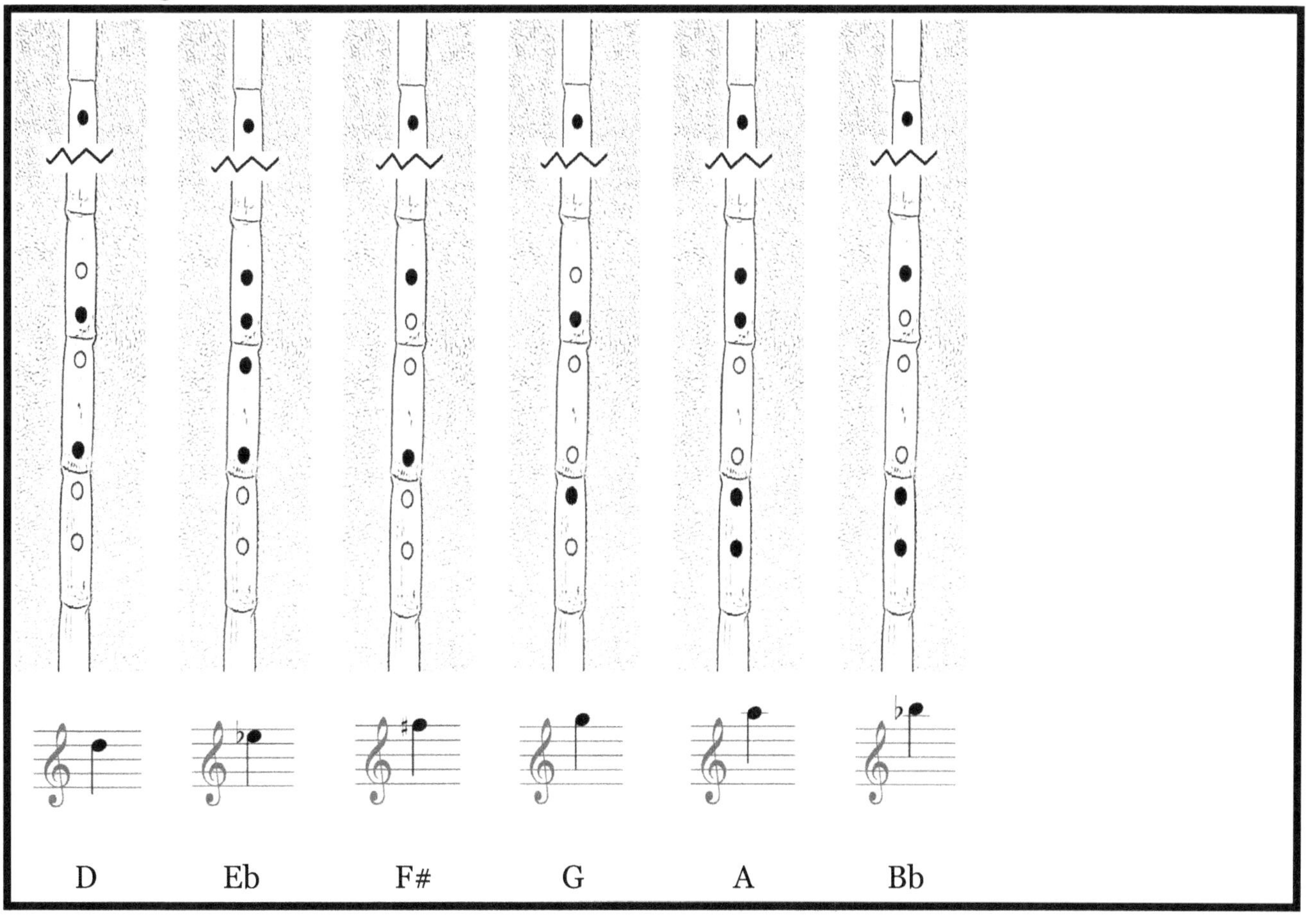

D	Eb	F#	G	A	Bb

Maqam Hijaz Awji

Closely Related Maqamat: Hijaz, Hijaz Masri, Araba (old name)

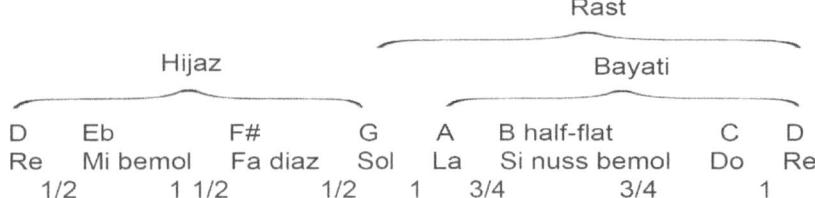

D	Eb	F#	G	A	B half-flat	C	D
Re	Mi bemol	Fa diaz	Sol	La	Si nuss bemol	Do	Re
	1/2	1 1/2	1/2	1	3/4	3/4	1

With brackets: Hijaz (D–G), Rast (G–D), Bayati (A–D)

Possible Descriptions: Hijaz tetrachord on bottom; rast pentachord on 4th; bayyati tetrachord on 5th.

Many songs are played in this maqam. Older sources make it clear that this was the basic form of the maqam "hijaz" until a few decades ago when it began to become common to assume a Bb instead of a B half-flat. But now musicians may simply state that the song moves from "Hijaz on Re" to "Rast on Sol" at some point during the song without actually knowing the name "hijaz awji."

Low Kabá Register:

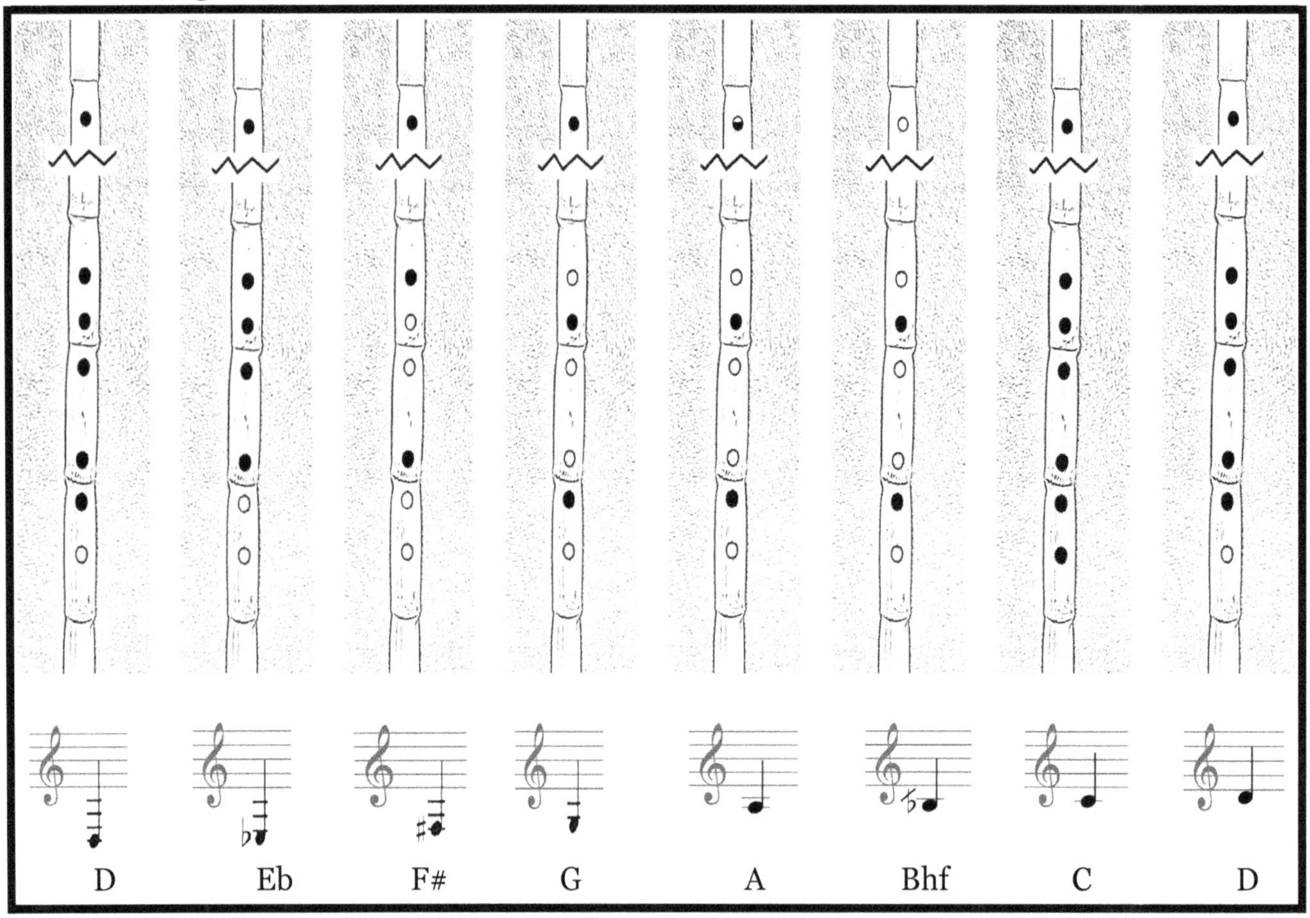

| D | Eb | F# | G | A | Bhf | C | D |

Main Register: 99

D	Eb	F#	G	A	Bhf	C	D

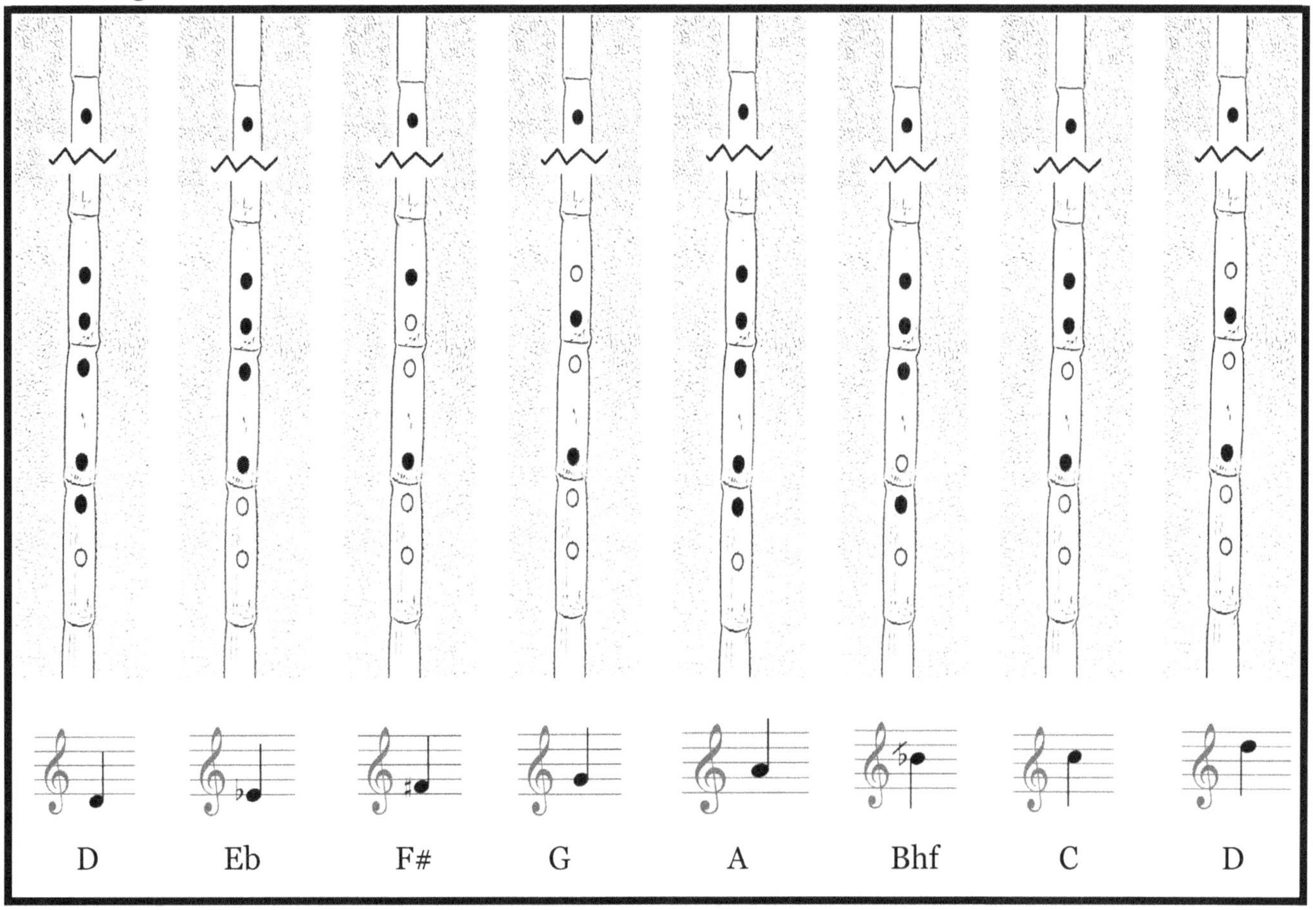

Second Register:

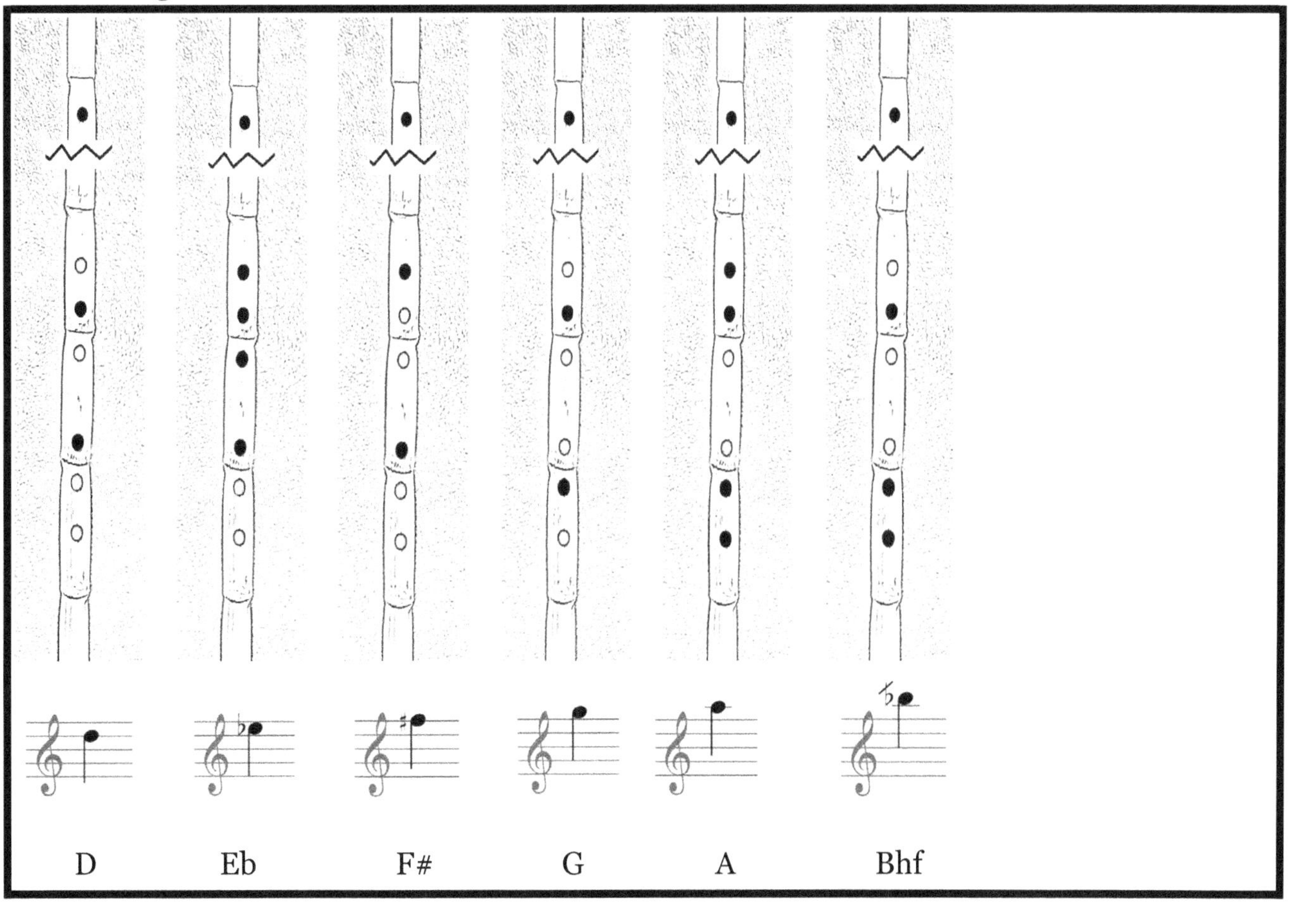

D	Eb	F#	G	A	Bhf

Maqam Shehnaz

Closely Related Maqamat: Sikah Baladi, Zirgule Hijaz, (Turkey)

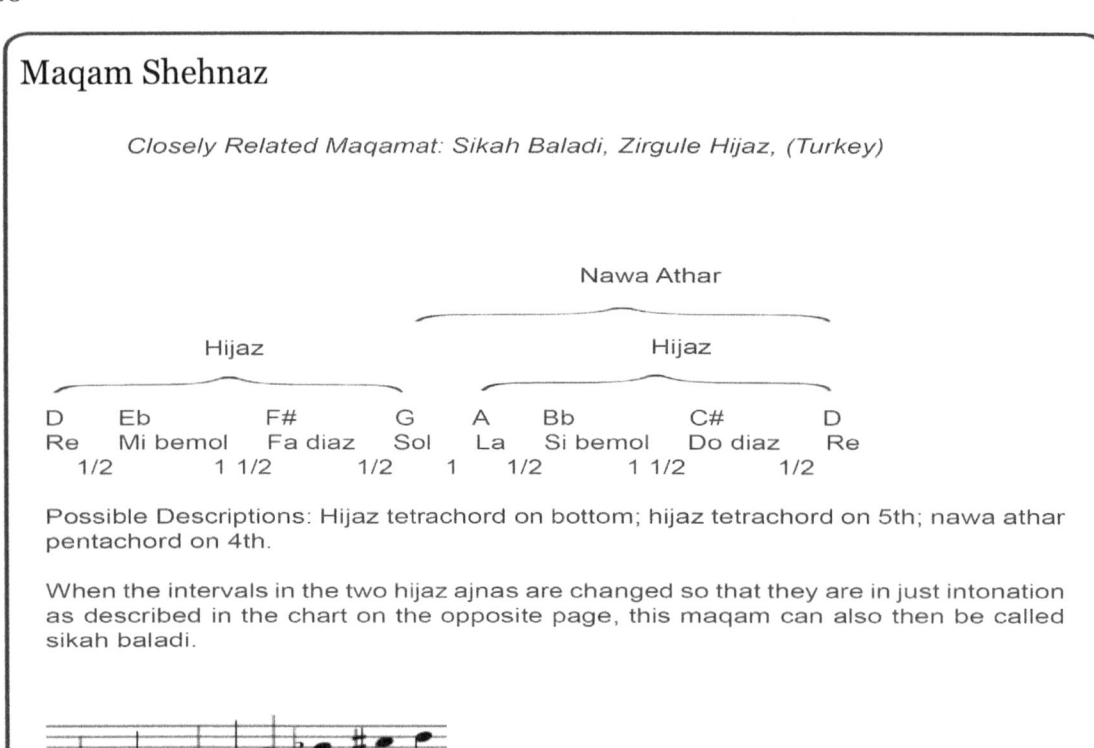

Possible Descriptions: Hijaz tetrachord on bottom; hijaz tetrachord on 5th; nawa athar pentachord on 4th.

When the intervals in the two hijaz ajnas are changed so that they are in just intonation as described in the chart on the opposite page, this maqam can also then be called sikah baladi.

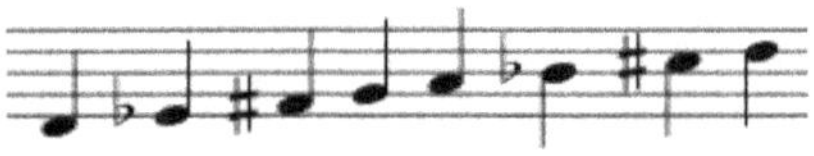

Maqam Shehnaz may also be described as Maqam Hijaz Kar with its tonic raised from C to D.

Low Kabá Register:

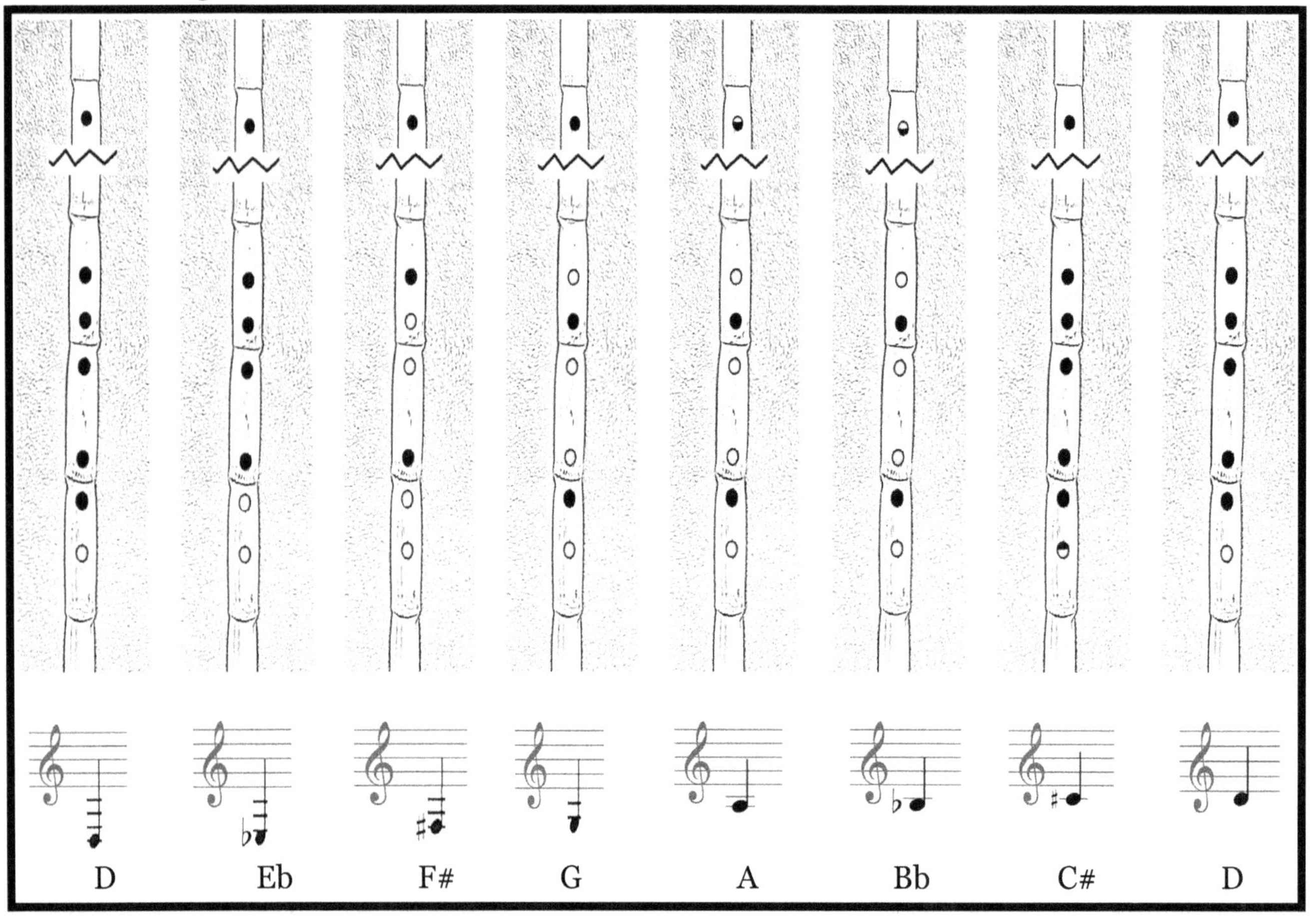

Main Register:

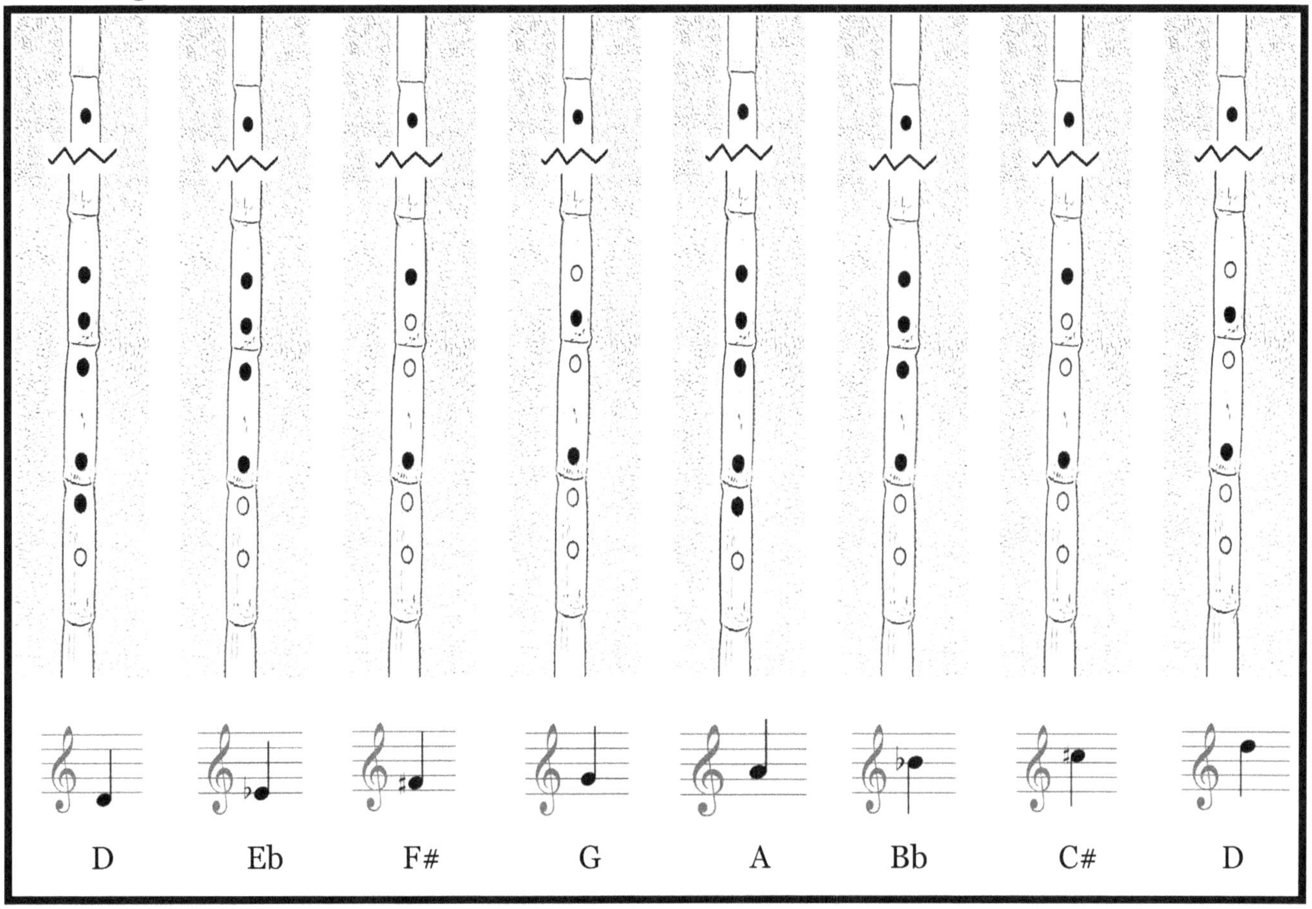

| D | Eb | F# | G | A | Bb | C# | D |

Second Register:

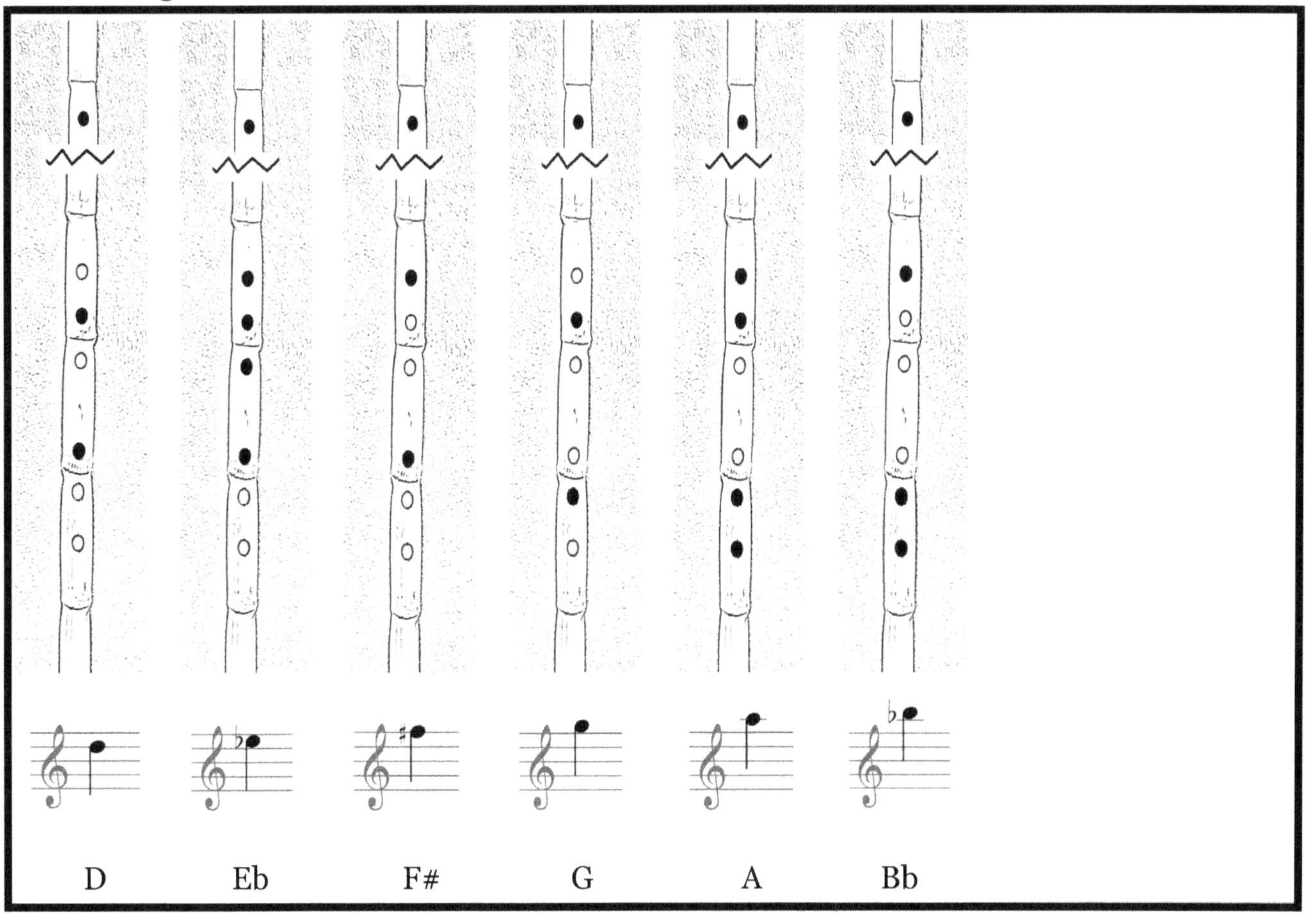

| D | Eb | F# | G | A | Bb |

Maqam Kurd

Closely Related: Phrygian Mode

```
                          Nahawand
              ┌──────────────────────────┐
         Kurd                    Kurd
     ┌──────────┐           ┌──────────┐
     D    Eb    F    G      A    Bb    C    D
     Re   Mi bemol  Fa  Sol La   Si bemol  Do   Re
        1/2    1    1    1    1/2   1    1
```

Possible Descriptions: Kurd tetrachord on bottom; nahawand pentachord on 4th; kurd tetrachord on 5th.

Ghammaz on 4th.

Low Kabá Register:

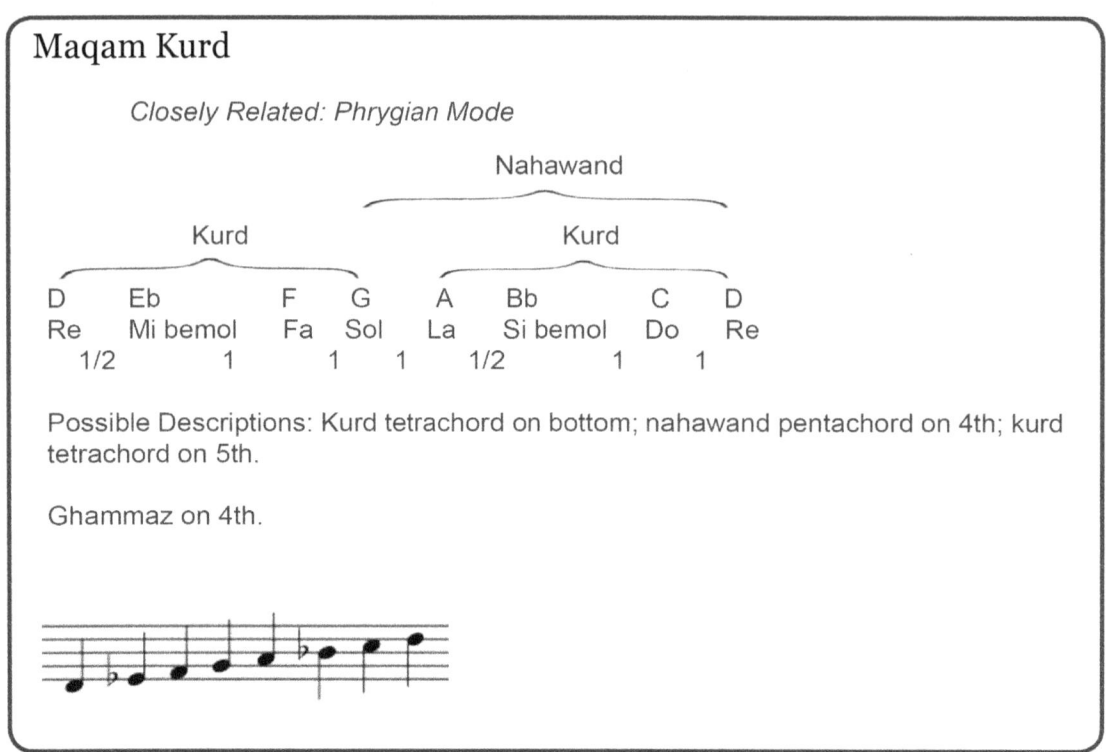

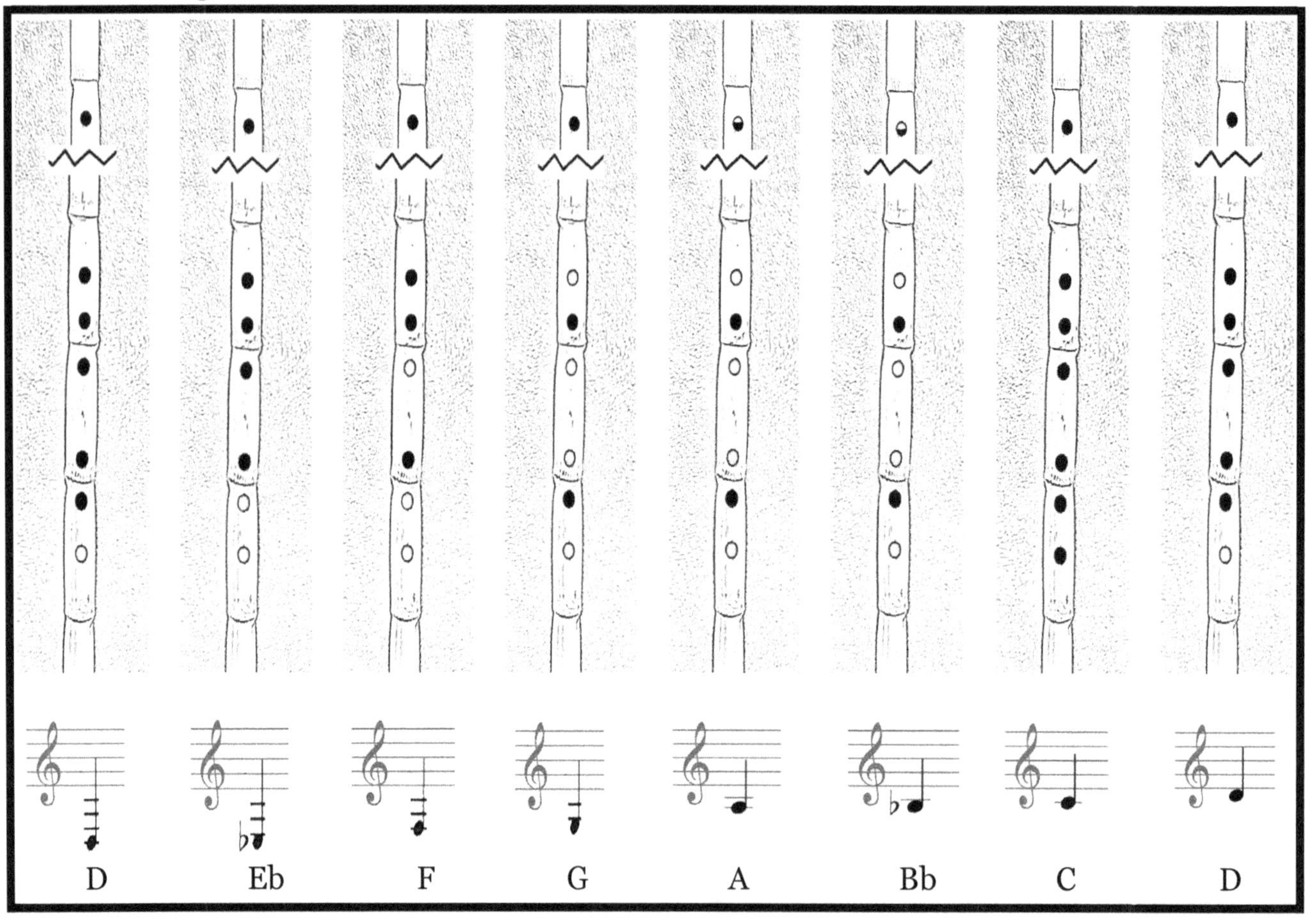

| D | Eb | F | G | A | Bb | C | D |

Main Register:

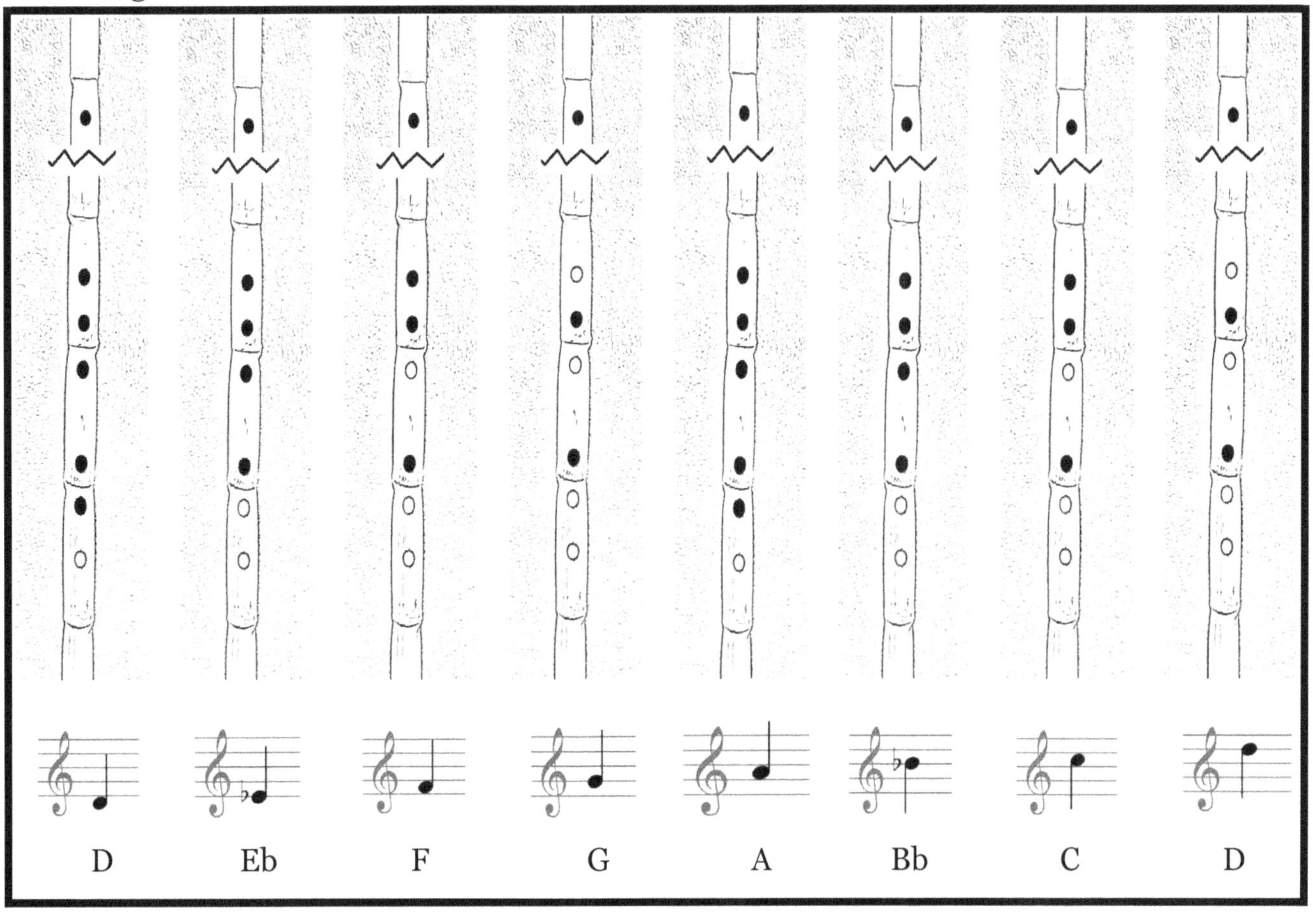

| D | Eb | F | G | A | Bb | C | D |

Second Register:

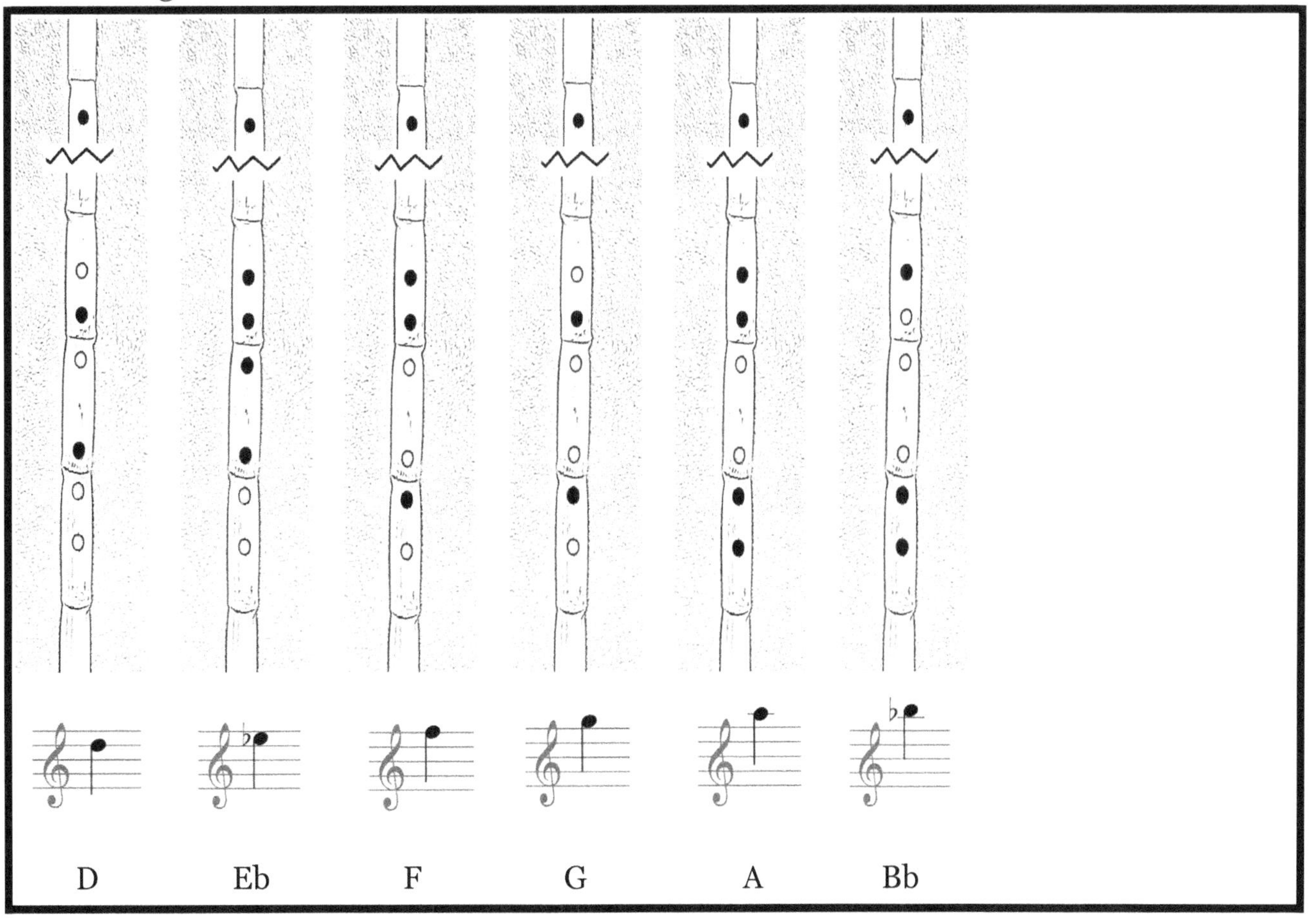

| D | Eb | F | G | A | Bb |

Maqam Shehnaz Kurdi

Nawa Athar

Kurd

Hijaz

D Eb F G A Bb C# D

Re Mi bemol Fa Sol La Si bemol Do diaz Re

1/2 1 1 1 1/2 1 1/2 1/2

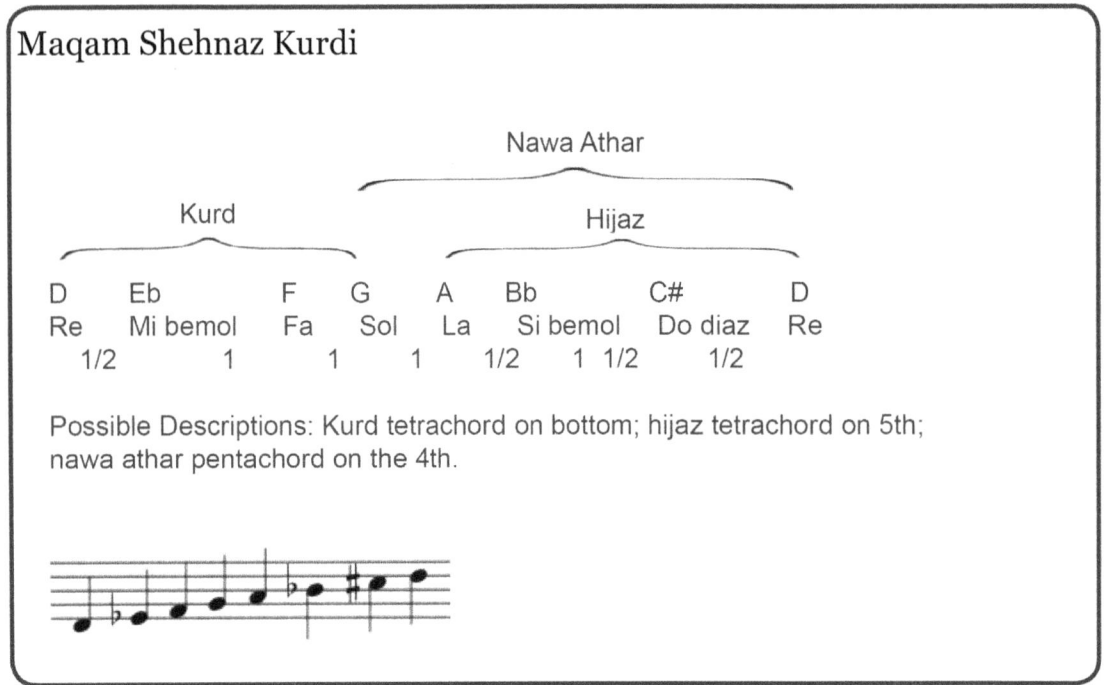

Possible Descriptions: Kurd tetrachord on bottom; hijaz tetrachord on 5th; nawa athar pentachord on the 4th.

Low Kabá Register:

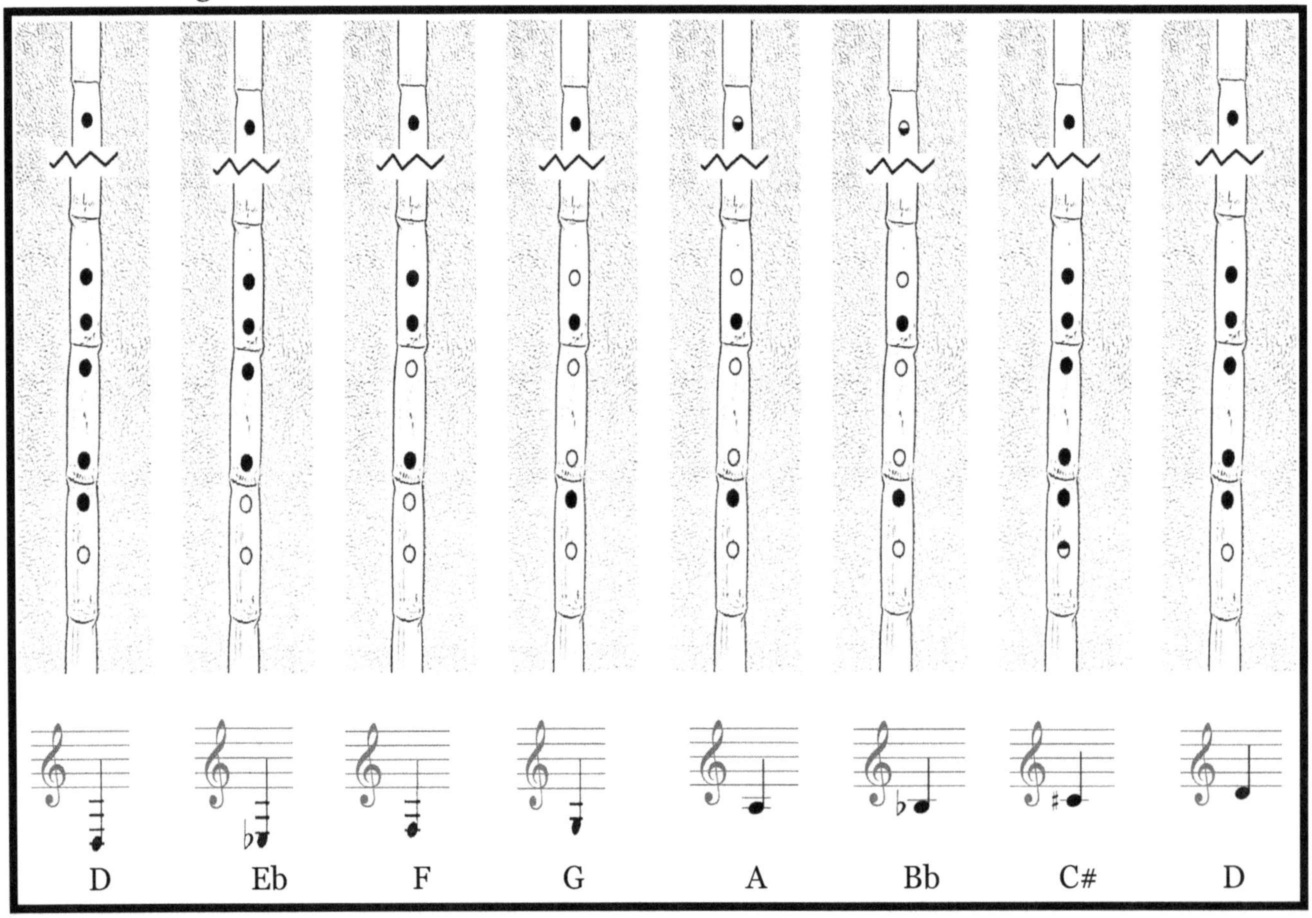

Main Register:

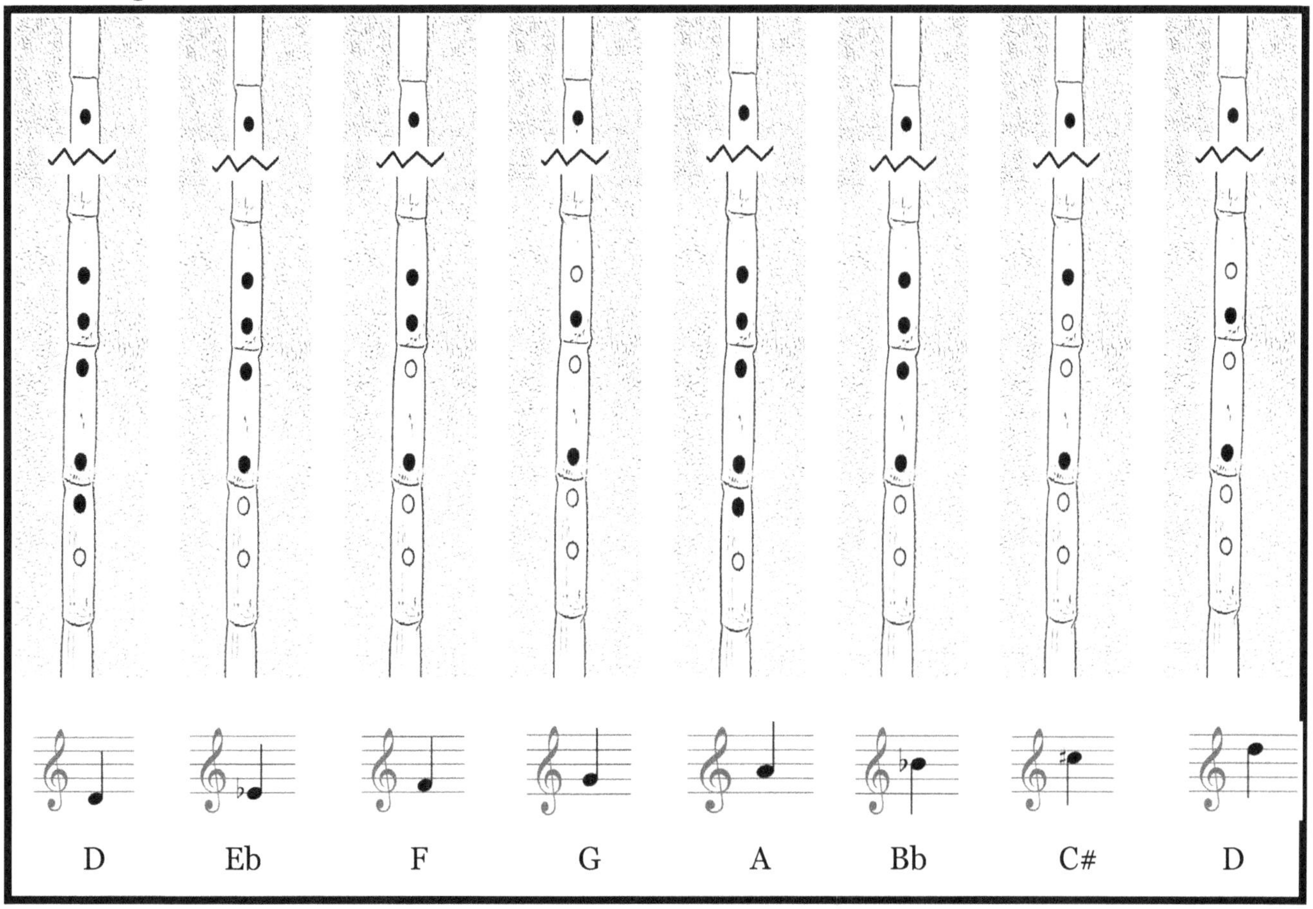

| D | Eb | F | G | A | Bb | C# | D |

Second Register:

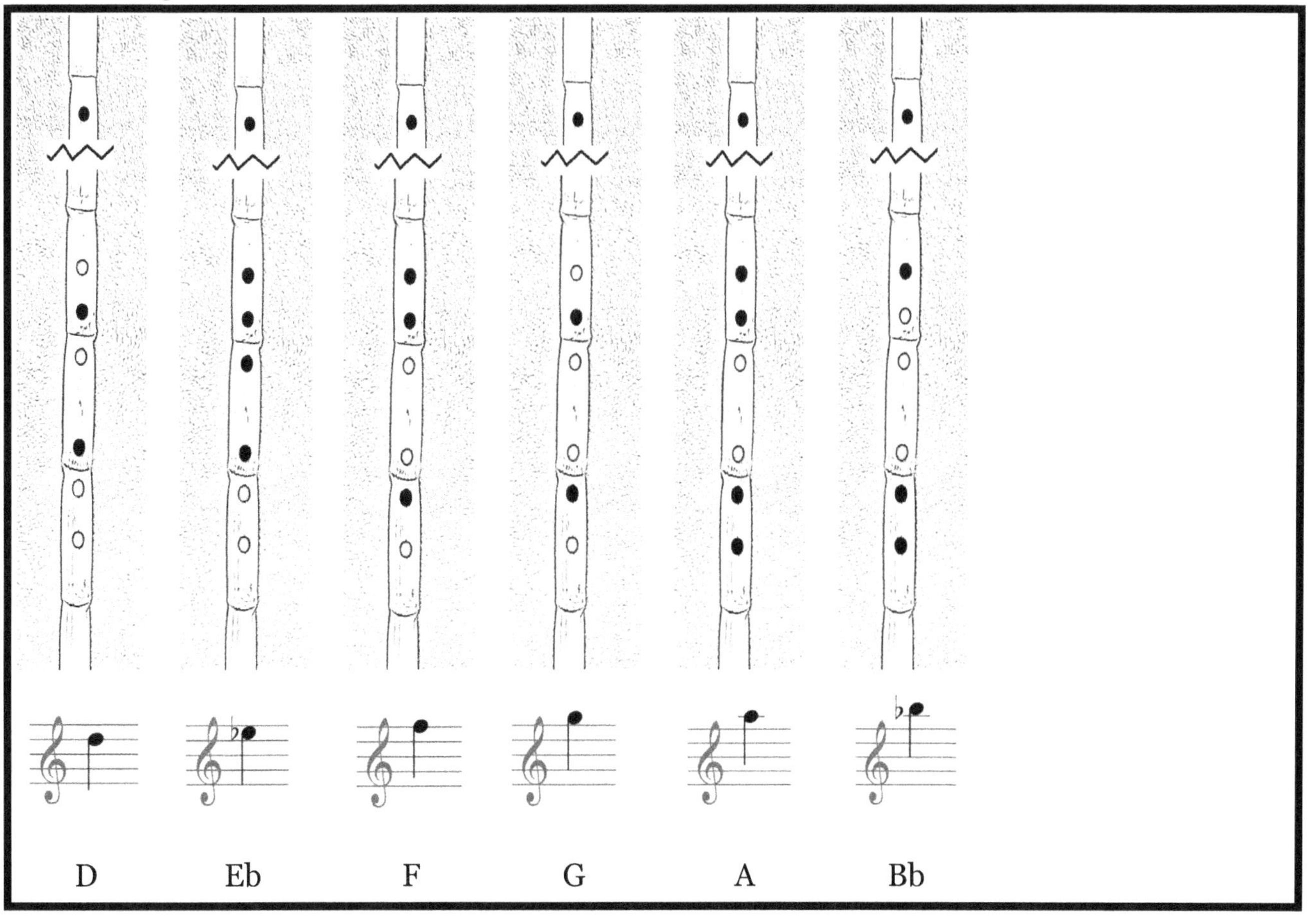

| D | Eb | F | G | A | Bb |

Maqam Ajam on Eb (Eb Major)

Closely Related: Huezawi (Iraqi), Ionian Mode, Eb Major Scale

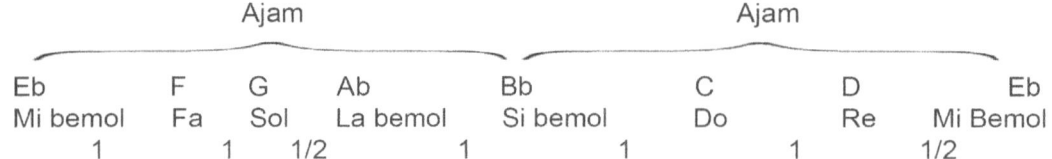

	Ajam				Ajam			
Eb	F	G	Ab	Bb	C	D	Eb	
Mi bemol	Fa	Sol	La bemol	Si bemol	Do	Re	Mi Bemol	
1		1	1/2	1	1	1	1/2	

Possible Descriptions: Ajam or "Jaharka" pentachord on bottom; Ajam or "Jaharka" tetrachord on 5th; Nahawand maqam on 6th.
Ajam on Eb is "relative major" to Nahawand (C minor scale).

Low Kabá Register:

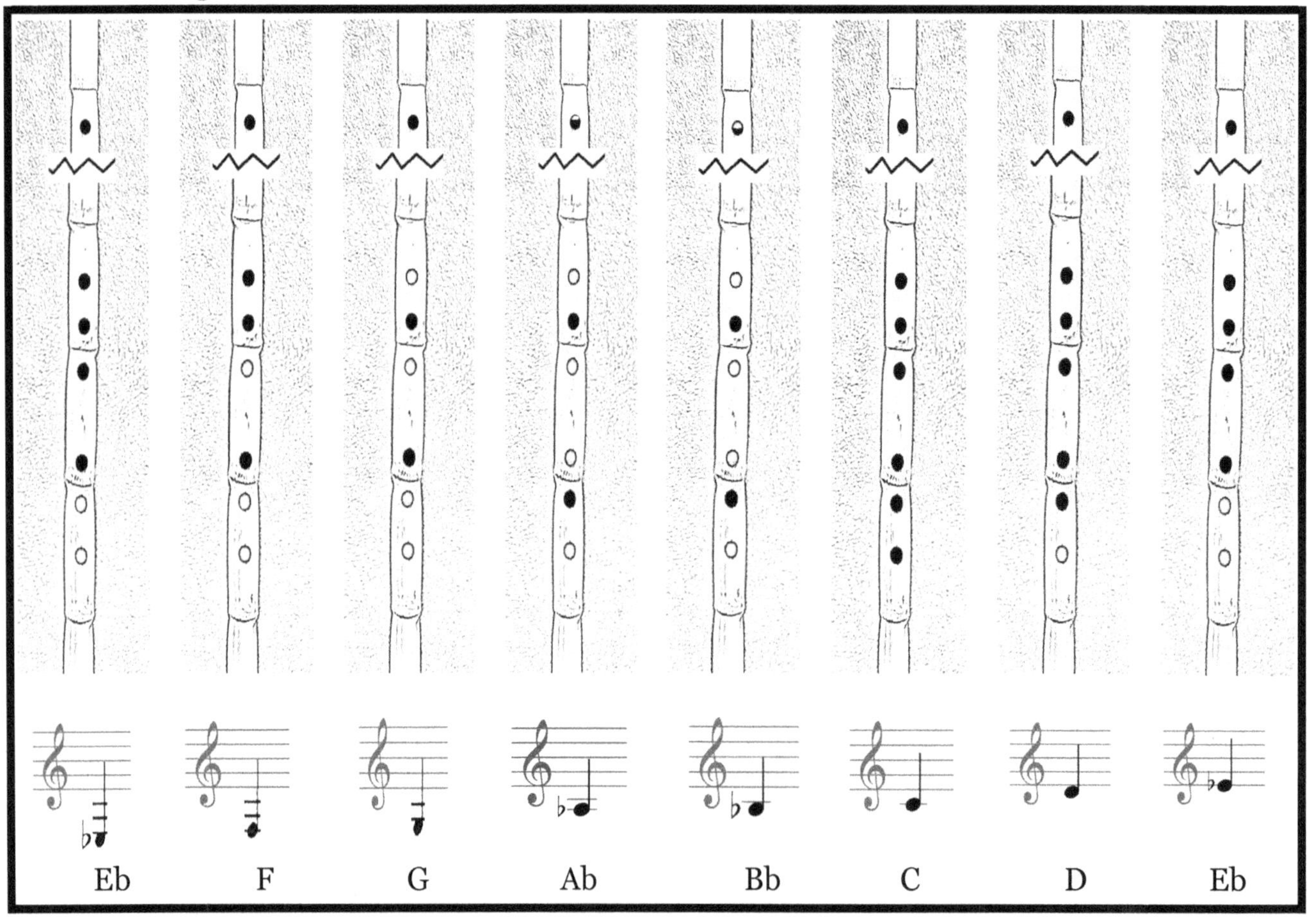

| Eb | F | G | Ab | Bb | C | D | Eb |

Main Register:

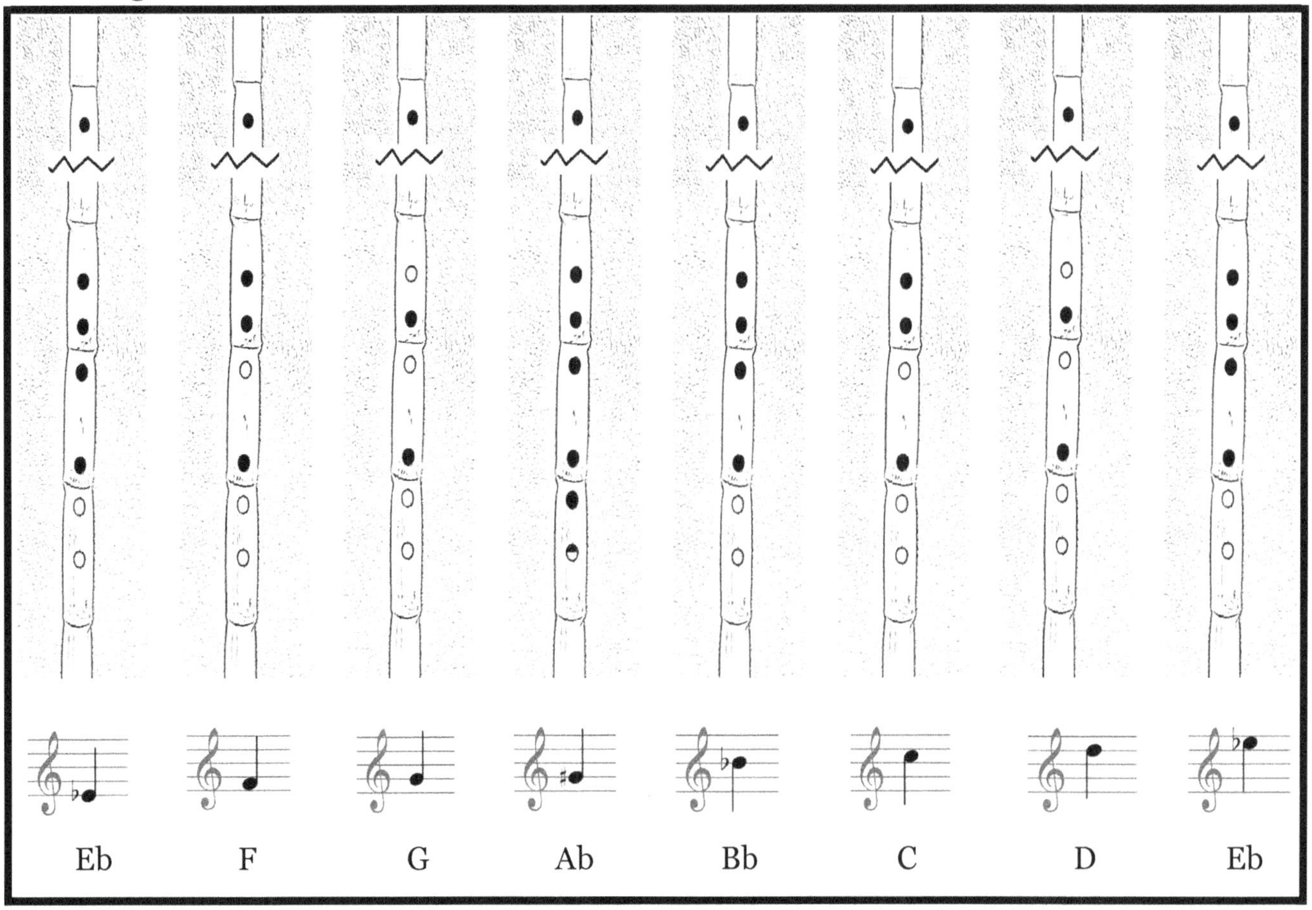

Eb	F	G	Ab	Bb	C	D	Eb

Second Register:

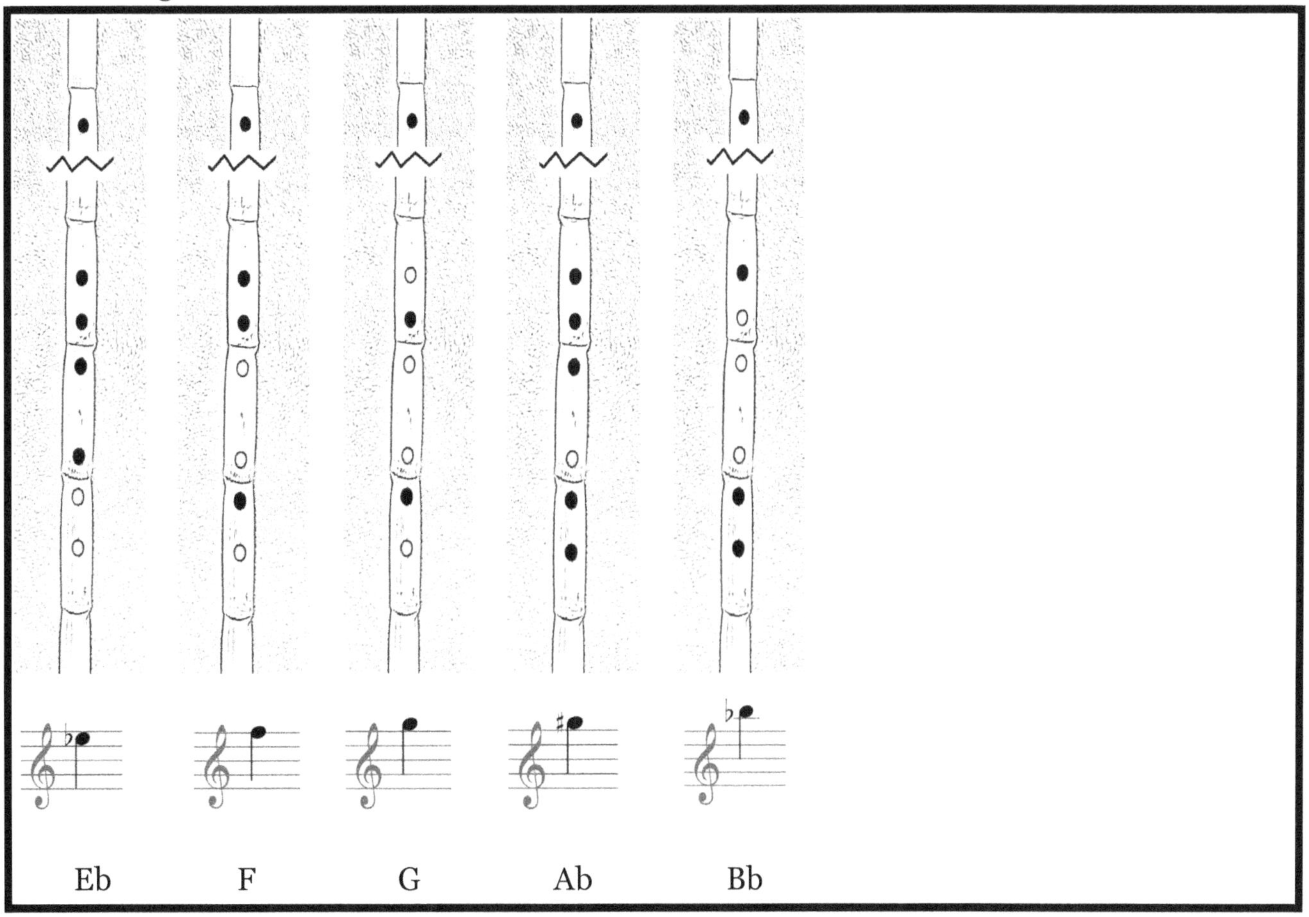

Eb	F	G	Ab	Bb

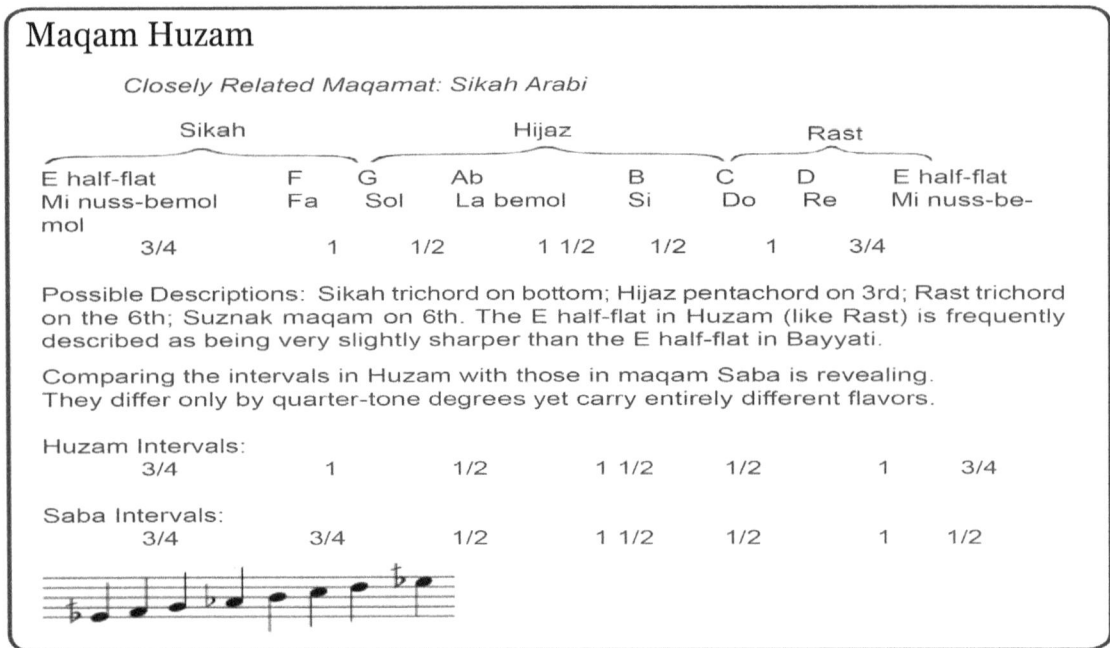

Maqam Huzam

Closely Related Maqamat: Sikah Arabi

Sikah		Hijaz			Rast		
E half-flat	F	G	Ab	B	C	D	E half-flat
Mi nuss-bemol	Fa	Sol	La bemol	Si	Do	Re	Mi nuss-be-mol
3/4	1	1/2	1 1/2	1/2	1	3/4	

Possible Descriptions: Sikah trichord on bottom; Hijaz pentachord on 3rd; Rast trichord on the 6th; Suznak maqam on 6th. The E half-flat in Huzam (like Rast) is frequently described as being very slightly sharper than the E half-flat in Bayyati.

Comparing the intervals in Huzam with those in maqam Saba is revealing. They differ only by quarter-tone degrees yet carry entirely different flavors.

Huzam Intervals:
  3/4   1   1/2   1 1/2   1/2   1   3/4

Saba Intervals:
  3/4   3/4   1/2   1 1/2   1/2   1   1/2

The notes in Huzam are the same as the notes in Suznak, but the tonic is on E half-flat instead of on C.

The leading tone or "zahir" for this maqam is a D#, which is only 1/4 tone lower than the tonic on E half-flat.

The musical lore around maqam Huzam is rich and extensive and is commonly found in many styles of Arab music.

Low Kabá Register:

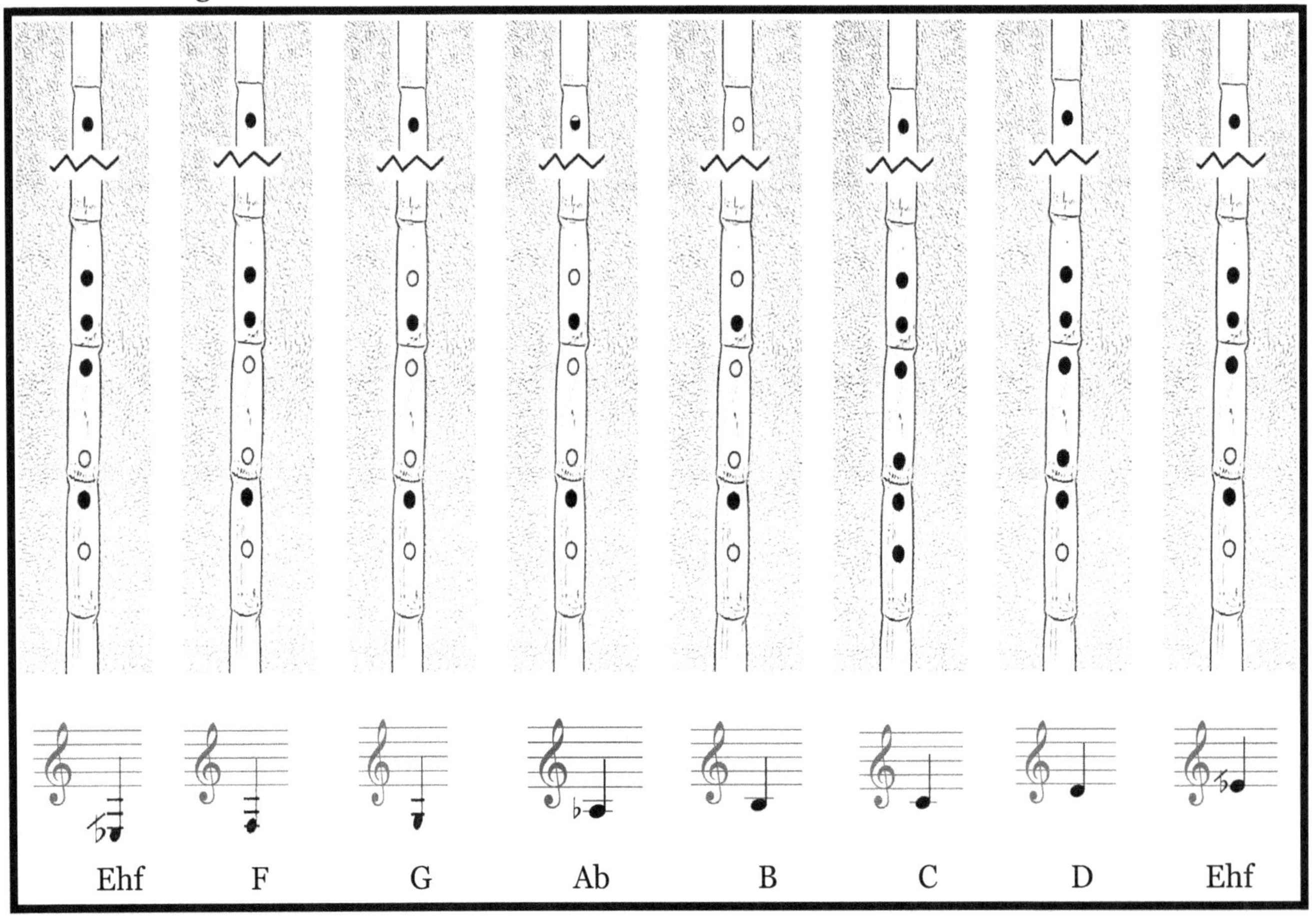

| Ehf | F | G | Ab | B | C | D | Ehf |

Main Register:

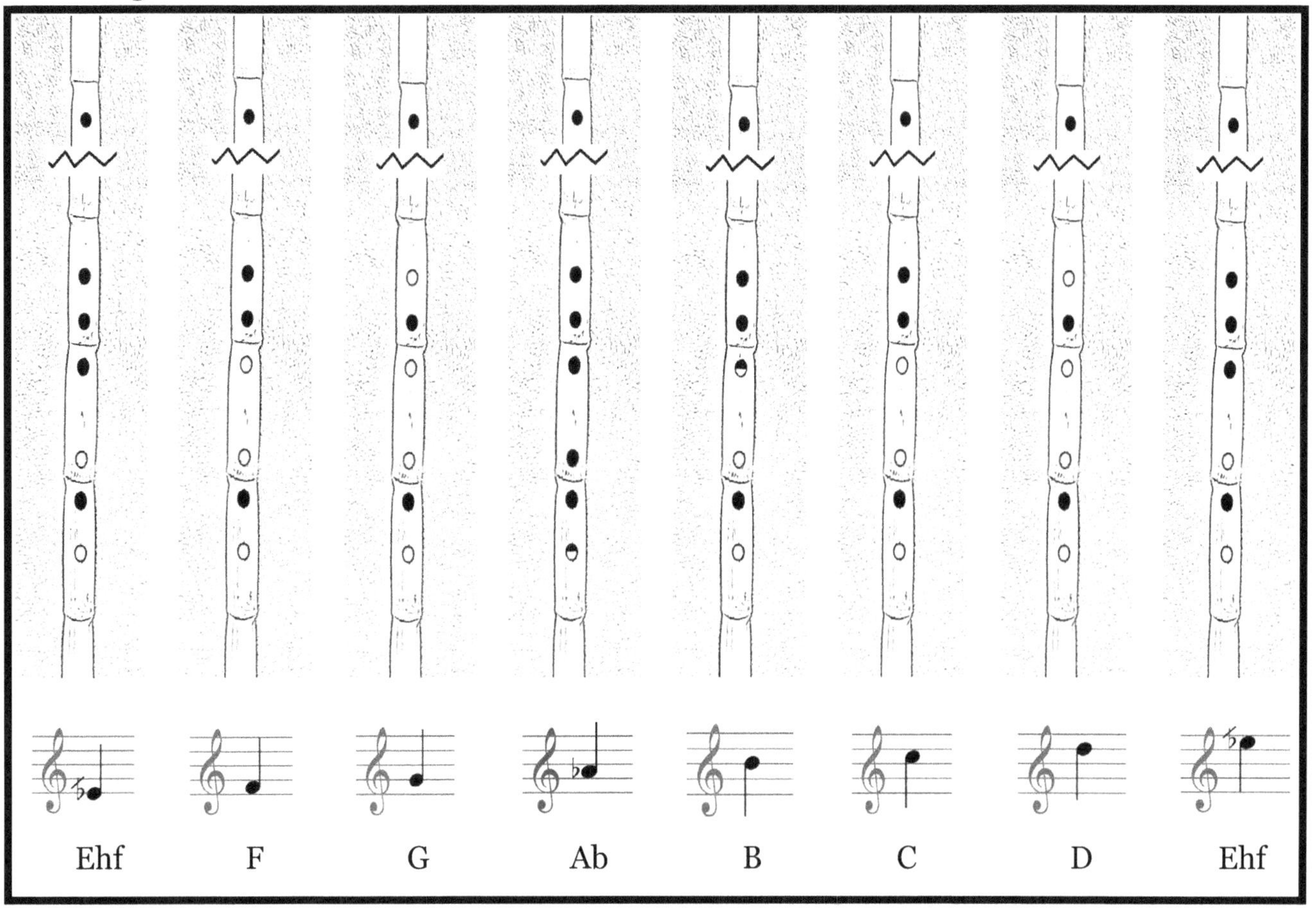

| Ehf | F | G | Ab | B | C | D | Ehf |

Second Register:

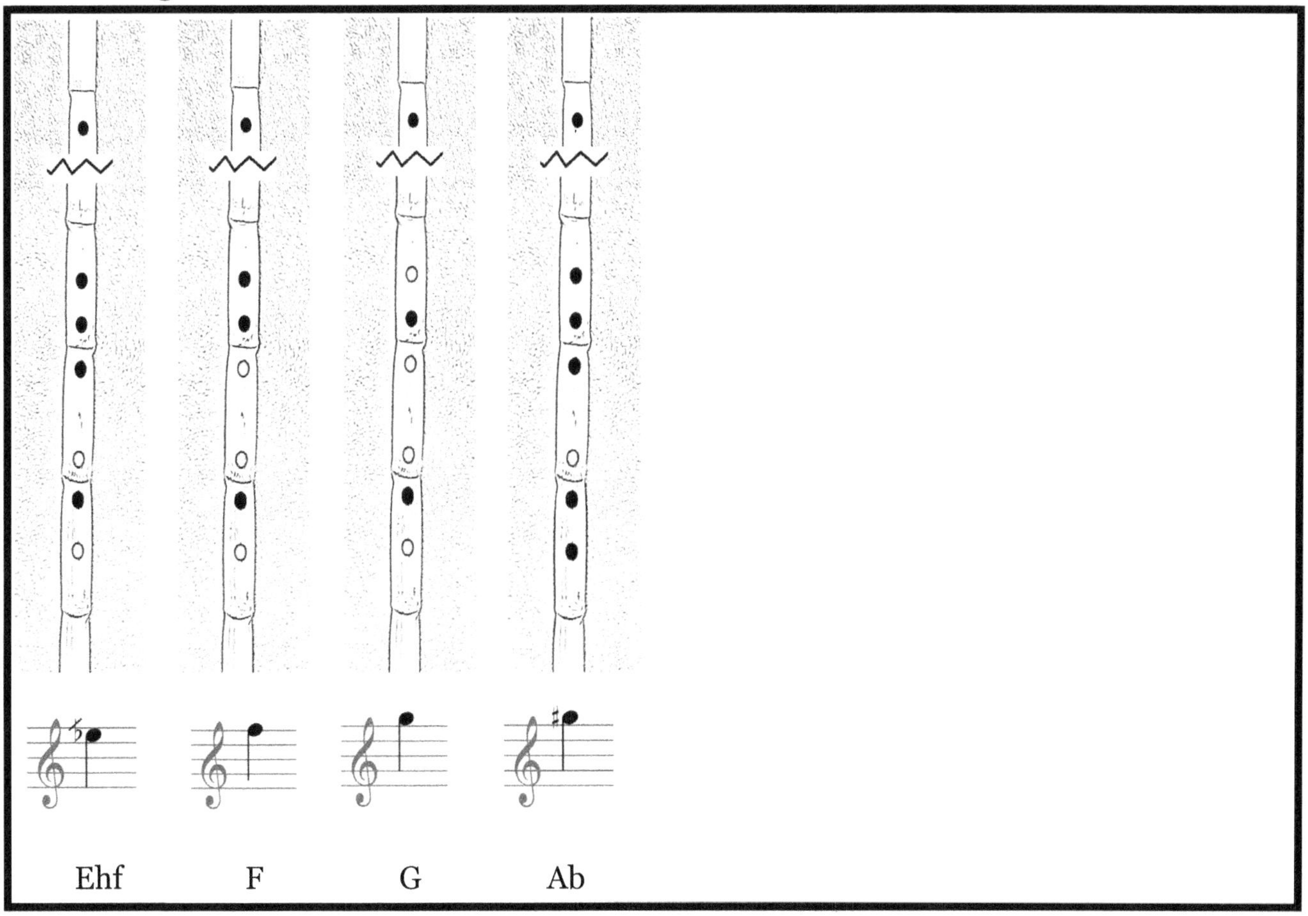

| Ehf | F | G | Ab |

Maqam Sikah

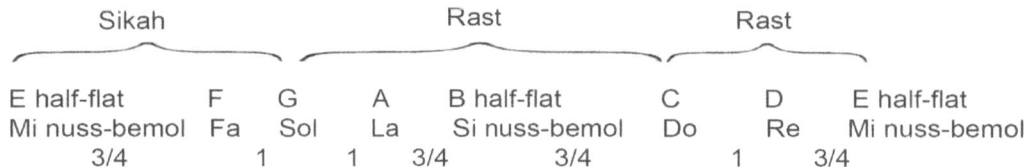

Sikah			Rast			Rast		
E half-flat	F	G	A	B half-flat	C	D	E half-flat
Mi nuss-bemol	Fa	Sol	La	Si nuss-bemol	Do	Re	Mi nuss-bemol
3/4	1	1	3/4	3/4	1	3/4	

Possible Descriptions: Sikah trichord on bottom; Rast tetrachord on 3rd; Rast trichord on 6th; Rast maqam on 6th. The E half-flat in Sikah (like Rast) is frequently described as being very slightly sharper than the E half-flat in Bayyati.

The notes in Sikah are the same as the notes in Rast, but the tonic is on E half-flat instead of on C.

The leading tone or "zahir" for this maqam is a D#, which is only 1/4 tone lower than the tonic on E half-flat.

Low Kabá Register:

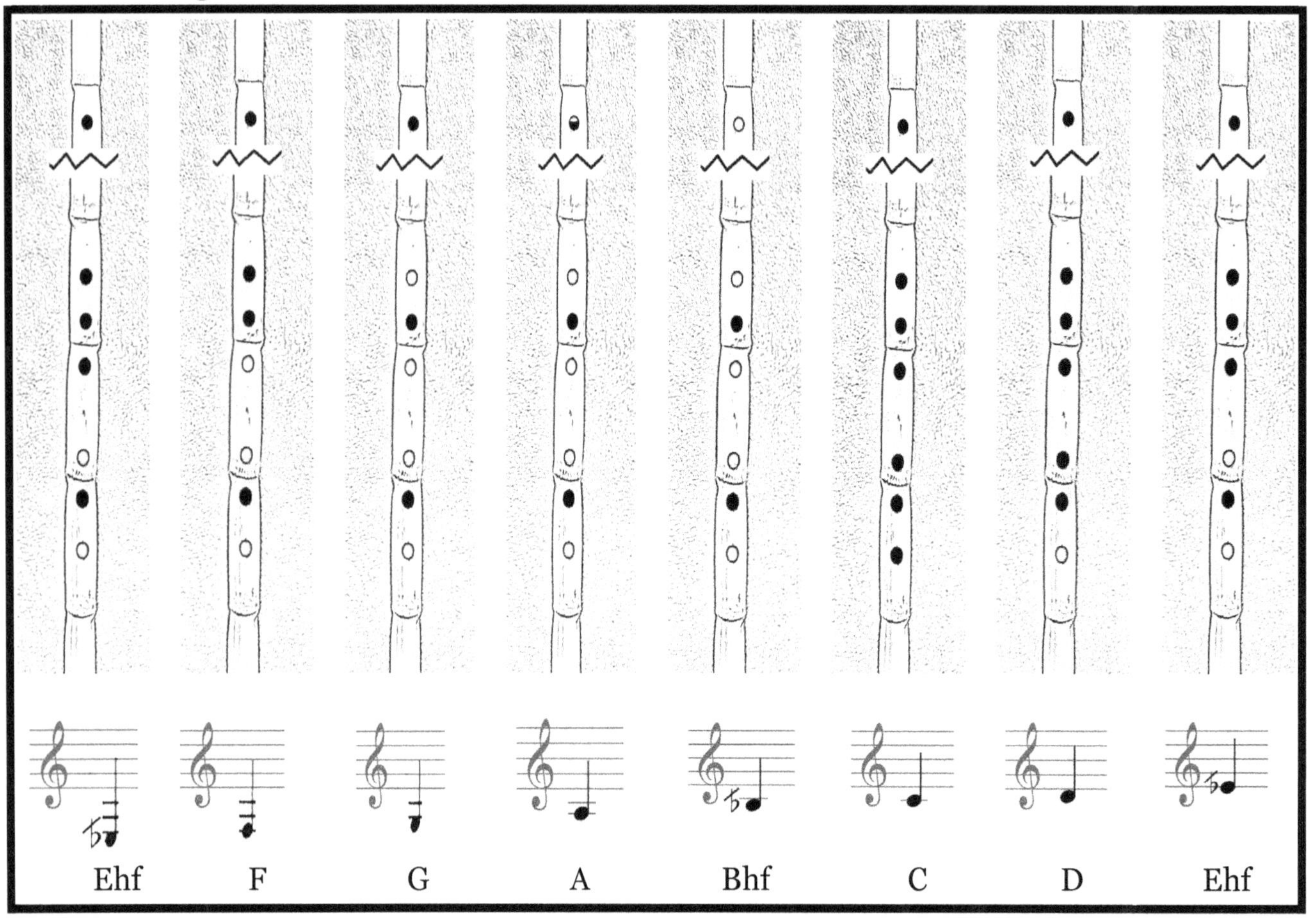

| Ehf | F | G | A | Bhf | C | D | Ehf |

Main Register:

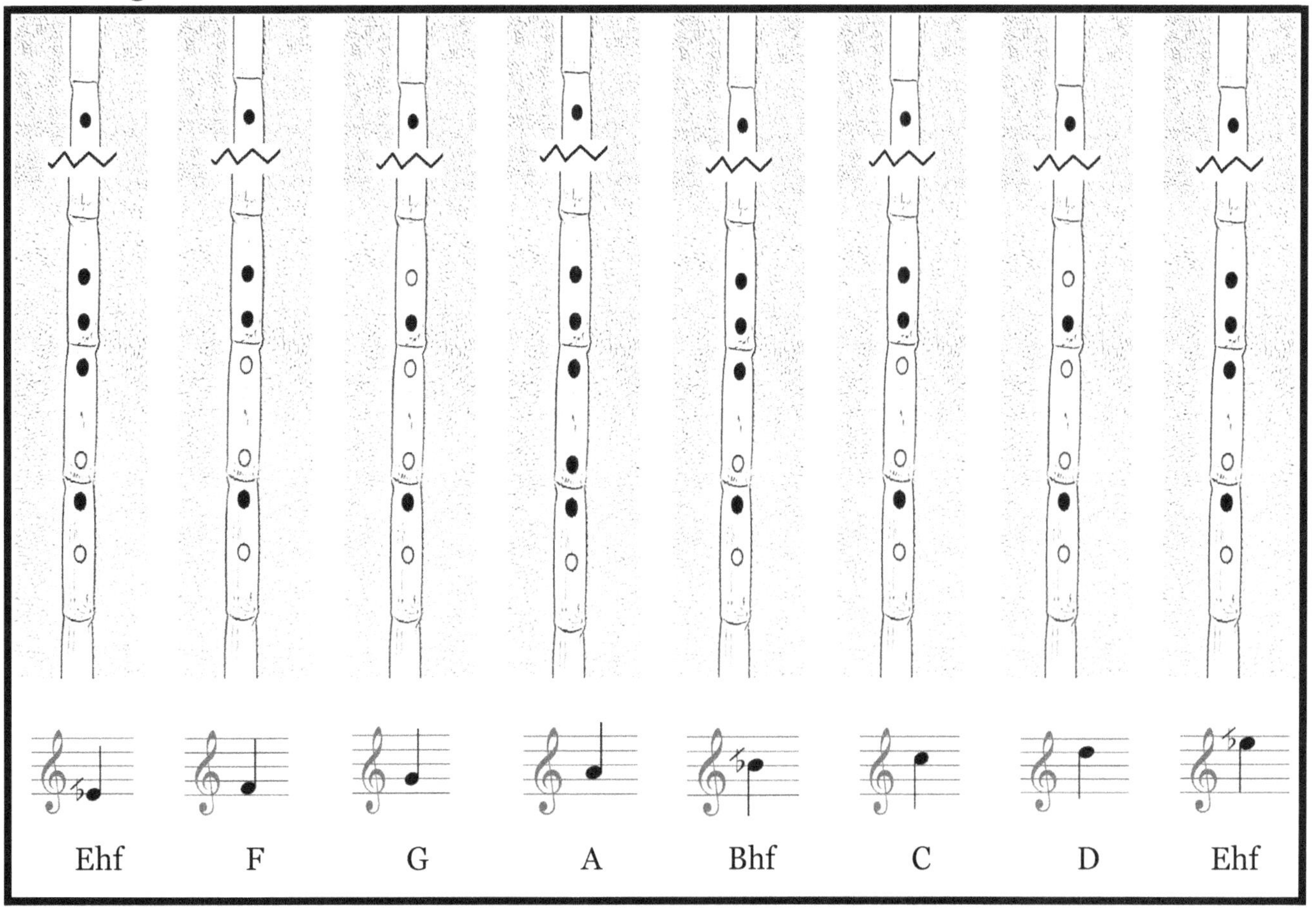

Ehf	F	G	A	Bhf	C	D	Ehf

Second Register:

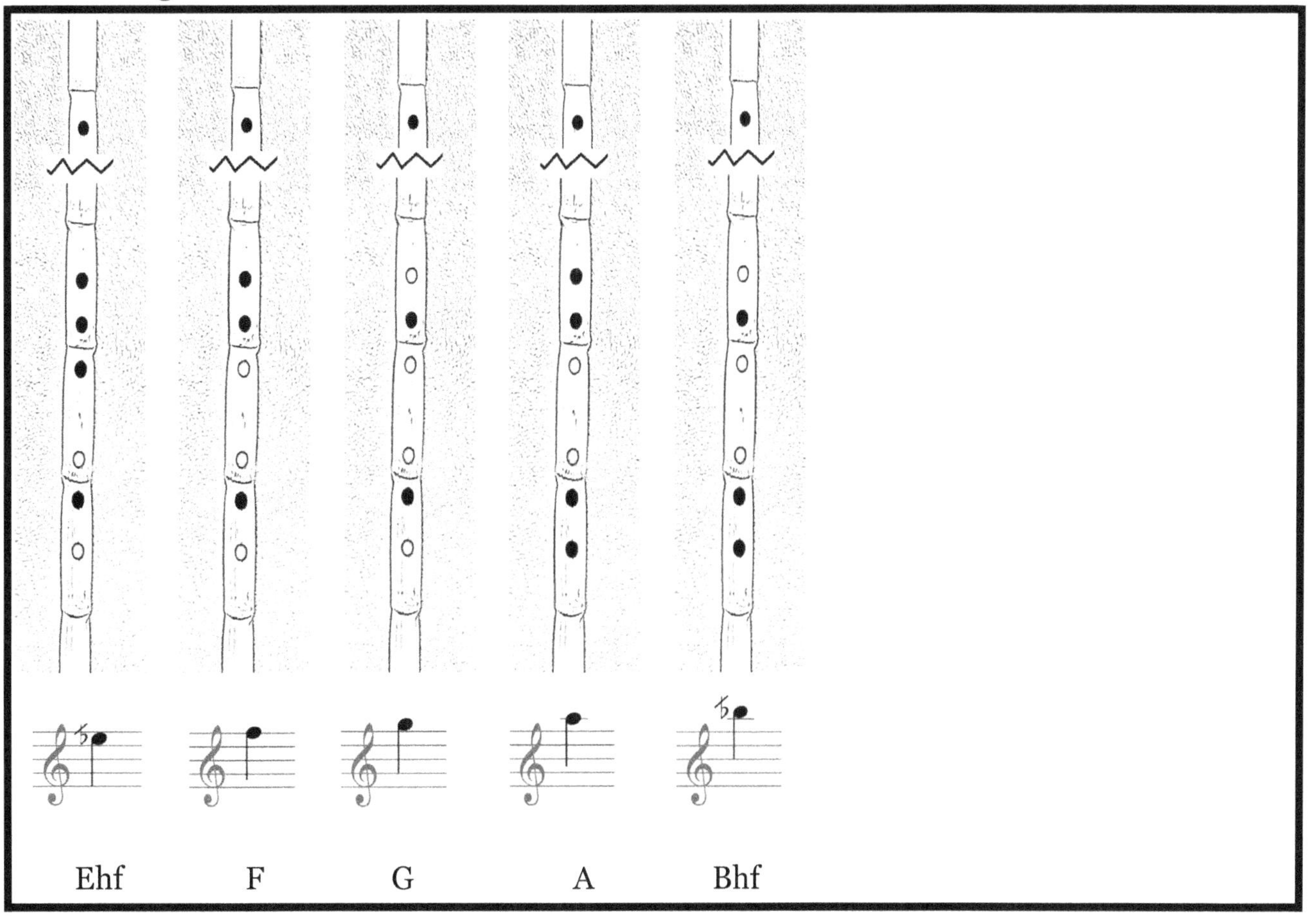

Ehf	F	G	A	Bhf

Maqam Awshar

Closely Related Maqamat: Sha'ar, Mayah, Wajh 'ardibar

Sikah			Nahawand			Rast		
E half-flat	F	G	A	Bb		C	D	E half-flat
Mi nuss-bemol	Fa	Sol	La	Si bemol		Do	Re	Mi nuss-be-mol
3/4		1	1	1/2	1		1	3/4

Possible Descriptions: Sikah trichord on bottom; Nahawand tetrachord on 3rd; Rast trichord on 6th.

Low Kabá Register:

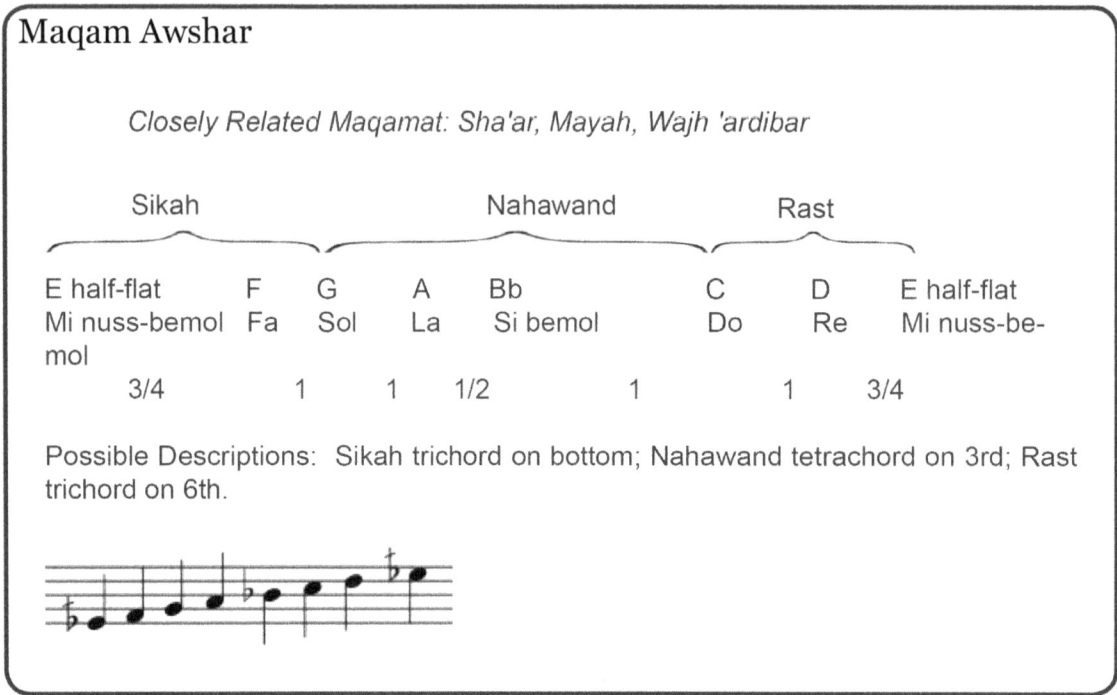

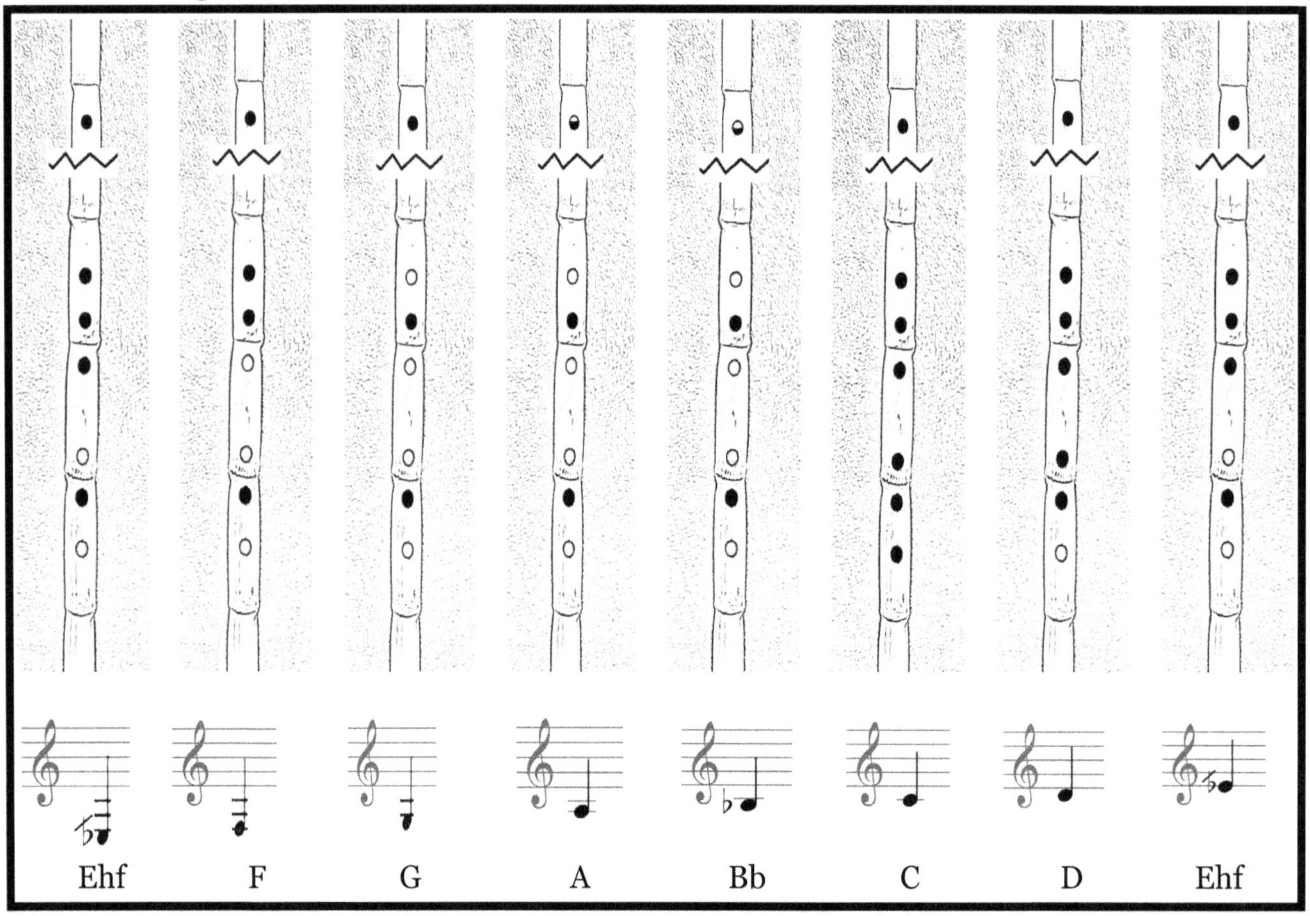

| Ehf | F | G | A | Bb | C | D | Ehf |

Main Register:

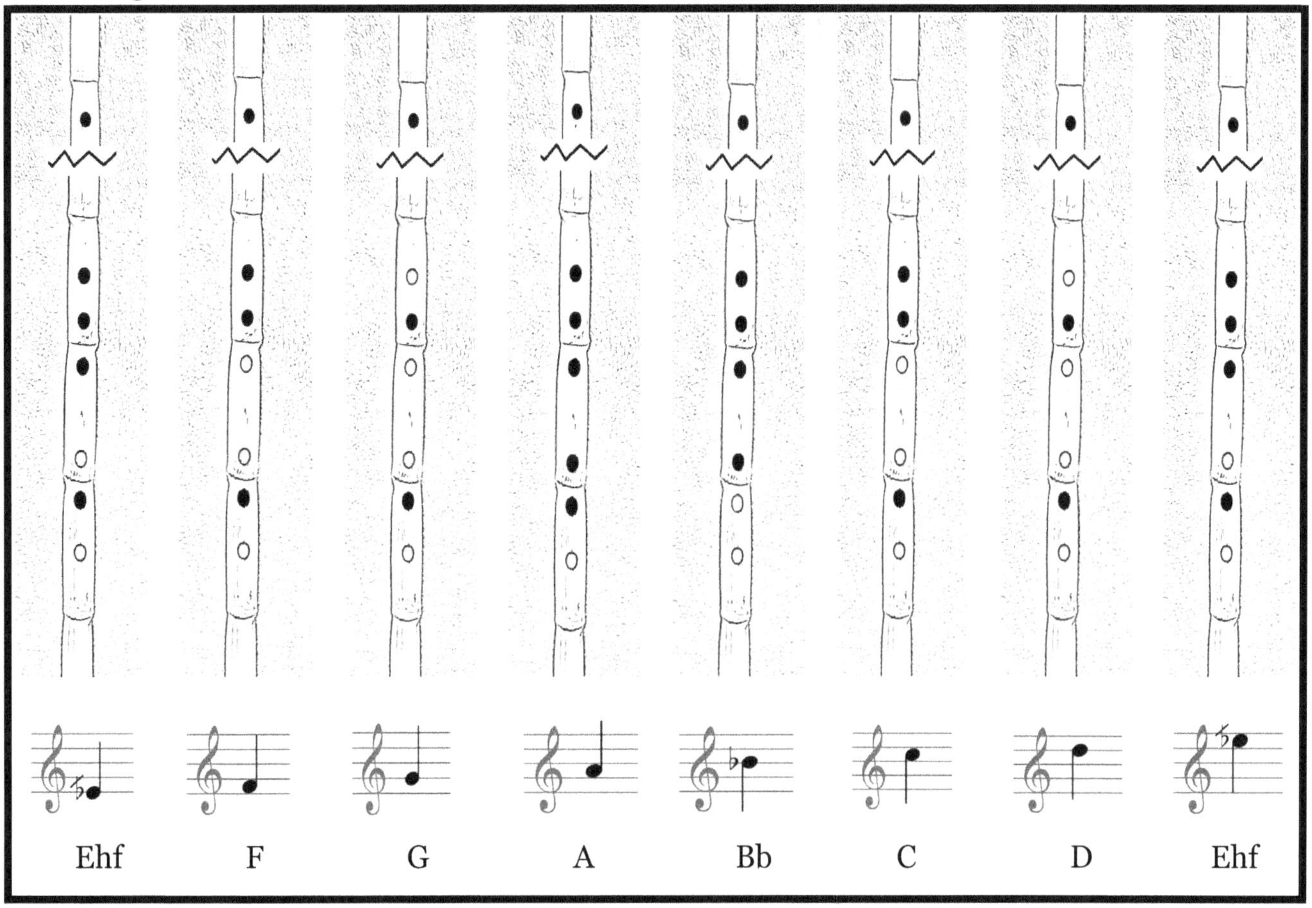

Ehf	F	G	A	Bb	C	D	Ehf

Second Register:

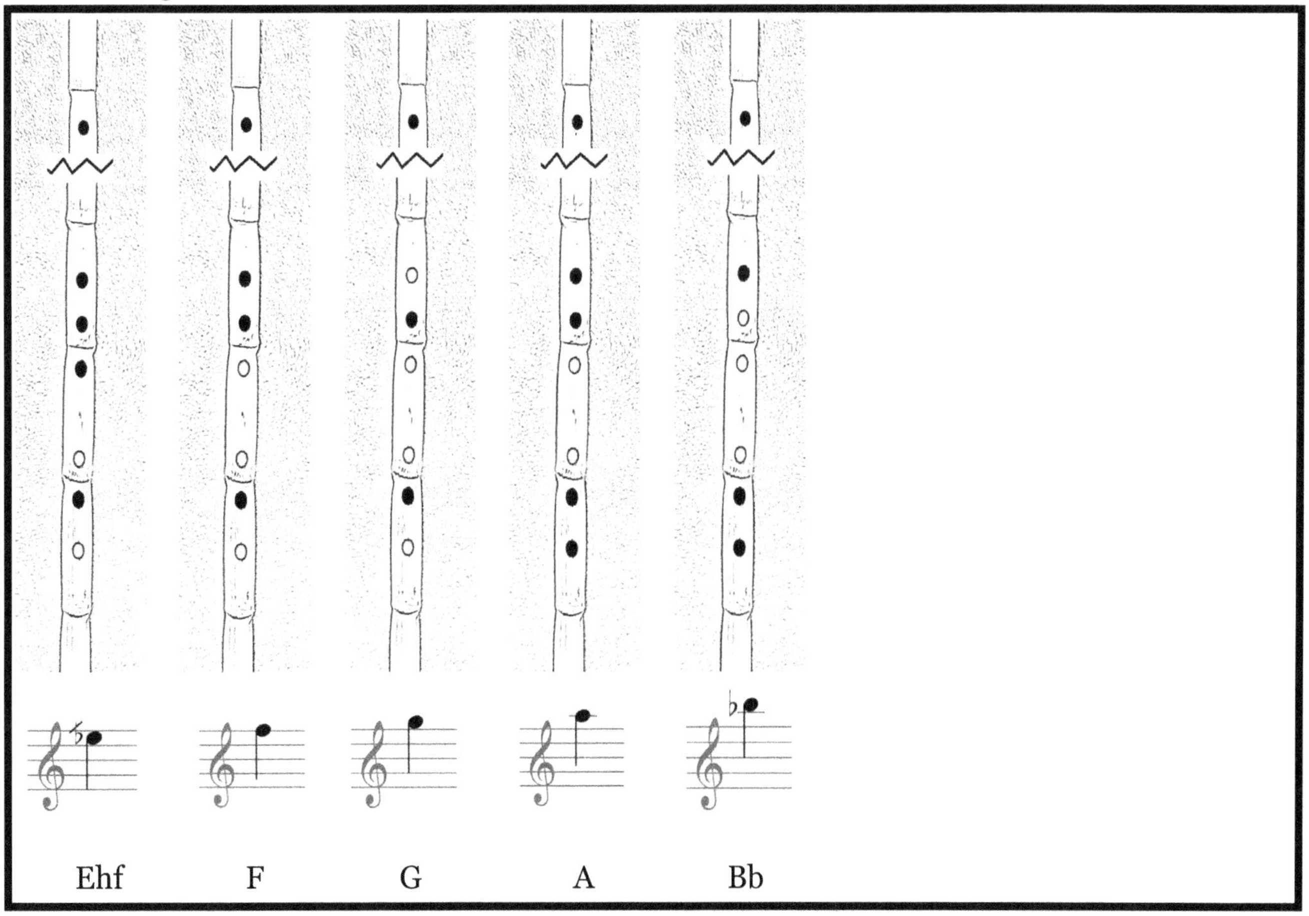

Ehf	F	G	A	Bb

113

Maqam Jaharakah

Closely Related Maqamat: Shahwar

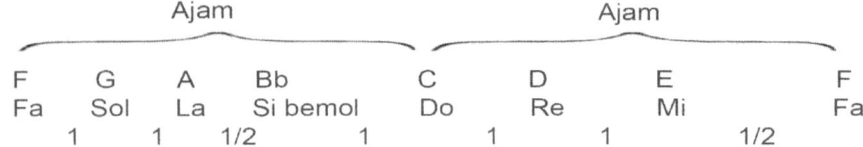

Ajam				Ajam			
F	G	A	Bb	C	D	E	F
Fa	Sol	La	Si bemol	Do	Re	Mi	Fa
1	1	1/2	1	1	1	1/2	

Possible Descriptions: Ajam or "Jaharka" pentachord on bottom; Ajam or "Jaharka" tetrachord on 5th.

In Western terms, Jaharka is "relative major" to the Nahawand on D (D minor scale).

Another, perhaps older, definition of maqam Jaharka requires a replacement of the E with an E half-flat which transforms the upper Ajam jins into Rast.

And some say that the 3rd note in Jaharkah is slightly flatter than the 3rd in Ajam. Since Ajam has become strongly associated with the ET major scale intervals, this is likely another way of saying "back to just intonation please!"

Low Kabá Register:

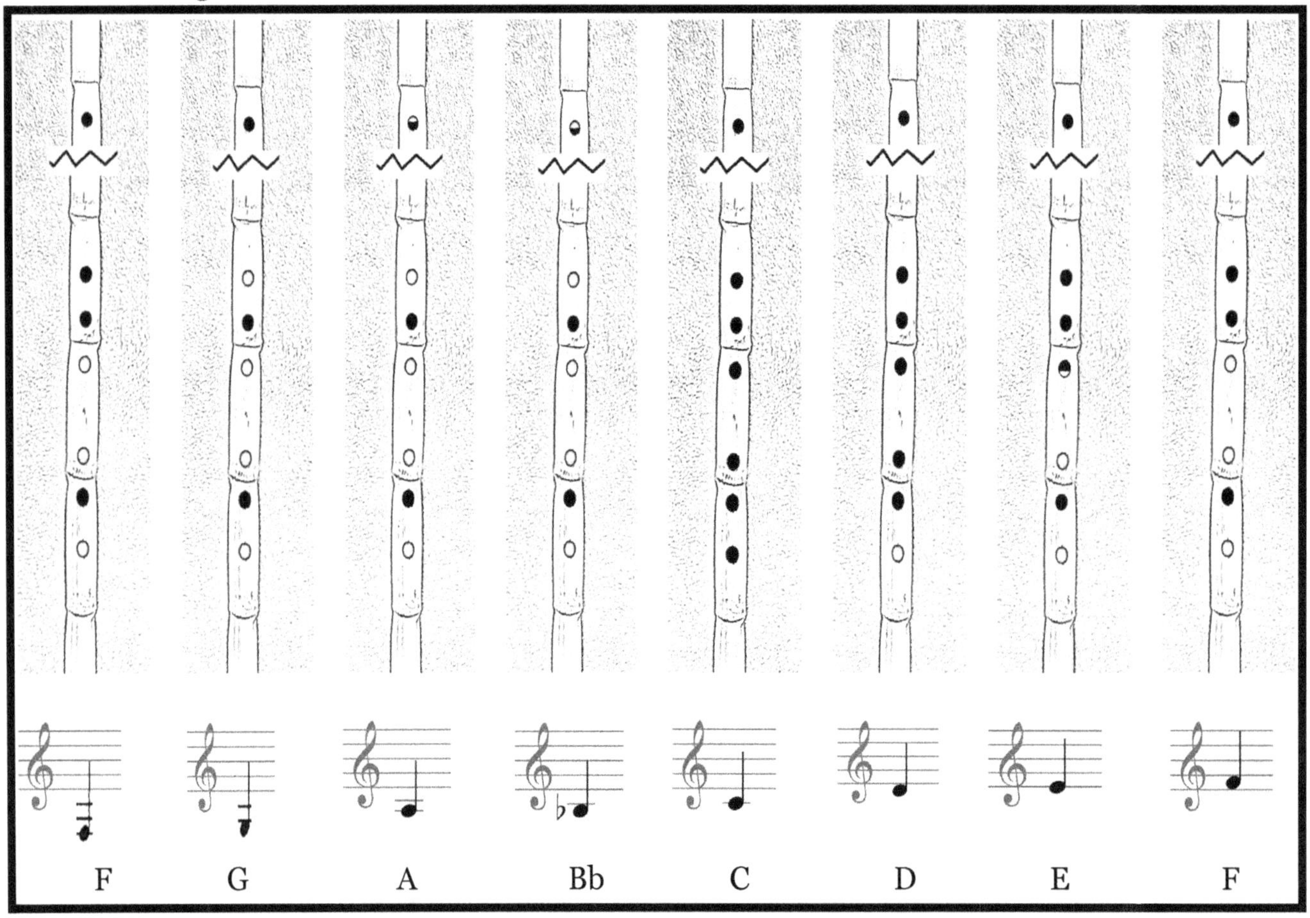

| F | G | A | Bb | C | D | E | F |

Main Register:

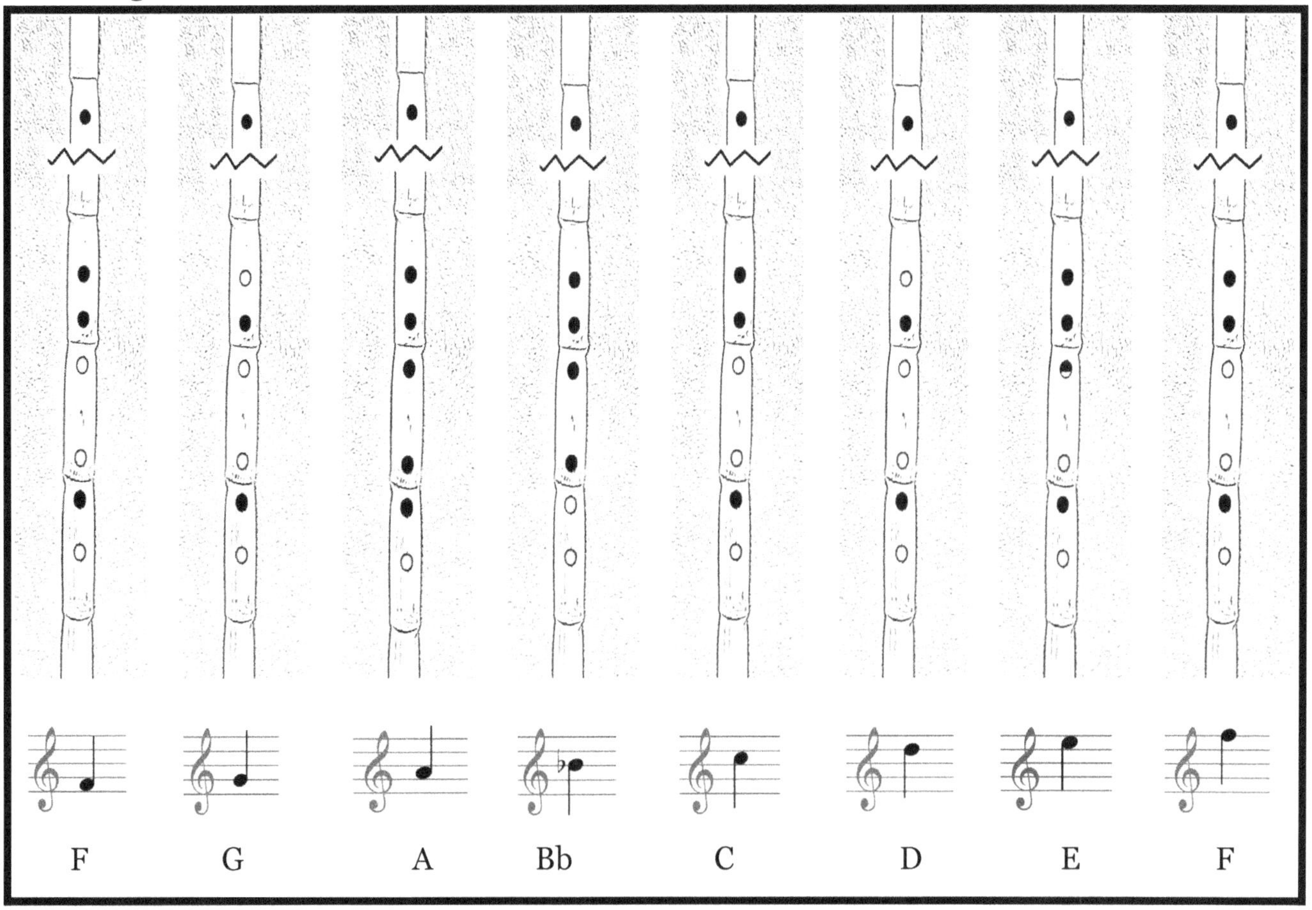

| F | G | A | Bb | C | D | E | F |

Second Register:

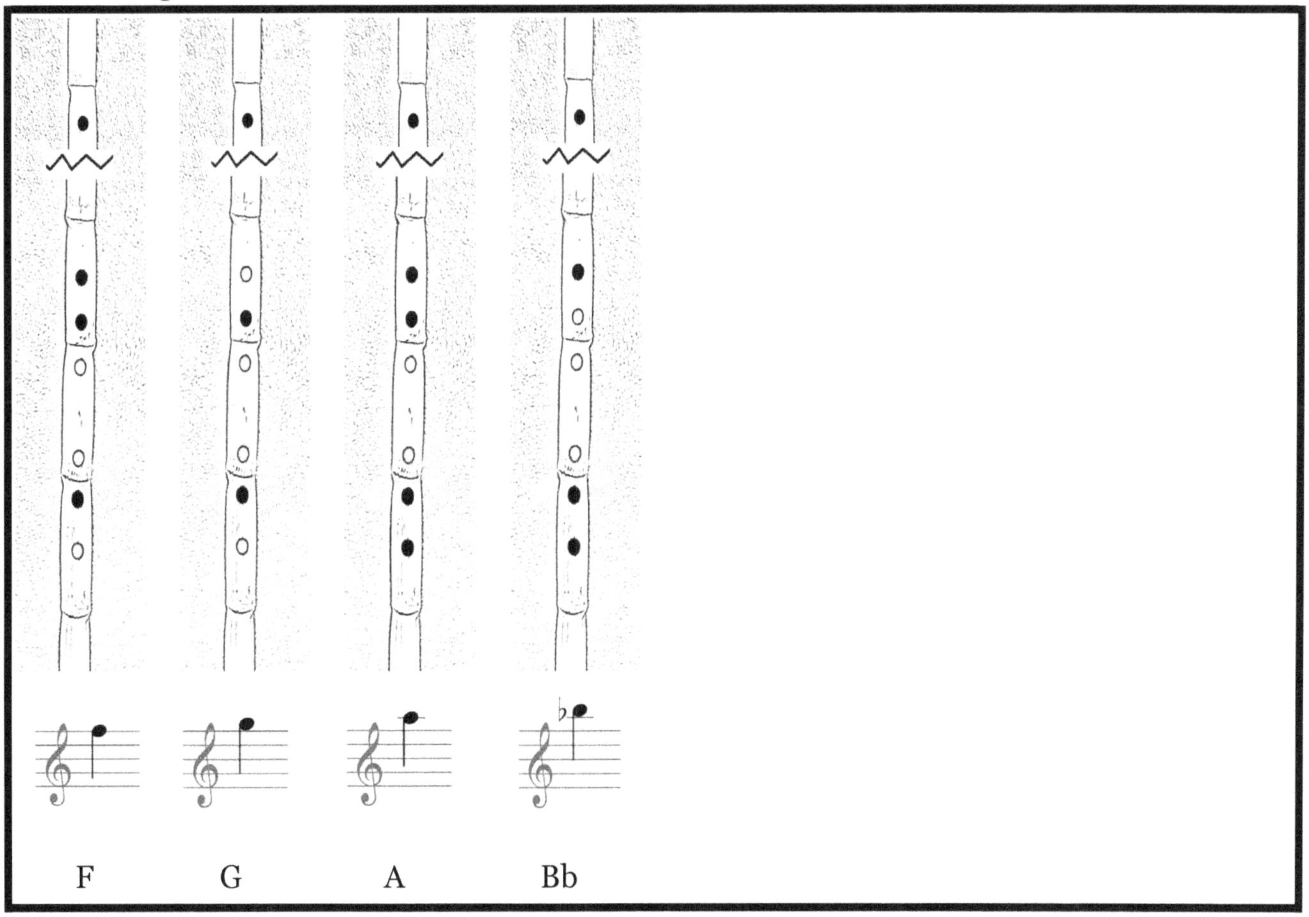

| F | G | A | Bb |

Maqam Jaharakah Turki (Shehnaz on F)

```
                              Nawa Athar
                         ⌢――――――――――――⌢
              Hijaz                  Hijaz
         ⌢―――――――――⌢             ⌢―――――――――⌢
   F    Gb      A      Bb    C    Db      E     F
   Fa   Sol bemol La    Si bemol  Do   Re bemol Mi   Fa
        1/2   1 1/2   1/2    1    1/2   1 1/2   1/2
```

Possible Descriptions: Hijaz pentachord on bottom; Hijaz tetrachord on 5th. The upper Hijaz tetrachord can also be replaced by a Rast tetrachord.

Low Kabá Register:

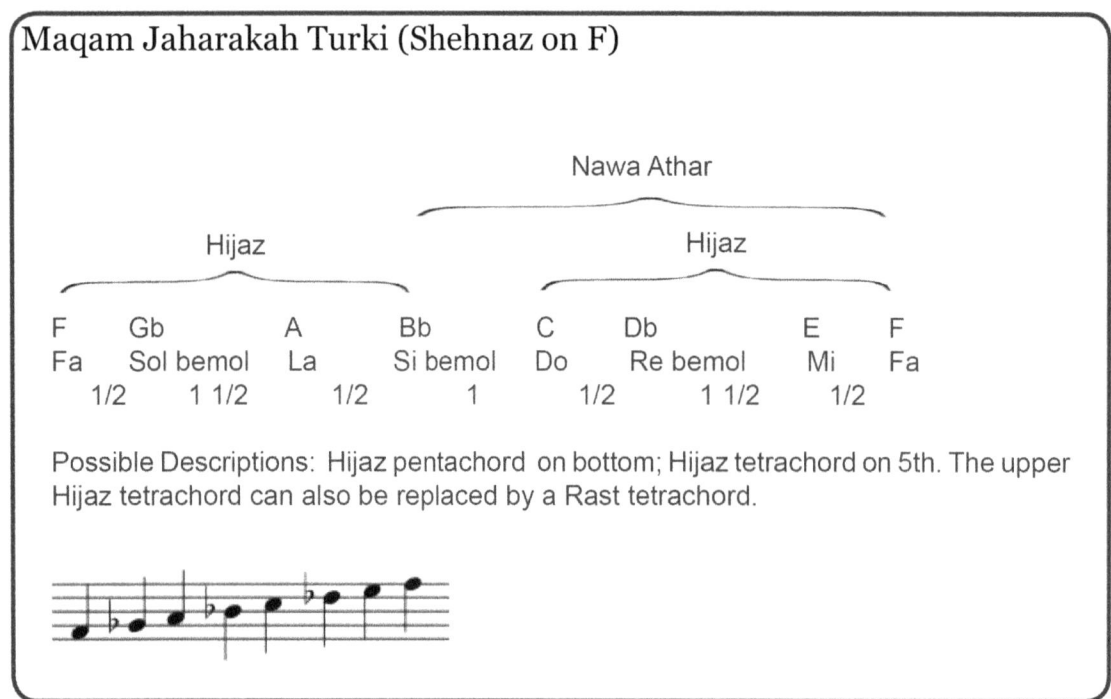

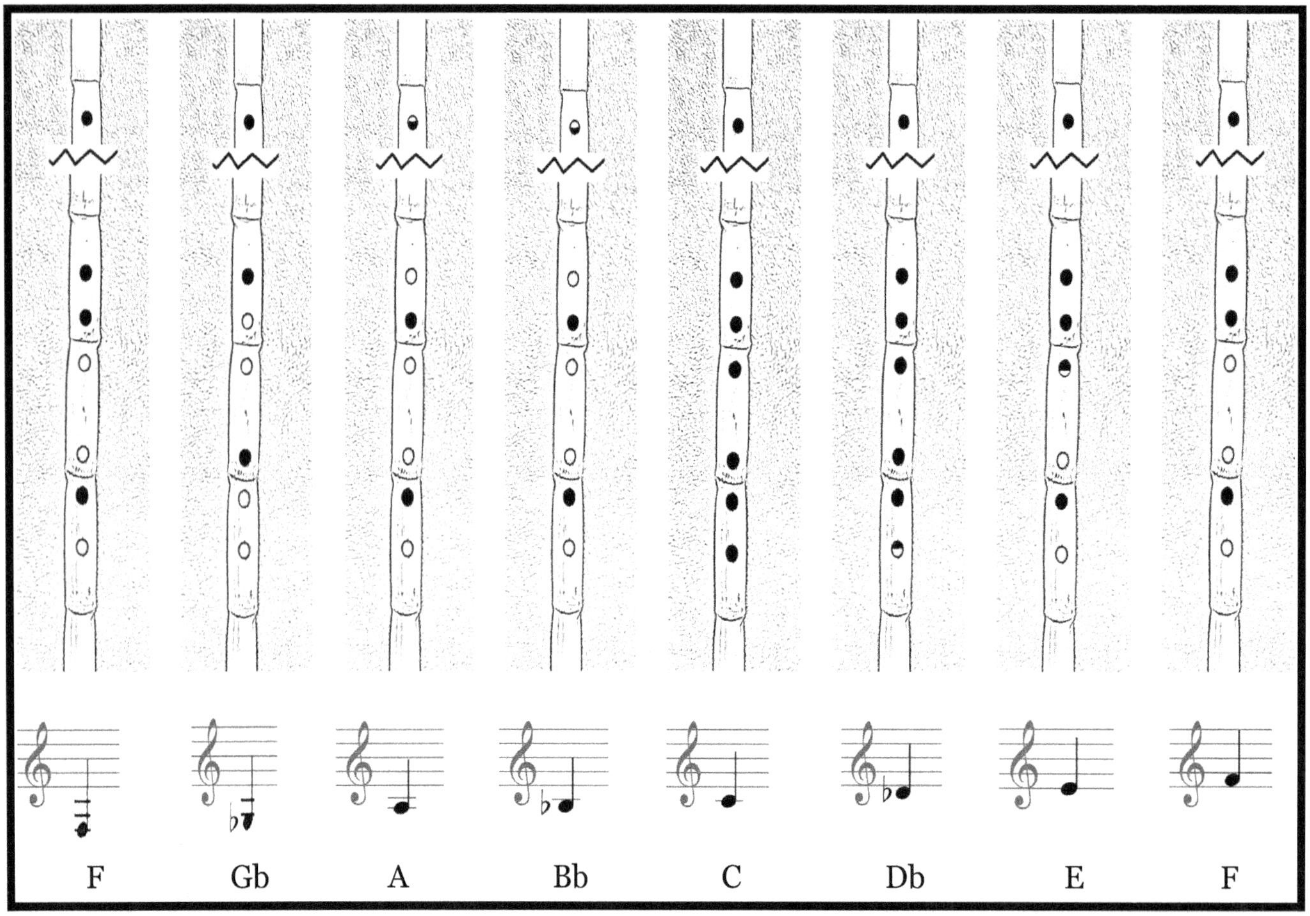

| F | Gb | A | Bb | C | Db | E | F |

Main Register: 117

F   Gb   A   Bb   C   Db   E   F

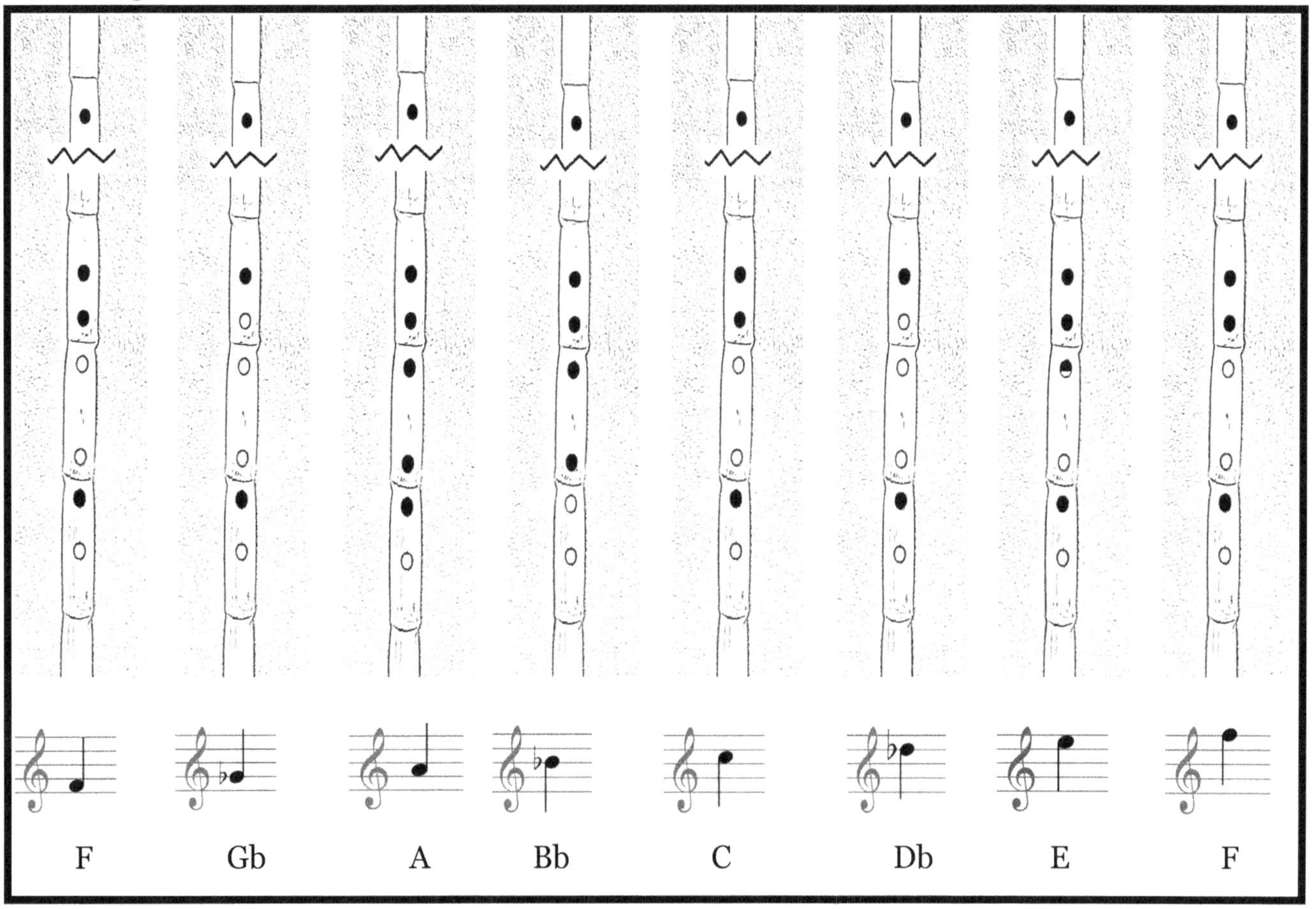

Second Register:

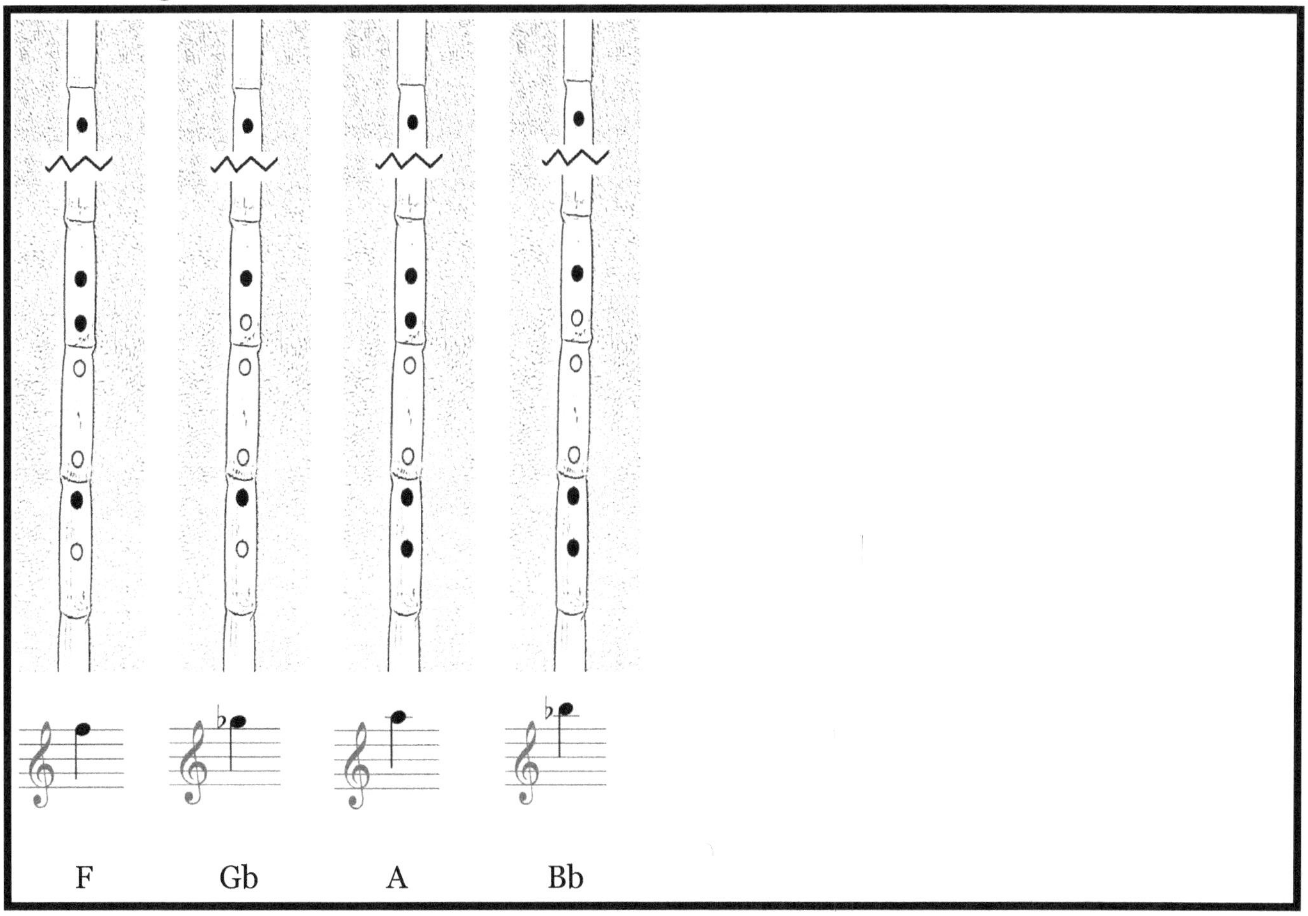

F   Gb   A   Bb

Doubled Low Notes - The Bridge

When the nay calls us to discover its secrets it is frequently that complex rich low sound which is like some kind of deep amplification of the human breath. If we were only interested in playing the notes we might have picked up a silver flute or something else. But the nay has its own unique voice. How can we bring this to life? It is not so easy. We try to play the lowest register as beginners and find it barely audible and weak. That is not what we were hoping for. So where do we discover that magical sound which seems like the cosmic voice of a whirling galaxy? It is hard to find words to describe that foggy throaty full and powerful low sound. When played, it makes the Nay sound other-worldly. Combined with a specific scale, or "maqam," called Saba, it is the most popular form of playing in the middle-east. Unfortunately, the "bridge" is just as difficult to play as it is to describe. This, of course, only to make us more ecstatic when we finally begin to find it!

The secret seems to be revealed when we discover that the nay can actually play and mix two octaves at once. The lowest notes refuse to come to life until they are invited into the octave above over what is called the "bridge." This seems to happen when we adjust the exact position of the edge of the tube across which we are gently blowing in a very microscopic way. There is a certain place on the edge of the mouth nipple across which your stream of air passes. X represents that spot. It can help to visualize this.

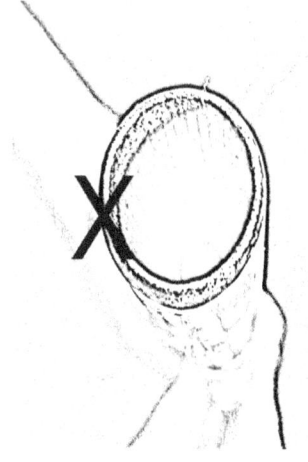

You will find that the middle octave comes to life most easily and that the instrument is somewhat forgiving with regard to how far to the right or the left your lips are placed. The instrument is a little bit forgiving also with regard to how much air you are producing and the highest register and the half register above that actually require a fairly forceful stream of air. But to bring that low register to life and mix it into the middle register is what produces that elusive magic. So experiment with reducing your air flow even more so that you are blowing ridiculously softly and then moving your lips microscopically to the left or the right until suddenly the two notes from the two registers begin to mix. Now you are entering the magic zone and it is so very delicate and subtle. The lowest notes remain the most difficult so it may be best to try this with something like the F# or the G. It is there somewhere and you will eventually find it. If you have more than one nay you can experiment as each has its own preferences.

Once you have achieved this magic you will feel very happy but also be disappointed to find that what you found on Monday refuse to manifest on Tuesday. It is a very subtle and delicate realm and the nay seems able to detect changes in your inner mood and sometimes just refuse if it doesn't like what you are emanating. Perhaps this is part of the reason for the instrument's reputation as some kind of spiritual vehicle.

But once you have begun to produce these mystical low sounds then you will discover that there are also some alternate fingering which enable some of these notes. This is especially true of the low notes between G and C: like the A and the Bb and B half-flat. Try them. It is even possible to use these alternative fingerings in the next higher register but with higher notes we are less likely to be seeking to make that magical mystical sound.

Alternative Low Note Fingerings Illustrated

| Standard Fingering | Alternative Fingering | Standard Fingering | Alternative Fingering |

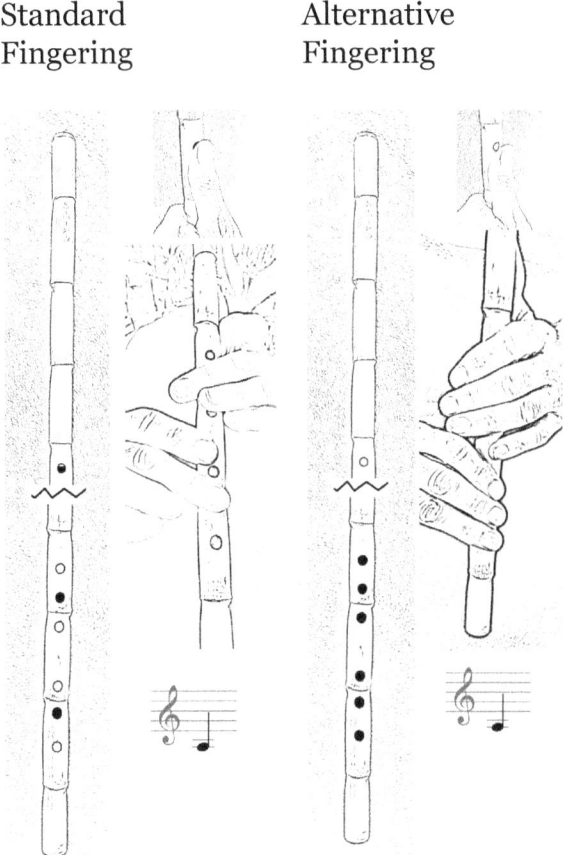

This fingering is the first one usually learned for the low A. It requires a very precise control of the thumb position.

This fingering requires the softest breath imaginable. Otherwise the pitch rises and becomes too sharp. But it can more easily enable the magic low sound.

This fingering is the first one usually learned for the low Bb. It requires a very precise control of the thumb position.

This fingering requires a very soft breath although not so extremely soft as for the A. But it can be used to easily enable the magic low sound.

Collection of Nays

This illustration shows the basic set of seven nays used by professional performers in the Middle East.
From left to right they are:

Bb or Ajam Nay
A or Husayni Nay
G or Nawa Nay
F or Jaharka Nay
E or Busalik Nay
D or Dukah Nay
C or Rast or Kirdan Nay

Also shown in this illustration are the Turkish Sufi Nay or "Kiz Ney" which is in B and the long Mansur Nay which is in a low A.

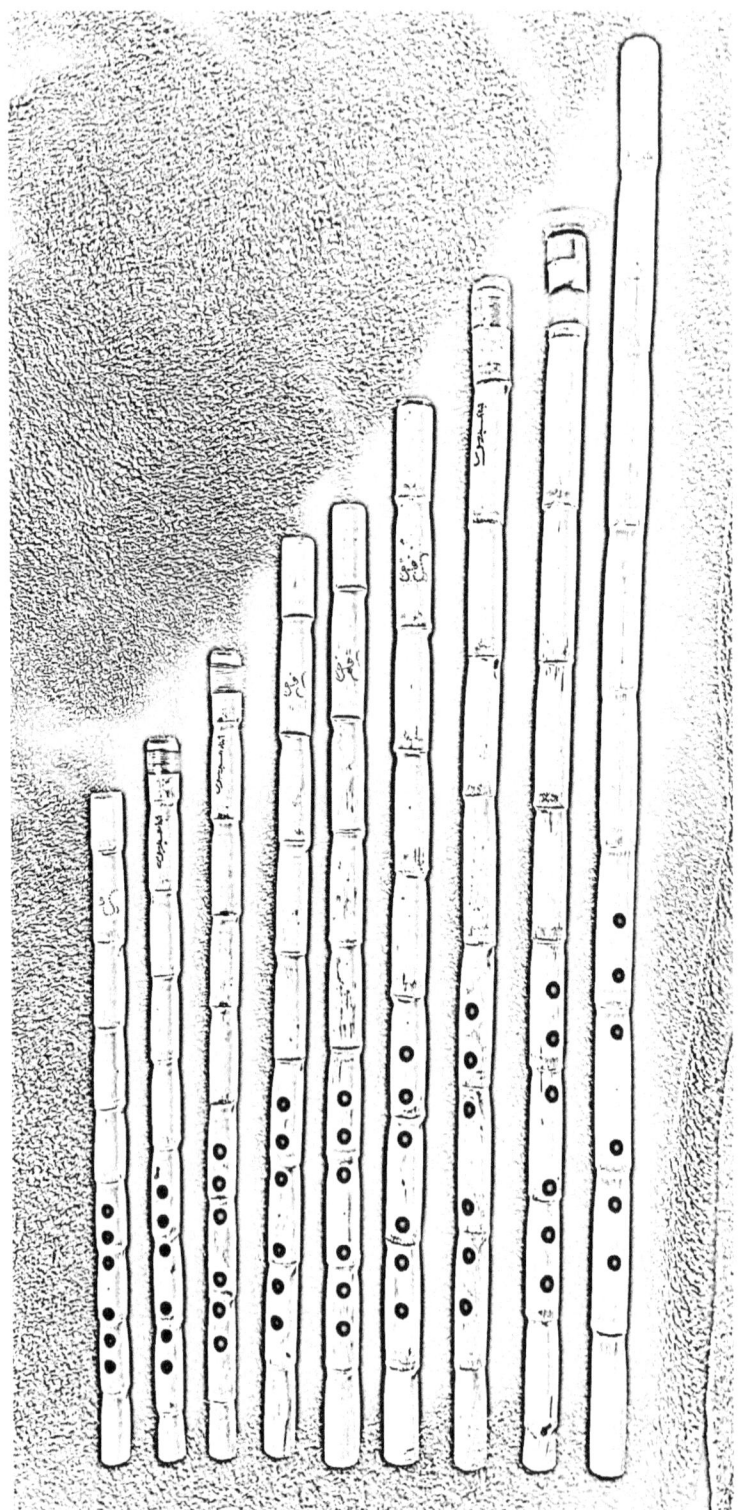

Curled Nays

There is a Nay maker in Cairo named Adil Fuad who personally manufactures great numbers of nays for professional players. He has created an amazing thing.

Shown in these illustrations are a Mansur nay in A and a long Nawa nay in G. They are entirely made from the same reeds as are straight nays. But Adil has managed to cut the reeds into little wedge-shaped sections and fasten them together with super glue and make short easy-to-reach-and-play nays which are tuned and work perfectly.

I have not seen products such as these from any other maker.

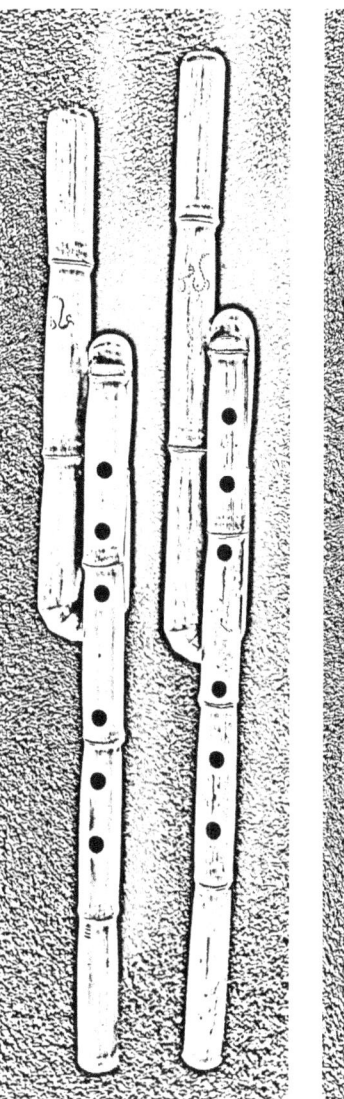
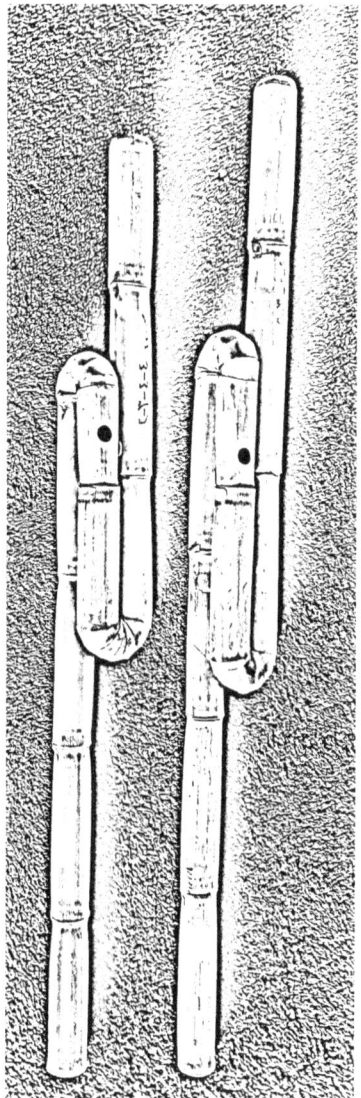

Nays in Different Keys

Turkish Sufi Kiz "B" Nay

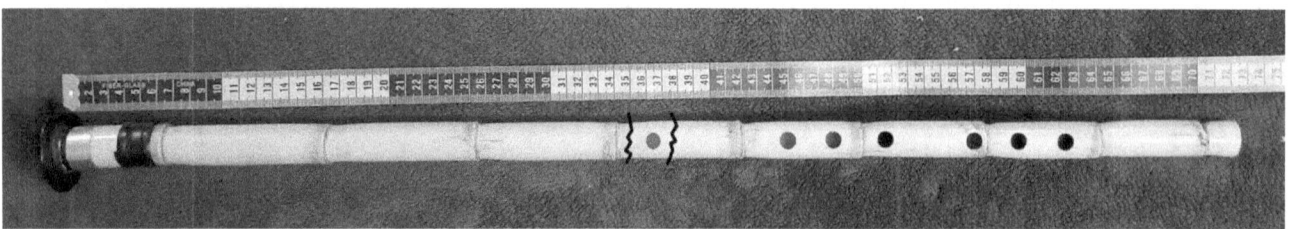

List of Maqams for Turkish Sufi Kiz "B" Nay

E Farahfaza (Nahawand 1)
E Sultani Yaka (Nahawand 2)
E Yakah (Yah-Gah or Rast Nawa)

F# Shawki Tarab (Kurd on A with Saba)
F# Busalik Ushayran (Bayati on A)
F# Bayati Ushayran (Bayatayn on A)
F# Hijazi Ushayran (Shuri on A)

G Ajam Ushayran
G Shawq Afza

Ghs Rahat al Arwah (Huzam)
Ghs Irak
Ghs Bastanikar

A Rast
A Suznak
A Dalanshin
A Nahawand 1
A Nahawand 2
A Nakriz
A Nawa Athar
A Athar Kurd
A Basandidah

B Bayati
B Husayni
B Saba
B Saba Zamzama
B Shuri
B Hijaz
B Hijaz Awji
B Shehnaz
B Kurd
B Shehnaz Kurdi

C Ajam

Chs Sikah
Chs Huzam
Chs Awshar

D Jaharka (Ajam)
D Jaharka Turki (Shehnaz)

Rast "C" Nay

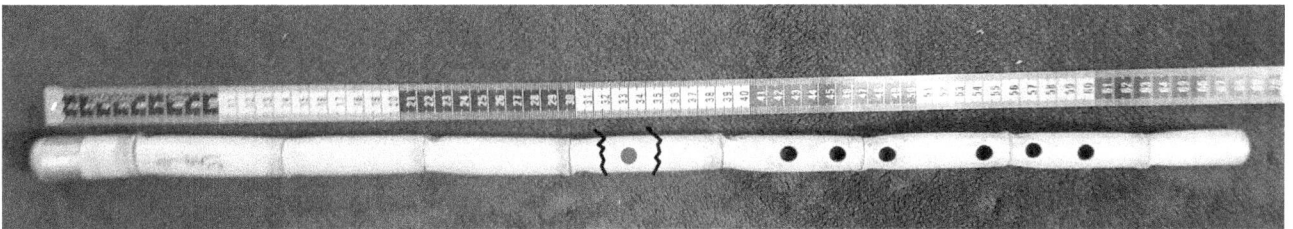

List of Maqams for Rast "C" Nay

F Farahfaza (Nahawand 1)
F Sultani Yaka (Nahawand 2)
F Yakah (Yah-Gah or Rast Nawa)

G Shawki Tarab (Kurd with Saba)
G Busalik Ushayran (Bayati)
G Bayati Ushayran (Bayatayn)
G Hijazi Ushayran (Shuri)

Ab Ajam Ushayran
Ab Shawq Afza

Ahf Rahat al Arwah (Huzam)
Ahf Irak
Ahf Bastanikar

Bb Rast
Bb Suznak
Bb Dalanshin
Bb Nahawand 1
Bb Nahawand 2
Bb Nakriz
Bb Nawa Athar
Bb Athar Kurd
Bb Basandidah

C Bayati
C Husayni
C Saba
C Saba Zamzama
C Shuri
C Hijaz
C Hijaz Awji
C Shehnaz
C Kurd
C Shehnaz Kurdi

Db Ajam

Dhf Sikah
Dhf Huzam
Dhf Awshar

Eb Jaharka (Ajam)
Eb Jaharka Turki (Shehnaz)

Dukah "D" Nay

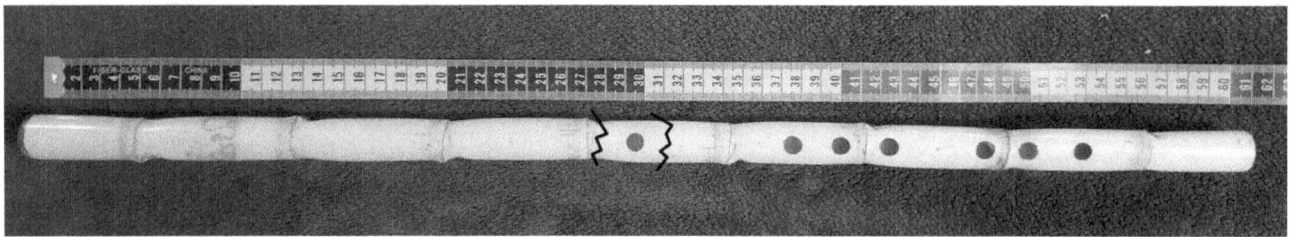

List of Maqams for Dukah "D" Nay

G Farahfaza (Nahawand 1)
G Sultani Yaka (Nahawand 2)
G Yakah (Yah-Gah or Rast Nawa)

A Shawki Tarab (Kurd with Saba)
A Busalik Ushayran (Bayati)
A Bayati Ushayran (Bayatayn)
A Hijazi Ushayran (Shuri)

Bb Ajam Ushayran
Bb Shawq Afza

Bhf Rahat al Arwah (Huzam)
Bhf Irak
Bhf Bastanikar

C Rast
C Suznak
C Dalanshin
C Nahawand 1
C Nahawand 2
C Nakriz
C Nawa Athar
C Athar Kurd
C Basandidah

D Bayati
D Husayni
D Saba
D Saba Zamzama
D Shuri
D Hijaz
D Hijaz Awji
D Shehnaz
D Kurd
D Shehnaz Kurdi

Eb Ajam

Ehf Sikah
Ehf Huzam
Ehf Awshar

F Jaharka (Ajam)
F Jaharka Turki (Shehnaz)

Busalik "E" Nay

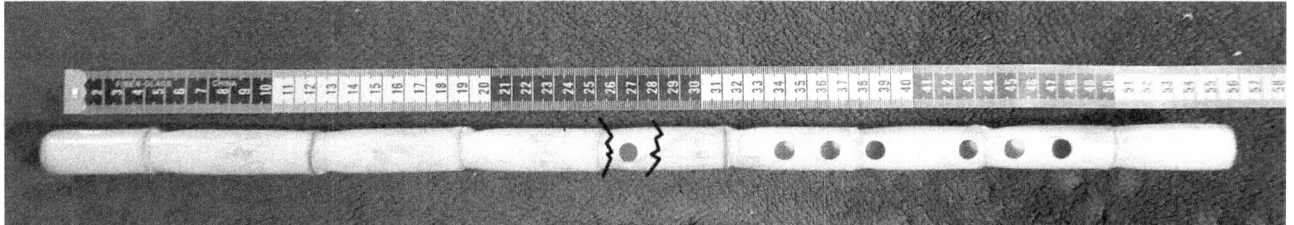

List of Maqams for Busalik "E" Nay

A Farahfaza (Nahawand 1)
A Sultani Yaka (Nahawand 2)
A Yakah (Yah-Gah or Rast Nawa)

B Shawki Tarab (Kurd with Saba)
B Busalik Ushayran (Bayati)
B Bayati Ushayran (Bayatayn)
B Hijazi Ushayran (Shuri)

C Ajam Ushayran
C Shawq Afza

Chs Rahat al Arwah (Huzam)
Chs Irak
Chs Bastanikar

D Rast
D Suznak
D Dalanshin
D Nahawand 1
D Nahawand 2
D Nakriz
D Nawa Athar
D Athar Kurd
D Basandidah

E Bayati
E Husayni
E Saba
E Saba Zamzama
E Shuri
E Hijaz
E Hijaz Awji
E Shehnaz
E Kurd
E Shehnaz Kurdi

F Ajam

Fhs Sikah
Fhs Huzam
Fhs Awshar

G Jaharka (Ajam)
G Jaharka Turki (Shehnaz)

Jaharka "F" Nay

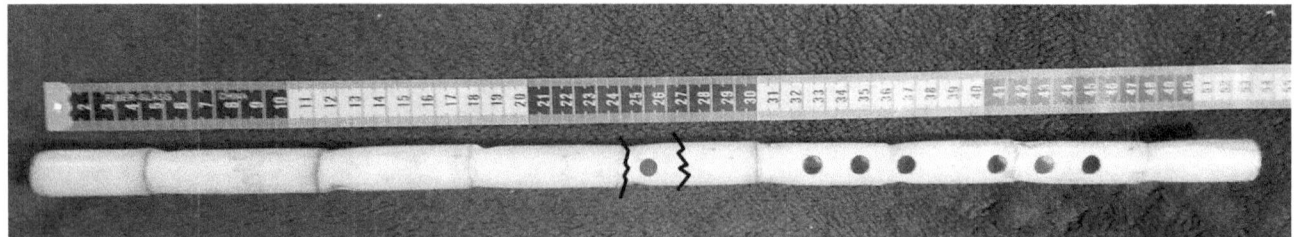

List of Maqams for Jaharka "F" Nay

Bb Farahfaza (Nahawand 1)
Bb Sultani Yaka (Nahawand 2)
Bb Yakah (Yah-Gah or Rast Nawa)

C Shawki Tarab (Kurd with Saba)
C Busalik Ushayran (Bayati)
C Bayati Ushayran (Bayatayn)
C Hijazi Ushayran (Shuri)

C# Ajam Ushayran
C# Shawq Afza

Dhf Rahat al Arwah (Huzam)
Dhf Irak
Dhf Bastanikar

Eb Rast
Eb Suznak
Eb Dalanshin
Eb Nahawand 1
Eb Nahawand 2
Eb Nakriz
Eb Nawa Athar
Eb Athar Kurd
Eb Basandidah

F Bayati
F Husayni
F Saba
F Saba Zamzama
F Shuri
F Hijaz
F Hijaz Awji
F Shehnaz
F Kurd
F Shehnaz Kurdi

Gb Ajam

Ghf Sikah
Ghf Huzam
Ghf Awshar

Ab Jaharka (Ajam)
Ab Jaharka Turki (Shehnaz)

Nawa "G" Nay

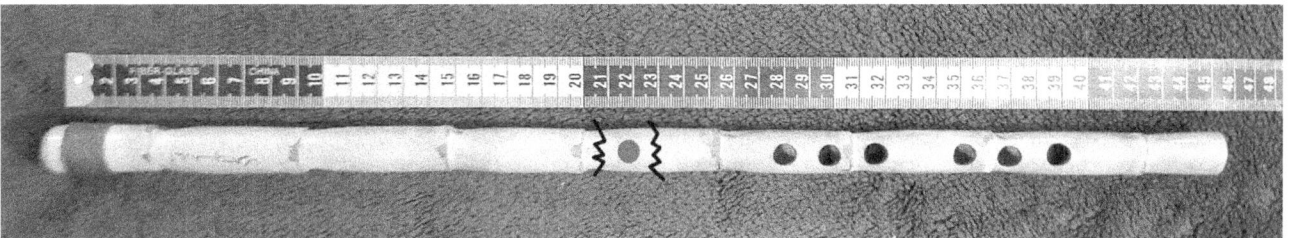

List of Maqams for Nawa "G" Nay

C Farahfaza (Nahawand 1)
C Sultani Yaka (Nahawand 2)
C Yakah (Yah-Gah or Rast Nawa)

D Shawki Tarab (Kurd with Saba)
D Busalik Ushayran (Bayati)
D Bayati Ushayran (Bayatayn)
D Hijazi Ushayran (Shuri)

Eb Ajam Ushayran
Eb Shawq Afza

Ehf Rahat al Arwah (Huzam)
Ehf Irak
Ehf Bastanikar

F Rast
F Suznak
F Dalanshin
F Nahawand 1
F Nahawand 2
F Nakriz
F Nawa Athar
F Athar Kurd
F Basandidah

G Bayati
G Husayni
G Saba
G Saba Zamzama
G Shuri
G Hijaz
G Hijaz Awji
G Shehnaz
G Kurd
G Shehnaz Kurdi

Ab Ajam

Ahf Sikah
Ahf Huzam
Ahf Awshar

Bb Jaharka (Ajam)
Bb Jaharka Turki (Shehnaz)

Huseyni "A" Nay

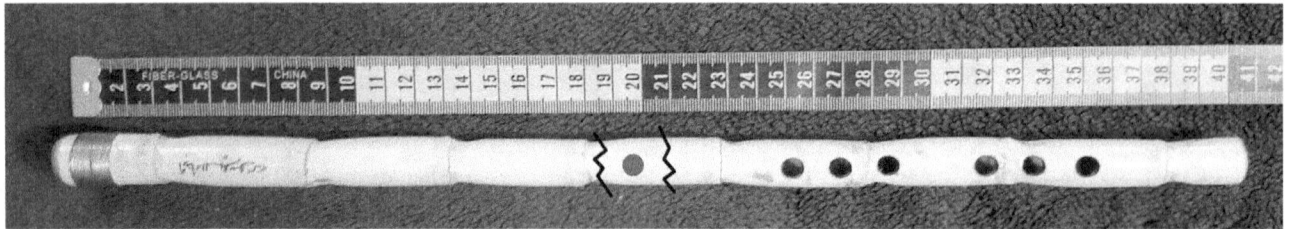

List of Maqams for Huseyni "A" Nay

D Farahfaza (Nahawand 1)
D Sultani Yaka (Nahawand 2)
D Yakah (Yah-Gah or Rast Nawa)

E Shawki Tarab (Kurd with Saba)
E Busalik Ushayran (Bayati)
E Bayati Ushayran (Bayatayn)
E Hijazi Ushayran (Shuri)

F Ajam Ushayran
F Shawq Afza

Fhs Rahat al Arwah (Huzam)
Fhs Irak
Fhs Bastanikar

G Rast
G Suznak
G Dalanshin
G Nahawand 1
G Nahawand 2
G Nakriz
G Nawa Athar
G Athar Kurd
G Basandidah

A Bayati
A Husayni
A Saba
A Saba Zamzama
A Shuri
A Hijaz
A Hijaz Awji
A Shehnaz
A Kurd
A Shehnaz Kurdi

Bb Ajam

Bhf Sikah
Bhf Huzam
Bhf Awshar

C Jaharka (Ajam)
C Jaharka Turki (Shehnaz)

Ajam "Bb" Nay

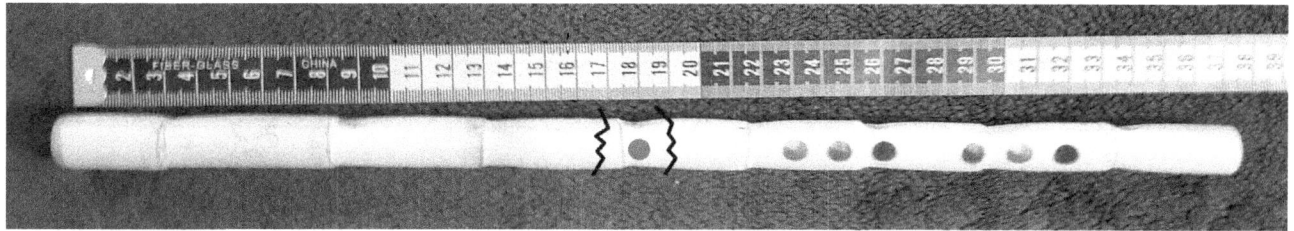

List of Maqams for Ajam "Bb" Nay

Eb Farahfaza (Nahawand 1)
Eb Sultani Yaka (Nahawand 2)
Eb Yakah (Yah-Gah or Rast Nawa)

F Shawki Tarab (Kurd with Saba)
F Busalik Ushayran (Bayati)
F Bayati Ushayran (Bayatayn)
F Hijazi Ushayran (Shuri)

Gb Ajam Ushayran
Gb Shawq Afza

Ghf Rahat al Arwah (Huzam)
Ghf Irak
Ghf Bastanikar

Ab Rast
Ab Suznak
Ab Dalanshin
Ab Nahawand 1
Ab Nahawand 2
Ab Nakriz
Ab Nawa Athar
Ab Athar Kurd
Ab Basandidah

Bb Bayati
Bb Husayni
Bb Saba
Bb Saba Zamzama
Bb Shuri
Bb Hijaz
Bb Hijaz Awji
Bb Shehnaz
Bb Kurd
Bb Shehnaz Kurdi

B Ajam

Chf Sikah
Chf Huzam
Chf Awshar

Db Jaharka (Ajam)
Db Jaharka Turki (Shehnaz)

Nay Construction

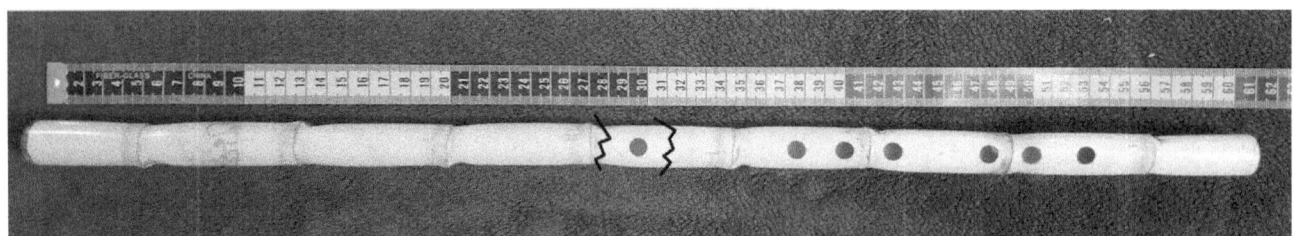

As you can see from the measuring tape laid beside the Dukah nay pictured above, there is a very specific formula applied when these instruments are made and the finger holes drilled.

Comparisons with the overall lengths and hole placements shown in the preceding section shows the repeated scaling of the same basic formula from the lower-keyed nays on up.

During one of my visits to Cairo, Dr Qadri Sourour, who teaches nay at the Arabic Music School on the Nile Island of Zamalek and who is also a world-class performer, was kind enough to make me a nay from scratch and allow me to take notes and photos so that the world could learn these construction secrets.

Clean inside of reed so air can enter cut and dry until brown. This may take several months.
You should start by first cleaning the outside of the cane carefully using fine sandpaper. Count 9 sections and decide on the key for this piece of reed. Then, with a long drill the same diameter as the interior of the cane, remove all of the membranous disks around the nodes that could obstruct the air channel except for the disk at the mouth hole or "nipple" end.

Then clean inside the nipple end and drill a small .5 CM diameter hole through the end segment disk to create the "khazna" or "bughaz" (as it's called in Turkish.) This creates a "passage" or "vault" or "reservoir" which keeps air from passing through too rapidly. The thin ring of reed node left sticking to the inner surface of the tube will vibrate when the musician blows into it.

Cut off the nipple end 4.5 to 5 CM from the first joint.

Shape this node both outside and inside to create a beveled outside edge using a knife and file and sandpaper.

Mark a straight line on one side of the reed for holes.

For Dukah nay measure from nipple end to last hole 52.5 to 53.5 cm (shorter for fat reeds.)

> For Turkish "kiz" B nay measure 62.5 CM;
> For Rast C nay: 60 CM;
> For Busalik E nay: 47.5 CM;
> For Jaharka F nay: 45 CM;
> For Nawa G nay: 39 CM;
> For Huseyni A nay: 35.5 CM;
> For Ajam Bb nay: 32 CM.

Measure 6 - 2.2 CM intervals back from the 53 CM mark for other five holes skipping one in the middle which will be used to measure distance X1.

Create same distance in other direction and call it X2.

Mark bottom end at X2 and cut off and file and sand.

Drill or burn 6 holes at marked 2.2 CM intervals. Skilled nay makers might make slight adjustments in these hole positions to avoid drilling right through a node or for other reasons.

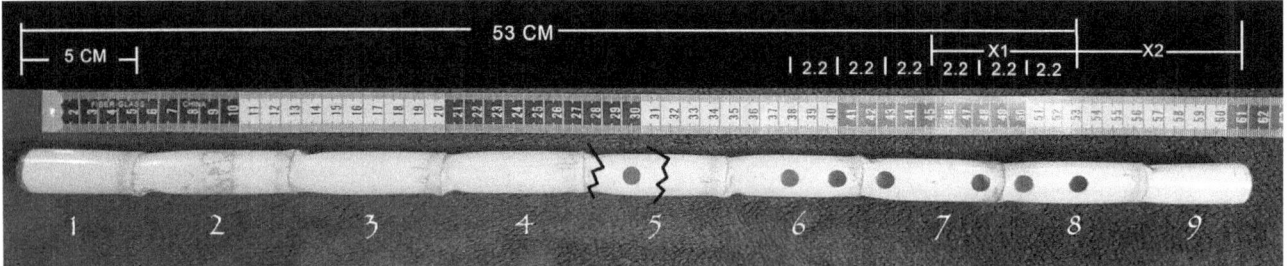

If you do not have an appropriate tool to make the holes, you can use a metal rod heated at one end. Here Qadri is using one of the special drilling tools shown in the next picture.

Since the ratio of the finger hole diameters relative to the interior diameter of the tube should be about .25 to 1, Qadri has drilling tools of different sizes for making the finger holes.

Use a file to smooth edges of finger hole openings.

Open the seventh or thumb hole on the back side of the nay at halfway along the whole length. Arabs like to open it a little closer to the nipple end so that when only the thumb hole is closed a low B half-flat is produced. Turks like it a little closer to bottom end so it is not B half flat but closer to B. First we mark the spot.

Then we drill it.

Use long rat tail file to make sure all joints except for the "khazna" at the nipple end are wide open.

You may then oil the finished nay. Walnut oil is good.

Some makers will wind the nipple end with wire or thread to retard cracking but this is really more just for decoration.

Where Everything is Music
We have fallen into the place
where everything is music.

The strumming and the flute notes
rise into the atmosphere,
and if the whole world's harp
should burn up,
there will still be hidden instruments
playing, playing

This singing art
is sea foam.
The graceful movements
come from a pearl
somewhere
on the ocean floor.

Poems reach up like spindrift
and the edge of driftwood
along the beach
wanting, wanting

They derive from a slow
and powerful root
that we cannot see.

Stop the words now.
Open the window
in the center of your chest,
and let the spirits fly
in and out!
-- Jalāl al-Dīn Rūmī (Jalalu'ddin Rumi, Maulana), 13th century Persian poet, founder of Mevlevi order / Whirling Dervishes of Sufi tradition. Translation by Coleman Barks.

Glossary of Terms

Ajnas (singular: jins)
: Arabic word meaning "basic maqam building blocks" or sequences of notes. Translated as "tetrachords" or "trichords" or "pentachords."

Amal
: Arabic word meaning "the work." The creative process brought by a musician to building a musical improvisation.

Bemol
: French word imported into modern Arabic: "flat."

Diaz or Diese
: French word imported into modern Arabic: "sharp."

Dulab
: An introductory musical melody which is specific to a particular maqam.

Ghammaz (has two meanings in music)
: Arabic word literally meaning "the wink of an eye."
: This term is used to label delicate musical decorations.
: Also means the 2nd most prominent note in a maqam: usually the 5th but sometimes the 4th or 3rd note.

Half-flat
: A note played somewhere between the pitch of the "natural," above, and the "flat," below.

Half-sharp
: A note played somewhere between the pitch of the "sharp," above, and the "natural," below.

Interval
: Musicians frequently talk about intervals such as "5ths," meaning the 5th note in the scale. More strictly speaking, "harmonic intervals" are based on dividing musical intervals such as a whole octave into equal parts. A "harmonic 5th," for example, results from just such a division. However, since specific notes in a scale don't always fall on pitches defined by strict harmonic theory, the student should be aware that terms like the "2nd," "3rd," "4th," etc, can simply refer to the number of a note in a particular scale. When intervals are used to describe pitch differences less than a whole step, terms such as "half-step," "three-quarter-step," "quarter-step" or "quarter-tone" arise.

Jins
: A building block of 3 or 4 or 5 notes which can be assembled with other Ajnas (Jins plural) to create a maqam. The lower jins may be called al-jusa and the upper jins may be called al-fara. Commonly translated as Tetrachord (or Trichord or Pentachord). The plural of Jins is Ajnas.

Koma
: An interval defined in Pythagorian musical theory but commonly used in Turkish maqam teaching literature to mean an increment of pitch equal to one-ninth of a whole step. Very precise pitch descriptions can be made using this term.

Mabda
: Usual starting note of a maqam.

Maqam
: An Arabic or Turkish musical scale or mode. In older traditions, learning to perform and improvise in a particular maqam meant learning a whole world of standardized embellishments and phrases, beginnings and endings which are specific to a given maqam. Given the depth of each maqam, very few artists could manage to master more than a few in one lifetime. Specific emotions are typically associated with each maqam. English plural: "maqams." Arabic plural: "maqamat." Turkish spelling: "makam" and "makamlar" (plural).
: Maqam names frequently reflect geographic locations and towns and landscapes, tribal identities or scalar note positions from Maqam Rast or other Arabic music note names.

Markaz
: A note which can be a resting place in the middle of a maqam.

Modulate
: To change from on maqam to another. Sometimes the tonic, or "home base" note, remains the same during modulations and sometimes it changes.

Nuss Bemol
: Half flat.

Nuss Diese
: Half sharp.

Penta-chord
: A sequence of 5 notes which form a building block or "jins" in a maqam.

Qafla
: A traditional ending musical flourish for a particular maqam.

Qarar
: Tonic note or Home Key of a maqam.

Quartertone
: Pitches approximately halfway between the equal-tempered notes. Equal tempered notes are all defined by either "whole-step" or "half-step" intervals. "Three-quarter-step" intervals create what we are calling "quartertones."

Reboton
: Half flat.

Shakhsiyyah
: A traditional opening musical flourish for a particular maqam.

Sikah
: Half flat. This term, although becoming common, is based on the Arabic note name for E half-flat. It is now becoming common to use it to refer to any half-flat. "Si sikah," for example, can refer to "B half-flat."

Solfege
: European syllables, Do Re Mi Fa Sol La Si, used to name notes in a scale. Unlike note names A B C D E F G, Do is portable and can be assigned to be the tonic of a scale at any absolute pitch. The note names in Indian music, Sa Re Ga Ma Pa Da Ni are roughly equivalent to Solfege syllables.

Taqasim
: Improvisation performed in Arabic music. Turkish spelling: "taksim" or "taxim."

Tetra-chord
: A sequence of 4 notes which form a building block or "jins" in a maqam. The term "tetra-chord" is used generically to refer to any sequence of 3, 4 or 5 notes.

Tonic
: The "home base" note of a maqam or scale.

Transpose
: To move the "tonic" of a scale from one pitch to another. This can be done to accomodate the range of a singer's voice, in which case the whole framework of maqamat becomes portable. Or it can be done by designating a new "tonic" for a particular maqam so that it can interplay with other maqamat in pleasing ways.

Tri-chord
: A sequence of 3 notes which form a building block or "jins" in a maqam.

Equal-tempered
: The scale which has become familiar in Europe and the Western world: 12 notes composed of equal "half-steps" which make up an octave.

Zaghrafa
: Musical ornamentations or decorations.

Zahir
: Leading tone of a maqam. Usually a step below the Qarar.

Acknowledgments

I have been personally shown the nay secrets or simply inspired by Omar Faruk Tekbilek, Qadri Sourour, Scott Marcus, Bassam Saba, AJ Racy and Fadi Aziz. Thank you!

I would also like to acknowledge the many teachers who have helped me with maqam study. They include Haig Manoukian, George Lammam, Simon Shaheen, Nabil Azzam, Joe Zeytoonian, Naser Musa, Rachid Halihal, Chakib Hilali as well as many others who have taken the time to hang out with me in the music stores, music schools and personal homes in Cairo, Aleppo, Amman and many other places in the Arab world. Ibrahim Sukar in Aleppo and Qadri Sourour on Zamalek and Naser on Mohammad Ali Street in Cairo are among these.

Very special acknowledgment must go to Scott Marcus. His doctoral dissertation, "Arab Music Theory in the Modern Period" is a treasure of detailed information. The Arabic note name tables are also from his work.

Jesse Manno, James Hoskins, Pete Jacobs, Scott Bears and Korey Wylie, dear musician friends in Colorado, have shared in the fascination of maqam study and helped shape this book.

I would like to invite my teachers, as well as other teachers and students, to make corrections and additions to this work.

Maqamat vary from region to region. The ones in this book are reflective of what is popular in Egypt, Jordan, Palestine, Syria and Lebanon. I have not attempted to focus on the Iraqi maqam system nor on Turkish makamlar.

Very special thanks go to Jihad Ibrahim from Amman, Jordan, Saadoun Al Bayati from Baghdad, Iraq, and Atef Abd elHameed from Cairo, Egypt, for offering me the opportunities to record their oud playing and present them as part of the teaching materials which accompany my Harmonic Secrets of Arabic Music book.

Many Thanks to Eva Soltes for gifting me a Residency at Harrison House in Joshua Tree, CA, for time and space for recording and mixing.

Cameron Powers
cameron@rmi.net

> *Rumi is not so interested in language, more attuned to the sources of it. As such, he has great appreciation for silence and emptiness. According to Rumi, language and music are possible only because we are empty, hollow, and separate from the source.*
> *The Reed Flute's Song ends with a reference to silence. The reed flute was also Rumi's favorite musical instrument and he has a whole theory of language based on the reed flute.*
>
> *In the heart is a flute*
> *Which plays the melody of longing.*
> *-Rumi*

Cameron Powers -- Biography

Cameron grew up with Mississippi River Blues Beginnings as a 14-year-old electric guitar-playing band member in St Louis, Missouri... Cameron was there on the dance floor while Ike and Tina Turner were presenting their first scorching hot music in the Chuck Berry friendly ecstasy of alcoholic rural party-times in the Afro-American dominated youth scene... Then on to the Tear-Soaked musical majesties of the Peruvian Andes... To the Time-stopping hesitation Black Hole musical mysteries of Athens, Greece... To the Divine Feminine Eternal Worship Dance in the Telepathically-Jeweled Musical Venues of Cairo, Amman and Damascus... To 70,000 miles of Touring the Amalgam Mix of the Cauldron called the USA... An amazing wild ride of a lifetime spent playing for people to dance!

Fascination with Peruvian Indian peoples encountered on mountaineering expeditions led Cameron to spend 8 years going to and from Andean villages back in the 1960's and 70's. He immediately discovered the value of learning to play their music with them as an easy aid to bonding in trust and friendship.

Cameron graduated with BA in Anthropology and Linguistics, University of Colorado, Boulder, with an emphasis on the study of Quechua, the language of the Incas.

Cameron also received a fellowship to attend a two-month intensive immersion program in Quechua at Cornell University. It was there that he began to realize the value of being a musician as well as a linguist.

Cameron also received a scholarship to work on a Doctoral program in Linguistics at the University of California, Berkeley. He continued to study the Inca language and began studies of the Tibetan language.

In 1973 Cameron lived in Greece with the Papanastassiou family and studied Greek language and Greek music.

Returning to Boulder, Colorado, Cameron performed Greek music and began the study of Arabic music with various local bands: "The Silk Route," "The Boulder Bouzouki Band," "Solspice," and "Sherefe."

He created Musical Instruments, built Houses, and helped produce a Spanish Language Teaching Program in Boulder while raising his children.

Cameron has a long association with Middle Eastern Music Camp which takes place every summer in Mendocino, California.

After the events in New York on 9/11, a pall was cast on his role as an American musician playing Middle Eastern Music. "Terrorism" had somehow entered the music. Gigs were canceled; people became nervous about producing Middle Eastern Music-oriented shows.

Knowing full well from his travels in the Middle East and from his extensive chain of friendships with Middle Eastern musicians that there is a warm reception available to anyone, including Americans, who wish to travel the Middle East, he realized the importance of continuing his "musical missions."

Now back from additional travels in Iraq, Egypt, Jordan, Lebanon, Syria and Palestine, he is working to help American people understand the Arab psyche. Cameron's wife, Kristina Sophia, has been a big part of all this work. Her beautiful singing voice, percussion skills and endless cheerful companionship both at home and on the road have helped make this creativity fun and possible.

The 501c3 non-profit organization, Musical Missions of Peace, now better known as "Musical Ambassadors of Peace," has been built around his and Kristina's international work. Through the Musical Ambassador programs founded by Musical Missions of Peace help has been provided to other American musicians who have traveled and performed in Iran, Iraqi Kurdistan and Indonesia. Through the Iraqi Refugee program support has also been provided for Iraqi refugee musicians in Syria to facilitate the teaching of traditional Iraqi music to young Iraqi children.

Musical Fun by the Red Sea in Aqaba, Jordan

Other Books and CD's by Cameron Powers

Harmonic Secrets of Arabic Music Scales
Fine Tuning the Maqams – With 2 Audio CDs

Play Modern Music with Ancient Tunings

If you are in love with a Middle Eastern sounding music scale and want to learn Arabic music and related Indian music scales, you need genuine Middle Eastern music theory which is Arabic music theory.

How to write Middle Eastern music? It involves using Eastern modes, Middle East instruments, and genuine Arabic music scales.

When I was only 5 years old I listened to the piano and I could tell there was something wrong: it should sound good but for some reason it didn't. They all thought it was in tune but I could tell that it wasn't... quite right...

When I was 14 I bought my first guitar. I could tell that it never sounded quite in tune. I tried to hear it as in tune but really... it wasn't quite right...

When I was 35 I bought the ancient grandfather of the guitar, a fretless Egyptian oud. Eventually, with practice, I learned to make it sound really good! Really in tune! And I learned so many beautiful ancient Egyptian scales!

Eventually I noticed: every time I changed to a different key, not only did the first note in the scale change but all the other notes did too!

Then I realized why the piano and the guitar had never sounded right. They were tuned in equal temperament!

But with modern electronic keyboard tuning technologies and with slinky strings on my guitar all that has changed. Now I can play perfectly harmonious ecstatic music on lots of instruments. What a difference!

Secrets of Magical Music Explained in Detail! What are the harmonic secrets of Egyptian Music? Whatever your instrument... Whatever your skills... Whatever your singing style...

You can put this information to use and become the musician or performer you really want to be!

You will be able to rock the world with this knowledge!

In addition to full disclosure of the ancient secrets of perfect harmony, more than eighty ancient scales are taught.

This is enough material for lifetimes of musical creativity!

Secrets derived from Indian, Persian, Chinese and other ancient music traditions prove to be exactly the same!

Don't miss out on this opportunity to leap beyond the limitations of current Western musical songwriting and composition!

Arabic Musical Scales
Basic Maqam Teachings - With 2 Audio CDs

Enter the Exotic World of Quartertone Scales
Designed for both the beginner and the professional musician, Arabic Musical Scales is the ultimate guide to 45 of the most popular Maqams

"Excellent book. I would highly recommend the CDs that are sold separately as well. They are very well done. Very informational and also have improvised demonstrations of the scales so you can hear each scale in a musical setting."

"All I have to say is 'WOW'!

You just put together what I was looking for, a concise yet comprehensive material for someone like me to study and get on with my ultimate passion, Arabic music!"

"I bought your CDs and book of basic maqam techniques. It was a wonderful surprise... it put everything I was looking for in my hands with no effort!"

"Your book on Middle Eastern scales has been invaluable to me. I lead a Middle Eastern musical ensemble but I'm the only Arab in the group, so your book has been the standard by which I teach my musicians. It really is a great book."

Maqam Practice Tracks
Perfect Harmony of Just Intonation

** Beyond Quartertones **

We return to the true ancient roots of Perfect Harmony; 21 Different Arabic Music Modes; Available on 6 CD's; Additional Track Included: Modulation Practice; A total of 22 Tracks: Six Hours of Practice Material

Arabic Musical Scales and most other maqam teaching systems rely on the "quartertone" concept for determining pitches of notes in various maqam intervals.

These teachings are a great start, but quartertones do not take us to the heart of the matter.

We must return to the laws of physics which determine the harmonic roots of all ancient indigenous music systems...

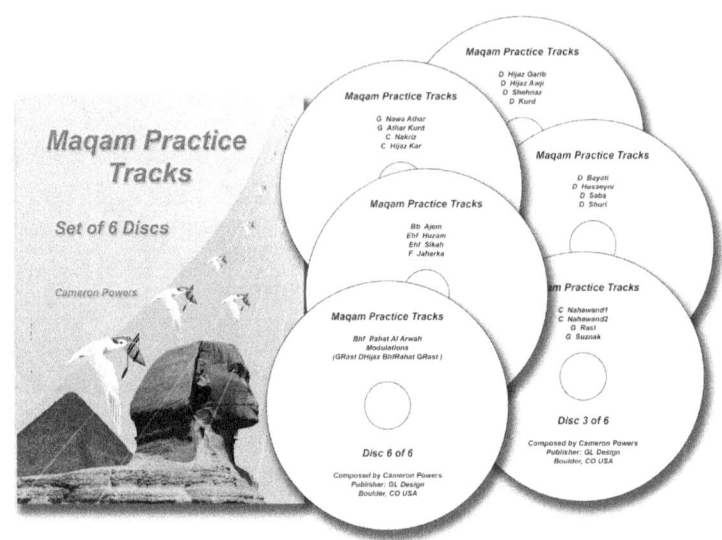

These musical laws of harmony are called "just intonation."

If you already purchased one of my books:

Arabic Musical Scales

or

Harmonic Secrets of Arabic Music

...or if you have approached from some other direction and are learning to play Arabic music with its fascinating and beautiful maqam system, then you are already trying to find the musical intervals on your instrument or with your voice...

I have designed this series of 15 minute tracks to try and help you...

Each Practice Track Moves Slowly Through Musical Phrases — Sometimes with Rhythm and Sometimes without — So the Student has Plenty of Time to Practice by Playing Along with any Instrument of Choice — Great for Singers Too —

Each Track is Actually 15 Minutes Long!

Arab Musicians Insist on These Intriguing Musical Facts:

"I've identified at least 12 notes between my lowest e-flat and my highest e-natural."

– Sami Shumays, Arab Violinist

In order to play the microtonal pitches accurately we must learn to hear and produce the justly intonated pitches. That is what these teachings are about.

Soulscapes
Sacred Meditation Music in absolutely perfect harmony!

These vibrational soundfields are unique!

They literally vibrate your energy fields into place!

Even those who have spent years working with other popular meditation soundfields are switching to Soulscapes after trying them out!

Perfectly Tuned Music Intervals!

These cd's contain something never before produced: ancient music scales from Egypt in mathematically perfect harmony created with modern technology which allows perfection!

The intervals between the cello, dulcimer and vocal notes which you will hear on these cd's can work a magical alignment in your being because the vibrational laws of physics are in action.

The wavelengths of the different notes actually nest together! They amplify and reinforce each other according to the physical principles of "just intonation."

Just intonation creates the same harmonies which are found in the sacred traditional musics of Egypt, Mesopotamia, and India!

These compositions not only use modern electronica to create perfect harmony, but are the artistic product of the composer's forty years of immersion in sacred music traditions in Peru, Egypt, Mesopotamia and Greece!

The listener can enter the deepest kind of meditation and become one with a resonant field of vibrational perfection. This has literally never before been possible and can lead the meditating listener into a place of effortless surrender to what is. There is infinite potential for the power of a perfectly harmonious vibrational reality to dissolve our word-based thinking and allow us to enter an enlightened place wherein there is no judgment.

The adventurous meditator can literally disappear into the sound fields contained in this series of 5 cd's. And the fact that the perfectly harmonious musical scales presented are primarily from the Egyptian tradition gives access to another fountain of traditional ancient wisdom.

Some say that the perfection of these harmonies resonates within the stored memories in our DNA!

To find out more information on this set of CD's go to:
https://www.sacredmeditationmusic.com/

Love Without Borders
From Inca Lands to Iraqi Sands

"Whatever you do, don't go there!" When some hear that admonition they don't go. Others might be enticed but enter only with weaponry and caution. But it can also serve as a siren call to simply brace oneself for a lot of romantic encounters, smile-infested dance parties and open-ended hospitality. No guarantees of course... but more often than not it somehow works out.

In this autobiography Cameron Powers charts a course through America, Mexico, Peru, Bolivia, Syria, Iraq, Egypt, Greece and more. Early in life, back in the 1960's, he founded a small travel guide service called "Cameron's Terrible Tours" and yes, a few 'happy campers' came along for the delightful mountaineering and cross-cultural adventures. Being a self-taught musician and a university-trained linguist didn't hurt. Cameron sings in 14 languages and speaks five and a non-profit organization called "Musical Ambassadors of Peace" has been built around his and his wife Kristina's work

Is it something about being willing to go meet others on their terms and absorb and learn their values? Love Without Borders is the story of a life-long evolution into the conviction that "sacred flirtation" is the way forward for humanity.

Cameron's lifestyle led to an article about his adventures with his wife, Kristina, being included in the May, 2009 Lonely Planet Guide to the Middle East. The article was entitled "Musicians for Peace" and was written by Anthony Ham.

"It's not every American musician who can claim to have learned to play the oud (Middle Eastern lute) like an Iraqi and then played local popular love songs on a Baghdad street in the dangerous aftermath of the US invasion of Iraq. But then Cameron Powers is not your ordinary musician.

Together with his partner, singer Kristina Sophia, Powers was showing the Iraqi people that Americans could invade with music instead of bullets. A performance before 60,000 people in Cairo, Egypt, followed the same year."

Partnering with females who desired to travel with him and share his experiences led to the opening of windows into the women's worlds through which they passed. Lisa, Leda and Kristina have contributed immensely to Cameron's ability to explore realms which would have been difficult for a lone male to enter. The chapters in this book have been named after these women so that they may be honored.

Singing in Baghdad
A Musical Mission of Peace

The story of events leading up to and including a journey to Baghdad, Iraq made at the same time as the US Marines were entering the city in the spring of 2003. The success of this journey illustrates the capacity of the Iraqi people to distinguish love-based invasions from fear-based invasions. The story told in Singing in Baghdad illustrates the possibility of expanding cross-cultural musical study and performance into a new kind of people-to-people international diplomacy.

Review: "I have had the good fortune of reading two of Cameron's books. Just like his and Kristina's visionary simplicity in connecting with peoples our culture habitually misconstrues, they are replete with profound insights. It is not often that I get entirely new perspectives on how our world is shaped through culture. Cameron's works are chock full of them. For example, so many Americans take the oppression of women in the Middle East as a given, without ever imagining that below the head scarf, the veil or the burka there is a human being and a feminine expression of Life that deserves to be discovered before it is summarily and casually dismissed under the reductive epithet "oppressed." Cameron's books speak of the amazing power of feminine presence in the Middle East, a feminine enchantment that, in the United States, people hardly have an inkling of, much less deep, experiential appreciation for. To read Cameron's books is to feast upon delicious new territories of the heart, it inspires taking the next flight to the Middle East so that we ourselves might become a little bit more roundly human.

I recommend Cameron as someone who is an expression of the change our world inspires. When you meet him, you realize that he is the change wherever he is, always ready to sing and travel widely with spirited gentleness into the landscape of the human heart. And all of his words lead toward that knowing that there is a realm which is fully human that we can dwell in together in a way that words can't express – but a voice, a drum or an oud can... And that is the disarming genius that Cameron expounds; rather than taking us through more thought processes about how we might think ourselves into having a different perception of other, Cameron takes us directly into ecstatic song, directly into shared ecstasy which, once shared, radically softens the very sense of other and opens us to mutual discovery through the bliss that inhabits our core and is yearning for release and connection. He is not out in the world resisting fear; he is out in the world inviting fear directly to the party and the feast which always awaits us in the communion of hearts.

Cameron's vision of turning the "missionary efforts" of the West inside out is brilliant: rather than sending Western young men and women out to the far corners of the Earth to spread Jesus and Tupperware, Cameron has a vision of sending young men and women out to learn songs, wisdom and culture from global inhabitants. When I think of that, I am astounded by its brilliance: nothing to teach, nothing to propagandize – simply the willingness to learn from others a new way of being human together." -- Olivier Tryba

Spiritual Traveler
Journeys Beyond Fear

Musicians have long held many of the keys to cross-cultural journeying as a spiritual path. Along the way many things are learned. In this book we find many clues about Arab-world people and the beauties of their ancient ways. With fear removed from our perceptions, we find a way paved for endless cross-cultural love affairs.

Review: "I sure enjoyed your book and learned so much from it. I will read it a second time to learn more. I wish I could pass it along to many other people, it has so much truth in it."—Lois conklin

Review: Cameron Power's "Spiritual Traveler" book is fresh, insightful, heartfelt writing at its best. It is a feast of wisdom and humanity such that one seldom comes across in literature; a true invitation to imagine, not only that our Middle Eastern brothers and sisters are "human beings too," but that perhaps we can benefit profoundly by availing ourselves of the wisdom and love that men and women in the Middle East so readily offer those who allow that they too have something amazing to share from the depths of their experience.

"Spiritual Traveler" is a powerful antidote to the corporate media and government misportrayal of the inhabitants of ancient and profoundly relevant Middle Eastern civilizations and invites us into recognizing that other people's human experience may be as rich, as loving, as human and as generous as ours – and that we can courageously and lovingly enrich our lives with others. "Spiritual Traveler" is full of enlightening insights into how the language which we use to describe others might also be limiting our experience of our earthly sojourn.

I recommend "Spiritual Traveler" without reservation. Read it and you too will want to open your heart to others in news ways, with new appreciation of the wonder that we are as human beings, as cultural participants, as lovers, as singers, as friends. -Caminante Olivier

Review: The Spiritual Traveler book is incredible!! You just might be the wisest man I know! I really love how you write. I want every Bellydancer who trains with me to read it!! – Sadie Marquardt

Review: I love that the tone of his Cameron Powers' writing is also characteristic of his speaking tone (obvious for those of us lucky enough to witness his speech firsthand). Not all writers achieve this, and that, in and of itself, IS an achievement!

To read his words is indeed a journey beyond fear regardless of the range of your geographic and cultural travel. In fact, the heart of this book hearkens you on an adventure of relating to yourself and others regardless of who the 'others' are (and who 'you' are, for that matter) at any point in time and space. And Powers' approach is unique. The chapter and sub-chapter headings are enough to shake ya awake and getcha moving! I mean, how can you not be drawn forth by such chapter titles as 'Do We Speak Language or does Language Speak Us?' or "'Civilization'–Whose?" or 'Sacred Flirtation' or 'Do We Really Want to Waste this Precious Lifetime?'

There's such an immediacy, urgency, insight and exuberance to the content of this book that it should always be within reach.

Oh yeah…don't you dare put this book down until you read the 'Tomatoes' poem at the end!
– F. Medina

Naked Wild and Free in the Grand Canyon
Rowing and Roaming

Venturing down the rivers and canyons of the American West we touch sacred and primal worlds, both outside and inside ourselves. Anyone who has enjoyed such an adventure knows about this. This journal gives a taste of how it looked and felt to our crazy crew.

The author was fortunate enough to be included on four river trips which took place between 1969 and 1975.

This book contains an expanded version of the written journal kept by the author during a passage through the lower half of the Grand Canyon in 1975. Some of the photos included are from other earlier trips.

These adventures involved descents of the Colorado River through Cataract Canyon and the Grand Canyon, the Yampa River through Dinosaur National Monument and Echo Park, and the Green River through the Gates of Lodor, Grays Canyon, Desolation Canyon and Canyonlands National Park.

The rafts were of our own design and took a lot of muscle to row through the numerous white water rapids. The pace was leisurely, with plenty of time allowed for each trip. Our passage through the Grand Canyon, for example, was designed to take more than a month. Riding the river for only 2 or 3 hours a day meant plenty of time for hiking, climbing, caving and enjoying the endless varieties of pools and waterfalls which can be found sometimes far up in the side canyons. Spending weeks at a time on the river also meant getting to know each more deeply and allowing the spirit of the canyon rock-scapes to enter our beings more fully. It felt like we were truly living in those canyons, not just passing through.

Photographic and adventure document. Rowing rafts and hiking and climbing with lots of time to do it. Feeling at home living in the Grand Canyon. Communal living in the wild. Back to nature at its best.

River runners are a notoriously wild and crazy bunch. This book contains a small taste of the adventures enjoyed by a communal group of friends from Steamboat Springs, Colorado.

Review: Naked wild and free magically transported me back to the excitement of the 60s and 70s. It was a time in my life when the universe was wide-open, every day offered new opportunities, and subtle energies ruled. The greatest high was connecting with another soul whether it be human, plant, or animal. Even though I didn't know the characters, I could feel them and know their experiences. Really?! Yes, this is a fun, easy read – yet profoundly deep. Thank you for sharing your adventure with us.
— John, Boulder Colorado

Cameron Powers Project CD
Dance Music - Egyptian Music Scales

Middle Eastern Dance Rhythms...

Review: Your Cameron Powers Project instrumental CD is incredibly on-target! It's one of the only truly "in-tune" performances I know of. The shift to the soul-stirring ancient harmonies is now complete in you. They are so internalized that you can dance freely there, and the result is breathtaking. The "minor" thirds and sixths sound so much more powerful than the same minor intervals in western tuning. The sevenths are incredibly evocative. I know you studied and practiced hard to find these notes, but now that the heavy intellectual lifting has been done, you have uncovered a treasure trove of brilliant sound that far surpasses any academic or intellectual achievement. This is no academic exercise, it's a bringing to the surface the radiant jewels that had been buried in our hearts for too long.
Love always,
Chris Mohr – Microtonal Composer

Review: I'm just getting the chance to listen to the Cameron Powers Project CD! WOWIE! It's wonderful. I'm taking it with me to Vegas for driving music. I'm shimmying in the car. Its gorgeous. I'll use it in dance church as DJ soon! So proud of your accomplishments Cameron. You AMAZE ME!
Christine Stevens - Sounds True

Review: Congratulations. Good stuff. I enjoyed the CD. Thank you for sharing.
Naser Musa – Jordanian Oud Player – Songwriter

Review: For my Birthday I received the new Cameron Powers CD caution: do not try to drive listening to it! I found myself in another world and had to park! It transports one straight to the heart and beauty! I LOVE cut 3 Breath of an Angel. Master musicians exploring rhythms and maqams!
Diane Eger

Review: Your new album sounds GREAT!! I mean gorgeous!
Ariana Saraha – Singer Songwriter

This CD is a reflection of Cameron's years of immersion in the music of Egypt, Iraq, Syria, Turkey and Greece.
Cameron Powers: Composer, Vocals, Oud, Nay, Cumbus; James Hoskins: Cello; Gilly Gonzalez: Percussion; Pete Jacobs: Upright Bass; Scott Bears: Oud, Cumbus; Kristina Sophia: Vocal Textures; Meg York: Clarinet

Baghdad & Beyond CD
Cameron and Kristina and Sherefe

This CD features four of the popular Arabic songs sung frequently by Cameron & Kristina in the Arab world. A couple of Greek songs add icing to the musical cake!

Review: Thank you so much for sharing the CD Baghdad and Beyond with me. I have been listening to it for the last two days and I really like the way that you have done these songs. Kristina's voice is very beautiful and your two voices go together very well. Cameron did a great job at singing and playing these hard styles of Arabic music. I did not expect to hear what I heard. Congratulation on a job well done and I am sure that many Arabs just like me appreciate all this great effort and hard work that you both have done and still doing. You are doing our culture a big favor. I love you both and wish you all the best. May God keeps on blessing you and using you as part of his beautiful-hearted angels. Love, — Naser Musa

Review: I don't usually write fan letters, but I have to tell you your latest cd, Baghdad and Beyond, is really amazing. They're all good, but this one has something extra about it. Lots of interesting subtlety. And I always get a kick out of the last cut, the one with the Bedouins. Ha! — Doug

Middle Eastern Moods
4:01 am CD

The sun sets, a flurry of evening activities come and go...

As midnight passes the quiet deepens...

Somewhere, in a few living rooms, in a few taverns or restaurants or around the campfires in the forests... a few people stay... conversations dwindle...

The time for music is arriving... The musicians are slowly melting into their instruments, becoming one with their sounds...

It's 4:01 a.m...

The painter paints, the sculptor sculpts, the writer writes, the musician plays and sings, the dancer dances... What is left? We have paintings, statues, books from centuries past... The musicians and dancers weave their magic and it vanishes.... until the advent of recording devices... So here it is: captured on Cameron's recording device and offered on CD plates... threads of live song... flavors of Greek harmonies and Egyptian oud moods.

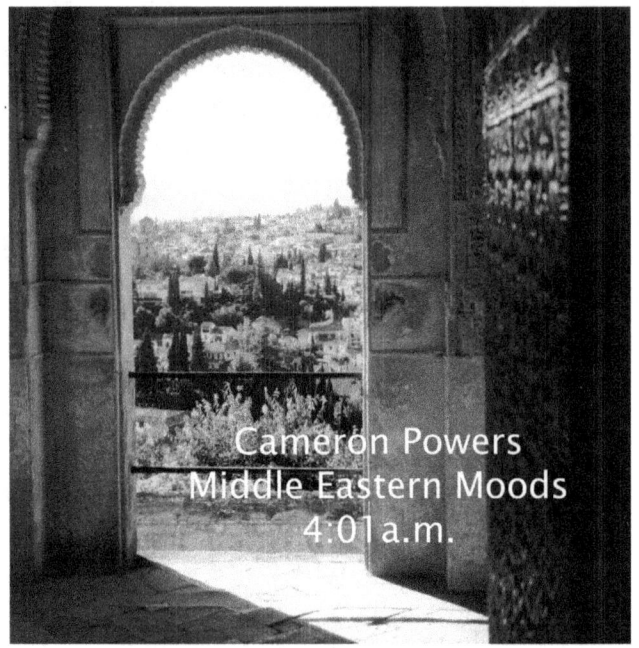

Contributors are too numerous to mention: musicians in Athens, Cairo, Fes, California and, yes, right here in Colorado, who have taught and inspired over the last 30 years...

This view through this thousand-year-old arched doorway in the Alhambre in Granada in Spain frames the still lingering vapors from countless such moments... Now under the warm afternoon sun the musicians are just finishing their breakfasts...

Dancing with Your Soul
Arabic Nights

Let your body gently move by itself to this music and see what happens...

Editor's Pick on Indie-Music.com: "...recognition that our screeners found your music of high quality..."

Review: "Hey I've become totally addicted to your tune Damascus... I'd like to download this one to my collection which I'm playing while driving in my car. Please send me a link to buy this... I just can't wait until I add it to my list of favourites!!!" — Denis

Review: "I absolutely LOVE Dancing with your Soul!!! Listening all the time to it and singing along... great tool for my learning maqamat." — Ynyra Oshea

Review: "Erotic, a desert flower in bloom... for making love, not war..." — Tessalin Green

Review: "I received your new CD in the mail and it is incredible !!!! Dancing with Your Soul is one of the most amazing CDs in my collection!! Thank YOU. — Lynnie Zsidov-Steiner

Cameron and Kristina have been deepening their musical and cultural connection to the Arabic-speaking people of the Middle East by making several recent journeys through Egypt, Syria, Jordan, Lebanon, Iraq and the West Bank of Palestine since 2002. They sang Iraqi love songs on the streets of Baghdad in solidarity with the Iraqi people in the spring of 2003. They performed Egyptian music for an audience of 60,000 in the Cairo Stadium in the fall of that same year. They were gifted a non-profit corporation in 2003 which is devoted to supporting Iraqi Refugee Children in Syria as well as helping to fund American musicians who work as Musical Ambassadors. Damascus, Aleppo, Lattakia, Beirout, Amman, Aqaba, Ramallah and Cairo have become fascinating new realms for their musical explorations. They have been busy traveling in the US and helping people better understand the Middle Eastern, Arabic, psyche. Well over 300 musical and multi-media presentations have recently been completed in more than half of the American states as well as in Panama, Venezuela, Ecuador and Mexico.

Smooth and Slow and Sensual...

The books and CD's listed above can be ordered from:
https://www.gldesignpub.com
or
E-Mail: distrib@gldesignpub.com

www.ingramcontent.com/pod-product-compliance
Lightning Source LLC
Chambersburg PA
CBHW082124230426
43671CB00015B/2800